CLASSICAL PRESENCES

General Editors
LORNA HARDWICK   JAMES I. PORTER

CLASSICAL PRESENCES

Attempts to receive the texts, images, and material culture of ancient Greece and Rome inevitably run the risk of appropriating the past in order to authenticate the present. Exploring the ways in which the classical past has been mapped over the centuries allows us to trace the avowal and disavowal of values and identities, old and new. Classical Presences brings the latest scholarship to bear on the contexts, theory, and practice of such use, and abuse, of the classical past.

GREECE ON AIR

Frontispiece. A drawing by Eric Fraser for the 1963 production of Sophocles' *Philoctetes* (*Radio Times*, 21 February 1963, 49). Reproduced by kind permission of the Fraser family.

Greece on Air

*Engagements with Ancient Greece
on BBC Radio, 1920s–1960s*

AMANDA WRIGLEY

OXFORD
UNIVERSITY PRESS

Great Clarendon Street, Oxford, OX2 6DP,
United Kingdom

Oxford University Press is a department of the University of Oxford.
It furthers the University's objective of excellence in research, scholarship,
and education by publishing worldwide. Oxford is a registered trade mark of
Oxford University Press in the UK and in certain other countries

© Amanda Wrigley 2015

The moral rights of the author have been asserted

First Edition published in 2015

Impression: 1

All rights reserved. No part of this publication may be reproduced, stored in
a retrieval system, or transmitted, in any form or by any means, without the
prior permission in writing of Oxford University Press, or as expressly permitted
by law, by licence or under terms agreed with the appropriate reprographics
rights organization. Enquiries concerning reproduction outside the scope of the
above should be sent to the Rights Department, Oxford University Press, at the
address above

You must not circulate this work in any other form
and you must impose this same condition on any acquirer

Published in the United States of America by Oxford University Press
198 Madison Avenue, New York, NY 10016, United States of America

British Library Cataloguing in Publication Data

Data available

Library of Congress Control Number: 2015937256

ISBN 978-0-19-964478-0

Printed and bound by
CPI Group (UK) Ltd, Croydon, CR0 4YY

Links to third party websites are provided by Oxford in good faith and
for information only. Oxford disclaims any responsibility for the materials
contained in any third party website referenced in this work.

For Dez, Matilda, Dylan

Acknowledgements

This book is a revision and expansion of my doctoral thesis, titled 'Engagements with Greek Drama and Homeric Epic on BBC Radio in the 1940s and 1950s', which was submitted to The Open University (OU) in 2009.[1] First thanks are owed to Lorna Hardwick (Department of Classical Studies, OU) and Oliver Taplin (Faculty of Classics, University of Oxford), both first-rate doctoral supervisors who created an encouraging atmosphere which was both supportive and inspiring, one in which I could with confidence 'Try again. Fail again. Fail better'.[2] I would also like to extend my thanks to my examiners Chris Emlyn-Jones and Christopher Stray for a viva that was not only stimulating but also enjoyable, to the Department of Classical Studies for running imaginative events for research students, and to the support staff at the OU for a consistently excellent service.

My part-time doctoral research over five years was stimulated by and ran alongside my final years in post as Researcher at the Archive of Performances of Greek and Roman Drama (APGRD) in the Faculty of Classics at the University of Oxford. Funding from the Arts and Humanities Research Board (AHRB), and later Council (AHRC), made the APGRD's activities possible and thus provided me with a professional environment which was enormously enriching for my studies; I am very grateful to the AHRC for granting special permission for me to pursue doctoral work alongside my nominally postdoctoral position. I also owe thanks to many APGRD colleagues for the encouragement and opportunities they offered, especially during my early years in post.

The final push in revising and expanding my thesis for publication took place in parallel with my first year's work on another AHRC-funded research project, Screen Plays: Theatre Plays on British Television, based in the Faculty of Media, Arts and Design at the University of Westminster. I like to think that this move from classics to media studies, together with the expansion in focus from Greek drama and literature to the full stage repertoire and the shift in focus

[1] Wrigley 2009a.
[2] Quotation from *Worstward Ho* by Samuel Beckett 1983, 7.

from radio to television, have contributed to making this a stronger book. Certainly, the intellectually engaging and hugely supportive environment created by my colleague John Wyver, the project's principal investigator, has been extremely enjoyable and enriching; I am also particularly grateful to him for allowing me to concentrate on bringing the book to completion in the summer of 2012. I would also like to acknowledge the support of Pete Goodwin, David Hendy, and other current and former colleagues in the Communication and Media Research Institute (CAMRI) and the Centre for Research and Education in Arts and Media (CREAM) at the University of Westminster. I am especially thankful to David Gauntlett and Jeanette Steemers, former co-directors of CAMRI, for the award of a grant to help with illustrations. I have also benefited greatly from membership of the Southern Broadcasting History Group through which I have enjoyed the support of an extremely congenial network of colleagues.

It gives me great pleasure to thank many other friends and colleagues in classics, classical reception studies, English literature, media studies, radio studies, and television studies who have been a rich source of intellectual inspiration, practical advice, and friendly support at different points over the years. I risk important omissions by naming names but, in addition to those acknowledged elsewhere, I must mention Jonathan Bignell, Amanda Bloore, Hugh Chignell, Robert Davis, Heather Ellis, Vasiliki Giannopoulou, Katherine Harloe, Stephen Harrison, David Hendy, Michele Hilmes, Fiona Hobden, Tony Keen, Kate Lacey, Natalie Papoutsis, Leah Panos, Jo Paul, Amanda Potter, Kim Shahabudin, Billy Smart, Chris Stray, Seán Street, and Michael Walton.

I am grateful for excellent assistance over a number of years from the staff of the Bodleian Library, especially Colin Harris of Special Collections; the BBC Information and Archives Department, especially Simon Crosthwaite; the BBC Written Archives Centre (WAC), especially Jeff Walden; and the British Library, especially Paul Wilson and his Sound Archive colleagues (BLSA). The radio-related materials deposited in the APGRD's collections by Pete Hartley, Philip Hooker, Colette King, and others were extremely useful at the start of my research; and the studies in the second part of the book were made much more possible by the kind help of several people, including Gabriel Josipovici, Graham Nelson, Beaty Rubens, and John Theocharis.

I offer warm thanks to Geoffrey and Mary Fraser for their kind permission to reproduce Eric Fraser's wonderful drawings for the

Radio Times in this book (the frontispiece and Figures 4.1, 4.2, 4.3, 6.2, 7.1, and 7.3). I am also grateful to the BBC Photo Library for permission to reproduce Figures 2.1, 5.1, and 7.2 and to the Henry Moore Foundation (HMF) regarding Figures 6.1, 6.3, and 6.4.

It has been extremely exciting to locate and explore such an uncharted and important area of research at the intersection of so many enriching lines of thought. Some of the emerging results of my doctoral research were therefore published as the thesis progressed and I am grateful to Wolfgang Haase of the *International Journal of the Classical Tradition*, Christopher Stray, editor of *Remaking the Classics: Literature, Genre and Media in Britain, 1800–2000*, and Dunstan Lowe and Kim Shahabudin, editors of *Classics For All: Reworking Antiquity in Mass Culture* for valuable opportunities to publish work-in-progress essays.[3] I am also grateful to Tim Wall, editor of *The Radio Journal: International Studies in Broadcast and Audio Media*, for permission to publish here (in Section 6.1) much of the material on *The Rescue* which first appeared in issue 8.2 (an article which won the Comparative Drama Conference's Philadelphia Constantinidis Essay in Critical Theory prize in 2011).[4] I am also indebted to Lorna Hardwick and Stephen Harrison for the timely opportunity of contributing material from Chapter 1, below, to their edited volume *Classics in the Modern World: A 'Democratic Turn'?*[5]

At Oxford University Press Hilary O'Shea and her colleagues Taryn Des Neves, Annie Rose, and Cathryn Steele have been, as always, extremely helpful, flexible, and patient. I am also thankful to the Press's external readers for insightful suggestions for improvement in their enthusiastic reports, and to Dorothy McCarthy for sensitive copy-editing.

On a personal note, I offer thanks to Christine, David, and Andrew Hilton for their love and encouragement over the years. It is with an enormous sense of happiness and gratitude that I dedicate this book to my husband Dez Sandiford and our brilliant and beautiful children. From our first conversation, just weeks before I submitted the doctoral thesis on which this book is based, my husband has been the most wonderful support and very timely reminder that life is more than book-work. Dez, Matilda, Dylan, my loves, my life: this book is for you.

---

[3] Wrigley 2006, 2007*b*, and 2009*b*.
[4] Wrigley 2010*b*.   [5] Wrigley 2013*b*.

Contents

List of Illustrations	xv
List of Abbreviations	xvii
Note on Conventions	xxi

PART ONE

Introduction: Broad(-er)casting Ancient Greece	3
1. Mass Media and Classics, the Public and Cultural Élitism	17
2. The Contexts of Programme-Making	35
2.1 Cultural broadcasting: origins and aims, networks and 'brows'	35
2.2 Departmental, collaborative, and literary historical contexts	59
3. 'Listening in'	75
3.1 Practical access; or, the democratic and educative medium	77
3.2 Imaginative access; or, the popularizing medium	97

PART TWO

4. Gilbert Murray: 'Radio Hellenist', 1925–1956	117
4.1 Murray's popular verse translations of Greek plays in performance	117
4.2 Talks on classics and international politics	142
5. Greek History in the Wartime Propaganda of Louis MacNeice	151
5.1 Poet and classicist, radio writer and producer	152
5.2 *The March of the 10,000*, *The Glory that is Greece*, and *Pericles*	157

6. The Poetry and Drama of Homeric Epic, 1943–1969   173
    6.1 Edward Sackville-West and Benjamin Britten's
       The Rescue (1943)   184
    6.2 Robert Graves's *The Anger of Achilles* (1965)   207

7. Greek Tragedy: The Case of Aeschylus' *Agamemnon*,
    1946–1976   221

8. Post-War Greek Comedy   247
    8.1 Louis MacNeice's *Enemy of Cant* (1946)   250
    8.2 Patric Dickinson's Aristophanic adaptations   263

Conclusion: Public Property; or, Classics for All   273

Appendix: Production Chronology   279
Bibliography   297
Index   321

List of Illustrations

Frontispiece A drawing by Eric Fraser for the 1963 production of Sophocles' *Philoctetes* (*Radio Times*, 21 February 1963, 49).   iv

2.1 Stephen Murray and Elsa Vergi perform the roles of Jason and Medea in the Third Programme's 1962 *Medea*.   65

4.1 Eric Fraser's drawing for the 1936 *Hippolytus* (*Radio Times*, 16 October 1936, 21).   124

4.2 Eric Fraser's drawing for the 1940 *Seven against Thebes* (*Radio Times*, 23 August 1940, 11).   129

4.3 The 1947 Home Service production of *Frogs*, illustrated by Eric Fraser (*Radio Times*, 31 January 1947, 10).   138

5.1 Louis MacNeice in rehearsal, script and pencil in hand.   154

6.1 'The Death of the Suitors' by Henry Moore (HMF 2305, printed in Sackville-West 1945).   186

6.2 'The sleeping Odysseus is laid ashore on the island of Ithaca': Eric Fraser's drawing for Edward Sackville-West's article 'The *Odyssey* in Terms of Modern Radio' (*Radio Times*, 19 November 1943, 4).   190

6.3 'Phemius and Telemachus' by Henry Moore (HMF 2300, printed in Sackville-West 1945).   195

6.4 'The Shadow on the Wall' by Henry Moore (HMF 2304, printed in Sackville-West 1945).   200

7.1 'To me this hour was dreamed of long ago': Eric Fraser's drawing for *Agamemnon* in 1946 (*Radio Times*, 25 October 1946, 12).   223

7.2 Brothers John and Val Gielgud rehearsing *Oedipus at Colonus* in 1959.   235

7.3 Eric Fraser's illustration for an article introducing the 1962 *Oresteia* in the *Radio Times*, 25 January 1962, 26.   237

List of Abbreviations

AB	Arthur Bliss
APGRD	Archive of Performances of Greek and Roman Drama, University of Oxford
AW	Amanda Wrigley
BB	Barbara Burnham
BBC	British Broadcasting Corporation
BBC WAC	BBC Written Archives Centre
BBC WAC SL	BBC WAC Script Library
BLSA	British Library Sound Archive
CEMA	Council for the Encouragement of Music and the Arts
DSCR	D. S. Carne-Ross
ERD	E. R. Dodds
ESW	Edward Sackville-West
FF	Felix Felton
GM	Gilbert Murray
HLJ	Hugh Lloyd-Jones
HMF	Henry Moore Foundation
LG	Laurence Gilliam
LM	Louis MacNeice
n.d.	no date (describing letters, manuscripts, etc.)
OU	The Open University
OUDS	Oxford University Dramatic Society
PA	Penguin Archive, Special Collections, University of Bristol
PD	Patric Dickinson
PV	Philip Vellacott
RG	Robert Graves
RGA	Robert Graves Archive, St John's College, Oxford
RGC	Robert Graves Collection, Special Collections, University of Victoria
RH	Rayner Heppenstall
RR	Raymond Raikes
TSE	T. S. Eliot
VG	Val Gielgud

Abbreviated and expanded references for files in the BBC WAC:

AH/C	Antony Hopkins: Composer, 1944–1962
AT/T1	Anthony Thwaite: Talks file 1, 1954–1962
BB/C	Barbara Burnham: Copyright, 1948–1962

List of Abbreviations

CAT/S1	Constantine A. Trypanis: Scriptwriter file 1, 1957–1962
CL/C1	Christopher Logue: Copyright file 1, 1955–1962
CP/C	Christos Pittas: Copyright, 1975–1979
GJ/S3	Gabriel Josipovici: Scriptwriter file 3, 1972–1982
GM/S	Gilbert Murray: Scriptwriter, 1936–1966
GM/T1	Gilbert Murray: Talks file 1, 1926–1941
GM/T2	Gilbert Murray: Talks file 2, 1942–1945
GM/T3a	Gilbert Murray: Talks file 3a, 1946–1952
LM/C	Louis MacNeice: Copyright, 1934–1962
MG/S1	Mary Garrett: Scriptwriter file 1, 1937–1962
PD/S1a	Patric Dickinson: Scriptwriter file 1a, 1939–1954
PD/S2	Patric Dickinson: Scriptwriter file 2, 1963–1967
PD/S2a	Patric Dickinson: Scriptwriter file 2a, 1955
PD/S2b	Patric Dickinson: Scriptwriter file 2b, 1956–1957
PD/S3	Patric Dickinson: Scriptwriter file 3, 1968–1972
PD/S3a	Patric Dickinson: Scriptwriter file 3a, 1958–1960
PD/S3b	Patric Dickinson: Scriptwriter file 3b, 1960–1962
R16/1463/1	R16/1463/1 Schools Programmes: Kenneth Cavander, Correspondence, 1966–1969
R19/307	R19/307 Entertainment: C146 *Enemy of Cant*, 1946–1948
R19/393	R19/393 Entertainment: *The Four Freedoms*, 1942–1943
R19/440	R19/440 Entertainment: *The Golden Ass*, 1944–1951
R19/456	R19/456 Entertainment: Greece, 1941
R19/457	R19/457 Entertainment: Greek Independence Day, 1940–1943
R19/925/1	R19/925/1 Entertainment: Plays, Head Office Memos, 1931–1936
R19/947	R19/947 Entertainment: *Portrait of Athens*, 1951
R19/976	R19/976 Entertainment: *Prometheus Bound*, 1948
R19/1026	R19/1026 Entertainment: *The Rescue*, file 1, 1942–1951
R34/602	R34/602 Policy: Programme 'C', 1945–1947
R101/323/1	R101/323/1 Radio Re-Organisation: The Campaign for Better Broadcasting
RG/S1	Robert Graves: Scriptwriter file 1, 1939–1962
RG/S2	Robert Graves: Scriptwriter file 2, 1963–1967
RG/T1	Robert Graves: Talks file 1, 1941–1962
S452/2/1	S452/2/1 Raymond Raikes: Personal Correspondence A–Z, 1949–1961
S452/3/1	S452/3/1 Raymond Raikes: Personal Correspondence A–Z, 1962–1975
S452/11/1	S452/11/1 Raymond Raikes: Plays. Production Papers, 1942–1948
S452/23/1	S452/23/1 Raymond Raikes: *Iphigeneia in Aulis*, 1949–1975

List of Abbreviations

S452/29/1	S452/29/1 Raymond Raikes: The *Oresteia* of Aeschylus, 1954–1956
S452/36/1	S452/36/1 Raymond Raikes: *Dyscolos* (Menander's *Misanthrope*)
S452/40/1	S452/40/1 Raymond Raikes: The *Medea* of Euripides, 1962
S452/48/1	S452/48/1 Raymond Raikes: *The Anger of Achilles*, 1964
S452/63/1	S452/63/1 Raymond Raikes: *Women in Power*, 1970
S452/S4/1	S452/S4/1 Raymond Raikes, Italia Prize 1965
T5/2160/1	T5/2160/1 *Lysistrata*, 1964

Note on Conventions

Ellipses in square brackets indicate omissions from quotations made by the author of this book.

In quotations from sources such as radio scripts or Listener Research Reports, ellipses which are not enclosed by square brackets indicate intentional pauses or unfinished sentences by the original author. For example, 'The moment has come to fight for the independence of Greece... to fight for our honour as a nation' in Louis MacNeice's 1941 radio script *The Glory that is Greece*.

Part One

Introduction: Broad(-er)casting Ancient Greece

This book explores the rich and fascinating history of creative engagements with ancient Greek literature, history, and thought on BBC Radio from the birth of broadcasting in the domestic sphere in the early 1920s up to the 1960s, with one or two forays beyond. In this period, the BBC regularly produced and broadcast a rich range of radio programmes drawing on ancient Greece and (rather less often) Rome.[1] These programmes included scores of performances of Greek tragedy, comedy, and their modern adaptations (whether written for the stage or for radio); creative re-workings of other ancient texts such as Homer's epic poems and the Socratic dialogues, often for dramatized performance; individual talks or series broadcast as part of the school curriculum or adult education schemes; and a significant number of creative re-imaginings of (usually historical) ancient Greek texts and topics in the form of feature programmes, a significant number of which were written and broadcast as propaganda in the Second World War.

This radio activity includes some of the most interesting, creative, and political engagements with ideas from and about ancient Greece in twentieth-century Britain. The various institutional aims and personal objectives underpinning these broadcasts, which are well documented in the BBC's written archives, are of particular significance to the discussion, especially when, for example, programmes were

---

[1] Louis MacNeice was one of the primary figures to adapt Roman texts and themes for British radio: for a selection of scripts, with discussion, see Wrigley and Harrison 2013.

written for a propagandistic agenda in wartime or part of educational series for broadcast to schools or adult learners. Behind the making of these programmes lies an illuminating and important account of how broadcasters, creative writers, and classicists worked collaboratively over many decades to bring to the general public informative, educational, and entertaining broadcasts deriving from the stories, histories, and ideas of ancient Greece. These broadcasts worked alongside and often in tandem with other cultural and educational activities (for example, the publication of relatively cheap Penguin paperback translations from 1946) to give works from ancient Greece a new and strong public identity away from the school and university classroom where, over the course of the twentieth century, the study of ancient Greek was becoming increasingly marginalized.

These programmes and associated talks and publications constitute one strand in what has been interpreted, often rather negatively, as the BBC's Reithian mission to grant a large and diverse public common access to an ambitiously wide range of works from what was perceived to be the nation's cultural wealth.[2] The audiences for these programmes were of an astonishing size, sometimes running into millions, with even the so-called less popular broadcasts being heard by hundreds or tens of thousands. Almost all of the various types of programme drawing on ancient Greece were created specifically for the non-specialist listener (that is, the listener without a classical education) and, accordingly, many programmes were accompanied by illustrated introductory essays in the *Radio Times*, versions of broadcast talks were often printed in *The Listener*, and educational programmes were accompanied by the publication of pamphlets, thus ensuring that listeners of all ages had a good chance of accessing a ready supply of contextual information with which to complement their listening.

In these terms, radio is a cultural sphere of great significance for a full understanding of ancient Greece in the public imagination in twentieth-century Britain. English translations, adaptations, and creative reinterpretations of Greek literature, history, and thought were,

---

[2] John Reith's (1889-1971) formative leadership of the BBC ran from 1922 to 1938; however, his influence lasted much longer than his BBC career. On the perceived potential of the idea of cultural heritage to unite society and the related missionary enthusiasm for 'humanizing the masses' after the First World War, see Scannell and Cardiff 1991, 12-13.

via radio, accessible more readily, more widely, and to far larger and more diverse audiences than has previously been taken into account. The fact that a great amount of archival evidence exists in the BBC's written archives both for production processes and also listeners' responses to these programmes brings other new, and extremely important, dimensions to current debates within the field of classical reception studies (for example, with regard to the idea of the 'democratic turn': see Chapter 1).

Underpinning the discussion in this book is the foundational argument that ancient Greek literature, history, and thought were to a significant degree both democratized and popularized via regular dramatic presentation on radio in this period. 'Democratization' and 'popularization' are contested terms which are sometimes superficially conflated; here, however, they are used specifically to refer to distinct processes which are represented by the two sections of Chapter 3. Section 3.1 argues that BBC Radio, as a mass medium, made the stories, histories, and ideas of ancient Greece *practically* accessible to a huge audience which was extremely diverse in terms of, for example, prior educational and cultural experience and demographic and geographical spread. Section 3.2 discusses how BBC Radio, as a distinctively exploratory and imaginatively stimulating medium for the presentation of established cultural works, made such aspects of ancient Greece *imaginatively* accessible to this audience in a vital and powerful way. Thus can ancient Greece be said to have been both democratized *and* popularized via radio in this period. Furthermore, there is evidence that this activity also made a reciprocal impression on the various cultural and educational forces which had contributed to its existence, thus subtly changing the landscape for classics in Britain for the later twentieth century.

This book, in so short a span, could not hope to provide an exhaustive account of the hundreds of relevant radio programmes broadcast from the 1920s to the 1960s. The aim is, rather, first to establish the subject as a significant area for further research through detailed discussion in Part One of some of the important and interrelated contexts in which this cultural activity may be productively examined; and then to present a compelling series of studies in Part Two which focus the lens on some particularly interesting and interrelated movements and personalities in this period, studies which are broadly organized around some major genres of extant

Greek texts—namely, Homeric epic, tragic drama, comic drama, and historical works.[3]

Chapter 1 uses the existence in the BBC's archives of a wealth of evidence for production processes and audience experience as a springboard for a re-consideration of the dominant methodological practices of classical reception studies. A shift away from the Jaussian terms 'production' and 'reception' in favour of a model of 'engagement' is advocated. This shift necessitates a more inclusive (described as an 'in the round') approach as opposed to the dominant one- or two-track approach which has been commonly used in the critical evaluation of modern engagements with the ancient Mediterranean world. It is argued that privileging one or two, albeit important, perspectives (such as the literary, artistic, or political) over several important others may be a critical practice with significant deficiencies. It tends to resist the necessary challenge of negotiating and integrating the more untidy and sometimes conflicting histories which can, from close consultation of a broader range of sources, be told about a cultural work; it may also overlook the significance of the autonomy with which individual members of the audience engage with a cultural work. The one- or two-track tendency in methodological practice seems therefore to ignore the full, *actual* life of a cultural work in the public imagination in favour of telling a more partial, but doubtless more seamless, history.

Building on this foundational argument, the second chapter considers several crucial contexts in which the writing and production of a radio programme drawing on ancient Greece may be considered. Section 2.1 outlines the changing contexts for cultural broadcasting before, during, and after the Second World War, beginning with a critical assessment of John Reith's formative conception of broadcasting as a force for providing the national audience with access to high quality information, education, and entertainment. The place of programmes using translated forms of ancient Greek texts within the broader idea of the nation's cultural wealth is addressed: first, within the context of other immediately post-war national 'improving' educational and cultural schemes (in which Greek tragedy, for example, featured prominently); secondly, at this point in time when the study of ancient Greek was beginning to be marginalized within the

---

[3] See also *Ancient Greece on British Television* (Hobden and Wrigley 2016).

curricula of the Universities of Oxford and Cambridge following the abolition of 'Compulsory Greek'; and also, very briefly, in relation to the concurrent project to establish English literature (as opposed to Greek and Latin texts in the original language) as the foundation stone of British national culture. Through vital processes of translation, adaptation, and contextualization (using techniques and ideas drawn from teaching, scholarship, theatre, oral performance, and acting), the stories, histories, and ideas of ancient Greece were broadcast for the enjoyment and informal education of massive numbers of radio listeners. Thus, it is argued, did ancient texts achieve an unprecedented public identity beyond the school and university classroom—a radically, if subtly, political act in terms of the prior educational and cultural status of classics within Britain.

A significant point of discussion in this regard is the post-war segmentation of the audience by cultural 'brow', especially as it operated through the foundation in 1946 of the Third Programme as a network specifically for 'highbrow' cultural works. Most programmes relating to ancient Greece henceforth appeared on the Third, although the Home Service broadcast many Drama Department productions of Greek plays as part of its monthly *World Theatre* series, for example. The anticipated audience for the Third's avowedly 'highbrow' cultural fare was deemed to be already sufficiently *au fait* with this kind of work. However, this expectation was not mirrored in actual listening patterns: a substantial part of the Third's audience was found to come from beyond the target demographic. This point demonstrates the extremely open and, one may say, democratic nature of the radio medium (a point on which Chapter 3 will expand).

Not uncommonly, listeners felt sufficiently moved by a production to write a letter to the BBC's production team, and the existence of a wealth of this kind of correspondence in the written archives offers hugely valuable sources of information on how listeners engaged with individual programmes. In addition, from 1936 the BBC regularly canvassed detailed opinions on programmes from its Listening Panels. The resulting Listener Research Reports offer statistical data on the size of the audience and how listeners rated a programme, with this numerical 'Appreciation Index' richly illustrated with a good range of comments on several different aspects of a programme (the music, acting, etc.) from listeners who were identified by occupation (and thus, sometimes, by gender—for example, 'Seamstress'). It is argued that the rich mine of sources that exists for the public's engagement with these radio programmes not only provides evidence for an uncharted realm of activity that by any measure is of great importance to cultural history, but the very existence of these sources for radio—which do not seem to exist to the same extent for other realms of cultural activity—also enables reflection on broader classical reception studies practices and methodological possibilities.

The political power of radio was harnessed especially during the Second World War when public figures, scholars, and creative writers contributed to the 'war of words' propagandist talks and feature programmes, a significant number of which drew on the literature, history, and thought of ancient Greece.[4] The Drama Department, too, fought for the preservation and promotion of what were described as 'civilised values' and 'civilised culture' through the increased broadcast of works from the established dramatic and literary canon—the radio dramatic equivalent, perhaps, of the 'Art for the People' programme of the Council for the Encouragement of Music and the Arts (CEMA)—a number of which were from the Greek tragic repertoire.[5] This wartime programme of cultural propaganda—the last topic discussed in Section 2.1—boosted the sense of patriotic morale whilst garnering support for the Allied cause through an appeal to a shared European cultural tradition.

Section 2.2 considers the departmental, collaborative, and literary historical contexts for these programmes. First, it traces how institutional policy with regard to cultural broadcasting found expression in the different kinds of programmes that staff from the BBC Departments of Drama and Features created for broadcast. Secondly, it discusses how the personal preferences of BBC writers and producers, together with their creative collaboration with freelance contributors (such as scholars, translators, creative writers, composers, and theatre practitioners) were instrumental in giving shape to a programme's intended purpose(s) in terms of, for example, entertainment, education, propaganda, or theatre-on-the-air; the sustained links that were forged between radio and other intellectual and creative professions are therefore also explored with reference to particular programmes. Finally, the discussion engages with the complexities of the

---

[4] The phrase 'war of words' was used by the BBC: see, for example, British Broadcasting Corporation 1946, 7.

[5] Val Gielgud's phrase 'civilised values' is quoted in Rodger 1982, 55–6; 'civilised culture' is a quotation from a BBC memo, printed in Briggs 1970, 113.

relationship between radio programmes drawing on ancient Greece and the literary and theatrical histories of the original ancient works. Chapter 3 shifts the focus to the experience of the listener. How the radio medium enabled what might be termed practical access to the stories, histories, and ideas of ancient Greece in this period is the first point of discussion in Section 3.1. The democratic aspects of radio broadcasting are examined with reference to considerations such as the ubiquity of radio sets in the domestic sphere, the low cost of the activity, what is known about patterns of listening across age, gender, class, and geographical lines, and the absence of listening etiquette (despite the efforts of early radio practitioners to impose it), resulting in a characteristic lack of those boundaries (pertaining to economics, class, education, and geography, for example) which may be variously perceived or experienced as conditioning access to and engagement with cultural activity in other spheres. The various methods of 'translation' that a Greek text underwent prior to being broadcast as a radio programme is then explored using the example of Greek drama: these include the use of an English translation or adaptation, the degree to which the text is manipulated for the specific dramatic conventions and dramatic possibilities of the radio medium, and the contextual information provided by introductory talks and illustrated articles in the *Radio Times* and *The Listener*.

The discussion then explores how radio throughout this period functioned as an educative medium, the most formal aspect being the large number of broadcasts to schools across the entire period under discussion. Furthermore, adult listeners in the 1920s and 1930s could take advantage of scholarly series of talks on ancient Greek literary, historical, and archaeological topics, many of which were accompanied by inexpensive pamphlets designed to facilitate discussions in the huge number of organized listening groups across the country. Also under discussion is the more informal educational impact of broadcasting, as it is reflected in letters sent to the BBC by listeners, many of whom happened to be educators who testified to the ways in which they themselves had been further educated by such broadcasts and stimulated to introduce Greek texts in translation in the classroom and conduct amateur performances in schools. Finally, radio's collaboration with another educational and cultural sphere beyond broadcasting—that is, reading and publishing—is examined with particular reference to the mutually supportive relationship between radio programmes drawing on ancient Greece and Penguin Classics, a paperback series which was operating from the same ideological ground and had, the evidence shows, a similar liberating effect on its readers.

The second section of Chapter 3 examines the close affinity between radio dramatization (used not only in the presentation of drama but also in, for example, documentary-style features) and other 'storytelling' forms such as the novel, Homeric poetry in ancient performance, and the messenger speech in Greek tragedy; it also explores the distinct differences between the performance of ancient texts on radio and on stage or screen. It argues that the absence of physical impersonation or visual representation of the action on radio requires no compensation of language to conjure a visual surrogate in the imagination; rather, the soundscape of words, music, and other noises is interpreted in a cumulatively impressionistic way, with the natural intimacy of the medium bringing the listener into a psychologically close connection with the ancient character or story. Furthermore, it is argued that the ease with which radio effects imaginative transports into another/another's world and the psychological intimacy achieved between listener and character serve to sharpen the sense of the constancy of human nature across time, geography, and cultures, which is a particularly important trait for engagements with cultural works arising from Greek communities living over two millennia ago. In short, then, Chapter 3 argues that value can be found in the fact that individual listeners from a wide range of social and educational backgrounds were drawn to engage on their own terms with radio representations of the ancient world and that these acts of engagement had the potential to be culturally informative, educationally enriching, *and* imaginatively stimulating.

The five chapters that make up Part Two present and discuss the evidence which exists on a wide selection and variety of programmes drawing on Greek stories, histories, and ideas in this period, with an emphasis both on the contexts and processes of programme-making and also on the response to the programmes from individuals listening at home and critics writing in the press. This concentrated focus on a selection of programmes offers examples of cultural traditionalism, creative collaboration, artistic and technical innovation, a variety of internal and external influences on the processes of programme-making, and a number of fascinating formal and informal collaborations with cultural spheres beyond the BBC. On this basis, the case studies demonstrate the methodological points made in Chapter 1 that not only is it possible to study these radio programmes as cultural events 'in the round' which manifest considerable tensions and contradictions, but also that these multiple perspectives and rather untidy aspects of the cultural history actually enrich our understanding and make the history more, rather than less, meaningful. The studies amply demonstrate that the subject of this book cannot be adequately represented by an uninterrupted narrative (by which is meant one that is seamlessly and progressively evolving), but that it is instead done fuller justice as one which embraces shifts, contradictions, challenges, and tensions. As detailed windows on exceptional conjunctions of circumstances, the case studies in these five chapters confirm the complexity of the subject and enrich the general argument.

These chapters are not primarily or even especially concerned with making qualitative assessments on where individual programmes fall on any line of 'evolution' of radio broadcasting.[6] All sought to engage the listener within particular institutional, technological, creative, and broader cultural and educational contexts and what is interesting is how they variously went about this and what the listener thought of the programmes. Two important observations arise: first, there could be interesting differences between the programme-makers' intentions for a programme and the way in which listeners actually engaged with it; secondly, there could be a wide diversity of response amongst the body of listeners to one programme. These observations suggest the autonomy of the listener and the personal nature of the listening experience, both of which reinforce the argument made in Chapter 3 for radio as a democratic and imaginatively engaging medium. Therefore, as argued in the Conclusion, these radio programmes may be considered to be in a significant sense 'public property', in that they brought ancient Greece potentially within the reach of all.

Chapter 4, the first of these studies, considers the significant contribution made by the classical scholar Gilbert Murray (1866–1957) to the task of putting ancient Greece on air, both in terms of the many

---

[6] With regard specifically to radio drama Lewis 1981*a*, 6–7 makes the important point that 'The scholar or critic who approaches radio from Literature or Drama is usually interested in serious and original radio writing of considerable artistic achievement. He looks to Louis MacNeice, [...] Samuel Beckett and other distinguished literary figures, and equates radio drama with the finest work the medium [...] has to offer. With regard to a mass medium like radio, this stress on "high culture" is of course unswervingly élitist; and although there is nothing immoral or reprehensible in this viewpoint, it can lead to falsification since it is likely to ignore that what goes under the heading of "radio drama" is extremely varied indeed.'

Drama Department productions of his translations of Greek plays from the 1920s to the 1950s (many of which benefited from his expertise during the production process and rehearsal) and also his introductory talks to these broadcasts and associated articles in the *Radio Times*. It is testimony to the BBC's Reithian project to broadcast the nation's cultural wealth—of which Murray's Greek play translations from the 1920s were themselves undoubtedly a part— that his translations continued to be a popular choice for radio production long after they fell out of favour on the professional stage. Over this period Murray also wrote and delivered a great number of general talks on classical and political subjects for broadcast both at home and overseas, a significant number of which drew on ideas from ancient Greece. Owing to his status as a considerable public figure (through his high-profile work for the League of Nations, for example), his collaborations with the professional stage, and, also, the sustained popularity over several decades of his verse translations of Greek drama, Murray was uniquely placed to make hugely effective use of radio to share his enthusiastic passion for ancient Greece (especially Greek drama as poetry and in performance), his political ideals, which were rooted in an ideological marriage between Hellenism and Liberalism, and his pursuit of harmony on the world stage.

A number of Murray's political broadcasts in the Second World War drew on ideas, and ideals, deriving from ancient Greece—as did many of those by the poet and writer Louis MacNeice (1907–63), some of which are the subject of Chapter 5. A crucial difference is that whereas Murray offered, in the main, translations or talks (for the Drama, Education, or Talks Departments), MacNeice worked ancient material into more creative dramatizations for Features. The name of Louis MacNeice may not be amongst the first to spring to mind when thinking about the afterlife of the ancient world in twentieth-century mass media. From 1941, however, when he began writing wartime propaganda scripts for the BBC, he wrote (and very often produced) some of the most interesting and animated radio dramatic adaptations of Greek and Roman literature broadcast by the BBC since its inception, thus revitalizing aspects of the ancient world for a modern, mass audience. Chapter 5 first considers his multi-layered career as poet, classicist, critic, radio writer, and radio producer before examining some of his early scripts which responded to the contemporary international situation during the Second World War, with a particular focus on *The March of the 10,000* (1941), *The Glory that is Greece*

(1941), and *Pericles* (1943), all of which rework ancient Greek historical texts for contemporary political purposes. It will be argued that MacNeice's educational background in classics together with his interest in modern Greece, combined with his skills as a creative writer and innate talent for exploring radio's potential for creative work, resulted in programmes which not only made the ancient world practically and imaginatively accessible to the huge, non-specialist audience but also (and increasingly, it seems, throughout his radio career) worked pragmatically to turn certain assumptions about the perceived inaccessibility and remoteness of classics on their head.

The Homeric epic poems have been an extremely rich source of material for radio presentation. Chapter 6 outlines how, in the early years of broadcasting when radio was very much concerned to serve as a channel for established cultural works (with a resulting fidelity to original performance forms), programmes drawing on Homer seem to have been delivered *as* oral poetry, in one voice, as if the listener were seated before the rhapsode; indeed these programmes were often broadcast to schools or as part of poetry series. From the late 1930s, however, the *Iliad* and the *Odyssey* were increasingly 'radio dramatized', by which is meant that certain dramatic aspects of the poems were teased out and developed in interesting ways, with the text delivered by different actors playing the various characters rather than one performer taking the responsibility of delivering all. A preliminary overview of some of the early dramatizations pays particular attention to *Twenty Years is a Long Time* (1949), Mary Garrett's 'light satire' of the *Odyssey* in which the returning war hero makes a painful and ultimately unsuccessful attempt to assimilate into his old, and now not-so-familiar, domestic environment, a scenario which could not fail to strike a familiar chord with the personal experience of some of those who had served both in battle and on the home front in the Second World War.

The remainder of the chapter focuses on two works: Edward Sackville-West and Benjamin Britten's *The Rescue* (1943), a retelling of the second half of the *Odyssey*, and Robert Graves's prize-winning 'epic for radio', *The Anger of Achilles* (1965), which reworks the *Iliad*. Sackville-West and Britten's collaboration on *The Rescue* (1943), the first substantial treatment of Homeric epic on BBC Radio and also the most enduring (with six further productions to 1988), resulted in a distinctive exploration of the dramatic potential of the medium which also examines how the close association of words and music suggest a reflective awareness of *The Rescue*'s relationship with ancient epic performance, especially through the character of the bard Phemius. Furthermore, the narrative resonates with the contemporary international situation and makes a persuasive case for the humanizing potential of aesthetic experience. Its exceptional status as a thoughtful meditation on the relationship between ancient epic performance and radio as a dramatic and storytelling form also plays a useful part in the thinking behind Section 3.2. By contrast, Robert Graves's *The Anger of Achilles*, broadcast over two decades later, was not written expressly for radio. Graves had intended to turn his version of the *Iliad*, first published in America in 1959, into a stage play, then a television work, and ultimately a film. While these initial, ambitious plans continually faltered, and other film versions of the *Iliad* meanwhile made it onto the big screen, a BBC Radio production of *The Anger of Achilles* proved to be extremely popular with its audiences and also a critical success, winning the prestigious Prix Italia in 1965.[7] It is observed that, however many scholarly feathers Graves ruffled with his sometimes eccentric interpretations of the ancient world, his lively re-writings of antiquity held enormous popular appeal.

Chapter 7 presents a diachronic survey of radio productions of Aeschylus' *Agamemnon* from the inaugural Greek tragedy on the Third Programme in 1946 (the first known BBC production of the play) to the production of Gabriel Josipovici's experimental *Ag* on Radio 3 thirty years later. Productions of tremendous variety, using translations and adaptations of the play by Louis MacNeice, Raymond Postgate, Constantine Trypanis, and Philip Vellacott, are discussed as far as the evidence allows in terms of the production process and the supportive programming, and also the response of the listeners and critics. Several productions involved important collaborations between the translator/adaptor with the radio producer, but what is clear from the extant recordings is that the dramatic preference of the producer is the most significant factor in determining the nature of the production. The landmark production of Josipovici's *Ag* was broadcast beyond the chronological span of this book but its inclusion in this penultimate chapter serves to illustrate the creative freedom that writers and producers would, in the decades following the end of Val Gielgud's culturally conservative leadership of the

---

[7] Established in 1948, the Prix Italia recognized talented creative writing for radio and, later, television.

Drama Department, come to exert on stage-plays, thus serving to throw into sharper relief the characteristic traditionalism of the department's output up to the mid-1960s.

The final chapter in the volume turns to comedy. Discussion of Gabriel Josipovici's 1976 *Ag* prepares the ground for the first section of Chapter 8, which offers a detailed exploration of one approach taken by the Features Department thirty years earlier towards the radio representation of Greek drama—but this time, perhaps significantly, the genre is Greek comedy rather than tragedy. Louis MacNeice's *Enemy of Cant* (1946) offers fresh translations of scenes from most of Aristophanes' plays which emerge from the 'real-life' situation of the playwright as he, over the years, converses about contemporary affairs with characters such as his lover, his slave, fellow playwrights, and a maskmaker. Such fictional interludes function—simply and brilliantly—to provide socio-political background and context for the scenes from the plays. The second section considers the considerable number of Aristophanic translations and radio adaptations which the BBC commissioned from the poet and playwright Patric Dickinson (1914–94) for broadcast in the 1950s, with a particular focus on his *Lysistrata*, which was not only produced on radio in 1957 but also on television in 1964 (much to Mary Whitehouse's chagrin, one imagines).

This book attempts to make a contribution both to classical reception studies and the history of broadcasting in Britain, but when looked at 'in the round' the radio programmes under discussion are also clearly part of a broader cultural history, not only in terms of their social and educational implications but also in the way radio practitioners worked hand-in-hand with educational and creative professionals in spheres beyond broadcasting. Formal links with other cultural and educational channels include the important connections with education (such as the listening groups of the 1920s and 1930s and the embedding of radio programmes in school curricula) and publishing (the circulation of talks in print via the *Radio Times* and *The Listener*, for example, and the mutually supportive relationship between the BBC and Penguin). In employing the services of classical scholars, the BBC ensured that the latest translations and ideas from scholarship were made available to a massive audience and scholars consequently learned how to communicate their work in an engaging way to an audience largely not schooled in classics. It is absolutely clear from an examination of all this activity that BBC Radio was not a second-rate channel of communication for the stale, unimaginative broadcast of cultural activity that actually belonged elsewhere. Nor was the perceived cultural influence one way: indeed, radio's relationship with the spheres of education, publishing, and the stage may more accurately be observed as creatively symbiotic.

It is welcome that radio has, in the last few years, begun to attract scholarly attention amongst those working under the aegis of classical reception studies.[8] It is hoped that the present volume will stimulate and encourage further rigorous work: there are very many more radio topics ripe for exploration by those working in the field of classical reception studies, for example, and several other productive angles of study may be brought to bear on the material discussed in this volume.[9] I will take forward my work on the life of Homer in radio performance, the educational potential and value of the radio medium, and the different ways in which radio and television media engage with Greek drama.[10] I hope that some topics touched on only briefly here will attract more detailed examination by others with the relevant expertise: most obviously, there is much more to be said about the important musical dimension of radio programmes, for example; an in-depth discussion of the many and varied radio dramatizations drawing on Greek philosophy demands to be written; and a study of radio engagements with ancient Greece after the 1960s could make excellent use of many more practitioner interviews and engage with the important complexities of the multi-platform information landscape of the twenty-first century.[11]

---

[8] This includes Morris 2007 on Gilbert Murray and the BBC, Hodkinson 2010 on, amongst other things, the association of Sparta and Nazi Germany in radio talks by classicists and ancient historians before and after the Second World War, and Papoutsis 2011 on Greek tragic productions on Canadian radio. M. McDonald 2007 (subtitled 'Oedipus in Opera, Radio, Television and Film') offers only a page or two on radio.

[9] I estimate the international history to be equivalent in size to that of the ancient world on film, an area of scholarly endeavour which is now happily well established (see, for example, J. Paul 2008 and 2013, Shahabudin 2006, and the extensive bibliographies therein).

[10] See, in particular, this book's companion volume *Greece on Screen: Greek Plays on British Television* (Wrigley 2016a, forthcoming).

[11] To cherry-pick just a few examples: the four-part series *An Odyssey Round Odysseus* (Radio 4, 1989), produced by Beaty Rubens and presented by Oliver Taplin, which was accompanied by a BBC Books volume (Rubens and Taplin 1989); Simon Armitage's dramatization of the *Odyssey*, commissioned by BBC Radio 4 and broadcast over a weekend in 2004 and later published as Armitage 2006; and Timberlake Wertenbaker's re-telling of Sophocles' *Trachiniae* as the radio play *Dianeira* (Radio 3, 1999; later published in Wertenbaker 2002).

1

Mass Media and Classics, the Public and Cultural Élitism

My mother, sister and I have just finished listening to *The Hippolytus* on the wireless, and we feel that we cannot do other than ask you to accept our thanks for having brought this play within our reach by translating it into English.

From the moment when we began reading this work in preparation for to-day's broadcast, we found ourselves taking a spontaneous interest in it, and felt in particular that we were making contact with the characters. We were very grateful for last Thursday's Introduction, since it left us with a deeper and wider sense of the significance of the play than we had before it.

To-night we are full of wonder at the vivid and sustained tragedy which we have heard, and we realise that this has been for us yet one more of life's unforgettable experiences.[1]

This is an extract from an unsolicited letter written by one Mary Jameson of South Norwood, London to Gilbert Murray, the classical scholar who did much to encourage and enable those beyond the academy to engage with Greek drama in translation and in performance (as discussed in Chapter 4). The 'wireless' broadcast to which Jameson refers was a 1936 production of Euripides' *Hippolytus* in Murray's verse translation, which had been prefaced a few days earlier by a twenty-minute programme designed to give the listener 'some idea of the play's content and history' (see Figure 4.1).[2] Jameson's appreciative letter provides (far from rare) evidence that listeners valued the potential of radio to broaden cultural and educational

---

[1] Letter from Mary Jameson to GM, 18 October 1936 (GM/S).
[2] *Radio Times*, 9 October 1936, 62.

horizons and, thus, it retrospectively justifies the BBC's endeavours to broadcast to the nation (and indeed beyond) what it believed to be its cultural wealth (on which concept see Section 2.1). It also demonstrates the willingness of some listeners to do preparatory work before the broadcast of a play and (a connected point) it testifies to the impact of radio on reading habits, as well as documenting the practice of communal domestic listening.

Much of the discussion in Part One of this book is founded upon the existence in the archives of a substantial amount of this kind of evidence for the audience's opinions on radio engagements with the stories, histories, and thought of ancient Greece. Of course, not all of this evidence is as wholly appreciative as Jameson's letter and much is more measured, ambivalent, and negative. These opinions, too, are useful and important, but I have chosen this particular example to open this chapter for what it usefully says about the powerful and long-term positive impact that mass media engagements with antiquity could have on the cultural life of individual listeners and, therefore, we may say, the public imagination.

These sources present us with something fascinating and valuable: contemporary evidence about how the general public—dressmakers, cooks, lawyers, railway operatives, shop assistants, civil engineers, nurses, professional classicists, factory workers, clerks, school pupils, housewives, university students, and library assistants among them— themselves engaged with creative engagements with ancient Greece over several decades. Coming across this evidence and trying to make sense of it led me to reflect on how I, and others, were practising classical reception studies. Faced with such rich and detailed evidence, it suddenly seemed rather short-sighted to write as if the public audience, for whose enjoyment and interest modern cultural works drawing on antiquity were at least to some extent created, was not a significant topic within critical discourse. Such practice seemed to diminish the actual life of these works in the public imagination—in other words, to miss an extraordinary opportunity to discover the agency of the individual in creating meaning and obtaining something positive (or not) from cultural encounters with the stories and histories of ancient Greece.

Furthermore, it became clear that the public's spectrum of engagements with creative works drawing on antiquity was to a considerable extent more diverse than the determining institutional or practitioners' intentions behind the making of an individual programme.

Not to include the audience's experience within the realm of what is perceived to constitute 'reception' therefore (perhaps conveniently) ignores the distinct and potentially awkward possibility that neither the intentions behind the creation of cultural works nor the critical response of, for example, reviewers in the press map accurately onto audience experience. Not to include the voice of the audience in critical analysis results in the telling of only one or two strands of a much more complex cultural history: indeed, the classicist Simon Goldhill has recently established that it is 'potentially a damaging oversimplification to exclude audiences from [Classical] Reception Study'.[3]

In this context, the work of Hans-Robert Jauss has particular significance.[4] Jauss's terminology of 'production' and 'reception' is implied and inscribed in the very name of classical reception studies, and is neatly mirrored in the traditional model of broadcasting, which involves the dissemination of information from an institution to a passive audience which does not send any information back. The evidence available in bountiful supply in the archives on audience engagement and response challenges this traditional top-down model of broadcasting to the extent that Jaussian terminology appears to require substantial modification in order to accommodate the full possibilities of exploring this important aspect of cultural history.

First, then, this chapter argues for the promotion of an alternative model of reception founded on the idea of 'engagement' in which all participants in a cultural event are valued as active and autonomous. Leading on from this is a discussion of the idea that modern cultural works drawing on the stories, histories, and thought of ancient Greece are most productively studied 'in the round'—that is, from as many

---

[3] See Goldhill 2011, 10, on such 'failures of [...] memory' that occur in the writing of cultural history: 'what has to be *forgotten* in the construction of a past' (original emphasis). He goes on (14 ff.) to state that one of the 'particular hermeneutic problems for reception studies' is 'How are we to evaluate the impact of *Ben Hur* when it reaches an audience whose cultural knowledge is so different from the usual educated audience envisaged by Reception Studies?', declaring an interest in something that is often neglected in Classical Reception Studies—'the messy business of how meaning or significance [...] takes shape in society, over time, and between genres', a point that is taken up later in this chapter.

[4] Hans Robert Jauss's Rezeptionsästhetik ('aesthetics of reception') promoted the idea of a channel of communication between the acts of 'production' and 'reception': see Hardwick 2003, 6–8 for a summary, Holub 1984, 57–63 for discussion, and Jauss 1982 himself, in English translation.

different perspectives and in as many contexts as the available evidence allows. This practice involves addressing not only the work in and of itself (be that a translation, painting, theatre performance, modern dance, film, television programme, or radio broadcast), the nature of its relationship with the ancient model(s) on which it draws, and the creative forces who contributed to its existence, but also the particular historical and political circumstances and the practical processes of its creation, in addition to how individual members of its various audiences engaged with it (so, not just the critics). Studying cultural works 'in the round' in this way necessarily involves carefully analysing the tensions and contradictions that exist between different kinds of source and the alternative perspectives they bring, and it therefore respects the many different acts of engagement that can be perceived to occur with a cultural work. This kind of multi-lens study is, I can confirm, untidy and a challenge to handle, but it undoubtedly yields a fuller and, therefore, arguably more valuable cultural history. This approach stands in contrast to 'grand narrative' scholarship which, in order to achieve its goal smoothly, can sometimes be seen to skim over sources which pose difficulties of interpretation. It also seeks to encourage more complex studies than those which seem possible through the traditional one- or two-track approach along well-trodden literary, aesthetic, or political paths utilized by many existing studies in classical reception. This shift towards greater equality in the treatment of different kinds of source and stronger engagement with the perspectives and practices of other kinds of cultural histories may be interpreted as something of a 'democratic turn' within classical reception studies.[5]

The chapter then moves to consider the democratic qualities of the mass medium of radio (in terms of practical and imaginative access to a broad spectrum of cultural works and political discussion, for example, and the relatively cheap and domestic nature of the medium) and the ways in which the BBC documented and archived the response of the audience to its programmes. The existence of such a rich mine of sources for audience engagement may, it is suggested, add something else of value to current debates in classical reception studies: not only do such sources provide evidence for a hitherto

---

[5] For the variety of ways in which this phrase is currently being interpreted within classical reception studies see Hardwick and Harrison 2013, a volume in which an earlier version of this chapter appears as part of a longer essay (Wrigley 2013*b*).

uncharted realm of engagement that by any measure is of great importance to cultural history, but the very fact of their existence for some spheres of cultural activity may also serve to encourage consideration of the 'silence' of the public voice in research on other spheres of cultural activity that genuinely have nothing extant by way of evidence for audience engagement.

Equality of engagement

Let us now turn to an example of a radio work that engages with the literary remains of the ancient Mediterranean world to consider how the term 'engagement' can be productively used in practice. Louis MacNeice's *Enemy of Cant: A Panorama of Aristophanic Comedy* is a dramatic feature programme that was broadcast in 1946 on BBC Radio's Third Programme network. This programme (the focus of Section 8.1) offered MacNeice's fresh translations of scenes from most of Aristophanes' extant comedies, which he situated within his own fictional scenarios in which the playwright, over the years, converses about contemporary affairs with characters such as his lover, his slave, and fellow playwrights. These 'real-life' interludes serve to provide effective and useful social and political context for the scenes from the Aristophanic plays. MacNeice was not only the writer of the script but also the programme's producer, working with the composer Antony Hopkins and its many actors, among whom was the poet Dylan Thomas.

Enemy of Cant may be interpreted as MacNeice's own act of literary and (radio) dramatic engagement with Aristophanes, and his collaborations with the composer, actors, and other creative forces in the realization of the script in the form of a radio programme offer other enriching realms for study; such a study must be mindful of the institutional and departmental contexts that, to an extent, impacted on creative possibilities and practical choices. The sources to be consulted for a broad understanding of this programme are not only, therefore, the script, the score, and the archival recording of the performance but also the available letters between MacNeice and his departmental colleagues and the other creative forces involved in the programme, as well as his private letters to friends such as T. S. Eliot and an introductory essay he wrote for the *Radio Times*. Those who listened to the three radio broadcasts of *Enemy of Cant* in

December 1946 were undoubtedly involved in their own acts of engagement with the programme as broadcast—with this 'version', we may say, of Aristophanic drama. Many responses from individual listeners are documented in the archives of the BBC (as noted in Section 8.1, a teacher reported that 'it was received with great relish by a class of non-classical senior girls here', but another listener considered it 'a bit of wimsy wamsy put on by the Senior Common Room');[6] other perspectives are represented by critics writing in newspapers (for example, Hopkins's musical engagement with Aristophanes, via MacNeice's script, received high praise: 'There were moments in *Enemy of Cant* when he seemed to take over a mood or a situation which had baffled the ingenuity of MacNeice').[7]

When viewed in this way, the cultural event of the radio programme manifests several different layers of engagement with Aristophanes which are too complicated and subtle to be described adequately by Jaussian terms of 'production' and 'reception'. These terms may, at first glance, seem to fit the activities of making radio programmes ('producing') and listening to radio programmes ('receiving') rather well; however, they are too loaded with the sense that 'producers' of a cultural work are active and 'receivers' passive to be accurate and useful. I therefore propose that the various activities that may be studied under the broad span of classical reception studies could be much more productively understood as 'acts of engagement' with aspects of Greece and Rome.

This alternative terminology better captures the active (rather than passive) imaginative and creative aspects of coming into contact with the literature, history, and ideas of and about the ancient Mediterranean world. Language of 'engagement' not only moves away from the unhelpful active/passive power balance embedded in the terms 'production' and 'reception', but it also usefully permits some space for the complexity of the prior educational and cultural experience of all individuals involved in the Jaussian acts of 'production' and 'reception'. Not all 'producers' are so because of their privileged knowledge and experience of ancient Greek source material and neither are all 'receivers' lacking in prior knowledge or experience of these ancient works. For example, some of those involved in programme-making at

---

[6] Letter from Mary Warry to LM, 29 June 1948 (R19/307); BBC WAC LR/6842 (R19/307).
[7] W. E. Williams 1946.

the BBC (such as MacNeice) had received a classical education, but many producers, writers, composers, and other creative forces had not. Similarly, the evidence demonstrates that whereas a significant number of listeners attest to not having received a classical education, a proportion do report some experience of having studied, researched, or taught ancient texts in the original language or in translation, for example.

Jauss's suggestion that a person engaging with a cultural work approaches it from a 'horizon of expectation'—or, in other words, from an individual position firmly rooted in a social and cultural context which cannot help but shape their interpretation of the cultural work—is, however, useful.[8] Educational and personal contexts are also aspects of life experience which can be said to be operational and relevant when engaging with cultural works. These four aspects—educational, cultural, social, and personal—are, of course, interactive and even overlapping, but they are sufficiently distinct and individually important to deserve consideration. Working with Jauss's notion of 'horizon of expectation' in the more complicated arena of 'engagement', as outlined above, leads to an appreciation of each individual's educational, cultural, social, and personal experience, as well as their expectations of and aspirations for the act of engagement—whether that person be Val Gielgud, the culturally conservative head of the Drama Department at the BBC for over thirty years, or Mary Jameson, who, as seen in the opening paragraph of this chapter, wrote to Gilbert Murray to share her own and her family's experience of first preparing for and then listening to a BBC Radio production of Euripides' *Hippolytus* in 1936.

In this way, free from the passive/active power balance inscribed in the Jaussian model, it is more easily observable that the nature and quality of the engagement of a member of the listening audience is influenced, but not governed, by the contribution of those who brought the work into being through their own acts of engagement with the ancient world. So Louis MacNeice, in writing and producing *Enemy of Cant*, was free (within the wide confines of the BBC's cultural broadcasting policy and with regard to the programme

---

[8] The term 'horizon' was already active in German philosophy: Hans-Georg Gadamer, for example, used the term to refer to 'the range of vision that includes everything that can be seen from a particular vantage point', and at a particular point in time (quoted by Holub 1984, 59).

needs and values of its Features Department and the limits of the budget and available technologies) to engage with Aristophanic comedy as he saw fit, drawing on his literary creativity and his own educational experience (his original intention with the programme had been 'to have a crack at the teaching of classics [...] in this country'),[9] and perhaps also his lack of success as a traditional lecturer in a university environment.[10] Equally, each listener was free to experience the programme as broadcast on his and her own terms. In other words, although members of the audience could only engage with the material selected for broadcast and in the way that it had been presented, they were otherwise free to experience it according to their own (educational, cultural, social, and personal) knowledge, experience, interests, and sensibilities.

The concrete evidence for the fact that an enormous number of individual listeners from a wide range of social and educational backgrounds were drawn, over several decades, to engage on their own terms with radio representations of ancient Greece is fascinating, but it also makes an important contribution to what is known about the cultural history of Britain and the cultural life and experiences of the British public. It is clear from the sources that these acts of engagement could be both culturally enriching and imaginatively stimulating (as well as, of course, boring, disappointing, and so on). A statement by Donald Low on radio adaptations of classic fiction may easily be extended to that proportion of the audience who got something positive out of radio presentations relating to ancient Greece:

> In common with other forms of 'serious' entertainment on radio [they] tend to be taken for granted. Yet they make a notable contribution to the nation's cultural life, giving fresh currency and immediacy to the words of great novelists, introducing individuals to books they did not previously know, recreating literary works in a new medium by a process that can be compared to translation.[11]

Furthermore, individual members of the listening audience display, in the sources, a notable level of autonomy in their engagements with what was broadcast, a fact which proves beyond doubt that these

---

[9] Memo from LG, 21 May 1946 (R19/307).
[10] Of his students at the University of Birmingham, MacNeice 1965, 131 wrote 'They were all so unresponsive, so undernourished', to the extent that he 'could not be bothered [...] no more desire to be a good teacher'.
[11] Low 1981, 134–5.

Jaussian 'receivers' were anything but passive. These observations from the example of radio may be productively extended to engagements with other cultural forms drawing on the ancient world—perhaps especially, but not necessarily exclusively, those in mass media.[12] For, as argued above, to write cultural history as if the public, the general reader, the theatre-goer, the radio listener, the television viewer, and the film-goer—in other words, the audience for which, at least to an extent, the cultural work was created—does not exist is to miss an extraordinary opportunity to discover the agency of the individual in creating their own meaning from cultural encounters with the literature, history, and thought of ancient Greece. In other words, it is to fail to engage with the *actual* life of ancient Greece in the public imagination.[13]

Classical reception studies 'in the round'

In working on radio engagements with the remains of ancient Greek culture, I am concerned with the literary afterlife of (mainly, but not exclusively) Greek dramatic, poetic, and historical texts as they have passed through the hands of creative writers and translators such as Kenneth Cavander, Patric Dickinson, Gabriel Josipovici, Louis MacNeice, and Gilbert Murray; but I am also interested in both the institutional policies and creative production processes that influence the choice and treatment of ancient texts for British radio, and also—equally—the life of the resulting works in the public imagination, as discussed above. The approach, as already indicated, is to look at these cultural works 'in the round', so far as the evidence permits. This means considering the evidence that exists on the writing of the script, the composition of the music, the making of the programme,

---

[12] The publication of *Classics for All: Reworking Antiquity in Mass Culture* (Lowe and Shahabudin 2009) was a significant milestone in the study of mass media forms within classical reception studies.

[13] It is interesting that classical reception scholars who are concerned with engagements with the material or visual cultures of ancient Greece and Rome have been among the first to take a broader perspective: examples include R. Davis 2013 on classicism at the 1893 Columbian Exposition, Shelley Hales's Crystal Palace Project (see http://sydenhamcrystalpalace.wordpress.com; accessed 4 May 2012), and Nichols 2012 on the Elgin Marbles at the Crystal Palace. On the inherent élitism within the academic subject of classics, which, to be engaged with at the deepest level, requires knowledge of Greek and Latin, see the following section.

institutional policies, the impact of economic factors, the publicity and the 'positioning' of the programme via the press, accompanying (introductory or educational) programmes, the political circumstances of the broadcast, the relationship of the work to contemporary, related productions on stage and film, and on radio networks in other countries, the views of the critics and the widely diverse spectrum of engagements with the programme amongst individual members of the audience listening at home.[14]

This approach is grounded in the reality of the event within cultural history, broadly conceived. It does not ignore the fact that programmes emerged from an institutional setting with active policies and cultural politics regarding the broadcast of works created many centuries before that technology existed. It also embraces the fact that the resulting productions have an undeniable literary pedigree and a relationship with prior translations, adaptations, and performances in these and other cultural forms, and that sometimes the scripts themselves made a new and vivid contribution to literary history through publication (and art, too, via the illustrations in these publications—see, for example, the wonderful drawings by Henry Moore for Faber's print of *The Rescue*, a radio *Odyssey*, in Section 6.1—and via the stunning illustrations by Eric Fraser accompanying *Radio Times* listings over many decades). In addition, it also considers the masses of evidence on actual individual reactions to these cultural events, despite the challenging fact that they often span a wide spectrum of personal critical opinion, with some audience assumptions and experiences being quite contradictory to the creative team's intentions behind a particular programme.

To approach the programmes 'in the round' in this way is, in truth, to expose the messy history of perhaps all cultural works, and not just those in mass media, but embracing these tensions, contradictions, and multiple perspectives may well enrich our understanding and lead to a fuller and more meaningful historical interpretation of the life and significance of cultural works. Studies taking this approach may still attempt to place a string of cultural events in the larger

---

[14] Interestingly, Lewis 1981a, 3 writes that the purpose of his 1981 edited volume was to consider the whole range of radio drama, and 'from several different viewpoints: the BBC producer, the radio writer, the professional reviewer, the literary critic, the cultural historian, and the sociologist of mass communication'—but not, evidently, the listener.

landscape of cultural history, but they will not do so in an unproblematic way; rather, they will demonstrate a critical awareness that for each cultural event the story is bound to be complicated and the audience's engagement with it mixed. Furthermore, it is suggested that the possibility and productivity of studying radio programmes from a multiplicity of perspectives and demonstrating an open acceptance of the sometimes considerable tensions and contradictions that lie within and between these perspectives is a methodological approach which may hold something of value for all work being done under the umbrella of classical reception studies, since it throws some significant 'silences'—areas that are not being included or even acknowledged in research methodologies—into sharp relief.

It is, of course, acknowledged that for a great number of cultural works which lie beneath the lens of classical reception studies the evidence for production and creative processes and audience engagements simply does not exist in such great abundance as it does for BBC Radio output. Some studies appear to bypass this perceived or actual dearth of sources by marrying the contemporary intellectual and critical response to a work (recorded in press reviews, and the archival and reprinted letters and diaries of literary and political figures, and others in a position of cultural authority) with the scholar's retrospective perception of the contribution or influence of the work in literary, political, or aesthetic terms.[15] However, from my experience of working on engagements with ancient Greece in a number of areas—namely, theatre, radio, television, education, and publishing—I can report that remarkably often some evidence for production processes and audience engagement *does* exist. The difficulty may therefore be not so much the absence of evidence but rather how to accommodate the often challengingly alternative perspectives that it offers within or alongside traditional scholarly interpretations. The understandable concern may be that the messy results of audience analysis (especially when the evidence cannot be

---

[15] This criticism may to an extent be directed at my own work (for example, my book on the performance history of Greek drama in Oxford: Wrigley 2011*b*). But that book does not attempt to construct an overarching narrative; rather, it is concerned to record and interpret a wide variety of responses to individual theatrical events, gleaned from careful sifting of contradictory opinions recorded in primary sources such as correspondence, diaries, autobiographies, and critical opinion in a wide range of periodicals and newspapers, always with an eye on the experience of the audience (albeit often recorded second-hand).

statistically robust, on which point see Section 2.1) or an inclusion of the nitty-gritty of production processes may create a far more uneven (and therefore, it is feared, less compelling?) story than the one that may be told by focusing on only one or two aspects of the cultural history.

This book intends to demonstrate that the more complicated or challenging aspects of cultural engagements with antiquity have the potential to enrich, rather than weaken, the cultural studies being written. When there is simply no observable evidence but the text (whether this 'text' is a translation, a playscript, a film, or a radio or television programme), it is hoped that the broader model of classical reception studies suggested here may encourage a more rigorous conception of, and more critical honesty about, what the available sources allow and what the unavailable evidence does not permit. Approaching the cultural event 'in the round', therefore, acknowledges the several acts of engagement which can be perceived to occur with respect to the ancient work. To privilege one angle of critical analysis—such as the literary—without taking into careful consideration such aspects as the commission behind the work, the intended audience, and the actual audience is to miss a rich opportunity to place the work fully within the reality of the circumstances of its composition and its subsequent life.

From twentieth-century cultural élitism to fresh perspectives

The fact that [radio] served a mass audience led easily to the intellectual canard that it could not be of any cultural significance. The fact that while it could provide serials and series of little intellectual importance it could also give, through Rudkin's translation, *The Persians* of Aeschylus the largest single audience this play had ever known, was overlooked. The single broadcast of a radio play, followed by one solitary repeat performance, does not create the sense of social occasion to be found in the theatre and has not attracted the attention of many dramatic critics. The reception of a radio play by the listener is a very private occasion and does not stimulate the kind of debate which can attend a theatrical production.[16]

---

[16] Rodger 1982, 155. The reference is to the dramatist David Rudkin's translation of Aeschylus' *Persians* (Third Programme, 1965), on which see Rodger 1982, 121.

The intellectual and critical prejudice against mass media, especially in the first half of the twentieth century, has roots in the reaction of the intelligentsia to the effects of late nineteenth-century educational reforms which by 1881 had made elementary education both free and compulsory for every child. As the literary critic and scholar of English literature John Carey has observed, 'The difference between the nineteenth-century mob and the twentieth-century mass is literacy. For the first time, a huge literate public had come into being, and consequently every aspect of the production and dissemination of the printed text became subject to revolution.'[17] It was for this newly enlarged literate public that the popular newspaper was born, a medium which was also subject to the contempt of intellectuals such as the literary critic F. R. Leavis. The spread of literacy and education was also regretted by writers such as T. S. Eliot and D. H. Lawrence; Aldous Huxley claimed that 'universal education has created an immense class of what I may call the New Stupid'.[18] The reaction of the intelligentsia to mass literacy was, argues Carey, the evolution of a new genre of difficult, anti-realist literature in the movement which came to be known as modernism:

> the principle around which modernist literature and culture fashioned themselves was the exclusion of the masses, the defeat of their power, the removal of their literacy, the denial of their humanity. What this intellectual effort failed to acknowledge was that the masses do not exist. The mass, that is to say, is a metaphor for the unknowable and invisible. [...] The metaphor of the mass [...] denies them the individuality which we ascribe to ourselves and to people we know.[19]

Louis MacNeice (pictured in Figure 5.1) himself openly confessed to negative feelings against radio before he started working for the BBC: he admits, 'I was, like most of the intelligentsia, prejudiced not only against that institution but against broadcasting in general.'[20] A common complaint—made, for example, by Leavis in 1930—was that mass media, in opening up the 'higher' arts to too

---

Earlier productions of *Persians* had been broadcast in 1939 (in Gilbert Murray's translation, with Sybil Thorndike as Atossa) and 1958 (in Trypanis's translation).

[17] Carey 1992, 5.   [18] Huxley 1934, 101.
[19] Carey 1992, 21. See Guthrie 1931*b*, 10, who distinguishes the individuality of the radio listener from the 'single crowd personality' of the theatre audience.
[20] MacNeice 1947*b*, 11. Rodger 1982, 5–8 offers a good discussion of the intellectual bias against the medium and radio drama in particular.

many, somehow risked levelling them downwards. Leavis believed that high culture should be the preserve of a minority in society, and not everyone:

> upon this minority depends our power of profiting by the finest human experience of the past; they keep alive the subtlest and most perishable parts of tradition. Upon them depend the implicit standards that order the finer living of an age, the sense that this is worth more than that, this rather than that is the direction in which to go, that the centre is here rather than there.[21]

Belief in an innate cultural aristocracy was widespread amongst intellectuals. It enabled them to defend 'the existence of a small group of people of exquisite sensibility, who know how to respond to works of art'—in other words, it was how they distinguished themselves from the rest of society.[22] In the 1940s, Virginia Woolf was clear in her dislike for the 'middlebrow' who increasingly had the means and the desire to follow the cultural life of those of 'higher' brow, like her. She specifically derided the BBC as being the 'Betwixt and Between Company' in, as she saw it, pandering to this part of society.[23] Carey argues that this cultural élite was concerned largely with the detection of 'pure form' in works of art and largely unconcerned with 'the human interests or emotions which artworks might seem to arouse'—and so, perhaps, concerned with form, tradition, and innovation, rather than engagement, personal experience, and emotional response.[24] Fascinating in this regard is a comment about radio and television broadcasts of established cultural works, made by the scholar of English literature and cultural studies Richard Hoggart in the early 1960s: 'mass communications do not ignore imaginative art. They must feed upon it, since it is the source of much of their material; but they must also seek to exploit it. They tend to cut the nerve which gives it life [...] but they find the body interesting and useful. Towards art, therefore, the mass media are the purest aesthetes; they want its forms and styles but not its meanings and significance.'[25] It seems that neither the intelligentsia of the first half

---

[21] Leavis 1930, 5.   [22] Carey 1992, 80.
[23] Woolf 1942, 198. On spatial metaphors for culture, such as 'high' and 'low', see Carey 1992, 74 and Napper 2000.
[24] Carey 1992, 80.
[25] Hoggart 1961b, 147. He has also described 'mass' or 'processed' culture as 'rap[ing] its material, consum[ing] it in deference to the assumed needs of its block-

of the twentieth century nor the cultural critic of the early 1960s are able to imagine that individuals who engage with cultural works via mass media may consequently experience a meaningful human response, comprising interest, emotion, and personal significance. Rodger helpfully sums up the issues in his comments on radio versions of theatre plays:

> the advent of any form of entertainment which suddenly enlarges the size of the audience or readership has nearly always evoked hostility from those who regarded themselves as the established arbiters of taste. [...] A theatre play may be safely judged within the consensus of a relatively small and select social group but there can be no sense of a shared occasion when a play can leap into the ears of almost anyone who cares to listen. It is easy then to conclude that such a play on radio or television can only be of appeal to the despised mass audience and that it cannot therefore be possessed of any artistic merit.[26]

At this point, it is worth reflecting on the opinion that Greek and Roman texts can only be properly appreciated in the original language and so, by implication, only by those who have had a classical education. In his 1923 Presidential Address to the Classical Association, the classical scholar and literary critic J. W. Mackail (1859–1945) derided all other acts of engagement—including English translations—as being merely 'simulacra'. Mackail expands on this idea as follows:

> Translations of a Classic are at their best only commentaries; of great use as helps, but not substitutes. [...] Something has reached them which derives from Greece, but has become diluted or distorted or debased in transmission. It may retain enough of its value to act, but to act, according to the circumstances, as an intoxicant, or a narcotic, or a high-explosive.[27]

Mackail seems to suggest that nothing good can emerge from the translation of cultural works into other languages and different media (he mentions, in particular, film) for new audiences who would, by implication, only be engaged in a rather hazardous version of what Leavis and Denys Thompson would a decade later come to call 'Substitute-Living'.[28]

---

audiences' (Hoggart 1961a). These comments are particularly striking given that Hoggart was at this time serving on the Pilkington Committee on Broadcasting.

[26] Rodger 1982, 6–7.   [27] Mackail 1925, 197–9.
[28] Leavis and Thompson 1933, 99.

Arguing in this way for what some may term the cultural 'authenticity' of original works (and therefore the 'inauthenticity' of new works inspired by or drawing upon them) functions as a call for the preservation and the defence of the original from such creative interference. In her discussion of the reception of popular films drawing on antiquity, Kim Shahabudin perceptively notes that 'popular culture's infiltration threatens the privileged cultural status enjoyed by Greece and Rome as the "foundations" of western literature and art, leaving the classics community without a defence against pragmatic criticisms of their topic's utility'.[29] Objections to perceived 'inauthentic' engagements often draw on arguments relating to (i) the damage that is perceived to be done to the original work and (ii) the inferior quality of the cultural life of the audience for the new work. Whereas Woolf roundly derided the 'middlebrow', other critics more politely located their dissatisfaction in a concern for the perceived power of mass media 'to beguile the innocent, the uneducated and unwary'.[30] Mass media reach enormous numbers of geographically scattered and diverse individuals amongst whom the traditional boundaries conditioning engagements in other (non-mass) media or cultural forms do not apply, a situation which to some extent denies the critic and the intellectual their authoritative roles. The cultural critic's rather irrational fears concerning, on the one hand, the castration of the work s/he would wish to have the authority to critique and, on the other, the quality of cultural engagement by the naïve and gullible audience seem to mask the more understandable fear of personal powerlessness and irrelevance, explicable as a response to the shock of the challenge posed by mass media to long-established socio-cultural divisions and their own position as 'gatekeeper'. Bourdieu's theory that classification of cultural works by 'brow' is principally sustained by those in a position of educational and cultural power within society with a view to preserving their established authority is here pertinent.[31]

---

[29] Shahabudin 2006, 3.
[30] Scannell and Cardiff 1991, 17. Frattarola 2009, 449 accepts that 'One does not have to look far to find evidence of modernist writers wary of the invasiveness and mass appeal of the radio' as prelude to an exploration of the more nuanced aspects of the relationship between modernism and the medium, a topic also ably explored by Avery 2006 (who at 54 ff. discusses Woolf's three radio broadcasts).
[31] See, for example, Bourdieu 1985.

However, in the context of this book, the obvious and somewhat contradictory point should be made that a number of those involved in putting ancient Greece on the radio—classical scholars, translators, poets, creative writers, and radio producers—*had* themselves studied Greek at university and, in the case of scholars, were still very much a part of that élite academic community, yet were complicit in the project of making radio 'versions' of the stories, histories, and thought of ancient Greece practically and imaginatively available to Everyman and Everywoman, a keen and interested body of individual listeners which was geographically, socially, culturally, and educationally very much unbounded.

2

The Contexts of Programme-Making

2.1. CULTURAL BROADCASTING: ORIGINS AND AIMS, NETWORKS AND 'BROWS'

If broadcasting was a force for the improvement of taste and knowledge and manners, as well as a means of promoting social unity, the task was to enable men and women throughout the country to take an interest in things from which they had previously been excluded.[1]

BBC Radio was a mass medium at the very heart of British domestic life for more than three decades—from its birth in the mid-1920s until at least the late 1950s. As a public service broadcasting channel for news and entertainment, it served to raise public awareness of matters both political and cultural (and sometimes both at the same time). Under John Reith's long and formative leadership (1922–38) the BBC exercised a 'clear pedagogic function', devoting its energies to granting a wide public common access to the full range of the nation's cultural wealth and political debate.[2] As broadcasting historians Scannell and Cardiff point out, hitherto many of the political and cultural resources made available by domestic radio broadcasting had been available only to self-selecting publics who enjoyed some level of privilege: 'Broadcasting equalized public life through the principle of common access for all.'[3] The notion of the cultural wealth, or cultural heritage, of the nation embraced a very wide range of forms of

---

[1] Hendy 2007, 2–3, referring to Reith's ambition to broadcast high-quality programmes to 'the greatest possible number of homes' (Reith 1924, 61); a similar sentiment is expressed by Scannell and Cardiff 1991, 7.

[2] McKibbin 2000, 460. Reith (1889–1971) served as General Manager, 1922–3; Managing Director, 1923–7; and Director-General, 1927–38 (Briggs 1961, 135 ff.).

[3] Scannell and Cardiff 1991, 14.

expression—from what was termed the 'highbrow' to the 'lowbrow'—the single criterion applicable to all programmes was that they should be of a high quality. This was a venture with rather paternalistic undertones, growing out of Reith's firm belief that broadcasting had the potential to unite society and at the same time elevate educational, artistic, and even moral standards. However, the attempt to establish a national culture was not without its critics at the time, and historically it has been viewed as having the flavour of an educational and improving Christian mission, imposing the narrowly defined cultural tastes of one part of society on a wide public, ostensibly for their social advantage but without any actual shift in the balance of power within society.[4]

Reith defended his position thus: 'it is occasionally indicated to us that we are apparently setting out to give the public what we think they need—and not what they want—but few know what they want and very few what they need. [...] In any case it is better to overestimate the mentality of the public, than to under-estimate it.'[5] In 1930 J. C. Stobart (1878–1933), Director of the BBC's Education Department, warned of possible comparison between Reith's idealism and totalitarian regimes: 'Perhaps we cannot adopt the Mussolini pose and refuse to consider anything which does not accord with our aesthetic notions of suitable programme material. Besides, however broad our minds are, we are not as broad-minded as our many-headed audience.'[6] It was not the case that Reith ignored the tastes of listeners, but he was not prepared to let popular tastes dominate programming.[7] An important related point is that Reith's notion of public service broadcasting conceived of listeners not as a mass, but as a public or a series of publics, composed of individuals, 'irrespective of age and sex, tastes and education, religions and politics, wealth and status'.[8] Reith and his colleagues viewed the medium as potentially 'an instrument of public good', with education 'in the broadest sense' considered to be, alongside entertainment, 'an equally important objective'.[9] This was, of course, indicative of their own social philosophies, as Scannell and Cardiff note: 'Victorian ideals of service

---

[4] Ibid. 9; see also LeMahieu 1988. On Reith's Christian principles see Briggs 1961, 240–1 and 272–3.
[5] Reith 1924, 34.   [6] Quoted in Whitehead 1989, 8.
[7] McKibbin 2000, 465.   [8] Briggs 1961, 239; Reith 1928, 32.
[9] Ibid. 7–8.

laced with Arnoldian notions of culture suffused all aspects of the BBC's programme service in the thirty years of its monopoly. Such attitudes, in broadcasting, as elsewhere, did not outlast the fifties—or at least not with the degree of unself-critical aplomb that they had hitherto possessed.'[10] However, the fact that the emergence of radio broadcasting as a considerable social force roughly coincided with the establishment of gender equality in the matter of voting certainly underlines radio's potential as a positive instrument of social democracy in these decades:

> Radio, in an organised social form, seemed to be one significant and unprecedented means of helping to shape a more unified and egalitarian society. [...] A common culture might be established by providing listeners with access to music and other performing arts and cultural resources from which most had previously been excluded. [...] a conception of broadcasting as an instrument of democratic enlightenment, as a means of promoting social unity through the creation of a broader range of shared interests, tastes and social knowledge than had previously been the portion of the vast majority of the population.[11]

An important strand within the idea of the nation's cultural heritage was the ancient world, which consequently had a vigorous, varied, and fascinating life on radio, almost always in translation and very often in some form of dramatized presentation. That Greek and Roman texts and subjects should feature prominently within the project to broadcast the best of British national culture seems at first glance to make sense. Classics had long been so dominant a part of the British upper-class educational curriculum, firmly embedded within the wider cultural mind-set, and many radio producers had studied Greek and Latin at school and some had taken classics degrees at university. It is clear from internal memoranda that producers were very much at liberty to draw on their own educational and cultural experience and their contacts in cultural and educational spheres beyond radio when drawing up their programme ideas;

---

[10] Scannell and Cardiff 1991, 9; at 16 they define the national culture embodied by the National Programme as 'of the educated, south-east English variety' whereas the cultures of the Regional services emerged from local life and concerns. On regional broadcasting see Hajkowski 2010, ch. 4.
[11] Scannell and Cardiff 1991, 13. Women over 30 were granted the vote in 1918; in 1928 the Representation of the People Act permitted all adult women to vote on the same terms as men.

individual members of staff and their external contacts were therefore instrumental in shaping the cultural output of radio—as much as, if not more than, any top-down institutional objectives.

The educational study of classical subjects and the live performance of Greek and Roman dramatic texts were not within the reach of all within society. It was with the publication of paperback translations of Greek plays and repertory, touring, and amateur productions of these in the 1910s and 1920s (well beyond the London stage) that Greek drama, for example, had gradually become a more readily accessible aspect of the national culture.[12] It is also important that Greek tragedy in particular had been used as a powerful theatrical vehicle for socio-political, cultural, and (broadly speaking) educational projects which were driven by theatre practitioners, literary figures, academics, and undergraduate classicists (such as the Balliol Players and the Holywell Players at Oxford) for some years before domestic broadcasting from the 1920s began to take hold as the most readily accessible sphere for their performance. Penelope Wheeler, who had acted in several Greek tragedies at London's Court Theatre (1904–7) and the Gaiety in Manchester (from 1908), set up her own Greek Play Company to take Gilbert Murray's translations of Greek tragedy on tour far and wide across Britain in the years leading up to and following the First World War. In wartime, she performed Greek tragedies for British soldiers in France, setting up the Le Havre Repertory Company in 1917; after the war she acted in Euripidean plays for the poet John Masefield's (1878–1967) amateur Boars Hill Players, which sought 'to create a better England' by engaging local communities with verse drama from 1919.[13] Both Wheeler and Murray were for many years involved in other 'improving' schemes such as the University Extension Summer Meetings which brought hundreds of students to Oxford for several weeks over the summer vacation and where Greek (and other) drama often featured in the curriculum,[14] and the Oxford Recitations which Masefield had established in order to revive and encourage public interest in

---

[12] For example, by Gilbert Murray: see Section 4.1. Also noteworthy is J. M. Dent's (hardback) Everyman series, founded in 1906.

[13] Babington Smith 1985, 186–7.

[14] 'The Summer Meetings were, without question, important symbols of social solidarity. For a brief period each year the gates of learning were stormed by the underprivileged, and élite institutions could be seen to have recognized wider responsibilities to the community in a literally spectacular fashion' (Goldman 1995, 96).

poetry-speaking—a movement which Elsie Fogerty, who later directed the choruses in several radio productions of Murray's translations in the late 1930s (see Section 4.1), had done much to establish. The social, cultural, and educational idealism which lay behind this loosely connected network of activities also fired several student groups, including the Balliol, Holywell, and Osiris Players at Oxford, to take drama (and, in the case of the Balliol Players, almost exclusively Greek drama) on tour to towns and villages 'for the most part in districts where plays are not often seen'.[15]

The post-war, 'missionary' enthusiasm which fired such literary, theatrical, and academic figures, and indeed groups of students, to share what arguably had hitherto been a restricted educational subject and cultural activity with non-classically-educated public audiences far from the professional London stage seems clearly to foreshadow the frequent radio broadcast of much Greek drama in translation as part of BBC Radio's policy to offer the best of what was considered to be the nation's cultural wealth to the radio audience from the mid-1920s. Indeed both may be said to be related to the palpable intellectual anxiety about the imminent crisis of Western civilization which the historian Richard Overy has identified as being characteristic of the 'morbid age', the years immediately following the First World War up to the 1930s.[16] Concerns over such a crisis were evident in classical radio talks too: observe how Murray's six-part series *Why Greek?* in 1938 (discussed further in Chapter 4) encourages the listener to find within the remains of ancient Greek society valuable resources and qualities quite different from the 'dollars and miles and horse-power' of the 'complex material civilisation' of the twentieth century; several of his other talks attempt to ally aspects of Western civilization that are perceived to be worth fighting for in the Second World War with aspects of ancient Greek life and culture.[17]

In 1929, the *BBC Handbook* argued that radio could serve as a highly effective form of national theatre and many others came to view the medium as functioning in an important way as a 'national theatre of the air', at a time when an actual bricks-and-mortar

---

[15] *The Times*, 15 November 1926, 17. On these activities by Wheeler, Masefield, and the Balliol Players, see Wrigley 2011b, chs. 4 and 6. Wheeler later contributed to BBC Radio programmes on amateur acting.
[16] Overy 2009.   [17] Murray 1938a, 373 and 1938b, 434.

National Theatre was still some decades away.[18] David Wade observes that the appellation is appropriate in so far as the medium broadcasts 'British classics, ancient and modern' to an audience of listeners who enjoy drama but do not, for whatever reason, go to the theatre, but he considers it limiting in two senses. First, it should be termed an 'International Theatre of the Air', in light of its broadcasts of the classics of world theatre and the plays of living non-British dramatists; secondly, it makes many more dramatic productions accessible, and to far greater audiences—within these shores and beyond—than London's National Theatre.[19]

In these senses, the broadcast of programmes engaging with the literature and history of ancient Greece may be perceived as a radically, if subtly, political act in terms of the educational and cultural status of classics within Britain. The timing for this 'broader-casting' of Greek texts in translation to a wide public is also significant in that it came just a few years after the abolition of the entrance requirement of knowledge of ancient Greek at the Universities of Oxford and Cambridge following the First World War, a moment which, argues the historian of scholarship Christopher Stray, marked 'the end of the fifty-year process in which classics was marginalized in English culture'.[20] From the history of scholarship angle, then, the abolition of compulsory Greek may indeed be taken as symbolic of the end of the old order in which classics as a discipline held a privileged and powerful place in university education. Indeed, Stray goes on to argue that in the period from 1920 to 1960 Latin superseded Greek as the primary form of classical education in England: 'Latin discipline,

---

[18] British Broadcasting Corporation 1929, 74; Drakakis 1981*b*, 7; Lewis 1995, 899. Priessnitz 1981, 33 considers that radio's role as a 'National Repertory Theatre of the Air' was strong until the late 1950s when the term 'radio play' began to earn 'the same sort of meaning as the German *Hörspiel*'. Plans for what would become the National Theatre were in place from the end of the 1940s; the foundation stone was laid in 1951; the first National Theatre productions took place at the Old Vic in 1963; and the current building on the South Bank opened in 1976.

[19] Wade 1981, 219. It is interesting to note that the OU was founded upon the idea of a 'University of the Air', making good use of both radio and television in its distance-learning courses from the start. On 'the most extraordinary success-story' that is the OU's Department of Classical Studies see Taplin 1999, 4; and on the OU's use of television in the teaching of drama (including Greek plays) both as text and in performance, see Wrigley 2016*c*.

[20] Stray 1998, 269.

not Greek culture, was to be a symbol of the age of petty-bourgeois culture; at least until Oxford and Cambridge abolished [Latin] as a general requirement at the end of the 1950s.'[21] The point at which Greek came to be marginalized within higher education was, I suggest, closely followed by the democratization and popularization (terms which receive attention in Chapter 3) of Greek texts through English-language engagements with them on the very new mass medium of radio. If ancient Greek language-learning was thrown 'to the wolves' at this time, as Stray suggests it was in order to save Latin within educational curricula, then ancient Greek literature and history in translation and adaptation was simultaneously thrown open to the listening public in broadcasts which served as both entertainment and, broadly speaking, cultural education.

Significant also is the increasing centrality of what were considered to be the masterpieces of English literature—'a more relevant and less painful modern alternative to the classics'—in school and university curricula from the early twentieth century.[22] As Henry Newbolt (1862–1938), chair of a committee investigating the place of English in the national curriculum, put it in 1921, 'The time is past for holding, as the Renaissance teachers held, that the Classics alone can furnish a liberal education. We do not believe that those who have not studied the Classics or any foreign literature must necessarily fail to win from their native English a full measure of culture and humane training. To hold such an opinion seems to us to involve an obstinate belittling of our national inheritance.'[23] The underlying motive of this and similarly liberating cultural endeavours is said to have been, at least in part, the establishment of a sense of a common cultural identity which would, it was hoped, go some way to ameliorate national class-based social tensions. It is arguable that the concurrent increasing availability of much of the extant literature of ancient Greece in English translation both on the page and in some kind of performance on radio at this time was in an adjunct way related (and perhaps even a direct response) to this desire to make the great works of English literature accessible to all. At heart, both projects were working towards a common goal.

The production of Gilbert Murray's translation of Euripides' *Hippolytus* in 1936 provides a good example of a dramatic performance

[21] Ibid. 270.   [22] Scannell 2007, 97.   [23] Newbolt 1921, 18.

on radio being used as a vehicle for culturally educative purposes. The BBC had some months previously decided to broadcast a substantial introductory programme a day or two before each big Sunday drama: the purpose of this was 'to give the listener an introduction to the play, to show him its contents and appeal, and give some idea of the history of the play'.[24] The programme introducing *Hippolytus*, which had been written and delivered in part by Murray himself, discussed the play in its ancient performance context and in later translation and adaptation by Seneca, Thomas Newton (1581), Racine (1677), and finally Murray. In addition, Murray wrote an accompanying essay for publication in *The Listener* in which he explains aspects of the play which may 'puzzle a modern audience' (such as the Chorus and the goddesses) and encourages listeners to 'be patient, and give it a chance; do not reject things because they do not fit the fashion to which you are accustomed. Don't be frightened of long speeches— listen to them. Have faith that a work of art which still delights people 2,000 years after it first appeared must have something rather wonderful about it.'[25]

A decade later, in the Third Programme's first month of broadcasting, Racine's *Phèdre* was itself the focus of the first hour-long programme in the *International Drama: Comment and Action* series, the purpose of which was an examination of 'great classical dramas that are seldom performed in England': this programme included contributions from the French actor-directors Jean-Louis Barrault and Michel Saint-Denis, May Agate (who had the year previously published a biography of Sarah Bernhardt), and a recording in French of Sarah Bernhardt and Marie Bell performing extracts from *Phèdre* in French; in addition, extracts from an English verse translation of the play were performed by Margaret Rawlings (Phaedra), David King-Wood (Hippolytus), and others.[26] Yet another decade later saw a 3¾-hour Third Programme production of the *Oresteia* accompanied by a substantial amount of 'educational' programming: an introductory talk by the translator Philip Vellacott (1907–97) was

---

[24] Memo from FF to Mr Dowler, 1 October 1936 (GM/S).
[25] Murray 1936.
[26] Listing in the *Radio Times*, 11 October 1946, 24. Less than half of the listening sample had prior familiarity with the play; the programme nevertheless is said to have 'aroused considerable interest' (BBC WAC LR/6504).

followed in subsequent weeks by talks on the theological and moral aspects of the trilogy by the classicist Hugh Lloyd-Jones, and a programme in which Elsa Vergi of the Greek National Theatre read extracts from the trilogy in Greek which were interspersed with summaries in English. This kind of cultural programming, offered regularly over several decades, exemplifies how the BBC was not simply broadcasting with the assumption that each listener had the requisite amount of knowledge to enjoy ancient plays and their adaptations *au naturel*. Rather, on the whole, producers were concerned to translate, contextualize, and elucidate using methods from other realms such as teaching and scholarship (for example, pamphlets and talks) and the theatre (for example, directors in discussion and actors in performance).

The BBC realized the political power of radio long before it began using it for propagandist purposes in the Second World War. In 1934, D. G. Bridson (1910-80), who had just started writing and producing for the BBC North Region, wrote the play *Prometheus the Engineer* for broadcast. He describes it as follows: 'in the form of classical tragedy, and set in what I described as the Workshop of the World. Its hero, the Engineer, was vainly attempting to hold a balance between the factory floor and management. As was to be expected, he ended up as a victim of neo-luddite violence: the workers threw him to the machines.'[27] Bridson wrote the play to underline the need for economic reform and explore the potential of Social Credit. The North Region accepted it for broadcast, it was prominently billed in the *Radio Times*, and it even went into rehearsal with Ewan MacColl (1915-89) as the militant leader of the workers.[28] However, when it was submitted to Broadcasting House for approval the Controller of Programmes banned it, assuming that 'an argumentative play written around a revolt of the workers was manifestly inspired by

---

[27] Bridson 1971, 39.

[28] MacColl's father, an unemployed steelworker, had moved the family from Glasgow to Salford in pursuit of work in the 1920s. MacColl was 'discovered' whilst busking, singing Scots and Gaelic ballads outside a Manchester cinema; the BBC employed him both as a singer and as an actor (Bridson 1971, 35-6; Rodger 1982, 50). From the 1930s he was involved in experimental theatre projects with Joan Littlewood (1914-2002; his wife from 1935); in 1937 he wrote a version of *Lysistrata* entitled *Operation Olive Branch* for their Theatre Union; in 1948 she produced it in Manchester, Edinburgh, and London for their collective Theatre Workshop. See Denselow 2004, Warden 2007 and 2011.

the Comintern' and, therefore, 'dangerously seditious'.[29] When war broke out, however, the BBC applied for Bridson's military call-up to be indefinitely deferred, for they were keen for him—an experienced and skilled writer and producer for radio—to make propaganda programmes. Bridson rose to the occasion, believing that it was of great importance 'to get radio linked up purposefully behind the national war effort'.[30] In 1941 he moved from Manchester to London to organize Overseas Features, whose listenership he estimates was a couple of hundred million, and from around this time the BBC started receiving what he describes as 'a certain amount of editorial advice' from the Foreign Office.[31] He considers that the feature programme came of age in the Second World War:

> Feature producers had followed the armies, flown with the planes, sailed in with the ships, and had brought the new immediacy of sound to the impact of war reporting. They had dealt with every aspect of the war, and had brought to the microphone thousands of people whose personal stories had been an integral part of the war effort. No war had ever been reported and made real to a world audience in such vivid terms before, and a vital part in the process—emotional involvement of the listener by colourful re-enactment—had been played by the feature programme.[32]

During the war, whilst those responsible for drama productions built on pre-war foundations by using established works from the dramatic and literary canons in the BBC's project to preserve and promote what were considered to be 'civilised values', features staff worked towards similar aims in its broadcasts of newly written radio-specific works which often drew more creatively on the same canons and the Talks Department focused on more overtly political topics.[33] It was war-work that brought creative writers such as Louis MacNeice to the BBC to lend their talents to the creation of feature programmes which fulfilled 'propagandist' or 'morale-boosting' purposes.[34] The BBC had written

---

[29] Bridson 1971, 40; the BBC's ban encouraged T. S. Eliot to publish it in *The Criterion*. Briggs 1961, 269–70 notes that, although 'it is sometimes argued that the BBC helped to stifle the free discussion of public issues during the inter-war years and joined with other national agencies in imposing a blanket of silence', this was not true of 1922–6 when Reith sought to use radio to foster 'both industrial and political argument'.
[30] Bridson 1971 77.   [31] Ibid. 85.   [32] Ibid. 121–2.
[33] Quoted by Rodger 1982, 55–6.
[34] 'Propagandist' and 'morale-boosting' seem to have been used as synonyms by the BBC. Their propaganda programmes actively supported the Allied cause but they

to MacNeice in 1940 to ask whether 'some aspect of Nazism and its influence or its victims would appeal to you as the theme of a radio programme. [...] We in this country have not yet been able to secure a first class poet for such radio programmes and I feel convinced that your lines would speak well.'[35] As a former lecturer in classics who often turned to classical themes in his published poetry it is not surprising to find that much of MacNeice's wartime radio work in support of the plight of Greece drew creatively on stories from ancient Greek military history (as detailed in Section 5.2). 'The format which was required in straightforward propaganda features', writes Rodger of the early 1940s Features Department, 'involved narration, actuality recordings, dialogue inserts and music': this 'served as a model of instruction which producers like MacNeice, Bridson [...] then applied to the creation of dramatic entertainments. Some of these works would now be described as radio plays but their creators tended to refer to them as features.'[36] Thus, many of MacNeice's later radio dramatic works (such as *Enemy of Cant*) and Sackville-West and Britten's *The Rescue* were described as features despite clearly (also) being new and exciting forms of radio drama.

Around the same time that MacNeice joined the BBC, the writer Eric Linklater (1899–1974) was persuaded to write some dramatic dialogues by Val Gielgud (1900–81; see Figure 7.2, where he is pictured with his younger brother, the actor John). The first of these was *The Cornerstones* (1942), which was set, 'like some of the later dialogues, in the Elysian Fields [the final resting place of the great and the good in Greek mythology], where it was therefore possible to gather historical figures from different countries and periods and to allow them to engage in conversation. [...] The propaganda objective of the piece was to identify a common cause among those fighting Hitler's Germany.'[37] Linklater followed the pattern of *The Cornerstones* in his play *Socrates Asks Why* (also 1942) in which the character of Socrates discusses with Abraham Lincoln, Voltaire,

---

do not seem to have broadcast outright lies. For a contemporary account of radio in the Second World War see Rolo 1943 and on Lord Haw-Haw's broadcasts as Nazi propaganda and how they were received by the British public see M. A. Doherty 2000.

[35] Letter from T. Rowland Hughes to LM, 7 March 1940, quoted by Stallworthy 1995, 287. See Havers 2007 on the BBC as a source of information and propaganda during the war.
[36] Rodger 1982, 62.   [37] Ibid. 60.

Dr Johnson, and Beethoven whether the Allies are 'truly conscious of their purpose': Socrates asks Lincoln, for example, 'Why are you fighting Germany?' (p. 61) and many more Socratic questions follow as the play reaches the conclusion that the Allies must conduct the war with the aim of constructing a peace in which both justice and creativity can flourish.[38] The play strongly echoes the thrust of many of MacNeice's wartime propaganda pieces at the point when another character, Flying Officer Arden, after hearing Socrates extol the virtues of ancient Athens, wonders whether 'it may be a sort of omen that Greece was the first of the Allied nations to win a victory? When Mussolini threw those stuffed divisions of his into Albania, Greece came to life in the old way. [...] There was some quality in the Greek army, in the people of Greece, that was more than ordinary courage and determination. It was like a religion' (pp. 111–12). This kind of wartime dramatic dialogue inspired the producer of features Rayner Heppenstall (1911–81) to establish the *Imaginary Conversations* series which included *Aristotle's Mother: An Argument in Athens* (1946), a programme by Herbert Read (1893–1968) which featured the character of Aristotle in conversation with the Greek painters Apelles and Protogenes.[39] This important series opened up a new, flexible and experimental, form for which a wide variety of writers ('scholars, novelists and biographers') could write material on people and topics which were not necessarily attractive to dramatists but which could, on radio, through the skill of the producers, be presented in a dramatized form.[40]

The BBC, like other radio services during the war, was responsible for delivering to listeners at home and also overseas not only information and propaganda, but also entertainment:

> A range of entertainment which had to appeal to intellectual minorities as well as to the mass audience. There was a national mood which looked to the arts for solace and inspiration and, for the five years of the war, British radio was the main medium for this communication and education.

---

[38] Linklater 1942, facing title page. References in brackets are to this published version of the text. See Sommerstein 2007 on Linklater's 1938 novel *The Impregnable Women*, an adaptation of *Lysistrata*, and his Aristophanic stage-play *Crisis in Heaven* (1944).
[39] Read 1948. On Robert Graves and this series see Section 6.2.
[40] See further Rodger 1982, 80–2.

British radio became the national theatre. The fear that theatres might be bombed and the fact that their staffs were directed into more combative employment meant that most of the theatres in the country were closed for the duration of the war.[41]

The historian Asa Briggs considers that in wartime '"Art for the People" was canvassed more successfully by the CEMA than it ever had been before'.[42] CEMA indeed worked hard to address the increasing public demand for serious arts in wartime and to counteract the closure of the theatres by organizing tours, and these involved actors such as Sybil Thorndike (1882–1976) 'explaining the plot of *Medea* to miners' wives in the wartime Welsh valleys' and 'barnstorm[ing] her way through the valleys leaving in her wake a trail of audiences who knew that whatever they'd seen it was Acting'.[43] Val Gielgud sensed a remarkable opportunity for radio to help to fill the entertainment gap occasioned by the severe curtailment of many pre-war cultural activities. Writing to the BBC Home Service Board in December 1939 with a wartime drama policy proposal, he outlined his belief that 'few things can be more important during a war than the preservation of civilised values for which that war is being fought. [...] we should—as far as is possible—work to re-establish our pre-war standards of straight drama. Without ignoring in any way the demand for popular entertainment [...] we should find every means to represent the classic drama.'[44] Gielgud had, it is said, been waiting for this kind of opportunity ever since being appointed to lead the Drama Department:

> For many years, there had been a reluctance on the part of the administration to permit the broadcasting of the full classic repertoire because it was feared that some plays of this kind would not appeal to the mass audience. This had meant that the Greek classics, which are eminently suited to radio, and even some of the plays by writers like Ibsen were not thought acceptable. But in 1939 Gielgud was at last able to counter this

---

[41] Ibid. 54.   [42] Briggs 1970, 46.
[43] Morley 1977, 12 and 113. Only 2 per cent of the audiences for plays sponsored by CEMA had seen a theatrical performance before.
[44] Quoted in Rodger 1982, 55–6. The BBC's ability to provide a wide range of wartime entertainment was admired by one German commentator in 1942: 'London goes on with its radio programmes as if nothing had happened—people singing in the shelters; reports from a cricket match; nice and clever people make their talks; there is more dance music than before. [...] we must respect them for all this' (quoted in Briggs 1970, 45).

argument and relate his proposed expansion to the commonly accepted principle that the war against Hitler's Germany represented a struggle to preserve civilised values. He was aided by the fact that during the war the fairly persistent philistine attitude towards the arts in Britain was relinquished. [...] Seizing the opportunity of a change in the cultural climate, people like Gielgud were at last able to use radio to present the whole range of drama.[45]

The wartime policy for drama and features was, as a BBC memorandum outlines, to provide a 'contribution to the preservation of civilised culture in time of war' and 'implicit or explicit propagandistic contributions to national wartime activity'.[46] These two objectives were naturally somewhat overlapping both in practice and ideology. The drive to preserve 'civilised culture' may be understood as comprising complex motivations including the construction and maintenance of a sense of patriotism and community through the establishment of a sense of a common, national culture, which itself boosts morale in that it strengthens the feeling of 'us' against 'them', the identified enemy. It is arguable that radio had been involved in a form of 'nation-building' since the establishment of domestic broadcasting in the 1920s, in its presentation of a unified patchwork of life (encompassing music, drama, opera, politics, religion, royalty, sport, public speeches, and variety entertainments) newly available to all.[47] Furthermore, the Arnoldian use of works from the established canons of high culture to draw in new audiences also helped to give the extant texts of ancient Greece a new public identity beyond the schools and universities (where, as noted above, the study of ancient Greek was becoming increasingly marginalized). The employment of canonical works, including those from ancient Greece, to strengthen allegiance to the wartime cause in this way is especially interesting in the light of the broadcast of such material across Europe during the war—not only to Allied soldiers stationed abroad but also, for example, to German civilians. The BBC's work to capture 'hearts and minds' in this respect sought to counter similar mass media projects working to

---

[45] Rodger 1982, 56.
[46] Quotations from a BBC memo in Briggs 1970, 113.
[47] See Hajkowski 2010 on the role of the BBC in the construction of a pluralistic national identity in Britain in the period up to 1953; R. Dillon 2010 on how historical programmes on British television have contributed to the construction of national identity, and Anderson 2006 on the creation and transformation of nationalism through cultural artefacts such as novels and newspapers.

The Contexts of Programme-Making

sustain Fascist and Nazi ideologies.[48] In this regard the BBC's cultural propaganda can be understood as an active weapon in the 'war of words', garnering support for the Allied cause and boosting morale through an appeal to a shared European cultural tradition.[49]

The relationship between the BBC and its audience

During the war, radio had become a great cultural force and the focus of attention of any thinking man or woman.[50]

BBC Radio's audience had increased substantially during the Second World War because of its ability to function as a reliable channel for bringing both news and entertainment directly to the home and also to group settings such as pubs, restaurants, and schools.[51] This enlarged audience remained loyal to the medium in the post-war years, and the BBC responded with an expanded and revived broadcasting service. There was a confidence that broadcasting could continue to act—and with added vigour—as both an educational and a civilizing force, but in the post-war landscape the emphasis was on cultural broadcasting as an aid to social reconstruction and a palliative to the horrors of war. Interest in arts and culture had increased substantially during the war, and it seemed that for some years afterwards, too, 'ordinary people were demanding more "serious" programmes'.[52] Although, as Kate Whitehead continues, this demand could be interpreted 'as a temporary reaction to cultural deprivation rather than a genuine blossoming of interest in the arts *per se*', social changes such as those set in motion by the 1944 Education Act, which had raised the bar on educational standards across the board, were also influential on the educational profile and cultural tastes of the nation.[53] As Hinton observes in his work on Mass-Observation: 'For those liberated by education, leisure and the widening availability of high culture via the paperback, gramophone

---

[48] See Wyke 1997 on the use of antiquity on film as a tool to promote both fascist and liberal ideologies. Further study of the use of Greek literature, mythology, and history by the National Socialist regime on wartime German radio is needed. (This is not covered by Kris and Speier's 1944 *German Radio Propaganda*.)
[49] See Nicholas 1996, especially ch. 5.   [50] Rodger 1982, 69.
[51] See Briggs 1970, Illustrations 2(a), (b), and (c). On broadcasts to schools and adult listening and discussion groups see the following chapter.
[52] Whitehead 1989, 10.   [53] Ibid. 10–11.

record and radio, access to the classics of British and international fiction [...] offered routes to self-invention, ways of freeing the self from the closure of predetermined roles'.[54] In other words, in periods of social and educational mobility, especially following an event such as cataclysmic world war, audiences for cultural works are simply less predictable and more mobile.

The newly appointed Director-General William Haley (1901–87) may well have had such factors as the Education Act in mind when in 1944 he announced that post-war plans for the expansion of the BBC's broadcasting service, developed from the model of wartime broadcasting, would contribute to making Britain 'the best informed democracy in the world'.[55] Prior to the war there had been the single National Programme which was augmented with regional programmes to provide local variation. Upon the outbreak of war the National and Regional Programmes were collapsed into the Home Service, a channel for spoken-word programmes such as news, talks, and drama, which was retained post-war. The Forces Programme, established in February 1940 to offer light entertainment to the fighting forces, had proved hugely appealing to civilians as well and indeed it became the most popular of all networks on BBC Radio, not least because it was (unlike the Home) free from the pressure to broadcast propagandist programmes; it was transformed into the new Light Programme on 29 July 1945.[56]

On 29 September 1946, the entirely new Third Programme began broadcasting: its stated aim was to broadcast opera, musical concerts, drama, and talks of an unashamedly 'highbrow' nature to an audience which is 'already aware of artistic experience and will include persons of taste, of intelligence, and of education; it is, therefore, selective not casual, and both attentive and critical. The Programme need not cultivate any other audience.'[57] Joan Hassall's (1906-88) illustration for the cover of the BBC pamphlet *The Third Programme: A Symposium of*

---

[54] Hinton 2008, 219.
[55] Quoted in Briggs 1970, 723. The same sentiment is expressed in Haley 1947, 10.
[56] Briggs 1970, 46–7.
[57] 'Programme C: terms of reference (approved by D. G. [the Director-General, William Haley] 14.1.1946)', internal memo dated 16 January 1946 (R34/602). When the popular music network Radio 1 came on air in 1967, the Light Programme and the Home Service were renamed Radio 2 and Radio 4 respectively and the Third Network umbrella title, which included the Third Programme, became Radio 3 (the names they still have today).

Opinions and Plans (1947) used a cornucopia overflowing with literary, dramatic, and musical motifs—including a lyre, books, violin, horns, tragic and comic masks, and the inscription 'words words words' on the far right—to represent the type of fare the new network would concentrate on broadcasting. Classical references were also present within the content of the book itself. The first three months of the new network were described in the following terms: 'there emerged from the head of Zeus a most surprisingly fully-armed Athene. [...] Her armour may need a little modification, letting out here, taking in there, [...] but inescapably and securely herself, moving with greater certainty and grace as each month passes.'[58]

The post-war division of broadcasting into separate cultural channels implies the segmentation of the audience by cultural 'brow', with 'lowbrow' fare offered by the Light, and 'middlebrow' and 'highbrow' material by the Home Service and the Third respectively. After the establishment of the Third Programme, the national audience was divided up amongst the Light, Home, and Third as follows— approximately 66 per cent, 32 per cent, and 2 per cent respectively.[59] Such segmentation based on cultural hierarchy was in principle antithetical to Reith's vision of a single, elevating public radio service, embodied by the pre-war National Programme, since in responding to well-established cultural divisions within society it did not serve to broaden horizons.[60] Whereas Reith may be perceived as rather paternalistically treating the British public as an undifferentiated whole, giving listeners what he considered they ought to have rather than what they may have wanted, the 'concept of offering rather than imposing culture was [...] central to the Third Programme philosophy'.[61] On the other hand, the Director-General William Haley, whose brainchild the Third Programme was, hoped that the BBC's duty, as defined by the Royal Charter, to 'inform, educate, and entertain' would in the form of the new tripartite broadcasting structure lead the audience up a 'ladder' of listening, from 'low' to 'middle' to 'highbrow' material and thus by increments improve the cultural life of the nation.[62] This hierarchical structuring of cultural output, 'a

---

[58] Ridley 1947, 9. Athene was patron goddess of Athens, as well as arts and crafts, and the personification of wisdom; she was also the goddess of war, thus the reference to armour.
[59] Paulu 1961, 156.   [60] Whitehead 1989, 7.
[61] Ibid. 8.   [62] Briggs 1979, 76–7.

broadly based cultural pyramid slowly aspiring upwards', was sustained for a quarter of a century,[63] but it has been demonstrated that the pyramid or ladder theories of 'brow' were not actually representative of actual listening patterns:

> we found that, far from confining their listening to the Third Programme, most of those who valued it and listened to it frequently nevertheless spent more time in listening to the other services, the Home Service and the Light Programme. While there may have been people who fitted the highbrow-lowbrow stereotypes, there was in fact widespread catholicity in listening.[64]

Yet the reluctance within the BBC to accept that a substantial part of the Third's audience came from beyond the target demographic of listeners who were, as stated in an internal memorandum, those 'already aware of artistic experience [...] persons of taste and intelligence, and of education' clearly demonstrates how the institutional intention behind cultural broadcasting did not, and indeed could not, map accurately onto the reality of listener preferences and experience. The Third Programme succeeded in having a considerable impact on the listening public, but it was not the one that its architects predicted or intended. This well documented example of the unpredictability of audience engagement with radio networks and programming seems also to demonstrate unequivocally the relative impotence, and perhaps also ultimate irrelevance, of those we may think of as cultural gatekeepers who are traditionally perceived to have a greater degree of influence on the way the public engages with works in more 'boundaried' cultural spheres, such as the theatre.

Following the establishment of the Third Programme, what were perceived to be the more difficult dramatic pieces—including, for example, the majority of programmes drawing on Greek texts and subjects—would now more often appear on the Third rather than on the Home: 'there was a tendency on the part of the Drama department to concentrate on the production of more plays from the classic repertoire which could now find a convenient outlet on the Third'.[65] William Haley, writing in the *Radio Times*, informed listeners that the new network would broadcast on 'a high cultural level, devoted to the arts, serious discussion, and experiment'.[66] A tension would,

---

[63] Haley quoted by Paulu 1956, 147. See also Whitehead, 1989, 49.
[64] Silvey 1974, 125.   [65] Rodger 1982, 74.   [66] Haley 1945.

however, arise within these varied objectives—specifically between, on the one hand, the broadcast of established cultural works of music, drama, and literature, for example, and, on the other, more innovative and experimental fare. Still, this promising and heady mix of 'high cultural' programming led to a rapturous response: in the *Picture Post* Edward Sackville-West predicted that the Third would become 'the greatest educative and civilising force England has known since the secularisation of the theatre in the sixteenth century'.[67]

That is not to say that programmes drawing on Greek stories and histories were no longer broadcast on the Home Service. Its aim was, after all, to reach 'the broad middle stratum of the population' and there was therefore some overlap with the type of programmes broadcast both by the Light and the Third.[68] When Greek material did appear on the Home, however, it was mostly in the form of more traditional radio dramatic productions delivered under the *World Theatre* banner: indeed, the *World Theatre* series was inaugurated in October 1945 with a broadcast of Murray's translation of *Hippolytus*.[69] The audience for radio plays had doubled by the end of the war,[70] and the Home's *Saturday Night Theatre* and monthly *World Theatre* were established (in 1943 and 1945 respectively) to respond to this larger audience. And a large audience it was: the average number of listeners for *World Theatre* in 1955 was 1¼ million—a small figure, perhaps, in terms of broadcasting, but an enormous one for a dramatic performance and many other art forms.[71] Scannell perceptively notes that whereas the arts and literature have continually been 'ring-fence[d] [...] from ordinary life and experience', 'Radio and television tear down the fence: the distinction between life and art is no longer sustainable'.[72] Or, to borrow the idea of Martin Esslin, Gielgud's successor, radio offers truly a theatre of the mind.[73]

---

[67] Quoted in Briggs 1979, 71.   [68] Priessnitz 1981, 39.
[69] Some tragedies first produced on the Third would occasionally be repeated in the *World Theatre* series (for example, Euripides' *Alcestis* and Sophocles' *Antigone* in 1950).
[70] Briggs 1970, 46. Gielgud 1945: 'last year's Listener Research figures show one thing conclusively: that the radio play has become, under the influence of wartime conditions and certain changes of radio-drama policy, a "majority" programme item'.
[71] Gielgud 1957, 30. *Saturday Night Theatre* regularly attracted audiences of around nine million (British Broadcasting Corporation 1950, 145).
[72] Scannell 1996, 74.   [73] Esslin 1971.

In some obvious ways related to the nature of the medium and the size and demographic spread of its audiences, radio programmes which draw on the stories, histories, and ideas of ancient Greece can be thought of as democratic. The size of audiences, even for broadcasts of comparatively minority interest, was consistently larger than for any other educational or cultural activity: listeners to one programme were often counted in millions; even the supposedly less popular programmes were heard by tens or even hundreds of thousands of people. The near absence in the sphere of radio of boundaries (pertaining to economics, class, education, and geography, for example) which may be variously perceived or experienced as conditioning access to and engagement with other cultural spheres was a crucial factor in enabling and encouraging access to these programmes. It is clear from the BBC's own audience research that listeners for the kind of programmes discussed in this book were also from a wide range of socio-economic, cultural, and educational backgrounds. Practicalities such as the ubiquity of radio sets in the domestic sphere, the relatively low cost of the activity, the absence of audience etiquette, and what is known about patterns of listening across age, gender, class, and geographical lines are here relevant.

The BBC as an institution was fascinated with its audience. Consequently, there is an astonishingly rich mine of sources documenting the experiences of individual listeners in their engagements with radio programmes drawing on the ancient world. Of primary importance is the Listener Research Report which was compiled from large numbers of questionnaires, completed by individuals on the Listening Panel, in response to a particular programme. These reports offer some statistical evidence on the audience (for example, estimated size and an 'Appreciation Index') as well as a summary indication of how the audience engaged with various aspects of a programme (such as production, music, acting), illustrated with quotations from listeners (identified only by occupation and, therefore, sometimes by gender: for example, 'Seamstress') which support, nuance, and disagree with the dominant view. The Reports are therefore of great value in indicating the wide variety of opinion that a single radio broadcast could generate.

Before the BBC began collecting statistics and information on the audience's response to programmes in 1936, the opinions expressed in letters were the sole source for how the audience had experienced a programme. Individual listeners were often spontaneously moved to write to programme-makers with their reactions (ranging from warmly appreciative to highly critical, with some confidently offering suggestions on how producers might do it better in the future); the recipient's response, which is also in many cases archived, often provides valuable information on the intentions behind a programme, especially when production choices are explained in light of criticism. In addition to correspondence which is found in the archives, second-hand reports of the audience's experience are occasionally documented in the private correspondence of programme-makers: for example, MacNeice mentions his butcher's reaction to *Enemy of Cant* in a letter to another listener, and Gilbert Murray similarly writes of how his 'nice parlourmaid listened with shining eyes' to a 1953 radio production of his translation of Euripides' *Electra*.[74] In his book on the BBC's audience research, Silvey considers that:

> It may now seem extraordinary that the BBC did not set about studying its public systematically until ten years after it had become a public corporation [i.e. 1936]. But when anyone suggested that it was out of touch with its public, it would point to its postbag. Listeners had not waited to be asked their opinions; they had volunteered them. From the first the BBC had been inundated with letters from listeners. There were so many, they were so varied in what they dealt with and in the views that they expressed and they seemed so manifestly authentic that few questioned their adequacy as a guide to listener opinion.[75]

Reith considered that letters from members of the public were a valuable source of information about the opinions of listeners, noting that 'with us "minorities" are very important sections of the community, and a "limited appeal" may still involve many hundreds of thousands'.[76]

Conversely, Val Gielgud argued against relying on correspondence from individual members of the audience to gauge the impact of a programme: 'the plain listener is not a person who ever writes a letter, except under very startling circumstances, and we obviously do not wish to broadcast for the benefit of cranks and people with a great deal of spare time on their hands', he spiritedly argued.

---

[74] Letter from LM to J. Kershaw, 14 November 1944 (R19/440); letter from GM to Peter Watts, 14 April 1953 (GM/S).
[75] Silvey 1974, 28. [76] Quoted by Briggs 1961, 204.

Correspondingly, his opinion of letter-writers who did not agree with his production choices—expressed privately in correspondence with colleagues and friends—was usually dismissive. It is therefore not surprising that it was Gielgud who led the campaign within the Corporation for a more formalized method of gauging the impact of a production, claiming that there was much anxiety within his department arising from a lack of knowledge about how drama programmes were being received: 'it seems to me absolutely vital [...] to survey our listening public. [...] a body of real information would be, speaking personally, of the most immense qualifying value to me in framing dramatic policy and controlling production methods and I cannot help feeling that such information could not fail to be of the same value to anyone else responsible for any type of programme activity'.[77]

The archives hold very many examples of Gielgud's 'plain' listeners writing in to share their satisfaction, enjoyment, gratitude, discontent, and disappointment, and sometimes to make suggestions on how a production might have been improved. How better to gauge the impact of a production? What is particularly striking is the confidence of opinion expressed time and again by these 'plain listeners' on matters of ancient performance and modern radio performance, which leads to a consideration of whether dramatic performance on radio (and other mass media) was somehow 'public property' (a phrase that will reappear in the Conclusion) to a degree that theatre productions, for example, were not. The democratic and intimate nature of the radio broadcast meant that the individual's response must be considered to be an honest and valid response.[78] The broadcast had been done for her and for him, and if it raised strong feeling then this could easily be—and often was—communicated directly to those people who had been responsible for the production. Interestingly, when comparisons were undertaken between the reactions of spontaneous letter-writers and the much larger BBC audience sample in response to a television production of George Orwell's *1984* transmitted in 1955, the opinions of letter-writers were found to be in line with the ratio of those who strongly liked and disliked the programme on the listening panel. What audience reports also valuably capture in

[77] Memo from VG to R. H. Eckersley (Director of Programmes), 12 May 1930, quoted by Pegg 1983, 101.
[78] On the democratic nature of radio see especially Section 3.1.

some number, however, are responses from those who had voluntarily tuned in to a programme (for there was no enforced listening for the purpose of completing questionnaires) but who would not have been sufficiently moved by it to write a letter. There was also found to be a predominance of middle-class letter-writers, whereas the BBC endeavoured to make the listening sample representative of the national population.[79]

These sources cannot, of course, be statistically significant since questions of comprehensiveness, partiality, and bias in the collection of data for reports, the archiving of letters, and the use of anecdotes must be considered. However, perhaps it may be reasonable to suggest that each of these contemporary responses to programmes may represent some (albeit unquantifiable) proportion of the mass audience.[80] This information is incredibly useful in demonstrating the fact that, regardless of the intentions that fed into the collaborative process of programme-making (and, indeed, regardless of the historian's own estimation of the success or otherwise of a programme), individual listeners reserved the right to respond in a highly personal way which had roots in the their educational, cultural, and social background and tastes: for example, listeners regularly display a strong sense of security in their knowledge of the ancient world and how it should best be represented on radio, even when they may be considered to be factually wrong on some point of ancient Greek history, culture, or society. The underlying argument of this study is that it was the very nature of the radio medium which encouraged such subjective engagements. After the point when radio sets were affordable by all, such broadcasts were practically accessible to everyone who had a desire to listen, and the boundaries which were perceived or experienced as existing for other forms of educational enrichment or cultural expression were largely not in operation with radio; furthermore, the intimate and powerful nature of the radio broadcast meant that stories and characters from antiquity could be brought vividly to life in the listener's imagination, allowing the

---

[79] Silvey 1974, 28.
[80] Ibid. 29 corroborates the view that the opinions expressed in letters from individual listeners can be taken to be representative of the experience of a wider section of the audience but that the question is 'how *widely* they are shared' (emphasis added).

human dimension of these ancient tales to be readily experienced (points that are discussed further in Chapter 3).

Certainly, these valuable insights into the mind of the public substantially augment the published critical reviews more commonly used (for example, in theatre production histories) to illuminate the contemporary reception of cultural engagements with the ancient world.[81] These insights also demonstrate unequivocally that the public consciousness and experience of classics in Britain was significantly affected by these radio presentations. An important segment of the audience clearly valued the programmes and the associated introductory or background programming as a form of education and an encouragement to further reading; furthermore, for example, there is evidence that Greek plays produced on radio in many cases stimulated both amateur stagings and the teaching of the plays in translation in the classroom. The evidence demonstrates that listeners engaged with programmes on their own terms, making strong aesthetic and other kinds of judgement which demonstrate a confidence of approach and a level of engagement and criticism which is not always supported by accurate knowledge of a subject. My interpretation of this aspect of the evidence for listener experience is that it indicates a level of public 'ownership' that is operational in this mass medium: in other words, radio seems able to make cultural works public property in some significant way.

This interpretation may help to make sense of the strong critical and intellectual prejudice against various mass media, especially when they engage with already established cultural works. The rich mine of sources that exist for the production of these programmes and the public's engagement with them can, therefore, valuably add to current debates in classical reception studies: not only do they provide evidence for an uncharted realm of activity that by any measure is of great importance to cultural history, but the very existence of these sources—which do not seem to exist to the same extent for other realms of cultural activity—also has the potential to enable and encourage reflection on broader scholarly practice and methodological possibilities.

---

[81] See Hardwick 1999 on the strengths and weaknesses in using reviews in (classical) performance reception studies.

2.2. DEPARTMENTAL, COLLABORATIVE, AND LITERARY HISTORICAL CONTEXTS

Departments of Drama and Features

> Indeed, there was a time when the Drama Department of the BBC saw its main function as broadcasting stage plays—taking the theatre to the people—and from the mid-1930s to the mid-1950s it was the Features Department [...] that was really responsible for exploring the possibilities of radio as a dramatic medium in its own right.[82]

The Reithian principle of broadcasting the best of the nation's cultural heritage and political debate to a wide public held long after the man himself left the BBC in 1938. In terms of drama, this principle found a loyal advocate in Val Gielgud, under whose leadership the Drama Department for more than thirty years concentrated—with immense success—on broadcasting 'classic' plays and literature to massive audiences, especially through the productions broadcast in the *Saturday Night Theatre* and *World Theatre* series on the Home Service. The most potent reason for the observable decline of interest in producing programmes which drew on ancient Greek texts and subjects in the 1960s (for example, it seems that approximately half the number of Greek tragedies that had been aired in the 1950s were broadcast in the 1960s) may, at first glance, appear to be the detrimental impact of television broadcasting—the audience for which increased rapidly in the mid-1950s—on the size of the radio audience. Television certainly had an impact on radio production processes: for example, when the Features Department was broken up in the 1960s, many members of its talented staff (such as D. G. Bridson, Douglas Cleverdon, and Raymond Raikes) went to work in television, and much other talent and money was attracted to the new and increasingly dominant medium.[83] However, one of the more immediately causal factors may have been the retirement of the culturally conservative Gielgud in 1963, a man who is considered to have had 'more influence than any other single individual over radio drama in Britain from 1929 until 1962'.[84] It was he who, when Samuel Beckett offered the Third an English version of *En attendant Godot*, which was taking Paris by storm, famously dismissed the new play as 'phoney'; thus was the opportunity lost for the British première of *Waiting for Godot* on

---

[82] Lewis 1981*a*, 7.   [83] Wade 1981, 226–7.   [84] Low 1981, 135.

radio.[85] Such traditionalism was rapidly displaced by his successor Martin Esslin's (1918–2002) strong support of contemporary playwrights and modern theatrical trends. Under the leadership of Esslin—an expert on Brecht who had received training in direction at the Max Reinhardt Seminar of Dramatic Art in Vienna, c.1936–1937—the Department produced early plays by Samuel Beckett, Caryl Churchill, Joe Orton, Harold Pinter, and Tom Stoppard for the Third—even if it sometimes 'failed to pick up the crucial play (*Waiting for Godot*, *The Birthday Party*, and *Rosencrantz and Guildenstern are Dead*)'.[86]

Gielgud had in wartime been in charge of the joint Department of Drama and Features but, in acknowledgement of its wartime development, Features was in July 1945 made independent of Drama under the leadership of Laurence Gilliam (1907–64).[87] Generally speaking, the Departments of Drama and Features produced two different types of programme which engaged with ancient Greek stories and histories: Drama focused on producing English translations and modern adaptations of Greek plays as stage-plays-for-radio; and Features made more free and creative use of Greek sources in its programmes, often with the purpose of making the ancient world resonate in a direct and clear way with modern concerns. As will be demonstrated in Part Two, both Gilbert Murray and Louis MacNeice, for example, had a common interest in using the radio medium to encourage appreciation and enjoyment of classical texts amongst the listening public, but the very different nature of the radio programmes they worked on was influenced by their collaboration with the Drama Department in the case of Murray and Features in the case of MacNeice. Murray was an enthusiastic broadcaster, supplying both

---

[85] Instead it premièred at London's Arts Theatre in 1955, under Peter Hall's direction. Carpenter 1997, 152–3, Drakakis 1981*b*, 15, Rodger 1982, 112–14.

[86] Carpenter 1997, 242. In 1938 Esslin joined the Jewish exodus out of Austria, eventually arriving in England after internment in the detention camp on the Isle of Man (with many future BBC colleagues). On release in 1940 he joined the BBC European Service and began broadcasting news in German, becoming a scriptwriter and producer of imaginative programmes for German-speaking listeners. In 1955 he became Assistant Head of the European Productions Department, in 1961 Assistant Head of Radio Drama, and from 1963 to 1977 Head of Radio Drama. Later he held a Professorship of Drama at Stanford University, California.

[87] Briggs 1970, 711. The Features Department had its roots in an experimental studio set up in 1937 along the lines of the Columbia Broadcasting System's Columbia Workshop 'to explore the specific expressive possibilities of radio' (Priessnitz 1981, 34).

translations and associated talks which served as introductions to the productions (in addition to his work for the Talks Department), whereas MacNeice wrote a vast number of scripts for Features, a significant proportion of which drew on Greek and Roman stories and histories.

> Broadcasting is plastic; while it can ape the Press, it can also emulate the arts. Yes, people will say, that is theoretically true but in practice you will never get art—or anything like it—out of a large public institution, encumbered with administrators, which by its nature must play for safety and to the gallery. [...] I would maintain that in this country such an institution cannot be really authoritarian; with ingenuity and a little luck a creative person can persuade (or fool) at least some of the administrators some of the time.[88]

MacNeice, in this quotation, considers broadcasting to be a 'plastic' medium, able to accommodate a wide range of forms from news to the arts. Indeed, radio programmes themselves may also be considered plastic in a sense, too, in that the formal boundaries between such works as radio plays, features, and documentaries are fluid and adaptable to the nature of the content and programming aim. This being the case, the terminology used to describe these various styles of programme has also tended to shift shape—both in contemporary and later critical writing.[89] Strictly speaking, features may be described as radio documentaries or information programmes which utilized innovative combinations of dramatization, poetry, music, and sound for their effect; loosely speaking, a feature 'could be almost anything'.[90] It has been argued that it was the writer-producer (often the same person) of radio features rather than the producer of radio drama who was more free to explore and push the boundaries of radio dramatic form and technique in this period, since the Drama Department worked under the traditional obligation to

---

[88] MacNeice 1947b, 13–14.
[89] See Drakakis 1981b, 8–9, Holme 1981, 40 and 46, and Whitehead 1989, 109–11 on the lack of a clear distinction between some features and the radio play format. Priessnitz 1981, 32 notes that 'the term "radio drama" is used in England to cover very different fields' from adaptations of stage plays, novels, short stories, as well as drama written specially for the radio.
[90] Coulton 1980, 130. The term was borrowed from the cinematic feature film (Scannell and Cardiff 1991, 135). Whitehead 1989, 109–34 offers a thorough discussion of the nature of features.

produce radio adaptations of existing stage-plays.[91] As Rodger notes, 'the pattern of the feature encouraged the telling of a story in sequence with dramatic inserts as illustrations of the theme in a manner which resembled to some extent the form of the novel'—an interesting point which will become important in the next chapter's discussion of how radio dramatizations work with the listener's imagination.[92] Also, as the need for wartime propaganda evaporated, writers such as MacNeice turned their energies towards writing more creative works for radio, with the result that, for example, from around 1944 MacNeice had established himself at the forefront of the newly emergent art form of the radio play, a form of feature (termed *Hörspiel* in German) that had more fictional or dramatic content than historical or political thrust.[93]

Creative collaboration:
BBC staff and freelance professionals

> To found
> A castle on the air requires a mint
> Of golden intonations and a mound
> Of typescript in the trays.
>
> From Louis MacNeice's 'Autumn Sequel' IV.[94]

This section offers some examples of mutually stimulating working relationships between radio producers and academics, translators, creative writers, composers, and theatre practitioners in order to highlight the collaborative aspects of the production process and the sustained links that were forged between radio and other intellectual and creative professions.[95] An appreciation of the creative teamwork required in the creation of programmes deriving from ancient Greece is an important foundation from which evaluations regarding the nature and perceived success of programmes may be approached. The BBC's idealism with regard to broadcasting's potential to contribute to the nation's cultural and educational life directly

---

[91] Rodger 1982.   [92] Ibid. 88.
[93] See Holme 1981, 43.   [94] MacNeice 1954a, 28.
[95] See the media historian David Hendy's important work on the contribution that radio and other media have made to creative and intellectual life over the past one hundred and twenty years (Hendy 2009 and 2015).

informed programme policy within Departments. Plans for programmes to be made by the Drama Department, for example, had to be passed by the Script Editor, who was supported by sub-editors and readers, for approval.[96] Yet, as MacNeice indicates in the 'broadcasting is plastic' quotation above, individual producers had considerable freedom to generate their own ideas for programmes and to commission and work with their contacts in spheres beyond radio, selling the idea to departmental heads who would sometimes overrule script editors. Influences from several cultural and academic circles on programme form and content were therefore strong.

The personnel files in the BBC's written archives hold many examples of producers being inspired to create a programme around, for example, a particular translation of a Greek play after having seen it performed on the stage or reading it in print, but writers and translators also sent in new (unpublished and unstaged) work. These personnel files hold fascinating evidence for budding playwrights, writers, poets, and translators offering scripts for radio in an attempt to establish their careers. Kenneth Cavander is one example: his numerous published translations of Greek plays were often produced on radio and television in the 1950s and 1960s, but these are now somewhat overshadowed by his later international success with *The Greeks*, the ten-play cycle drawing on Greek tragedies which he wrote together with John Barton for performance by the Royal Shakespeare Company in 1980. Cavander began sending in his translations and adaptations of Greek tragedy and comedy to the BBC whilst an undergraduate reading classics at Oxford (where several undergraduate groups were staging them: five of his translations of Greek drama were performed in Oxford in 1955 alone), but they did not initially impress the BBC.[97] His first stroke of luck came when Val Gielgud accepted an invitation to see Euripides' *Hippolytus* performed by the Oxford University Dramatic Society (OUDS) which was in 1955 for the first time breaking with the tradition of performing Greek plays in the original language by using his English translation.[98] Gielgud was sufficiently impressed to accept the production

---

[96] Tydeman 1981, 17; see also Coulton 1980, 197–8.
[97] On the Oxford productions see Wrigley 2011*b*, 118–20.
[98] See Wrigley 2007*a* and 2011*b* on OUDS' tradition of staging Greek plays in ancient Greek, which lasted from 1887 until 1932, and the earlier production of Aeschylus' *Agamemnon* at Balliol College in 1880.

for performance on the Third later that year, with most of the Oxford actors. Cavander subsequently translated Euripides' *Women of Troy* (1958) and Sophocles' *Philoctetes* (1961) for BBC Television, radio versions of *Philoctetes* (1963; see frontispiece) and Euripides' *Bacchae* (1964), and eleven twenty-minute dramatizations from Homer's *Iliad* and *Odyssey* for broadcast in the *Living Language* series of BBC Schools Radio in the later 1960s (on which see Section 3.1).[99]

Radio's long relationship with the stage guaranteed a steady flow of professional stage actors who worked on radio programmes alongside the BBC's own repertory of actors, especially in productions of plays in which they had performed in the theatre. Section 4.1 discusses a number of radio versions of stage productions in the early days of broadcasting, noting how, when theatres were curtailed in wartime, Sybil Thorndike and Lewis Casson (1875–1969) from the Old Vic Company broadcast extracts from *Medea* for the *From the Theatre in Wartime* series (1942). Later, having struck up a firm working relationship with the Greek actor Elsa Vergi, the producer Raymond Raikes (1910–98) arranged for her to record dramatic extracts in Greek for broadcast following English-language productions of plays. She also performed Greek tragic roles in English translation as an experiment to see 'how much of her own powerful rendering of Medea could be made to come across in our language'.[100] Her visit to the UK to play the role of Medea in a 1962 radio production (see Figure 2.1) was well covered by the press and the production was awarded an extremely high Appreciation Index of 78 (calculated from the listener research sample; at this time reasonably successful Third Programme plays received an average of 60).[101] The production (in Vellacott's translation, which he was preparing for publication in the Penguin Classics series) was followed by Vergi reading extracts from the ancient Greek text in modern Greek pronunciation.[102] The justification of these rare programmes in the ancient language was said to

---

[99] On the BBC television productions see Wrigley 2016a. Expanded versions of the Homeric radio scripts were published as Cavander 1969.

[100] Quotation by Raikes in typescript of discussion on 'Greek Drama Today' by Raymond Raikes, Elsa Vergi, and Leslie Finer for the Transcription Service issue of *Medea* (S452/40/1). Finer was a foreign correspondent for several British newspapers, living in Athens and married to Vergi.

[101] The *Evening Standard* and *The Scotsman*, for example, covered her visit (cuttings in S452/40/1).

[102] The translation was published as Vellacott 1963.

Fig. 2.1. Stephen Murray and Elsa Vergi perform the roles of Jason and Medea in the Third Programme's 1962 *Medea*. © BBC. Reproduced by kind permission of the BBC Photo Library.

be that 'the small audience that listens to programmes of this sort on the Third like[s] to be able to "follow in the text"'.[103] But when W. R. Smyth, a Classics lecturer at the University College of Swansea, wrote a detailed letter to Raikes, calling the utility of these extracts into question and challenging the method of pronunciation, a rather uncharacteristically irate Raikes rapped him on the knuckles thus: 'It was an opportunity to hear a distinguished modern actress interpreting the classical Greek as an actress (not as a pedant paying careful note of every syllable and comma and by doing so failing to see the wood for the trees).'[104]

Christopher Whelen's music for the English-language production also came in for some criticism which is worth quoting at length, illustrating as it does the strong feelings to which unsatisfactory music in radio programmes could give rise:

> Much as I enjoyed Elsa Verghis' performance in *Medea* last night, the production as a whole was spoiled for me by the music. In 5th century Greece the chorus was accompanied only by a flutist who merely emphasized the rhythm of the lyrics. Simple prose spoken in unison would produce an effect much nearer the original, than loud, piercing, and incoherent singing. The musical accompaniment to the speeches was discordant both with their sense and with their word pattern; while

---

[103] Letter from RR to Leslie Finer, 5 May 1966 (S452/3/1).
[104] Letter from W. R. Smyth to RR, 18 May 1962, and RR's response, 29 May 1962 (S452/40/1). See Chapter 7 for Raikes's warning to the listener in 1956 that, in a similar programme of extracts from the *Oresteia* read in ancient Greek, Vergi would pronounce the language in the way it was taught at the University of Athens.

the music played at exits and entries only distracted the mind and broke the continuity of the play. In your productions of Greek plays the music has for years been becoming more unsuitable and irritating. Will your producers ever realize that these great works are sufficient in themselves, that their impact is utterly spoiled not enhanced by experiments in incidental music?[105]

Another dissatisfied listener wrote to Raikes to question whether the ancient Greeks would have performed *Agamemnon* in an operatic style, following a 1950 production of Louis MacNeice's translation of the play which featured music by John Hotchkis (1916–96). This listener 'was forced to switch off in disgust after about ten minutes—ten minutes during which I had heard nothing but background noises and moaning singing'. Raikes responded to explain why he chose to apply song and music to the choruses in this way: 'to sing the entirety of these lengthy choral odes would be more than the modern ear could assimilate and comprehend; and so I tried to strike a mean, having certain phrases sung and the remainder spoken to the accompaniment of music'.[106]

Raikes's response here indicates the collaborative nature of the working relationship between producers and composers. Producers of plays and features would often hand the script over to the composer with detailed instructions with regard to how much music and what sound effects were required, and often with encouragement to interpret the meaning of the script in musical terms. As MacNeice wrote to Antony Hopkins, the composer for his *Enemy of Cant*, in 1946: 'I am anxious that the essential bits of meaning should come over but apart from that please do what you like with these pieces, apportioning lines as you prefer among your different singers and working in any nice polyphonic convolutions that occur to you.'[107] Val Gielgud liked to involve the composer early on in the production process: it is clear from extant correspondence that Gielgud, the translator Constantine Trypanis, Colette King (who trained the choruses), and the composer John Hotchkis worked together to a remarkable degree on the 1962 Third production of *Oresteia*.[108] However,

---

[105] Letter from Henrietta Smith (Witney, Oxon) to RR, 19 May 1962 (S452/40/1).
[106] Postcard from A. Mackenzie-Smith to RR, 13 July 1950, and Raikes's letter in response, 21 July 1950 (S452/29/1).
[107] Letter from LM to Antony Hopkins, 19 November 1946 (R19/307).
[108] Hotchkis wrote music for at least twelve productions of ancient drama from 1950 to 1963.

Antony Hopkins—who wrote the scores for a considerable number of productions of Greek drama (as well as for the 1945 production of Sophocles' *Oedipus Tyrannus* at the Old Vic)—was to an extent critical of the method of briefing composers for feature programmes, considering that it usually permitted music to function merely as 'journalism'. He suggested a new form in which the programme was conceived by composer and writer together, music and words thus achieving an equal importance (as Sackville-West and Britten had managed in 1943 with *The Rescue*). The BBC were initially hesitant but in 1952, for example, a composite music/libretto work by Hopkins and Patric Dickinson, titled *Scena*, was broadcast.[109] Such creative collaborations have been described by Rodger as follows:

> a very rare and profitable association of composers and writers, actors and musicians. The artists of words and music had to work together. Composers like William Walton and Benjamin Britten [...] were not expected to create their music in isolation without knowledge of or care for the text. The convention of the opera, where the librettist is often the verbal servant of the music, did not apply. The convention of the cinema film, where the music was simply employed as a background effect, was also not applicable. The music sometimes had to become part of the dialogue and the words in performance had likewise to respond musically.
> This necessary association of writers and musicians was to lead to a remarkable creative rapport.[110]

In 1947 MacNeice wrote an essay through which he sought to win over writers who may have been prejudiced against writing for radio: 'The producer', he wrote, 'is nearly always a man with an open mind; he will welcome the author's co-operation up till the moment of transmission. The author therefore has far more say about the performance of his piece than in any other medium which involves teamwork.'[111] His own position was unusual: his work was not only

---

[109] Documented in AH/C.   [110] Rodger 1982, 50.
[111] MacNeice 1947c, 26. Many writers at this time despaired of the ephemeral nature of radio and considered it a second-class medium; on the intellectual snobbery against radio, see Chapter 1. Yet the financial rewards were attractive: MacNeice admits that three broadcasts of a piece submitted as an outside writer earned him 'rather more money than I once used to make in a year as University lecturer' (MacNeice 1947c, 28).

produced by several departments, including Drama and Features, but he also regularly functioned as both writer and producer for features, and with regard to programmes drawing on classical material he drew both on first-hand understanding of Greek and Roman texts and on modern poetic and dramatic forms. It is nonetheless true that writers were customarily invited to contribute in a number of significant ways to the production process. Translators or adaptors of Greek sources were offered the chance to make their published texts 'more suitable for broadcasting', as the producer Mary Hope Allen (1898–1970) suggested that the classicist and translator Rex Warner (1905–86) might do in 1948 with regard to his translation of *Prometheus Bound*, published by the Bodley Head in the previous year.[112] Such an invitation may have been met with suggestions for cuts (especially within choral odes), 'interpolations' to aid the sense and action in the absence of the visual clues of live performance, and updatings (for example, in the script for the 1947 production of his translation of the comedy *Frogs*, Gilbert Murray replaced the word 'obols', ancient Greek coins, with 'coupons', relating to wartime and post-war rationing). Furthermore, Murray and many others were extremely keen to contribute further to the production process, meeting the producer to discuss the realization of the text on air, writing notes on pronunciation for the actors, attending rehearsals, and writing an introductory piece on the play, either for broadcast and/or publication in the *Radio Times* or *The Listener*.[113] Murray also regularly offered a delightful mix of exalted praise and unsparing, detailed criticism in letters to the various producers of his translations after they had been broadcast.

[112] Letter from Mary Hope Allen to Rex Warner, 1 October 1948 (R19/976). Translators and adapters of Greek material for the page and the stage were primarily male in this period, an important exception being H. D. (Hilda Doolittle, 1886–1961) whose *Ion* was produced in 1954. In recent years, women have become prominent in the radio adaptation of Greek tragedies: Rosemary Southey's short story *Morning Story* (based on *Iphigenia at Aulis*) was broadcast in 1991; Timberlake Wertenbaker's *Dianeira* (based on *Trachiniae*) in 1999; and Phyllis Nagy's *Dolores* (after *Andromache*) in 2001 and 2003.

[113] For clarity, it should be noted that on radio the producer is 'the person who makes a radio play [...] director and producer both' (Tydeman 1981, 13). The *Radio Times* was first issued on 28 September 1923 with an initial circulation of 250,000; this increased to two million by 1934. *The Listener* was founded in January 1929, achieving an average circulation of around 50,000 copies per week (Pegg 1983, 106).

The extent to which the radio work of scholars such as Gilbert Murray had a reciprocal impact on the academic subject of classics and public perceptions of it is, naturally, difficult to evaluate. Later chapters detail how commissions from the BBC certainly impacted on the number of translations of Greek texts that were written and subsequently published. As discussed in more length in Chapter 7, in 1957 Val Gielgud struck up a fruitful working relationship with Constantine Trypanis, poet and Professor of Medieval and Modern Greek at Oxford, an association which began with the production of one Greek tragedy but which led to the commission and production of several more in Gielgud's last years at the BBC before retirement. Similarly, Patric Dickinson's translations of Greek and Roman comedy (considered in Section 8.2) were popular on the air and several were commissioned directly (and later published) once a good working relationship was secured.

Greek texts and subjects were doubtless, as a result of this kind of radio activity, positioned more centrally within the broader cultural life of the nation and made to exist more energetically in the public imagination, at a time when, as noted above, Greek as an academic subject in the school and university classroom was becoming marginalized. There can also be no doubt that from the 1970s the OU and other higher educational institutions offering extra-mural activities took advantage of this wider cultural conversance with Greek texts and subjects which had been effected by radio in tandem with other allied media such as paperback translations. The extent to which the OU in particular utilized both radio and television media as an important channel for educational content, in a formal way for registered students and informally for the wider public audience, is testament to this.[114] Today, of course, the academy uses the term 'outreach' to describe scholarly contributions to radio or television programmes (and other media such as websites, podcasts, etc.) which are designed to make academic subjects interesting and accessible to non-specialist audiences, but it is clear that this utilization of mass media extends right back through the twentieth century to the birth of domestic broadcasting in the early 1920s.

---

[114] It was from the start part of the OU's mission 'to promote the educational well-being of the community generally' (quoted in The Open University 2012*b*). See British Broadcasting Corporation 1974 and Wrigley 2016*c*.

Radio dramatizing the theatrical and literary canon

The process of adapting plays, novels, and short stories has, over the years, grown to such an extent that radio must be considered a primary means by which many people gain access to the literature and drama of the past.[115]

In a valuable essay which discusses Shakespeare on the radio, the scholar of stage and radio plays John Drakakis considers the complex processes involved in adapting for radio performance texts which have both an established performance history on the stage and literary history on the page. The example of Shakespeare is illuminating for the case of ancient Greek texts which, similarly, have enjoyed a long, canonical status and a considerable history both in performance and as literary texts for reading and study. Drakakis concludes that radio productions of such canonical works exist 'in a curiously complex *reflective* relationship both to literary text *and* theatre performance': the very reason these texts are chosen for radio performance, he considers, is their established status in literary and theatrical canons, and thus a radio adaptation of a stage play '*enacts* those values and aesthetic structures which are already in receipt of prior assent'.[116] Drakakis takes his argument so far as to ask 'to what extent all radio adaptation [of established canonical works] minimises this question of value judgement', concluding that the listener is 'participating in a ritual that is, in effect, self-validating'.[117]

This final step in the argument seems to cloud what may rather be perceived as a clear distinction between the intentions and choices of those involved in programme-making (and aspects of institutional broadcasting policy which may be operational here) and the quality of experience of individual listeners. Institutional policy with regard to what is worthy of air-time under the banners of cultural wealth or artistic experimentation and the various choices made by individual radio departments and producers, of course, determine which writers and which works receive air-time. An established work's cultural history—in terms of scholarship, literature, publishing, performance, etc.—is undeniably present in any radio re-creation, not only in, for example, the nature and degree of adaptation for performance on radio, but also in the critical reception of that presentation by

[115] Drakakis 1981*b*, 3.   [116] Drakakis 1981*a*, 130 (original emphasis).
[117] Ibid. 131.

reviewers and those listeners who have prior knowledge and experience of the original work or previous interpretations of it. It is arguable, however, that radio presentations of works from established canons do have the potential to be experienced from a fresh perspective, most obviously by those who do not bring to the listening experience existing knowledge of the work or comparative evaluations from other types of performance or media, and perhaps also by those who have prior knowledge or experience of the work but who are open to responding to its production on radio as a new work, or a fresh interpretation within the limitations and the opportunities of the medium. This last point is perhaps especially relevant to radio programmes which take a radically creative approach to adapting a text for radio performance, whether this involves dramatizing a section of one of the Homeric epics (for example, *The Rescue*) or bringing an ancient playwright to life within a drama in order to offer context and background for his works (*Enemy of Cant*).

Furthermore, as was noted above, whatever the *intended* aims and functions of an individual radio programme, this can never accurately predict or neatly map onto the *actual* engagement with it by the great diversity of individual listeners because of, amongst other things, the absence of boundaries conditioning the reception of cultural activity on radio and, indeed, in other mass media. Although on a case-by-case basis there is usually a wide spectrum in the nature of audience response to programmes and there are inevitably discrepancies between the intended and actual aims and functions of a programme, the evidence does nevertheless demonstrate that in this period the body of radio programmes under discussion had a considerable impact on public knowledge of Greek stories, texts, authors, and histories and experience of them in performance. This is not to say, as Drakakis states, that listeners are necessarily complicit in a ritual act of validation of the works' established status in literary and theatrical canons. It may be argued that the accessibility of the works through their translation from ancient Greek, their translocation from the schoolroom and the lecture theatre, and their transformation into a vernacular performance or other presentation which is readily accessible within the domestic context beyond the boundaries associated with many other modes of cultural consumption may remove them from associations with the canon and other forms of privileged cultural access. As will be argued in more detail in the following section, the contribution of BBC Radio to the cultural life and enjoyment of ancient Greek works seems to have been to open up both practical and imaginative roads to knowledge and enjoyment of them, potentially for the whole of society, against the wider cultural and political landscape in which classics was gradually moving away from the centre of the educational curriculum; but it was the listener's decision whether or not to tune in and whether or not to keep listening, and, regardless of the established canonical status of the work being broadcast, the listener reserved (and frequently demonstrated) the right to have a strong, independent view on the radio presentation of these works.

Drakakis's assertion that the broadcast of canonical literary and theatrical works is an enaction of their established aesthetic value and canonical status may be lent some weight by the fact that sometimes little energy seems to have been expended in adapting Greek plays to the radio medium. (By contrast, as will be seen in Section 8.1, when a writer such as MacNeice set about putting Aristophanes on radio, the fact that he was working for the Features Department gave him the freedom to consider the material afresh, in terms of radio, and not in terms of the Drama Department's concern to broadcast one entire play whole.) As Head of Drama for more than three decades, Gielgud's considerable achievements must not be dismissed—for example, he had enormous success in attracting huge audiences for radio productions of plays from the traditional repertoire of the stage—but, as noted above, under his management the Drama Department seemed to be somewhat resistant to the production of innovative and experimental works by contemporary playwrights as well as the imaginative re-creation of stage plays for the specific limitations and opportunities of the radio medium.

It may well have been the case that Gielgud's strong family connections with the stage left him with such a deep respect for theatre that he could not make the necessary leap to adapt plays for fully effective radio realization.[118] With regard to Greek tragedy, at least, his conservative, almost reverential, approach does not seem to have allowed him to explore the possibilities of the medium for the fullest expression of the drama, as discussed further in Chapter 7. 'This old

---

[118] On his mother's side he was related to Ellen Terry (1847–1928); his brother was the actor John Gielgud. Val directed drama at Oxford; he left without taking a degree and later acted before starting work for the *Radio Times* and then the BBC (Imison 2004).

problem of putting the necessary spotlight upon the identity of the speaking character is', Gielgud wrote to Murray in 1946, 'almost an inevitable one. It certainly demands a very considerable degree of concentration on the part of the listener, but I confess I shrink from anything in the nature of a sort of interpolation, stage direction, or running commentary, particularly when dealing with a verse play.'[119] Gielgud's reluctance to insert even basic 'stage directions' to enable listeners to make sense of the 'movement' of actors in terms of the narrative or through imaginative space was a point of discussion between the two men over several years, with Murray repeatedly making suggestions for noises such as 'a peal of thunder to introduce Artemis, otherwise one has a momentary feeling of "who the dickens is this?"' and the bang of a door 'to let the audience realise that the chorus cannot get in to help [Medea's] children'.[120] In this light, Gielgud's statement that Greek tragedy might be *best* done on radio, voiced as late as 1957, may therefore be understood not only as a rejection of the challenge posed by the live performance of an ancient play but perhaps also as the elevation of the text to a position of greater importance than its dramatic potential as a radio performance. It is paradoxical that the hugely important work done by the Drama Department in making plays from the canonical repertoire of the stage available to massive audiences under Gielgud's leadership may therefore have contributed to the critical dismissal of radio productions of drama as 'merely a crippled form of theater', a lesser cousin of the stage.[121] A more positive estimation of the potential of radio broadcasts of stage plays is offered by Rodger:

> radio required the adaptation of existing literary and dramatic forms of expression [...] this requirement stimulated experiments which have subsequently had considerable influence upon recent and contemporary writing, in both the new forms of expression and the traditional literary and dramatic forms.[122]

---

[119] Letter from VG to GM, 8 March 1946 (GM/S).
[120] Letters from GM to VG, 14 October 1946 and 21 August 1949 (GM/S).
[121] Guralnick 1996, p. xv. [122] Rodger 1982, 1.

3

'Listening in'

The singer alone does not make a song, there has to be someone who hears:
One man opens his throat to sing, the other sings in his mind.

Rabindranath Tagore, 'Broken Song'.[1]

This chapter focuses on the listener and the act of listening, discussing the ways in which the radio medium enabled, first, practical access to knowledge and experience of ancient Greece and, secondly, a particularly potent form of imaginative access to these stories and histories. In these two ways radio in the period under discussion functioned as both a democratizing and a popularizing force.[2]

Section 3.1 considers the democratic nature of radio, bearing in mind the sheer size of audiences and the evidence for how the listeners' experience of broadcast programmes was not hindered by age, gender, class, or geography. Furthermore, the evidence that exists for the diverse demographic composition of audiences for supposed 'highbrow' works strongly suggests that the absence of any tangible boundaries (financial, geographical, educational, etc.) or any kind of listening etiquette conditioning access to and engagement with cultural activity on the air was significant. Radio developed its enormous potential to function as a culturally educative medium through informal adult education series in the 1920s and 1930s and more formally, over several decades, to classrooms of schoolchildren. The evidence that exists from listeners about their own educative engagements with these programmes is useful

---

[1] Tagore 1985, 55.   [2] On the term 'listening in' see Briggs 1961, 242–3.

in this regard: even educators often found themselves to be further educated on the topic of ancient Greece, feeding this back into the classroom in the form of, for example, amateur productions of Greek drama. The mutually supportive relationship between paperback translations published by Penguin and radio performances of these translations is offered as a potent example of how the medium worked hand-in-hand with other ideologically similar enterprises.

The second section focuses on the way in which the nature of radio permitted a particularly special and powerful kind of imaginative access to the stories and histories of ancient Greece when they were presented in performance, a quality of access which, in effect, resulted in an important degree of popularization of the subject. As a new and distinctively evolving medium for the dissemination of cultural works, radio made the ancient Greek world come alive for the audience in a particularly vital and striking way. The close affinity between radio dramatization and other 'storytelling' forms such as the novel, Homeric poetry in ancient performance, and the messenger speech in Greek tragedy, plus the distinct differences between dramatic performance on radio and that on stage, film or television are briefly examined. In particular, the absence of physical impersonation or visual representation of the action requires no compensation of language to conjure a visual surrogate in the imagination; rather, in fact, the soundscape of words, music, and other noises is interpreted in a cumulatively impressionistic way, and the natural intimacy of the medium brings the listener into a psychologically close connection with the ancient character, a transportation which radio is able to manage effortlessly well.

Thus did radio widen accessibility to, and widen the appeal of, the stories and histories of ancient Greece in this period: or, in other words, it both democratized *and* popularized ancient Greece via regular radio presentation. This chapter therefore finds value in the fact that individuals from a wide range of social and educational backgrounds were drawn to engage on their own terms with radio representations of the ancient world, and that these acts of engagement had the potential to be culturally informative, educationally enriching, *and* imaginatively stimulating.

3.1. PRACTICAL ACCESS; OR, THE DEMOCRATIC AND EDUCATIVE MEDIUM

Most of the good things of this world are badly distributed and most people have to go without them. Wireless is a good thing, but it may be shared by all alike, for the same outlay, and to the same extent. The same music rings as sweetly in mansion as in cottage. [. . .] Broadcasting may help to show that mankind is a unity and that the mighty heritage, material, moral and spiritual, if meant for the good of any, is meant for the good of all. [. . .] It ignores the puny and often artificial barriers which have estranged men from their fellows.[3]

The audience

By 1939 three-quarters of British households owned a radio or, at least, were issued with a licence: the size of the listening audience was probably larger if licence evasion and listening with relatives or neighbours is taken into account.[4] It is estimated that in this period those identified as working-class listeners outnumbered middle-class listeners by two to one: in the last years of the Second World War the introduction of the cheap utility set made ownership of a radio more affordable to the working class, and once ownership was financially possible for the greater part of society, radio 'far exceeded any other medium of communication in its penetrative power, with the potential to reach the homes of the most isolated or disadvantaged'.[5] It is clear from the number of female respondents to the BBC's listener research panel over the decades and those women who spontaneously wrote in to producers and translators with their thoughts on a programme that gender does not seem to have posed any barriers to listening. Indeed, in 1933 Hilda Matheson (1888–1940), former Head of Talks at the BBC, wrote that 'it is difficult to exaggerate what broadcasting has done and is doing for women. [. . .] many women who are not only wives and mothers but also housekeepers, houseworkers and cooks, have little opportunity of enjoying outdoor or indoor recreations, of going to meetings, concerts, even cinemas'.[6] BBC Schools Broadcasting is likely to have reached as many girls as boys, and at least one schoolgirl is noted as being on

---

[3] Reith 1924, 217–19.　[4] Pegg 1983, 7 and 9.
[5] McKibbin 2000, 457; Pegg 1983, 219.　[6] Matheson 1933, 188.

the listener research panel. Her comments in the Listener Research Report for a 1950 Third Programme production of Sophocles' *Antigone* in translation identify her (perhaps uncommonly) as a reader of ancient Greek who was also aware of modern adaptations of the play: 'I am interested in the classics and am reading *Antigone* in the original Greek. I have also heard the French version of the story [Anouilh's *Antigone* was broadcast in English translation in 1949] and was interested to see how much it differed from Sophocles.'[7]

A questionnaire survey of 127,000 listeners in the summer of 1938 reported that radio plays, for example, were equally liked by listeners who were categorized as middle class and working class (with '"class" being based on the stated occupation of the heads of the household') but middle-class listeners favoured talks and discussions more than working-class respondents, who preferred musical comedy and serial plays; similarly, the tastes for different types of programme amongst urban and rural listeners, and across regions, did not differ markedly.[8] 'Radio has done more for rural life than all the reformers put together', considered one writer in the *Radio Times* in 1926: 'to-day there are whole villages remote from the great centres of population with a wireless set in every house. [. . .] There must be over a million radio sets in rural areas giving enjoyment and education to five times as many listeners! [. . .] most village institutes possess wireless sets and attract nightly crowds.'[9] As noted in the previous chapter, the boom in listening during the Second World War resulted in the audience for radio drama, for example, doubling by 1945; furthermore, the media and radio historian Peter Lewis makes the important point that 'during the 1930s and 1940s, the average person's experience of drama certainly came much more from radio than from the stage'.[10] Not only was regular attendance at the theatre beyond the financial and geographical reach of many, it was also arguably a culturally boundaried activity. In fact, as already established, since the radio was a relatively inexpensive device for the home, as a medium for the dissemination of cultural works it operated beyond almost all of the educational, financial, geographical, or other barriers which may have been variously perceived or experienced as surrounding many other modes of cultural activity.

---

[7] BBC WAC LR/50/2131.   [8] Silvey 1974, 68–9.   [9] White 1926, 522.
[10] Lewis 1981*a*, 2. See Briggs 1970, 46 and Rose 2001, 204.

By any standards the number of listeners for radio programmes on ancient Greek topics was impressive: Listener Research Reports declare that even the least popular were heard at each broadcast by tens or hundreds of thousands, with the most popular being heard by millions. Comparisons with audiences for other kinds of cultural programmes are possible, but they would perhaps be less meaningful than a comparison between, on the one hand, the astonishing size and diversity of the average audience for ancient Greek radio programmes and, on the other, audiences for other kinds of engagements with ancient Greece in the public sphere—for example, performances of these works on the stage and in translation on the page. (Although it should, of course, not be forgotten that the Penguin Classics series, for example, brought translations of classical literature to an extremely large and clearly enthusiastic audience from 1946. The first in the series, E. V. Rieu's (1887–1972) translation of Homer's *Odyssey*, had sold half a million copies by 1952: as one critic commented, 'these cheap editions of classical works have clearly drawn a response from a new public'.[11]) The crucial fact seems to have been that these radio programmes were, in large part, not broadcast for the specialist listener who had knowledge of ancient Greek texts in the original language: 'listening in' did not therefore presuppose a classical education (and indeed, as is argued below, there is evidence that for some listeners it served as such), nor even the confident level of literacy necessary for tackling English translations of classical texts on the page.

The post-war segmentation of the audience by cultural 'brow' meant that from 1946 most programmes concerning ancient Greece were considered appropriate 'highbrow' material for broadcast on the new Third Programme, the stated aim of which was to serve an audience 'already aware of artistic experience [...] persons of taste, of intelligence, and of education'.[12] Many years later the poet Geoffrey Grigson (1905–85) would highlight how such programmes gave

---

[11] Anon. 1952. The reviewer in *Greece & Rome* stated that it was a translation 'not primarily for "us", but for readers most of whom know no Greek, and for whom the past is not only dead but done with. The real proof of the pudding, then, will be found in the number of those who want to eat it, and it is to be hoped, both for Mr Rieu's sake and for that of the enterprising publishing firm who have offered it to the public at the price of one shilling, that they will be very many' (Newman 1946, 124).

[12] 'Programme C: terms of reference (approved by D. G. [Director-General, William Haley] 14.1.1946)', internal memo dated 16 January 1946 (R34/602). See Section 2.1 for the full quotation.

the Third a reputation for solemn erudition, with reference to the network's first Controller, George Barnes (1904–60):

> 'George will hire the Greek Ambassador to read, in Greek,
> All Aeschylus, in 99 instalments, week by week.'[13]

The Third Programme, however, presents something of a paradox which highlights the tensions inherent in the concept of a 'high cultural' mass medium. On the one hand, it positioned itself as an uncompromising arbiter of 'highbrow' cultural fare for a select and already educated listenership. On the other, in a practical way it broadcast material drawing on ancient Greek literature which had been subject to various forms and degrees of 'translation'—including acts of explanation and contextualization as well as rendering in the vernacular—in order to attract listeners without prior knowledge or experience of these works. Within the wider context of the BBC's cultural broadcasting output—which included music hall, comedy series, soap opera, etc.—programmes drawing on ancient Greece were undoubtedly at the 'higher' end of the 'brow' spectrum, but considerable efforts were made to ensure that these programmes were practically (and imaginatively) accessible to a much wider audience than merely those who had experienced a classical education.

Facilitating engagement: the example of Greek drama

Introductory talks and articles in the *Radio Times* and *The Listener* continued to be employed for programmes which presented performative engagements with ancient Greek topics broadcast on the Third Programme, as they had been on the National and continued to be on the Home, but the BBC was relatively stern in response to aspiring Third Programme listeners who wrote in specifically to ask for study guides or more background information on programmes. In firmly resisting what was derisively termed the provision of 'crutches' or 'hearing aids' for 'aspirants', Third Programme staff believed that

---

[13] Extract from the poem 'Remembering George Barnes', published in Grigson 1984, 140. Grigson is here quoting Barnes's enemies; the way in which the couplet is quoted by Carpenter 1997, 129 may be misread as suggesting, inaccurately, that Grigson himself is poking fun at Barnes. An earlier version of the poem had Aristophanes for Aeschylus, which does not work so well (see Grigson 1978, 54).

they were safeguarding programme content from 'dilution'.[14] The strength of feeling against providing more aids to comprehension and enjoyment for keen but struggling listeners (which seems somewhat to fly in the face of the fact that steps *were* being taken to broadcast Greek texts, for example, in already very 'translated' forms) is indicative of a wider reluctance fully to accept that a significant part of the Third's *actual* audience was composed not of listeners already within the target bracket but of a much more diversely educated and cultured listenership.[15]

In 1953 a BBC survey of Third Programme listeners reported that the audience on an average winter evening had shrunk to 90,000, but also that far fewer of those who might be expected to be listening—on the basis of their level of formal education and cultural tastes—were doing so and that instead many more outside of this bracket were tuning in.[16] The new network could not but make accessible to anyone who had access to a wireless and the desire to listen a rich range of what might otherwise be expensive and socially exclusive pursuits, and so the Third Programme—explicitly designed for an educated and cultured élite—proved in practice to be a democratic and affordable access route to cultural and artistic experience.

> Before the advent of radio, the cinema film and television, the audience for a play was socially limited and culturally homogeneous. The writer for the theatre could and did presume his audience to be possessed in common of certain received opinions and prejudices. [...] There was the obvious opportunity to broadcast plays from the classic repertoire as an educational service but it was not immediately realised that such productions sometimes required an additional education to explain their historical and social context.[17]

When considering the ways in which the radio medium facilitated practical access to Greek plays in performance, the first important (if rather obvious) point to be made is that they were almost always broadcast in English translation, adaptation, or re-working. (When

---

[14] Whitehead 1989, 48–50.   [15] On this reluctance see ibid. 61–2.
[16] Carpenter 1997, 109 (by comparison, the Home was attracting 3¼ million listeners). *The Economist*, 24 October 1953, commented that the Third 'has a far bigger market among the supposedly philistine than among the cultured', whilst the editor of an Oxford undergraduate magazine wrote that 'we do not listen much to the Third Programme, which is a curious thing when so much of its work must clearly be directed at us' (Hughes 1952).
[17] Rodger 1982, 11.

broadcasts on very rare occasions offered extracts from plays in ancient Greek, they were adjuncts to a performance in English.) Other acts of 'translation' pertain to the way in which the form of the original text was manipulated for broadcast on radio. In productions which presented relatively close translations, the degree to which the text was adapted to what may be considered to be the dramatic conventions and the dramatic possibilities of the radio medium is worth noting. Productions fall broadly into three categories. First there are performances of the translation almost straight from the page, and these occur as late as the early 1960s: in such productions there is often a high degree of polish in the acting and a considered amount of accompanying music and sound effects; sometimes an announcer prefaces the performance with a short and simple 'scene-setting' statement, which is particularly helpful since the script has not been subject to any radio-sensitive adaptation to provide verbal or other audio clues as to the opening character's 'social status, mental attitudes and previous history'.[18] In this category falls Val Gielgud's 1962 *Oresteia*, for example (discussed in Chapter 7). The next category involves productions where careful attention has been applied to the subtle adaptation of the translation to the dramatic conventions of the medium (as they emerged and developed over the decades) with, for example, the replacement of pronouns with proper names, the insertion of verbal 'signposts' to indicate the arrival and departure of characters, and the transposition, editing, and cutting of lines and passages for clarity and radio dramatic effect. Drakakis describes this process as 'converting those elements of its structure that depend for their effect upon visual realisation into appropriate aural equivalents, and the inevitable editorial adjustments of the text which such a process demands'.[19] Raymond Raikes was a master of this kind of work. The third category consists of productions in which the raw material of the translated playtext has been substantially refashioned in an attempt to realize the drama in terms of aural performance alone, often using the full range of radiophonic possibilities and techniques, such as the easy fluidity of time and space which, for example, leads to rapid changes of 'scene' (as in film) or the natural use of interior monologue. These productions embrace the full dramatic possibilities of the medium. Examples in

[18] Ibid. 149.   [19] Drakakis 1981*a*, 114.

'Listening in' 83

this category include Gabriel Josipovici's *Ag* (1976) and MacNeice's *Enemy of Cant* (1946).

Since radio productions of Greek plays were directed at the non-specialist, efforts were made to explain and contextualize aspects of the subject matter of which knowledge could not be widely assumed (especially in the first two of the three categories outlined above). For example, radio productions of Greek plays were often preceded by short illustrated articles in the advance issue of the *Radio Times* or *The Listener*; the broadcast might be introduced by a brief talk by the translator; and the performance itself prefaced by some words from a narrator-figure. Productions in the third category more inventively weaved the social and political context of the ancient plays into the script itself, as, for example, MacNeice did in his Aristophanic *Enemy of Cant*.

Listings and articles in the *Radio Times* were in very many cases illustrated by drawings which offered the potential listener visual clues about the subject matter of the broadcast. A great number of these were drawn by Eric Fraser (1902–83), a distinguished illustrative artist who accepted regular commissions from the *Radio Times* from 1926 to 1982 and who had a preference for illustrating Greek subjects.[20] His striking line-drawings became distinctively associated with radio engagements with ancient Greece. As can be seen from the many examples of Fraser's *Radio Times* work reprinted in this volume, he often drew upon the figurative simplicity and stylistic details of Greek vases (see, for example, Figure 7.3), and the more complex examples offer synopses of crucial scenes in the drama which convey a deep imaginative engagement with the subject (see, for example, Figure 7.1 and the brief accompanying discussion). His illustration for the *Radio Times* listing of the 1963 production of Kenneth Cavander's translation of Sophocles' *Philoctetes* has been chosen as the frontispiece of this book because of its intense concentration on some of the significant aspects of the play within the confines of the almost square frame—namely, Philoctetes' agony resulting from the infected wound on his leg and the central importance of Heracles' bow which is both

---

[20] Backemeyer 1998, 27. For further examples and discussion of Fraser's work see Backemeyer 1998, A. Davis 1974, and the frontispiece to Stray 2007*b* (an illustration from the 1965 Third Programme broadcast of Donald Cotton's comedy *The Tragedy of Phaethon*). On the art and the artists of the *Radio Times* see also Driver 1981 and Baker 2002.

Philoctetes' life-line and also what the Greeks need in order to win the ongoing war against Troy. This formal concentration speaks eloquently of the way in which radio's 'limitations' (as some would perceive aspects of the medium's form) serve to focus the listener's attention powerfully on crucial narrative aspects of the story being told—ideas which are expressed in more depth in Section 3.2.

The educative medium

> The art of entertaining and the art of educating have a common meeting-point, at any rate in their broadcast versions, in the art of arousing interest.[21]

The various forms and degrees of translation and adaptation of English versions of Greek texts for radio performance were all designed to widen accessibility to, and to widen the appeal of, these cultural works—so, to democratize *and* popularize them. Sufficient evidence exists to support the view that programmes drawing on ancient Greek texts and topics were largely successful on both counts; although it must be remembered that, of course, not all listeners expressed a positive response to programmes, as will be seen in Part Two. In order to contextualize the significance of the great amount of evidence for positive listener engagements with programmes it is useful to bear in mind the historian Lawrence Goldman's statement about the university extension programme in the nineteenth century: he notes that 'generations of working people did not reject the high culture of the universities; rather, they sought to open and democratize them so that they and their children could have access to that culture as well'.[22] Goldman's observation that individuals who had not enjoyed a traditional university education were, generally speaking, often open to availing themselves of opportunities for educational and cultural experience which had previously been unavailable to them is certainly applicable to and observable in other, similarly educative activities. There are countless responses from listeners in the Listener Research Reports which would seem to back this up: for example, in response to an English translation of André Gide's *Œdipe*, broadcast in English translation as *Oedipus* on the Third Programme in 1951, a School Meals Worker expressed the

---

[21] Matheson 1933, 176.   [22] Goldman 1995, 87.

view that such 'radio presentation of plays by foreign authors gives listeners an opportunity to extend their literary knowledge'.[23] In 1924 Reith stated that 'there is abundant evidence that broadcasting arouses interest and curiosity, and has caused large numbers of people to patronize performances in theatre or concert hall which otherwise they would not have attended'.[24] Writing in 1933, Matheson considered that 'even the most passive, unintelligent kind of listening may make people aware, in a dim way, of ideas, events, facts, places and people of whose existence they would otherwise never have dreamed'.[25] Some of her language may appear to be rather condescending, but my own listening experience testifies that the phenomenon she identifies remains a real one. However, much of the BBC's output was, as will be outlined, purposefully designed to be educational, and appreciated as such, and the educative potential of much other programming was valued in an equally positive way.

As early as 1928, the BBC broadcast a series of six twenty-minute programmes under the title *Greek Plays for Modern Listeners*. Presented by Archibald Young Campbell (1885–1958), Gladstone Professor of Greek at the University of Liverpool, these programmes almost constituted a crash-course in Greek drama. The *Radio Times* listing for the first programme in the series, 'The General Character of a Greek Tragedy', acknowledges that the appeal of Greek drama is, 'at first sight, somewhat incomprehensible to the average man', thus defining the hoped-for audience for this programme as one not already knowledgeable about, nor even sympathetic to, the topic; Professor Campbell will, it is said, 'explain how classical drama differs from that of our own time, and how it should be approached to enjoy it fully', further underlining the didactic nature of this series.[26] The next four programmes are introduced in the listings (all of which are illustrated by ancient artefacts) in terms which strive to make them more readily accessible to the listener with no prior knowledge of the tragedians: the listing for 'Æschylus and his *Oresteia*' describes Clytemnestra and Orestes as 'The Lady Macbeth and the Hamlet of the Greek world'; the hero of Sophocles' *Oedipus at Colonus*, the subject of the next

---

[23] BBC WAC LR/51/1010.
[24] Reith 1924, 169. Similarly, Rodger 1982, 29: 'in European countries like Britain and Sweden and Germany the radio actually stimulated listeners to go and read classic novels or visit the theatre'.
[25] Matheson 1933, 176.   [26] *Radio Times*, 24 February 1928, 400.

programme, is hailed as 'the King Lear of the ancient world'; the following programme on Euripides is introduced by a reminder that this ancient playwright is the 'most popular in our own age'; and, similarly, the subject of the penultimate programme, Aristophanes, is described as 'the unique, Gilbertian satirist of ancient Greece'.[27] The educational potential of such series may be most profitably observed from a consideration of their relationship with other, related programmes available to listeners in the months preceding and following. A few weeks before the *Greek Plays* series began, for example, the *Stories in Poetry* series broadcast a programme on 'Epic Poetry: the *Iliad* and the *Odyssey*' for schools (on which there is more detail in Chapter 6) and, whilst the series was on air, the radio play *Speed: A Tragi-Comic Fantasy of Gods and Mortals*, featuring divine characters include Cronos and Zeus, was heard; within weeks, two of Maurice Baring's Greek-inspired short dramas, *After Euripides' Electra* and *The Greek Vase*, were broadcast. In later months, substantial extracts from translations of Euripides' *Alcestis* and Aeschylus' *Persians* appeared in separate programmes and Euripides' *Electra* was given in a full production (see Chapter 4 for discussion of these productions); other plays inspired by the ancient world were also broadcast, such as John Drinkwater's *X = O: A Night of the Trojan War*.

Further series of talks were broadcast in 1929: the five-part *Classics in Translation* series for schools, covering translations from Elizabethan times to the present, was presented by the retired headmaster of Merchant Taylors' School, J. Arbuthnot Nairn (1874–1957), and the series *New Light on Ancient Greece* by Stanley Casson (1889–1944), Reader in Classical Archaeology at Oxford. The latter series consisted of six twenty-minute programmes, each of which focused on one ancient site—Sparta, Troy, Delphi, Mycenae, Corinth, and Olympia. Each week, *The Listener* printed an illustrated version of Casson's broadcast talk and at the end of the series it described the contents of a number of books on ancient Greek history, literature, and art to facilitate the further self-education of listeners.[28] This series was part of the BBC's Talks and Lectures Programme for 1929, which an article in *The Times* describes as being intended 'for the student, either as an individual or in groups', referring to the fact that over 160

---

[27] *Radio Times*, 2 March 1928, 454; 9 March 1928, 504; 16 March 1928, 554; 23 March 1928, 606.

[28] *The Listener*, 24 April 1929, 561.

'discussion groups' for radio's talks and lectures had been formed in the autumn of 1928 alone.[29] By the winter of 1931 the total number of such registered groups was 922.

These series were often accompanied by the publication of an Aids to Study pamphlet which, for the price of 1*d.* or 2*d.*, summarized the talks and offered illustrations, facts and figures, and a full bibliography for further reading.[30] One such pamphlet accompanied the *International Co-operation and What It Means* series in 1930 in which Murray delivered the first talk, which was entitled 'On Intellectual Cooperation' (and see Section 4.2, on his contribution to radio programmes on contemporary topics).[31] The pamphlets were intended to have 'independent value' of the radio series they accompanied and it was believed that 'listeners tend to pay a good deal of attention to lecturers' advice [...] and Libraries like a full bibliography so that they may have a range of choice in their supply to readers'.[32] Furthermore, these very programmes and pamphlets made up the 'curriculum' studied and discussed by the increasing number of Listening Groups being formed at educational institutes and settlements up and down the country.[33] Such listening groups, set up in the cause of what was termed 'broadcast adult education', flourished in this period, and many of the several hundred active groups were organized by Workers' Educational Associations.[34] Clearly, a common enough concern for some—but not, presumably, for those who were already actively involved in these groups—was that these discussion groups would result in 'mechanising thought' or bringing about the 'uniformity of general culture' and, in the light of such concerns, it is interesting that the drive behind the scheme was as much about inculcating a sense of citizenship and social responsibility as imparting knowledge and equipping listeners with debating skills.[35] Support for these organized adult education activities survived for a number of years but in 1937 there was a shift in

---

[29] Anon. 1929*b*.   [30] Anon. 1930, 405.

[31] Broadcast at 7.25 p.m., Wednesday, 5 March 1930. Later programmes, delivered by other prominent speakers, covered topics such as economics, labour, and health.

[32] Letter from Charles Siepmann to GM, 20 November 1929 (GM/T1).

[33] Siepmann anticipates that many new groups 'will be formed to hear this series' (letter to GM, 22 January 1930, in GM/T1).

[34] *The Listener*, 23 January 1929, 60.

[35] Ibid. On the higher sociopolitical intent behind listening groups see Bailey 2009 and bibliography there. See also Pegg 1983, 166–8 and Matheson 1933, 195 ff.

policy towards targeting educational talks at the individual adult listener and the programme was not re-established on the same footing after the war.[36]

The BBC was also very much concerned to broadcast educational programmes to schools, devising a system in which around 3,000 schools were listening by 1927, nearly 10,000 in 1939, over 14,700 in 1947, and more than 28,000 in 1958.[37] As with adult educational broadcasts, supplementary pamphlets were issued, containing 'notes, maps, diagrams, illustrations, book-lists, and so on, which cannot be given orally without great waste of time and repetition'.[38] In 1929 the *Radio Times* considered that these schools pamphlets 'will also be found [to be] of assistance to listeners generally' and in 1958 Mary Crozier noted that 'It is not uncommon for the housewife, or the worker kept at home for a few days, to enjoy following lessons about Chaucer's England or some great novel like *War and Peace*, or about how people live in distant lands'.[39] An early report based on the listening habits of seventy-two schools concluded that

> broadcast lessons effectively imparted a knowledge of facts, stimulated interest in ways which could be definitely observed, created impressions as durable as those produced by ordinary classroom lessons, and were particularly interesting to clever children. In addition they supplied views and information which teachers by themselves could not have supplied, gave teachers new ideas for lessons, and interested some hitherto indifferent parents in the work that their children did at school.[40]

Schools broadcasting covered subjects across the full curriculum, and classical topics were not neglected. Taking 1937 as an example brings up 'Socrates', a twenty-minute programme in the *Talks for Sixth Forms* series, delivered in February by classical scholar Richard Livingstone (1880–1960). Ancient philosophy was also the topic of a later *Talks for Sixth Forms* programme in October, in which the

---

[36] Scannell and Cardiff 1991, 83; Briggs 1965, 226. See also Jennings and Gill 1939, 17–18.
[37] Briggs 1965, 189; British Broadcasting Corporation 1947a, 55; Crozier 1958, 167.
[38] British Broadcasting Corporation 1929, 80.
[39] *Radio Times*, 29 March 1929, 772; Crozier 1948, 167.
[40] Briggs 1965, 191 (but see subsequent pages for the hard work that lay behind the BBC's efforts, especially under the guardianship of Mary Somerville (1897–1963), to refine broadcasting technique to create programmes that would always work this well in the classroom).

philosopher C. E. M. Joad (1891–1953) presented a programme entitled *How Philosophy Began: Socrates and Plato*. In the same month, Gilbert Murray gave his talk, again for sixth forms, on 'Euripides' (just a few months after his translation of *Trojan Women* had been produced by Barbara Burnham). Ancient topics were sometimes presented in dramatic format: for example, also in October that year the series *For the Schools* broadcast a twenty-minute 'dramatic interlude' under the 'World History' banner, entitled 'Greece and Persia: Salamis' by the historian and dramatist Hugh Ross Williamson (1901–78). The listing in the *Radio Times* indicates that this play celebrates Athenians as lovers of freedom who, with Greek allies, successfully warded off Xerxes and his Persian forces in the sea battle at Salamis in 480 BC.[41] This dramatization prefigures the use of this ancient historical topic in radio propagandistic contexts as Britain prepared to enter, and then was engaged in, the Second World War: see, for example, the radio production of Aeschylus' *Persians* in April 1939 (the topicality of which, as the storm clouds gathered over Europe, struck home in reviews); Murray's reference to Salamis in his wartime talk on 'Greece and her Tradition' (1940); and Louis MacNeice's use of the Battle of Salamis as a potent symbol to shore up support for the plight of Greece in his wartime feature programme *The Glory that is Greece* in the following year. Younger children, too, had Greek tales presented for them in suitable form: in the autumn and winter of 1937, for example, *The Children's Hour* included a series of Aesop's fables which were re-worked by the poet Henry Reed (1914–86). 'Try to read the story first', encouraged the *Radio Times*, 'then listen to this version with music and songs'.[42]

In the late 1960s Kenneth Cavander wrote eleven twenty-minute dramatizations from Homer's *Iliad* and *Odyssey* for broadcast in the *Living Language* series of BBC Schools Radio.[43] As Cavander noted in the introduction to the 1969 published version of these scripts, because of the original performative context of the epic poems, 'The medium of radio is therefore an appropriate way to reintroduce these tales to a twentieth-century audience. Composed for the listener, not the reader, these stories [. . .] created (like radio) moving pictures for

---

[41] *Radio Times*, 15 October 1937, 51.   [42] *Radio Times*, 3 September 1937, 73.
[43] The plays were first broadcast in 1966 and 1968, with a repeat of the *Odyssey* in 1969. See Cavander 1969 for expanded versions of these scripts.

the mind's eye.'[44] A selection of comments from teachers (identified only by the region in which they taught) on their pupils' responses to these Homeric programmes give a valuable, albeit second-hand, snapshot of how they were experienced:

> The pupils were completely engrossed in this broadcast and said they found it most exciting. The fight between Hector and Achilles excited the imagination of the boys, in particular. (Clackmannan)
>
> Most of the girls enjoyed the dramatized section of Hector and his wife and child on the battlements—it came over vividly. Boys enjoyed battle. (East Lothian)
>
> Excellent broadcast: pamphlet notes adequate; girls not quite as absorbed as boys. (Campbeltown)
>
> As good as your best! Pupils of varying ages listen spell-bound, touching their collar-bone when it's mentioned, really experiencing the story— and most especially the emotions. (Fleetwood)
>
> Not enough groundwork on Helen's abduction given to take up story when the broadcast did. Children very confused by so many characters with Greek names. Pupils' pamphlet excellent as ever. Not enough distinction between Gods and mortals. (Doncaster)

Other comments illustrate how teachers used the series as a springboard for further class activities: a teacher in Edinburgh noted that, after listening to the series, pupils wrote up the story of the *Iliad* 'in serial form in modern newspaper language'; a Plymouth teacher had recorded the series on audiotape in order to allow for pauses in which pupils, for example, voted on Achilles' likely response to the Greeks' request for him to rejoin battle. Another teacher from Plymouth considered that the series had been particularly successful in 'throwing the children's thoughts forward and encouraging imagination as against reception'.[45]

Clearly the impact of classical programmes broadcast within formal educational channels is an area for further study. As already established, however, the educational potential and effect of broadcasting was not only through formal educative channels, and the long-running 1933–4 series of half-hour *Readings from Classical Literature* on Sunday afternoons bears out the generally educative

---

[44] Ibid. 7.
[45] Three typescript pages with letter from Joan Griffiths (Producer, Schools Radio) to Kenneth Cavander, 6 February 1969 (R16/1463/1).

form and function of cultural broadcasting in these early years of the medium. The series began by moving gradually through the Greek playwrights, historians, and philosophers, before exploring Roman literature, the aim ultimately being 'to review the whole field of classical literature' from ancient Greece to present day 'classics'.[46]

The BBC WAC contains much evidence for the fact that individual listeners found programmes drawing on ancient Greece broadly educative. The long quotation at the top of Chapter 1 is worth bringing into discussion again here. It is from a letter written by a listener, Mary Jameson, to Gilbert Murray in response to a 1936 production of Euripides' *Hippolytus* which was prefaced by a substantial introductory programme and *Radio Times* article designed to give the listener some historical background to the play. Jameson wrote to Murray, who had translated the play, to thank him for having 'brought this play within our reach'. She refers to how she, her mother, and her sister had read the play in preparation for the broadcast, and how the introduction had 'left us with a deeper and wider sense of the significance of the play than we had before it'.[47] This letter is a far from unique example of unsolicited feedback which seems to underline the value of the BBC including accessible versions of 'highbrow' fare within its project to broadcast a broad spectrum of what was perceived to be the nation's cultural heritage. It also demonstrates the willingness of at least some proportion of the audience to do preparatory work before broadcasts, which suggests that some listeners actively valued the culturally educative potential of radio.

There is evidence that some educators, too, considered themselves to have been further educated by radio broadcasts and that some were stimulated by dramatic productions on radio to stage the plays with their students. After hearing *Iphigeneia in Aulis*, a 1951 Third Programme production of the Euripidean play, a schoolteacher wrote in her listener research questionnaire that 'I had not realised before how impressive and beautiful Greek tragedy can be'.[48] It is noteworthy that prior to this 1951 production, which was the very first BBC radio broadcast of the play (repeated in 1952 and 1954, demonstrating its perceived success), there seem to have been only occasional stagings of Euripides' *Iphigenia at Aulis* in Britain. The

---

[46] 'Microphone announcement', undated typescript (R19/925/1).
[47] Letter from Mary Jameson to GM, 18 October 1936 (GM/S).
[48] BBC WAC LR/51/1668.

wave of amateur performances, many in educational settings, which were directly stimulated by the radio production are, therefore, a striking illustration of the knock-on effect that radio dramatic performances could have on the stage. Listeners wrote letters to the producer Raymond Raikes mentioning productions which had been directly inspired by the radio version which had been staged by London's Attic Players, Reading's Progress Theatre, the Yorkshire college Bretton Hall, and the East Ham Grammar School for Girls.[49] A lecturer in English at St Mary's Training College in Bangor had been for some time searching for an 'effective and actable' version of the play for her students to perform before she had heard Raikes's own translation on the radio (of which he had subsequently sent her his own acting version to copy).[50] She also acknowledged another reason to be grateful to him for his additional offer of help with the text: 'I can see that some of the generalizations (based mainly on Aeschylus and Sophocles) which I have been making in my classes on Greek drama need pretty serious qualification [...] ignorance of Greek can be such a disadvantage when it comes to detailed interpretation of the text.'[51] This translation also attracted attention from overseas: the English-born Ben Iden Payne (1881–1976), an actor and director who had since 1946 been a drama scholar at the University of Texas, requested a copy of the script for use in his classes, specifically 'for the presentation of scenes in what are called Demonstration Labs', Friday afternoon sessions in which students taking the Period Play Production course directed scenes from plays.[52]

This was one of the early productions by Raymond Raikes, who would go on to specialize in producing Drama Department productions for broadcast on the Third. He was a producer for whom radio dramatic sense was of the utmost importance: he had studied classics and English at Uppingham School and the University of Oxford but he was no academic purist; indeed, he became renowned for liberal

[49] Various sources in S452/23/1. The sense that the production was considered a great success is reinforced by the fresh production broadcast as one of his last productions in 1975, before which the Hellenist Denys Lionel Page (1908–78) gave a 10-minute introductory talk.
[50] Letter from Gweneth Lilly to RR, 12 June 1954 (S452/23/1).
[51] Letter from Gweneth Lilly to RR, 18 July 1954 (ibid.).
[52] Letters from Ben Iden Payne to RR, 24 September 1951 and 30 January 1952 (S452/2/1).

cutting and rewriting of texts, including (at least) twenty Greek and Roman plays, to make them as accessible as possible. His *Iphigeneia in Aulis* translation was written (in metres which correspond with the Greek) whilst serving in the army during the Second World War. The production was generally very well received, with an Appreciation Index of 76 (comparing favourably with the current average of 66). The Listener Research Report summarized the response to it thus: 'the play was enjoyed by the majority of its Panel audience, including listeners to whom it was already well known and others to whom it was new. A Bank Cashier said, "I doubt whether I should have been able to enjoy it without the excellent introductory talk"; an Engineer, on the other hand, said the talk induced him to give the play a trial, and "it proved to be one".' Some listeners found the play to be 'long-winded', 'horrible', and 'bloodthirsty', but most enjoyed it, despite admitting some ambivalence to the idea of a Greek play:

> It is hard to find an exact reason why these Greek plays appeal. Their plots can hardly be called wonderful, in fact this particular play has just about enough for a one-act play, yet the padding doesn't seem superfluous. (Clerk, Transport)
>
> Strange, in my mind I say, 'What, all these ancients again?'. Yet I listen with bated breath and get fascinated and thrilled each time I hear them. (Retired Teacher)[53]

The evidence for the broad culturally educational impact of radio programmes on listeners, and especially the way in which radio programmes seem often to have had an impact on teaching and learning both in the classroom and via amateur stages, underlines Pegg's conclusion that the educational impact of radio was largely informal. Yet it was clearly not insignificant. The evidence for radio broadcasts stimulating individual listeners to read Greek plays in print (as Mary Jameson, her sister, and her mother did), and to stage them with their pupils in schools and colleges, is especially interesting in light of the increasing marginalization of ancient Greek in the academic curriculum during the course of the twentieth century. Writing at the end of the century, the classical scholar Oliver Taplin declared that 'the loss of confidence and of dogma in classical studies has paradoxically been a liberation. [. . .] Classical Education had become an isolated fortress, a place with high walls and exclusive

---

[53] BBC WAC LR/51/1668.

frontier controls.'[54] Indeed, fifty years earlier, in 1948, the historian E. L. Woodward observed that 'there is already a surprisingly large audience for Greek plays broadcast in translation. [...] I believe that the study of Greek and Latin literature may itself gain lost ground through educational broadcasts. A revival of this kind [...] might well have important political effects.'[55]

Collaborations between eye and ear, print and radio

At several points so far radio has been seen to work in tandem with affordable pamphlets, paperback translations, or academic books in the project of making classical literature both practically and imaginatively accessible to a wide public from the 1920s. Briggs notes that in the 1920s the sale of books increased substantially because of the impact of radio on the listening public and 'more than one local librarian in his annual report referred to wireless as a "new ally [...] creating and deepening the interest of the public in the higher forms of literature"'.[56] Mark Pegg has studied this phenomenon in detail in his book on broadcasting and society to 1938, emphasizing the characteristic informality of the educational effect of broadcasting and the subsequent difficulty in measuring its impact with precision. Nevertheless he considers that it is possible to conclude that 'radio could provide the incentive to read a book cited in a broadcast: there was evidence from libraries that novels dramatised for the radio were quickly put under heavy demand' and that, in the 1920s at least, 'librarians reported that there was a direct link between the specific volumes which were taken out on loan, and the personal enquiries for helpful books on the subject of a radio programme'.[57]

It is arguable that the decade of domestic broadcasting before the launch of Penguin Books in 1935 was a significant factor in the 'new reading public' that has been perceived to emerge at this time and it is likely that the near coincidence of the founding of Penguin Classics and the Third Programme in 1946 was mutually beneficial to both media.[58] Just as the radio listener was on the whole perceived to be a non-specialist (and, as noted above, for all the Third Programme's

---

[54] Taplin 1999, 8.   [55] Woodward 1948, 26–7.
[56] Briggs 1961, 16, quoting a library report.   [57] Pegg 1983, 209.
[58] Joicey 1993, 25. See also Rylance 2005.

desire to reach an already educated and cultured listenership, classical material was almost always translated and to some extent contextualized), so it was also the intention of the editor of the Penguin Classics series, E. V. Rieu, 'to commission translators who can [...] present the general reader with readable and attractive versions of the great writers' books in modern English, shorn of the unnecessary difficulties and erudition, the archaic flavour and the foreign idiom that renders so many existing translations repellent to modern taste'.[59]

In October 1947, some of the more dramatic of Plato's dialogues were broadcast in the new translation of Professor Hugh Tredennick which was intended for the Penguin Classics series.[60] This broadcast may not have been the first translation for Penguin to have been adapted for radio performance but the example illustrates how from an early stage it was not unusual for Greek and Roman titles in Penguin Classics to receive some sort of reading or performance on air. In 1969 Betty Radice (1912–85), who had read classics at Oxford and was by this point joint editor of the series with Rieu, wrote some scripts for the BBC on Socrates and Plato for broadcast to China on what was then called the Far Eastern Service; she had also submitted her translations of Terence's Roman comedies (published in the Classics series) for consideration by the Third (which, on this occasion, did not bite). Philip Vellacott was another Penguin translator whose translations were frequently broadcast by the BBC. Vellacott, who had read classics at Cambridge and was a teacher at Dulwich College from the early 1950s to his retirement in 1967, translated all the surviving plays of Euripides and Aeschylus for Penguin Classics, in addition to works by Theophrastus and Menander. A high proportion of his Greek play translations were adapted for dramatic performance on the Third around the time of their publication; indeed, his translation of Aeschylus' *Oresteia*, which was both performed on radio and published by Penguin in 1956, was initially commissioned by the BBC.[61] Vellacott wrote to the producer Raymond Raikes

---

[59] Anon. n.d.
[60] These do not, however, appear in Penguindex 109, the checklist of all Penguin Classics titles.
[61] In addition to the *Oresteia*, his translation of Euripides' *Iphigenia in Tauris* was broadcast in 1949 (published in *Alcestis and Other Plays*, 1953); Euripides' *Trojan Women* was broadcast as *Women of Troy* in 1952 (published in *The Bacchae and Other Plays*, 1954); in 1953 Euripides' *Hippolytus* was both broadcast and published in

thus: 'thank you for the moment of inspiration when you first said to me on the telephone, "Why not have a shot at the *Oresteia*?" and for the constant and patient help which you have given me since then in completing this work'.[62] The Penguin translation of the *Oresteia* accordingly prints a dedicatory inscription to Raikes, as well as a full list of cast and credits from the radio production. A letter from Vellacott to a Mr Glover at Penguin reports that 'the BBC propose to repeat the broadcast of it soon after the publication of the book'; Glover gladly responds that 'this will certainly give encouragement to the book sales'.[63]

The two media—radio and paperback publishing—were, therefore, both operating from the same ideological ground in a mutually supportive way. As *The Times* put it in 1952: the 'printed book and radio transcript popularize each other; it is sometimes a two-way traffic'; furthermore, the writer notes that the Penguin Classics are 'the most popular series that the firm has launched, judged by the test that every volume in the series has been reprinted'.[64] In terms of the audience, it is also worth noting that the positive feedback from readers of Penguin Classics often echoes that of listeners to radio programmes drawing on ancient Greece. Compare the nature of Mary Jameson's letter, discussed earlier, with the following sentiments written by a reader described as a 'a woman teacher' to Rieu in praise of Penguin Classics, indicating that the series expertly filled

---

Alcestis and Other Plays; in 1954 Euripides' *Helen* was both broadcast and published in *The Bacchae and Other Plays*; Euripides' *Medea* was broadcast in 1962 (published in *Euripides, Plays* in 1963). The work of such popular freelancers was not automatically accepted for broadcast, however: Vellacott's translation of *Medea* was only provisionally accepted in 1961 subject to alternations, and those of Euripides' *Ion* and Aeschylus' *Seven against Thebes* were rejected in 1950 and 1960 respectively; his play *An Island in Time*, drawing on Odysseus's relationship with Calypso in *Odyssey*, Book V, was only accepted for production in 1955 after several revisions and his *Oedipus Aware*, a version of Sophocles' *Oedipus Tyrannus*, failed to impress in 1968 (see correspondence and internal BBC readers' reports in S452/2/1, S452/3/1, and S452/40/1).

[62] PV to RR, 10 May 1956 (S452/29/1).

[63] PV to Mr Glover, 23 August [1956] and Glover's response, 24 August 1956 (PA, Editorial File DM1107/L69). Penguin was also supportive of its translations being used in other contexts: in 1953, for example, the company sent twenty-four copies of the galley-proofs of Vellacott's *Hippolytus*, shortly to appear in the volume *Alcestis and Other Plays*, to the Attic Players, who were to perform it at Toynbee Hall in May of that year (see correspondence in PA, Editorial File DM1107/L31).

[64] Anon. 1952.

'Listening in'   97

the gap in knowledge resulting from having gone to a school where Greek was not on the curriculum:

> For anyone like myself, whose bitter regret it has long been that Greek is not taught in girls' schools, this series of splendid translations has been more than a godsend. You yourself were <u>my</u> 'Chapman's Homer', and since then one new planet after another has swum within reach. Only recently I was reading Rex Warner's Xenophon, and I literally could <u>not</u> put it down.[65]

3.2. IMAGINATIVE ACCESS; OR, THE POPULARIZING MEDIUM

Radio's stimulation of the imagination

GILBERT MURRAY I think we fall into a deep defeatist trap
to regard poetry superseded by the slide show or the snap!
If it's to a modern appliance that you must go
I would sooner place my trust in the power of radio.
You know, I genuinely believe that I have often seen
vivider pictures on the wireless than the screen.

SYBIL THORNDIKE I know you've told me, Gilbert, Greek tragedians could,
had they wished to, like us, use buckets of stage blood.
They weren't theatrically backward, so why didn't they?
I know you think it's because they'd found a better way.

GILBERT MURRAY The messenger speech. A messenger speech
reaches depths in the heart mere pictures never reach.
If the messenger's on target, the mind's eye of the hearer
more than vision itself brings horror ever nearer.

From Tony Harrison (2008), *Fram*, 55.

---

[65] Quoted in memo titled 'EVR, ASBG', 23 January 1959 (PA, DM1819/27/7), with reference to Warner 1949. The poetic reference is to John Keats's 1816 sonnet 'On First Looking into Chapman's Homer' which relates how astonished the Greek-less Keats was on reading the Elizabethan George Chapman's free translation of the epic poet: 'Yet did I never breathe its pure serene | Till I heard Chapman speak out loud and bold: | Then felt I like some watcher of the skies | When a new planet swims into his ken'.

As this quotation from Tony Harrison's play *Fram* implies, in its presentation of characters and events that the audience cannot see, radio dramatization has a close affinity with the messenger speech in Greek tragedy, a dramatic device in which action which has taken place elsewhere is described verbally rather than presented visually to the audience.[66] In a similar way the ancient, oral performance of Homeric epic tells of characters and actions rather than enacting them. Although the radio actor is unable to use powerful aspects of his or her physicality which ancient performers may have drawn on (for example, gesture, and—as we might imagine in the case of rhapsodes, who were not masked—facial expression and eye contact), both must work hard to capture the imagination of the audience and hold it during the telling of an event or a story which is not itself physically enacted or visually illustrated. Some other aspects of Greek tragedy could also be said to lend themselves well to dramatic performance in a purely aural medium: for example, the small number of principal roles; the potential for a wide range of vocal delivery (speech, chant, song) by individual and multiple voices; and soliloquy, which on radio is often interpreted as interior monologue. Furthermore, choral odes are comfortably integrated into the dramatic whole through the ease with which music accompanying song and chant is accommodated into the dramatic 'soundscape'.

The 1929 production of Euripides' *Electra* in Murray's translation was considered by the BBC to be one of the most satisfactory productions done that year on account of its 'poetic value and classic purity of outline'.[67] For some time it was not an uncommon belief that Greek tragedy might be *best* done on radio: one critic considered in 1937 that 'their lack of action is then an advantage, and the power of the words is left to recreate the original *atmosphere* without the

---

[66] The messenger speech was often used to describe especially violent actions (suicide, murder, etc.) which almost always took place off stage; another device, the *ekkyklema*, was sometimes used to bring the results of those actions (e.g. the bodies of recently deceased characters) onto the stage. Drakakis 1981a, 119 discusses Shakespearean examples of the reporting of action not shown on stage: 'here, as elsewhere, a theatre audience is placed in the position of a radio listener'. The ancient Greek literary treatise *On the Sublime* (attributed to Cassius Longinus, c.213–273, until the early nineteenth century when it was dated to the first century AD) discusses the concept of *phantasia* (which may be translated as 'visualization') with regard to a speaker's capacity to imagine what he is describing so vividly that his audience share in the imaginative experience.

[67] British Broadcasting Corporation 1930, 73.

intrusion of a modern stage-setting'.[68] A decade later, similar sentiments were often expressed: for example, 'Greek drama is, at any rate structurally, peculiarly suitable for broadcasting [...] the movement is of emotion and plot.'[69] Even in the early 1960s, Val Gielgud asserted that the 'visual presentation [of Greek tragedy] in the theatre is always liable to teeter dangerously on a ledge separating too narrowly the sublime from the ridiculous [...] broadcasting presentation, compelled by circumstances to essay less, may on occasion accomplish more'.[70] Such statements may well be read as a rejection of the challenges posed by the live, bodily performance of a play inherited from a far distant time and culture, but they also suggest an advantage of the radio medium for the impersonation of ancient characters and the playing out of their stories. During the early decades of radio, at least, theatrically staged productions of Greek drama tended to use 'antique' designs for set and costume, thus flagging up antiquity—and therefore temporal and cultural difference—and creating a distancing effect. In the enforced absence of questions about the design of set and costume and about the representation and movement of the chorus, radio drama seems to have the potential to get more quickly to the human dimension of the drama. The same benefit holds for the radio performance or presentation of other ancient texts, especially bearing in mind the tendency of the radio producer of feature programmes to ensure accessibility of language and style.

Radio cut its dramatic teeth on plays from the stage, and in producing them it gradually discovered the different requirements and possibilities of radio as a new medium for dramatic presentation. The emerging radio form drew on the techniques used by oral literature to capture and hold the imagination through the power of words. It developed the use of non-verbal sounds, almost as 'stage

---

[68] Turton 1937 (emphasis added). This statement, in an article anticipating a radio production of *Trojan Women* with Lillah McCarthy as Hecuba, is particularly interesting in light of the fact that its author had, as an Oxford undergraduate studying classics, co-founded the Balliol Players, which toured Greek plays in translation around the English countryside (for a history of the group see Wrigley 2011*b*). The previous year Gilbert Murray had confessed in a *Radio Times* article accompanying a production of *Hippolytus* that he had 'never yet found a satisfactory way of presenting the Chorus on the modern stage' but that 'In broadcasting much of the difficulty will disappear' (Murray 1936).

[69] Ridley 1947, 15.

[70] Gielgud 1963. Radio plays were generally considered to be closer to reality than stage plays (see Drakakis 1981*b*).

properties', to suggest the scene and position the dramatic action in a meaningful sweep of time and space; and from opera and oratorio it observed how music can set the emotional register, signal changes of scene, and offer another language for the interpretation of the drama. Owing to the scope for powerful effects of counterpoint (which, of course, is not possible on the page), some have recognized a special affinity between radio drama and opera. Referring to the sung and musical aspects of a 1950 production of MacNeice's translation of *Agamemnon*, one reviewer said: 'Oratorio, opera? We had better not start beating the bounds again on that vexed no-man's-land which divides opera and radio play.'[71] Some radio dramas and features purposefully aspired to an equality between word and music: for example, in *The Rescue*, the 1943 dramatization of Homer's *Odyssey* by Sackville-West and Britten, music was considered to be 'part of the texture of the play, warp and weft, verse and music, neither complete without the other'.[72]

The building blocks of a radio dramatization can therefore be said to include the words of the script; the way in which these words are delivered (for example, in speech, chant, or song; by single or multiple voices; and in dialogue, monologue, or as interior monologue); music; non-verbal and non-musical sounds ('sound signs'); silence; and the temporal and spatial shifts in the narrative. But it is the complex combination of these elements which produces a dramatic effect greater than the sum of its parts: successful radio dramatization is a well-woven tapestry of meaningful noise. This 'soundscape' is, of course, created and manipulated (orchestrated, almost) by technological devices such as the dramatic control panel, the introduction of which, from the late 1920s, 'enabled radio drama to dissolve both temporal and implied spatial boundaries, thus extending its powers of aural suggestion, and offering parallels in sound only of what dramatists such as Strindberg and Brecht had already begun to explore in

---

[71] Hope-Wallace 1950.
[72] Crozier 1948, 167. Rodger 1982, 84 describes it as 'a kind of spoken opera'. Rattigan 2002, 2–3 considers that the use of music in radio drama is of one of two kinds: the first is external to the dramatic action ('that music has a role as an external structural framing device with possible extended significance in creating a sense of mood'); in the second kind it can be equal to words and all other noises in creating meaning ('can define and impart meaning on a sub-textual level as a paralanguage in its own right'). See Guralnick 1996, p. xiii and ch. 3 on radio plays which have 'affinities to music'.

the theatre and that film had utilised almost from its inception'.[73] This enabled sound to be faded in and out and more than one studio to be used for actors, choruses, musicians, and sound effects. After its introduction, 'the microphone became as versatile as the film camera was later to become'; furthermore, through its employment, radio 'could imitate the flexibility of the human mind itself, with the result that soliloquy, flashback, the cross-cutting of scenes, all became part of the "grammar" of the radio play'.[74] The application to radio of artistic techniques more usual in other cultural forms such as film (for example, montage) and the novel (stream of consciousness) meant that the listener could 'hold in his mind related sequences of sound for which there could be no objective visual validation'.[75] The technological advances over the course of the twentieth century therefore enabled snatches of conversation to be juxtaposed, two scenes could be inter-cut and broadcast with a sense of simultaneity, and internal thoughts voiced without artifice or awkwardness.

Some early radio practitioners demonstrated scepticism about the medium in which they were working. In particular, radio's early relationship with the stage meant that the critical focus was always on what was being *lost* in the process of transmitting stage plays via radio and the focus of much attention was radio's subsequent so-called 'blindness'—or, in other words, the absence of a visual or physical dimension. For example, in 1949 a radio critic wrote in the *Radio Times* that 'radio drama has always drawn what strength it has from its own most crippling limitation, blindness'.[76] Earlier, in 1934, Val Gielgud put the following question to readers of the popular newspaper *The Daily Mirror*: 'Do you listen to radio plays? And, mark you, I mean by that, do you *listen*?' He warned that if women, in whose domestic power he believed lay the key to good listening, 'insist on washing the baby or playing bridge, on chattering inconsequently, if amiably, through [...] the items of a radio programme, their households will inevitably come under the category of bad listeners'.[77] Thus in the early years of broadcast drama the listener was urged to adopt in the home the audience conventions for serious drama in the theatre—silence, darkness, and stillness. It is clear that

---

[73] Drakakis 1981*b*, 5. Drakakis dates the dramatic control panel to 1928, but Briggs 1961, 201 to 1927.
[74] Drakakis 1981*b*, 21.   [75] Ibid. 5.   [76] Hope-Wallace 1949*c*, 22.
[77] Gielgud 1934. See also Guthrie 1931*a*, 187, Scannell and Cardiff 1991, 371.

some did: in 1929, 'A Listener' contributed an article to the *Radio Times* in which he (presumably) described how he listens by the fire, 'with pipe', in darkness: 'it *must* have one's undivided attention', he considered, so that 'an imaginary world peopled with living characters actually looking, walking, and dressing' can be envisaged.[78] The fear seems to have been that, unless radio drama was given undivided attention by listeners who were actively resisting the intrusion of the domestic on the cultural experience, its impact, and therefore its value, would be lost. This fear had roots in a deep insecurity: the onus was firmly being placed on the audience to compensate, through 'good listening', for what radio practitioners themselves sensed to be the major shortcoming of the medium—its 'blindness', or rather its sole reliance on the sense of hearing. The anxiety on the part of the radio practitioner to control the listening experience through suggestions about listening etiquette also betrays a considerable anxiety about the ability of the listener to engage with a programme on their own terms in the domestic sphere. Two decades later the advice to listeners had mellowed somewhat, but still it emphasized the point that listening is something to be *worked* at: 'the part of the listener in securing his own enjoyment is an active one. The people at the producing end will do all they can to help him, but he must himself be alert to react to the aids, and learn by practice to make the impact on his ear stimulate the visual imagination', a concept which will receive further discussion shortly.[79]

From an early point, however, some radio practitioners noticed that radio's difference from the stage signposted a remarkable opportunity. In 1925 the great tragic actor Sybil Thorndike, writing in the *Radio Times* of her experience of reprising the role of Medea for radio broadcast, considered that: 'Surely it is not the least important aspect of the boon of wireless that it does not deny a people's imagination, but, instead, revivifies and, as I think, inspires it! [. . .] Each member of a wireless audience is required [. . .] to bring his own imagination into play, devising his own settings and conjuring up images of the situation based on his own emotional experience.'[80] A few years later, the theatre director and early radio producer Tyrone Guthrie (1900–71), considering that what he termed 'the microphone play' had possibilities which were 'inherent in neither the film nor the

---

[78] Anon. 1929c (original emphasis). [79] Ridley 1947, 14.
[80] Thorndike 1925, 50.

stage', elaborated on this train of thought. He believed that because the medium relies on only one sense,

> the mind of the listener is the more free to create its own illusion. Playwright, producer and actors combine to throw out a sequence of hints, of tiny clues, suggestions; and the mind of the listener collects, shapes and expands these into pictures. Admitted that this is difficult; it demands a great deal of creative energy and technical ingenuity of the artists, a great deal of imaginative concentration of the listener.

For Guthrie, the radio play is 'less substantial but more real than the cardboard grottoes, the calico rosebuds, the dusty grandeur of the stage; less substantial and vivid, because not apprehended visually, more real because the impression is partly created by the listener himself. From the author's clues the listener collects his materials, and embodies them in a picture of his own creation. It is therefore an expression of his own experience—whether physical or psychological—and therefore more real to him than the ready-made pictures of the stage designer.'[81] Guralnick has more recently restated this idea succinctly: the best radio drama can achieve 'a profound expressivity, not *despite* limitations in scale, but *because* of them'.[82] The absence of the visual and the physical dimension frees the creativity of both writer and production team, as well as the listener's imagination, in exciting ways.

When considered alongside other ways of realizing a story in the audience's imagination, radio dramatization seems to operate in a way that is closer to the novel than the more performative genres of stage, film, and television drama, all of which, considers Lewis, 'give us little or no choice about what we see and prevent our visual imaginations from functioning'.[83] As Denis Nowlan, then Network Manager of Radio 4, commented, 'it may be that the aural is a deeper, more primary way of engaging with reality than the visual'.[84] Both reading a novel and listening to a radio dramatization are intimate experiences which require a degree of attention in order for the imagination to be actively engaged. Lewis suggests that both activities stimulate the *visual* imagination, going so far as to claim that the act of listening to a radio play 'encourages the listener's imagination to visualise what he is listening to, to create for himself the visual dimension he is apparently deprived of, to construct the

---

[81] Guthrie 1931b, 8-9. [82] Guralnick 1996, p. x (original emphasis).
[83] Lewis 1981a, 9.   [84] Nowlan 2005.

settings and the appearances of the characters from the clues that words and sounds provide'.[85] This section follows Lewis in considering how other storytelling forms and media function in order better to explore what is distinctive about the imaginative access to Greek literary and performative texts enabled by radio. However, it will argue that the importance Lewis ascribes to the activity of the 'visual imagination' with regard to radio dramatization lacks subtlety and perhaps even obscures the nature of the peculiar intimacy between the listener and the radio dramatic character, which will be discussed shortly.

All representations of real or fictive experience make an appeal to the imagination, but the extent to which the visualizing imagination is active in response to a radio dramatization is, at least, debatable: certain aural stimuli may elicit a partial mental image, but sound drama is largely interpreted conceptually, without the creation of an inner, visual surrogate for the 'absent', outer object. Radio dramatization is certainly not *dependent* on the construction of coherently detailed mental images of the action (contrary to the belief of some early radio practitioners). As readily as the desolate island of Lemnos in a theatrical production of Sophocles' *Philoctetes* may be evoked by a single rock, so does the radio listener's imagination interpret the 'soundscape' of words, music, and other sounds conceptually rather than visually, constructing meaning in an impressionistic and cumulative way in response to the auditory signals. As Henry Reed wrote to George Barnes in 1947:

> It is a MYTH that Radio has any capacity for inducing in the mind of the listener anything in the nature of PARTICULARIZED VISUALIZATION. You might, once in an evening persuade him to see *one of* those great stage directions; but not, I think, more than one. For when radio has to suggest a *scene* to the listener, it does best to give only a brief powerful hint from which, with the help of specially written *dialogue designed to an end*, the listener can without effort and perhaps only half-consciously, construct a scene from [...] his own memory.[86]

In support of the notion of the listener interpreting the 'soundscape' in a conceptual and cumulatively impressionistic way we may draw on some key writings on the imagination. *The Oxford Companion to*

---

[85] Lewis 1981*a*, 9.
[86] Quoted in Drakakis 1981*b*, 22–3 (original emphasis).

Philosophy states that the aesthetic imagination is said to be engaged when the mind actively 'group[s] together what it literally perceives into a form with added significance'.[87] Drakakis usefully reminds us that 'in 1931 the psychologist T. H. Pear emphasised that hearing was a cognitive process—"Let us remember that we hear not with our ears but with our minds."'[88] The listener is, therefore, considered to be an active maker of meaning; or, in the words of the academic and radio playwright Frances Gray, 'the radio play [is] an act of co-operation between speaker and listener'.[89] Gray rightly places importance on the listener as an active maker of meaning, but the 'act of co-operation' that occurs is not quite as simple as that between the 'listener' and Gray's 'speaker'. Radio drama is composed of many more aural signifiers than simply the voice. As Fink notes, in a comment which harks back to the analogies between radio and, say, Homeric epic, 'radio, especially in its dramatic form, returns us to a preprint complexity of communication'.[90]

In some instances of radio drama, music is not merely incidental ('external to the internal dramatic action', for example, as a 'framing device', or 'creating a sense of mood') but an active contributor of meaning 'on a sub-textual level as a paralanguage in its own right', a description which certainly applies to Britten's musical contribution to *The Rescue*, discussed in Chapter 4.[91] If words, music, and indeed other sound signs can creatively work together in an orchestrated whole to form what we might call a sound drama, then it may be productive to think more carefully about what it is that the listener is in an act of cooperation with. Rattigan's concept of sound drama as 'aural performance literature' implies that the listener is required to 'read' the drama aurally, but he is sensitive to the fact that the human perception of a soundscape which is composed of verbal language supported by other 'paralanguages' such as music and sound signs is a complex phenomenon.[92] The reader of the text on the page creates meaning from words alone (sometimes supported by illustrations); whereas the listener to the sound drama may be

---

[87] Honderich 1995, *s.v.* 'aesthetic imagination'.   [88] Drakakis 1981*b*, 23.
[89] Gray 1981, 50.   [90] Fink 1981, 191.   [91] Rattigan 2002, 2–3.
[92] Ibid. 2. Cf. Lewis 1981*a*, 6: it is 'impossible for a producer to counterpoint what is seen with what is heard or to blend the visual with the aural in different ways, which a theatre director is doing all the time. Radio acting, unlike stage acting, is entirely vocal.'

listening to a complex orchestration of words, the sub-textual 'paralanguage' of music, and other sound signs.

The attempt on the part of the creative team to bring into imaginative existence the stories and histories of ancient Greece is met by the individual listener who does not listen to it or hear it so much as respond to or engage with it. As Tim Crook perceptively argues in his book on radio drama, the focus on the medium's perceived 'blindness' and surrogate visualization by 'the mind's eye' has distracted attention from the important fact that the listening experience is an emotional one, drawn from memory and mood.[93] The listener's imagination enters into dialogue with the sound drama, creating the meaning of it on her own terms. At this point it is useful to recall the classicist Egbert J. Bakker's 1993 study of discourse and performance in Homeric poetry in which he asserts the active participation of the listener in the poetic performance: 'the interlocutor is not the passive receiver of the linguistic, conversational "message" but actively contributes to it, by participating, not only in the context in which a discourse is uttered, but also in what it represents, or invokes'.[94] 'Listening in' to Homer on the radio could also, therefore, be described as a Bakhtinian participation, contribution, or dialogue. Nowlan goes on to consider that 'the fertile darkness of radio invites us into a more intimate and *active* encounter with the story. Radio is less of an external event and more of an inner, *interactive* experience.'[95] The 'inner' and 'intimate' qualities of this interactive experience will become important in the following discussion.

The workings of the imagination being shrouded in some unknowability, it is understandable that its function and effects should sometimes be described in easily recognizable, if rather indistinct and misleading, terms. This is, I would argue, why the language of visualization is often used by listeners themselves to describe their experience of engaging with effective radio broadcasts. The evocative and powerful combination of words and music in *The Rescue*, for example, left many feeling that the experience of listening had had a visual dimension. Stephen Potter (the member of BBC staff who made the first informal arrangement for Britten to conduct his score: see Chapter 6) wrote in his diary that 'all the time I was seeing. I saw Penelope watching from the pillar alone, saw Odysseus

---

[93] Crook 1999, 60-1. [94] Bakker 1993, 2-3.
[95] Nowlan 2005 (emphasis added).

as an old man being led forward, saw the profile of his shadow.'[96] In 1948, a critic considered that 'It paints a series of pictures [...] most skilfully'.[97] The 1962 production by Val Gielgud elicited similar responses:

> Some scenes, Telemachus' recognition of his father, were so vivid, it is hard to believe I hadn't seen them illustrated. (Profession not stated)
>
> The vivid imagery and strong characterization, the confident, unfaltering way the narrative was carried forward, closely following Homer, yet always giving a new dimension, and always in the background Britten's really superb music—all this set in motion in the inner eye a brilliantly coloured picture of Ithaca... and all the different actors in the drama, now afar off, now close up. (Commercial Artist)
>
> I was transported to Ithaca; I watched in the cavern and waited in the palace for the final victory. (War Pensioner)[98]

Here we return to *The Oxford Companion to Philosophy*'s description of what happens when the aesthetic imagination is engaged: the mind actively 'groups together what it literally perceives into a form with added significance'.[99] Human beings have been telling stories to each other for millennia and our minds are adept at comprehending words accompanied by whatever supporting signals the particular storytelling conventions include—whether gesticulation, facial expression, or music. The imagination has an innate visual memory or dimension which is spontaneously engaged in acts of imagining, and it seems that in popular, non-philosophical discourse we simply lack the facility or critical vocabulary to describe accurately and effectively the workings of the imagination. As Currie and Ravenscroft observe, 'visual imagery [by which is meant visual *imaginings*], for example, seems to be like visual experience in important ways; we naturally describe its content in terms appropriated from the description of things seen'.[100]

The classicist Emily Greenwood's important essay on Christopher Logue's poetic 'accounts' of Homer is thought-provoking in this regard. Building on earlier studies, she argues that Logue capitalizes on 'Homer's latent cinematography' by introducing further visual

---

[96] Reported in A. Porter 1995, who seems to suggest that Potter wrote this after hearing the first 1943 production.
[97] Anon. 1948.   [98] BBC WAC LR/62/413.
[99] Honderich 1995, *s.v.* 'aesthetic imagination'.
[100] Currie and Ravenscroft 2002, 11.

aspects into his poetry, both on the page (for example, in the typeface) and in the language (for example, references to photo-journalism). She considers that 'although the medium of film is completely alien to Homeric epic, film syntax proves extremely apt for clarifying aspects of the techniques and perspectives of narration in the *Iliad*, such as the gods' eye view, or the way in which the narrative pans from the view down on the plain to the gaze of a spectator on the wall of Troy, or vice versa'.[101] Such techniques and perspectives may, in retrospect, be termed 'cinematographic', but this runs the risk of downplaying the crucial point that they are, first and foremost, stock features of the epic storyteller's art. The 'scenes' described so vividly in the *Iliad* convince modern critics of Homer's 'latent cinematography', but it may be more interesting to think of how cinema has borrowed from, and developed in a true visual form, the ancient art of the epic storyteller, and how this functions in active collaboration with the listener's imagination. Greenwood is alert to the fact that Logue's first encounters with Homer were commissioned and broadcast on BBC Radio; the effect that his early engagement with this non-visual storytelling medium may have had on the 'visual' aspects of his poetic technique (poetry being, in essence, like radio, a medium lacking in visual images) awaits discussion.

Another intriguing line of thought is suggested by a comment that one member of the audience made in response to the 1962 production of *The Rescue*: for this listener it had been 'an object-lesson in *sound-picture making*'.[102] *The Rescue*, as other radio plays, does not strive towards 'sound-picture making' or, indeed, 'picture making', but it is clear from the reports of listener experience that the effect of the broadcast did in some way bring fragments of images to mind. Let us imagine how, if one person were to tell another about a male colleague who had proudly sported a particularly striking tie to work that day and how his colleagues responded to it, the actual words used would be a shorthand of that event, conveyed with the assistance of tone of voice, facial expression, gesticulation, etc. The listener brings to their engagement with the story factors such as prior knowledge of the man involved, his character and sartorial style, but he or she would have to imagine the look of the tie based on what detail was offered to convey what made it so striking. If a Messenger in a stage

---

[101] Greenwood 2007, 163.   [102] BBC WAC LR/62/413 (emphasis added).

production of Sophocles' *Oedipus Tyrannus* tells of how Jocasta—having recently discovered that Oedipus, her husband and the father of her children, is actually also her son—rushes into their bedroom tearing her hair, slams the door, and (as he later discovers) climbs atop the marital bed where she hangs herself from a noose, the audience member may bring to mind what that actor playing Jocasta looks like, but otherwise the details in Sophocles' *Oedipus Tyrannus* are quite scant. The Messenger does not describe the marital bed nor report in a detailed way how she arranged the noose sufficiently high above the bed, but the absence of these details does not hinder the hearer from filling in the gaps with their own remembered experience of what marital beds are generally like and (perhaps from film or television depictions) how nooses operate to bring about death, and then interpreting the information that has been given to allow the next stage of the drama to make sense.

Herein lies a small but usefully significant point. The modern theatre-goer probably does not know what *ancient* marital beds look like, nor what structural feature she may have hung the noose from. Whenever I imagine Jocasta rushing into her bedroom, on seeing and hearing the Messenger perform this speech on stage, I have vaguely (and anachronistically) in mind a high four-poster bed with white linen. This was undoubtedly not the same image of a bed that Sophocles had in mind, nor what the first ancient actor to play the Messenger in this play had in his mind, nor the subsequent Messengers to take this role over the centuries (ancient and modern). That is before we even begin to consider the doors and the beds that the members of the various ancient and modern audiences have subsequently had in mind on listening to this Messenger speech. The significance of this lies in the fact that when hearing—or, more usefully, engaging with—a story the listener brings to it actual knowledge (for example, the memory of what Jocasta looked like in earlier scenes of the play) and general knowledge, sourced from the listener's own experience. The absence of physical representation or visual illustration is, in other words, no barrier or hindrance to effective realization of a radio dramatized story in a listener's imagination. Furthermore, the mind actively supplies from its own store of memories from lived experience whatever has been covered by storytelling 'shorthand'. In the next section it is argued that it is in this way that ancient characters are constructed in the modern imagination, and that both the absence of the physical actor and some of the distinctive dramatic possibilities of the radio medium (such as the intimacy of interior monologue) can in some cases lead to a deep connection between modern listener and ancient character.

Ancient experience in the modern imagination

> at the sound
> Of which, an invisible audience listens,
> Not to the play, but to itself
>
> From Wallace Stevens, 'Of Modern Poetry'.[103]

As suggested above, the effect of radio dramatization on the imagination is more analogous to the experience of reading a novel than seeing a play staged: both listening and reading, for example, make an intimate appeal to the listener/reader via a complex of narration, description, dialogue, and interior monologue. Lewis considers that 'radio does seem to be the medium in which drama and fiction come closest to meeting, and the importance that the interior monologue assumes in both radio drama and modern fiction is indicative of this'.[104] But whereas the reader of the novel can 'pause' and 'play' the narrative at will, the listener (at least in the pre-digital age) must submit to the speed and onward motion of the performance (or switch off—the ultimate control). In its powerful engagement of the imagination, radio has also been likened to the practices of bedtime stories, oral literature, and dreaming.[105] In all these representations of real or fictive experience, characters are not bodily impersonated and the drama/action/narrative is not physically enacted. 'A' does not pretend to be 'B' before the audience 'C', as on the stage. In theatrical performance, the playing out and watching of the action is charged and heightened by the mutual knowledge and acceptance of the pretence that is taking place. In radio drama, 'A' does pretend to be (speaking in the voice of) 'B', in an audio-only performance which is later broadcast to the remote audience 'C'. Broadcasting technology does impose temporal and spatial distance between actors and audience, but the absence of the physicality of the actor in radio drama does seem to facilitate the potential for an intimate perspective on

---

[103] Stevens 2006, 209–10.   [104] Lewis 1981a, 8.
[105] For example, 'like a bedtime story, [the radio play] whispers in our ear' (Gray 1981, 51). Further useful studies in this direction include Esslin 1971, Drakakis 1981b, Rodger 1982, Shingler and Wieringa 1998, and Stanton 2004.

'Listening in' 111

the psychological unfurling of character and action—the human dimension of the drama. The relationship between the actor's voice and the listener's ear (or, rather, mind) is also subject to a spectrum of nuance resulting from the proximity of actor to the microphone, the use of 'acoustic baffles' (for example, screens and drapes) and either on-the-spot or later treatments of the sound to bring about effects such as echoes and distortion.[106]

The absence of the physicality of characters dramatized on radio (as, for example, in the performance of Homeric epic) dissolves the constructive layers of dramatic and narrative art. Here the scholar Mary Jacobus's careful meditation on what actually happens during the act of reading—in an exploration of how the reader is thrust into a mental state other than thinking, in which boundaries between self and other (character, story) dissolve to the extent that an act of dynamic union between the two takes place—is extremely useful also in the context of the listener's engagement with radio.[107] In the quotation which opens this section, Wallace Stevens likens the modern poet to an actor whose fully engaged audience identify with his words on a deeply personal level: 'an invisible audience listens intently, not only to the play, but also to itself as expressed in the play's events and gestures, which perforce bear the stamp of whoever envisions them. Thus do the audience and the playwright become one, united in their effort to realize a work that [exists] as a mutual "act of the mind".'[108] Reading an imaginative work and listening to imaginative radio both also seem to make possible a conflation of self and story, sometimes transforming the reader/listener into something like an 'extra' within the story. The children's author Michael Morpurgo captured this beautifully when discussing his childhood experience of reading Robert Louis Stevenson's *Treasure Island* (1883): 'I simply became the hero of the story. I *was* Jim Hawkins on the deck of the Hispaniola. I *did* hide in that barrel of apples. I *did* overhear that conspiracy. I was *there*. I was *right* in the middle of

---

[106] Stanton 2004, 96; see 97 on how proxemics at the microphone creates a dynamic between actors.

[107] Jacobus 1999, an intelligent discussion of 'the implicit assumptions about reading, whether considered as a process, a representation, or an ideology, that involve concepts or unconscious phantasies of inner and outer, absence and boundaries, and the transmission of thoughts and feelings between one self (or historical period) and another' (8–9).

[108] Guralnick 1996, 192.

it.'[109] In a seemingly identical way, some listeners to *The Rescue* reported feeling this sense of transportation *into* the story, *into* the position of a character: for example, 'I was transported to Ithaca; I watched in the cavern and waited in the palace for the final victory', said one War Pensioner.[110] Similarly, a listener identified only as being of 'Independent Means' considered that the poetic retellings from the *Odyssey* broadcast in 1960 (on which see Chapter 6) 'conjured up a room in an ancient Greek household, dark, gloomy, only lit by the fire where the women sat spinning and where the "bard" arrived and sang of heroes and glory. I was completely transplanted and loved it.'[111]

When interpreting narrative devices such as interior monologue, for example, listeners to radio dramatizations find themselves rather on the *inside* of a character's mind, exploring motivation and emotion from within: 'radio focuses very naturally on the interior workings of consciousness and can relay mental processes at length without any sense of strain [. . .] words seem to come straight from the mind, not the mouth'.[112] Or, as Gray describes this phenomenon: 'as soon as we hear a word in a radio play, we are close to the experience it signifies; in fact, the sound is literally inside us. To submit to this kind of invasion, to allow another's picture of the universe to enter and undermine our own, is to become vulnerable in a way we do not when we watch a film or a play, where the alien world is demonstrably outside.'[113] Making reference to Brecht's radio play *The Trial of Lucullus*, which charts the Roman general's descent into Hades and his trial there, Esslin perceptively notes that the radio play came into development at the significant literary moment when novelists were moving from 'the description of the surface of life into the inner landscape of the soul'.[114] Drakakis, too, points to contemporaneous experiments in literary form such as James Joyce's *Ulysses* (1922) and T. S. Eliot's *The Waste Land* (1922).[115] The facilitator in this blurring of boundaries between self and story/character is the imagination. As

---

[109] Michael Morpurgo and Anne Fine interviewed by Sarah Montague (Radio 4, *Today* programme, 27 April 2009, *c*.8.20 a.m.).
[110] BBC WAC LR/62/413.   [111] BBC WAC LR/60/2190.
[112] Lewis 1995, 897.   [113] Gray 1981, 51.
[114] Esslin 1971, 8. The radio play *Das Verhör des Lukullus* was commissioned shortly after the Nazi invasion of Poland; its broadcast by Swiss-German radio was coincident with the invasion of Norway and the Netherlands. It later became an opera to a score by Paul Dessau (see further Lucchesi 1993).
[115] Drakakis 1981*b*, 2.

Currie and Ravenscroft have stated, imagination enables us to occupy 'the perspective of another actual person. It might be the perspective I would have on things if I believed something I actually don't believe. [...] recreative minds recreate the mental states of others.'[116]

The radio producer John Tydeman has noted that after the first read-through of a script, 'a gift is made. The lines become the property of the actor; the character suggested through print becomes the living creation of a specific actor.'[117] This idea could be productively extended: when the dramatization is broadcast, it becomes 'the property' of the listener, and the character then becomes 'the living creation' of each listener. If, as is argued, the practical conditions of radio (such as the absence of the actor's physicality) and its artistic possibilities (such as the potential for intimacy between listener and character) bring the listener more readily in connection with the human dimension of the drama, then the suggested consequences are remarkable with regard to radio dramatizations of the stories and histories of ancient Greece. In the absence of potentially distancing effects of stage set and costume, the character is experienced as a voice, delivered in an informative and suggestive complex of other noises, including music and 'sound signs'. Thus radio has the potential to bring the modern listener in close psychological engagement with the characters and the stories first told and performed in antiquity. In fact, as Ralph Stranger suggests with the title of his 1928 book *Wireless: The Modern Magic Carpet*, the medium enables the listener to traverse landscapes of knowledge and take virtual journeys (as we would say today) all over the world and across time periods.[118] The ease with which radio effects such imaginative transports into another/another's world and the psychological intimacy achieved between listener and character sharpen the sense of the constancy of human nature across time, geography, and culture. As Hilda Matheson perceptively observed when radio was just a decade old:

> Something definitely happens by this act of translation. The concentration upon one sense, the inevitable sharpening of the ear to catch fine shades of voice and meaning, the impression that the speakers are close beside one, may all help to emphasize the human element, to bring one more intimately into touch with the thoughts and emotions which the players are interpreting.[119]

---

[116] Currie and Ravenscroft 2002, 1.   [117] Tydeman 1981, 19.
[118] Stranger 1928, a book on the technical side of the broadcasting process.
[119] Matheson 1933, 112.

Part Two

4

Gilbert Murray: 'Radio Hellenist', 1925–1956

4.1. MURRAY'S POPULAR VERSE TRANSLATIONS OF GREEK PLAYS IN PERFORMANCE

The very first drama on BBC Radio was a broadcast of extracts from the Shakespearean canon in February 1923 and further extracts and more substantial versions of individual Shakespeare plays followed in 1923 and 1924.[1] At first, and for a few years, such dramatic programmes featured performance conventions imported from the stage: costumed actors projected their voices as if in a large theatre and music was played before the performance began and between acts.[2] Furthermore, listeners were in these early years encouraged to practise 'good listening', behaviour modelled on that of a theatre audience for serious drama, which involved sitting in a darkened room and concentrating carefully.[3]

Shakespeare, unsurprisingly, was considered to be 'the indispensable ballast of respectable output', but Greek tragedy lay not far behind because of both its canonicity and its perceived 'poetic value' and 'lack

---

[1] On these early Shakespeare broadcasts see Briggs 1961, 280–1, Drakakis 1981*a*, 115, and Gielgud 1957, 17 ff.; valuable recent studies include Greenhalgh 2009 and Oesterlen 2009. Drakakis 1981*b*, 2 notes that 'the terms in which the debate about Shakespearean performance was conducted during the 1920s bear a striking resemblance to those in which the early broadcasters themselves defended the new medium. Issues such as the question of the intimacy of the relationship between actor and audience [...] the primacy of poetry and the rhythms of performance generated by the variety of the spoken dialogue, all appeared as part of the early justification for radio drama itself.'

[2] Drakakis 1981*b*, 4 and Gielgud 1957, 20.

[3] On 'good' vs. 'bad' listening practice see Gielgud 1934 and Section 3.2.

of action'.[4] Given radio's early reliance on the stage for both content and performance conventions, it is not surprising that the very first radio productions of Greek drama for which there is some evidence have strong links with the stage: for example, a 1924 radio production of Sophocles' *Antigone*, broadcast from Glasgow, appears to be a version of A. Parry Gunn's 1922 production of the play in the city's Hengler's Circus for the University of Glasgow. For BBC Belfast in May 1925, the young Tyrone Guthrie produced Gilbert Murray's translation of Euripides' *Iphigenia in Tauris*, a text which had enjoyed immediate and continued popularity on the stage since its publication in 1910 and which Guthrie went on to produce, again with Flora Robson (1902–84) in the title role, for the Cambridge Festival Theatre of Amner Hall.[5]

A month after the Belfast production, a condensed version of Murray's translation of Euripides' *Medea*, with stage luminaries Sybil Thorndike as Medea and Lewis Casson as Creon, was broadcast (perhaps surprisingly) on a Sunday at tea-time, just weeks after the husband-and-wife team had given a special performance of the play at Christ Church, Oxford which Murray himself had arranged in aid of the League of Nations Union and just a few days before they would perform the play to inaugurate the new open-air theatre at the County High School for Girls, Walthamstow.[6] The radio production of *Medea* was considered to have been rather poor by the critic in *The Times*, who advised that 'the voice that is suitable to the theatre is not always also the one that lends itself with success to transmission by wireless' but begged forbearance on the part of the listener 'in these days of experimentation'.[7]

These were indeed days of experimentation. Radio was working out its relationship with the theatre through its presentation of plays

---

[4] Gielgud 1957, 19; British Broadcasting Corporation 1930, 73; Turton 1937.

[5] BBC Belfast opened in 1924 (Briggs 1961, 218). The radio production is discussed briefly in Dunbar 1960, 67–8. The APGRD Database attests that Murray's translation of the play appealed particularly to amateur and touring companies in the fifteen years before the radio production; interestingly, just two months afterwards, Lennox Robinson (1886–1958) produced Murray's translation for the Dublin Drama League (Hogan and Burnham 1992, 380).

[6] See Wrigley 2011b, 104–5 on the Oxford production, Anon. 1925b and 1925c for Walthamstow, and Macintosh 2000, 19 for Thorndike's earlier mastery of the role on the professional stage. Casson produced several plays for radio in 1924; both he and Thorndike regularly appeared on air (Briggs 1961, 281).

[7] Anon. 1925a. Thorndike 1925 offers some thoughts on doing *Medea* for radio.

written for the stage (as well as, of course, trying its hand at plays written especially for the medium, the first of which, Richard Hughes's *A Comedy of Danger*, was broadcast in 1924). The *Radio Times* offered photographic images of the lead actors of some of its early Greek dramas in a regular page-length feature titled 'People You Will Hear This Week', including a portrait shot of Thorndike with two of her children (all four of whom had at some point appeared with her in stage productions of *Medea*) and another of Edmund Willard, who played Hector in the ninety-minute production of Murray's translation of Euripides' *Rhesus* in 1926.[8] This portrayal of the actors (out of costume in the case of the Greek dramas) seems to underline the theatrical provenance of the plays and also many of the performances; the practice would soon, however, be replaced by illustrations of listings and articles with imaginatively evocative drawings, perhaps as confidence grew in radio's potential as a bona fide medium for the presentation of plays originally written for the stage.

This was the case with a production of Murray's translation of Euripides' *Electra* which was produced in 1929 as number eleven in a series of twelve *Great Plays* (a predecessor of *World Theatre*). The *Radio Times* listing was accompanied by a magnificent art deco influenced illustration by the book illustrator John Austen (1886–1948), in which the stylized central figure appears with columns either side, while the fluid folds of the clothing and the Greek vase bottom right (showing a battle scene of Orestes' revenge) break up the symmetry. The production also benefited from a long article published in the same issue by W. A. Darlington, dramatic critic of *The Daily Telegraph*, which was itself illustrated by a bust of Euripides and a photograph of the ancient theatre of Epidaurus. Darlington introduces the production by covering the nature of Greek tragedy and its stage conventions and discussing other playwrights' treatments of the Electra myth and the modernity of Euripides' version.[9] He states that 'speech was everything and action comparatively unimportant', thus claiming that, whereas Greek tragedy on the modern stage is hampered, 'many of the difficulties disappear when broadcasting' and a 'Lack of swift action, and a dependence on language only [. . .] are

---

[8] *Radio Times*, 26 June 1925, 5 and 17 September 1926, 525. See Gielgud 1957, 39–41 for the contemporary importance of such acknowledgements to both audience and acting profession.
[9] Darlington 1929.

actually advantages to the listener'. However, he also seems to anticipate some negative critical attention in his warning that the delivery of Murray's poetic translation may come across as 'not merely unrealistic but stilted'. As already noted, the BBC considered this production of *Electra* one of 'the most satisfactory' in the series because of its 'poetic value and classic purity of outline',[10] but the Cambridge classicist J. T. Sheppard (1881–1968), who had himself directed a number of Greek plays for the University, in his review of the production for *The Listener* thought that the actors 'were always reverently aiming at the thing I call "the Greek Play voice and manner"' which he defines as '*stilted*, over-emphatic, declamatory convention'. He does, however, think that improvements can be made: 'The whole performance [...] was hardly a success, but it gave promise of success, and the experiment is worth repeating'.[11]

An article in *The Listener* in the following months was rather downbeat about the achievements of the *Twelve Great Plays* series: 'it has, on the whole, fallen short of what must be considered most desirable. [...] several proved, frankly, unsuitable for broadcasting purposes. [...] On the other hand, in the case of such plays as the *Electra* [...] the experiment was mainly justified in its results.' The anonymous writer concludes: 'while in the future radio drama must by no means neglect the debts it owes to literature, and the sterner, more ascetic virtues of classical plays, the greater part of its efforts are bound to be directed rather to the future than to the past—rather to the play written for the microphone than to the play written for the Elizabethans—to Mr Tyrone Guthrie rather than to Euripides'.[12] This critical opinion underlines the emergence of what would be a long-standing tension lying at the very heart of the concept of radio drama—a tension which, of course, illuminates different conceptions of the purposes and potential of cultural broadcasting—between the broadcasting of stage-plays and the development of a dramatic form specifically for radio, an endeavour which was being given a boost by work such as Guthrie's exciting radio plays *Squirrel's Cage* (1929) and *The Flowers Are Not For You To Pick* (1930).

---

[10] British Broadcasting Corporation 1930, 73.
[11] Sheppard 1929, 126; emphasis added. *The Listener* reproduced part of this review in its '50 Years Ago' column on 26 July 1979, 113.
[12] Anon. 1929d.

The day after the 1926 production of *Rhesus* was broadcast, Murray sent in to the BBC 'the sort of note I would make after a rehearsal, with a view to possibly improving the production next time'.[13] And Murray here was talking from experience, for over the last two decades he had spent much time and energy advising on both professional and amateur stage productions of his rhyming verse translations: indeed, later, when it was his habit to attend rehearsals in the studio, he admitted that he got great pleasure from it since it reminded him of 'the old pre-war days with Granville-Barker, at the Court'.[14] These close translations of Greek drama were first composed for the practical purpose of illustrating his lectures at the University of Glasgow (where he had held the Chair of Greek since 1889). His first published volume—comprising Euripides' *Bacchae* and *Hippolytus*, and Aristophanes' *Frogs*—appeared in 1902, three years before he became a Fellow of New College, Oxford.[15] Around this time he also read extracts before a variety of audiences in cities across the country and, by the time he became Regius Professor of Greek at Oxford in 1908, his translations of these and other Greek plays were well on their way to becoming outstandingly popular as both reading and acting editions.[16] The first quarter of the twentieth century saw at least sixty productions of Murray's translations on the British stage, with at least the same

---

[13] Amongst other things he wrote about the difficulty he (the translator!) had experienced in distinguishing the characters from one another, a complaint he repeatedly made in response to later productions which underlines an obvious potential problem in producing stage plays on air (letter from GM to J. C. Stobart, 23 September 1926, GM/T1).

[14] Letter from GM to BB, 20 April 1939 (GM/S). On his collaboration with Harley Granville-Barker (1877–1946) at the Court Theatre, London see Hall and Macintosh 2005, ch. 17.

[15] Several of the Euripidean translations have recently been reprinted: Murray 2005. Murray's first attempt to translate Greek tragic material to the modern stage was his version of the Andromache story, which, drawing mainly on Euripides, was published in 1900 as a play in three acts. Its performance by the Stage Society in London in February 1901 is reported to have been unsuccessful but the play itself drew interested attention from, among others, A. E. Housman, George Bernard Shaw, and Leo Tolstoy (D. Wilson 1987, 84–7).

[16] For example, at the Haslemere Microscope and Natural History Society (1900), the Fabian Society (extracts from several plays, 1901), Newnham College, Cambridge (*Hippolytus*, 1901), and the Socratic Society of Birmingham (*Trojan Women*, 1904). Hall and Macintosh 2005, 494 and Morwood 2007, 133–4 note the impact that the readings had on George Bernard Shaw and Bertrand Russell; see also D. Wilson 1987, 94 and 97. Morwood is also worth reading for his estimation of the virtues of Murray's translations and on T. S. Eliot's damning critique ('he leaves Euripides quite dead': Eliot 1920, 64).

number staged in the rest of the century.[17] Amateur groups, especially those led by and composed of women, seem to have been particularly attracted to performing them. In Oxford, for example, he gave permission for and assisted at rehearsals for many local amateur productions: the Oxford Students' Dramatic Reading Society read *Medea* in 1908;[18] the girls of Oxford High School staged *Iphigenia in Tauris* in 1910 (the year of its publication);[19] the Dramatic Society of the Society for Oxford Home-Students (which made provision for young women to live in private lodgings across the city whilst studying at the University) read *Hippolytus*, also in 1910;[20] second-year undergraduates of the all-women Somerville College staged *Frogs* the following year; and past and present students of the Society for Oxford Home-Students performed *Trojan Women* in the New Masonic Hall in 1912.[21]

In this last production the role of Andromache was played by Hilda Matheson, then a student of the Society reading History: her final words to her infant son before he was taken away by the Greeks to be killed are reported to have 'reduced the house to tears'.[22] Sixteen years later it was Matheson who, as BBC Head of Talks, worked with Murray on one of the first broadcasts of his translations on radio. This half-hour programme on Euripides' *Alcestis* in 1928 was not, as *Medea* and *Rhesus* had been, a full-length production but, rather, 'two or three bits of chorus + enough dialogue to make—with occasional comments—a connected story'.[23] Murray, rather than Euripides, was

[17] These figures, based on my own (as yet largely unpublished) research, should be thought of as a conservative estimate: his translations were particularly favoured by the smaller repertory companies, colleges, and schools whose production histories still require a considerable amount of archival investigation. On especially the professional London productions see Hall and Macintosh 2005, ch. 17 and on some of the amateur productions in Oxford and touring repertory productions see Wrigley 2011b, ch. 4.

[18] *The Fritillary*, March 1909, 791.

[19] Reviewed by Birch 1910. Murray's son Basil had been in the (mixed) kindergarten of the school in 1908/09.

[20] *The Fritillary*, December 1910, 901. In 1942 it became the St Anne's Society which in 1952 was founded as St Anne's College.

[21] The Society permitted a mixed-sex cast in this production (for example, the young lecturer Julian Huxley played Menelaus) at a time when most other student dramatic activities were segregated.

[22] Carney 1999, 8.

[23] Letter from GM to Hilda Matheson, 10 November 1928 (GM/T1). The idea for a partial reading of one of his Euripides translations was Matheson's (see her letter to Murray, 3 August 1928, GM/T1). On her careers in radio and in intelligence see

the star of this programme and, accordingly, the *Radio Times* illustrated the programme listing with a photographic portrait of the translator himself, alongside two other 'distinguished public men' who contributed to that December evening's entertainment.[24]

It was doubtless the rapid and sustained popularity of his texts on amateur and professional stages, and also—a closely related point—in print, in the two decades before the birth of radio that made Murray a natural choice in the early days of broadcasting when producers looked primarily to the stage and the literary canon for dramatic material. In the case of Murray, what is particularly interesting—and, perhaps, testimony both to the BBC's project to broadcast what was perceived to be the nation's cultural wealth and to the enduring popularity of Murray's translations amongst the domestic audience— is the fact that these works continued to be a popular choice for production on radio long after they fell out of favour on the professional stage. Also, the important element of symbiosis, or creative interaction, between radio, print, and live performance is here discernible (and it will arise again in later chapters). One only has to read how many listeners writing in to the BBC responded in a positive way to radio productions of his translations to understand how these broadcast performances served, in real terms, to increase his reading public and encourage further performances on, especially, school, college, and other amateur stages.

There appears to be quite a gap between Euripides' *Electra* in 1929 and the next known production of a Murray translation—Euripides' *Hippolytus* in 1936. It is, of course, possible that productions were broadcast during this seven-year period but that they have left little or no trace in the archives. Certainly there was interest in Greek plays and classical literature more broadly in this period. In 1932, for example, BBC Belfast broadcast a version of the Abbey Players' production of Sophocles' *Oedipus Tyrannus*, as *King Oedipus* in W. B. Yeats's translation (which had premièred in Dublin in 1926, and where it had subsequently been regularly revived). There was also the monumental *Readings from Classical Literature* series which, beginning in January 1933 and continuing well into 1934, started with Homer and moved through the Greek playwrights, historians,

---

Carney 1999 and Hunter 1994 and 2004; her 1933 book *Broadcasting* has an interesting chapter on 'Literature and Drama'.

[24] *Radio Times*, 30 November 1928, 609.

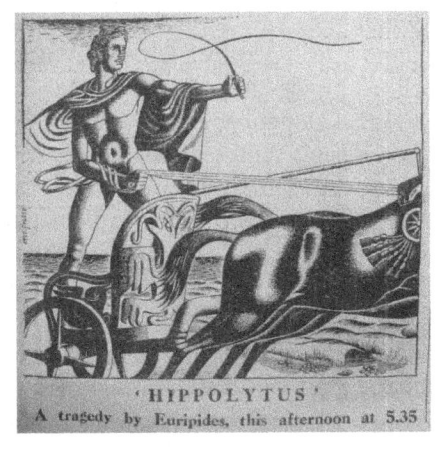

Fig. 4.1. Eric Fraser's drawing for the 1936 *Hippolytus* (*Radio Times*, 16 October 1936, 21). Reproduced by kind permission of the Fraser family.

and philosophers, before exploring Roman literature in a regular series of thirty-minute programmes on Sunday afternoons.

In 1929 the BBC had ensured that the potential audience for *Electra* had some introduction and background to the play by commissioning Darlington's illustrated article for the *Radio Times*. In October 1936, the BBC went further, broadcasting a substantial introductory programme a day or two before each big Sunday drama, the purpose of which was 'to give the listener an introduction to the play, to show him its contents and appeal, and give some idea of the history of the play'.[25] The programme introducing a production of Murray's translation of Euripides' *Hippolytus*, then, part of which had been written and delivered by Murray himself, covered ancient Greek theatrical conventions, with comments on the play in its ancient context, then moving on to Seneca, Thomas Newton (1581), Racine (1677), and finally Murray's own translation. Further elucidation was offered in Murray's accompanying essay in *The Listener*, titled 'A Love-Tragedy from Ancient Greece', which explains aspects of the play which he considers may 'puzzle a modern audience', such as the Chorus and the goddesses Aphrodite and Artemis. As already noted in Section 2.1, he concludes by encouraging listeners to 'be patient,

---

[25] Memo from FF to Mr Dowler, 1 October 1936 (GM/S). At least part of the script of this introductory programme survives in GM/S.

and give it a chance; do not reject things because they do not fit the fashion to which you are accustomed. Don't be frightened of long speeches—listen to them. Have faith that a work of art which still delights people 2,000 years after it first appeared must have something rather wonderful about it.'

In this essay Murray confessed that he had 'never yet found a satisfactory way of presenting the Chorus on the modern stage', but he believed that on radio difficult questions 'of dance and movement', for example, would 'disappear'.[26] The question of the representation of the Chorus was tackled by the reviewer in *The Manchester Guardian* who considered that 'the training and direction of Miss Fogerty and Miss Thurburn resulted in some fine cadences of sound'.[27] The production of *Hippolytus* was largely in the hands of women. As the reviewer observes, the Chorus was 'directed by' Elsie Fogerty (1865–1945), the major figure in theatrical training who had founded the Central School of Speech and Drama in 1906, and it was trained by Gwynneth Thurburn (1899–1993), first a student, teacher, and then principal at Central; the producer was Barbara Burnham, a cousin of Peggy Ashcroft, who was one of the team of producers working at this time under Val Gielgud on adapting plays and novels for radio.[28] In this period, producers were typically male, but Burnham and Hilda Matheson were significant exceptions, as was Mary Hope Allen, working in the late 1940s. With regard to Greek tragedy, the role of 'directing' or 'training the choruses' was almost always taken by a woman (for example, Fogerty, Thurburn, and, later, Colette King, on whom see Chapter 7). Women (for example, Cynthia Pughe, Dulcima Glasby, and Helena Wood) are also frequently credited with 'arranging' or 'adapting' the text for broadcasting.[29] The significant role that

---

[26] Murray 1936. As it turned out, Murray 'was frankly disappointed in the Chorus. It gabbled. I am going to write to Miss Fogerty about it. I want a quite different quality of voice in the lyrics from the dialogue' (letter from GM to FF, 19 October 1936, in GM/S; this letter contains many more suggestions for improvement which both Felton and Burnham addressed in letters to Murray, also in GM/S).

[27] Anon. 1936.

[28] Burnham had been adapting plays for the BBC since 1929; she began work as a producer in 1933 and by the 1960s was adapting plays for television (Anon. 1937*b*; Gordon 1940).

[29] What may appear to modern eyes to be the relegation of women to subsidiary roles in the production process perhaps plays down the important fact that in these early decades at the BBC women *were* permitted to climb to important positions perhaps not as easily attainable in other professional spheres. Briggs 1961, 254 points

women took in the radio productions of Murray's translations strongly echoes the popularity of his translations on the stage with amateur groups in women's schools and colleges and with the professional and semi-professional theatre groups led by women which included his translations of Greek tragedies prominently in their repertoire—for example, Penelope Wheeler's Greek Play Company, which energetically took his translations on tour to towns and cities across the country in the 1910s and 1920s.[30]

It is perhaps testament to Burnham's success with *Hippolytus* that she produced the majority of Murray's Greek plays thereafter, including *Trojan Women* (1937), *Persians* (1939), *Alcestis* (1940), *Seven against Thebes* (1940), *Medea* (1942), and the radio première of *The Rape of the Locks* (1942), his unpublished translation and reconstruction of Menander's *Perikeiromene*. In fact, the same Burnham–Fogerty–Thurburn team swung into action again just a few months later on the April 1937 production of Murray's translation of Euripides' *Trojan Women*, which also featured the two lead actors from the 1936 *Hippolytus*: Lilian Harrison and Hubert Gregg (Phaedra and Hippolytus) played Athena and Talthybius. Joining them were Belle Chrystall (Helen), Lillah McCarthy (Hecuba), Flora Robson (Cassandra), and Edith Sharpe (Andromache). The play was produced 'on the same lines' as *Hippolytus*, with only 'drums and musical trumpets' providing 'effects'.[31] Once again, the accompanying *Radio Times* article noted that some Greek theatrical conventions—namely the Messenger Speech, the formal diction (from very long speeches to stichomythia) and the choruses—may appear 'exotic'. The author wonders whether ancient plays might, however, be *best* done on radio: 'their lack of action is then an advantage, and the power of the words is left to recreate the original atmosphere without the intrusion of a modern stage-setting'. After a brief sketch of the three surviving Greek tragedians and an outline of the historical background to *Trojan Women*—the Athenian seizure of Melos in 416 BC, when all adult males were killed and women and children enslaved, which has often, controversially, been taken as a clue to the play's interpretation—the author touches on the topicality of this

---

to the 'willingness of the BBC to take women on to its staff on terms of complete equality'.

[30] On Wheeler see Wrigley 2011*b*, 93–100.
[31] Letter from BB to GM, 22 April 1937 (GM/S).

story: it is, he believes, 'too harrowing, and too modern in that the plight of the Trojan women resembles so closely that of many victims of the brutality of war today'.[32] It is noteworthy that the illustrator Victor Reinganum's (1907-95) striking image of a woman attempting to rush back into burning Troy but being seized by Greek soldiers was later re-used to illustrate the listing for the 1946 radio production of *Trojan Women* (discussed later in this section) and also in 1958 for the listing of a BBC Television production of the play (which happened to be the very first Greek tragedy to be transmitted on British television).[33]

This seems to be the first Greek play for which something in the nature of a Listener Research Report survives.[34] From this we learn that one quarter of the listening panel were sufficiently interested to tune in; just over half of respondents enjoyed it (reasons given include 'restrained', 'dignified', 'parts well spoken', 'acting exceptionally good', and 'initial interest in Greek drama') and just under half (consisting 'almost entirely of listeners to whom Greek tragedy makes little or no appeal') found it 'too heavy, dreary, gloomy, morbid or montonous', with the production too long and the pace too slow. A number of this latter group had difficulty distinguishing between characters and some thought the story difficult to follow. Half of respondents were critical of the chorus, 'the most frequent criticism being that the chorus was too reminiscent of a school recitation'. This brief selection of quotations offered by the report suggests a production which sought to capitalize on the poetry of Murray's verse translation, without employing music or 'sound signs' to make it work more effectively as radio drama. The following two comments suggest that, had efforts been made to adapt the text for broadcasting and to offer the listener more in the way of background to the play, a greater proportion of the audience might have got more enjoyment out of it:

> Length and pace must depend largely upon the original: can Greek tragedy be presented in such a way that the average listener, not

---

[32] Turton 1937.
[33] This seems to be a relatively rare recycling of artwork in the magazine. On the 1958 *Television World Theatre* production by Caspar Wrede and Michael Elliott, see Wrigley 2016a.
[34] 'Drama Reports Scheme: General Summary', 25 June 1937, pages entitled 'Memo', 263-4 (typescript in BBC WAC).

previously interested, will not find it rather long and slow? The construction of the plot seems to favour broadcasting, but it definitely needs help from the listener.

I found little pleasure in listening to *The Trojan Women*. I do not deny the literary or dramatic merits of the play. I pay tribute too, to the admirable cast and the manner in which they spoke their parts, but the action being so remote in time and space, and the historical background a little vague, I found myself unable to appreciate the broadcast.

The report concludes that '*Trojan Women* is clearly a broadcast for which a mass audience is not to be expected', but this did not deter Burnham from producing several more of Murray's translations in quick succession, although first, in November 1937, she turned to a new translation—not yet performed on stage—of Euripides' *Alcestis* by the Americans Dudley Fitts and Robert Fitzgerald. In response, the critic (and later innovative television producer) Grace Wyndham Goldie wondered why people were still concerned with Greek drama ('We swallow what is dead partly for the sake of enjoying what is still alive but partly, too, because it is interesting to hear a play by Euripides at all, and partly because there is a curious pleasure in seeing how the same emotions persist after two thousand years') and how this colloquial translation (so very different in style from Murray, of course) may have aided the audience in both its comprehension and enjoyment: 'Professors of classics can decide whether the colloquialisms [. . .] represent the satiric element in the play better or worse than the flowing verse of Professor Murray. To the ordinary listener there was a loss of dignity and a gain in life.'[35]

On 16 April 1939, in the period when Britain and France were negotiating with the Soviet Union over a potential political and military alliance designed to halt Hitler's aggression across Europe, Burnham produced Murray's as yet unpublished translation of Aeschylus' *Persians* in a prime-time Sunday evening slot. In this first production in a series of *Great Plays*, Sybil Thorndike took the role of Queen Atossa, Cecil Trouncer the ghost of Darius, and Ivan Brandt Xerxes. Murray provided a brief spoken introduction and Elsie Fogerty once again directed the choruses. The topicality of this Aeschylean tragedy of 472 BC, in which the Greek destruction of the Persian fleet at Salamis is narrated and the overall defeat of the

[35] Wyndham Goldie 1937.

Fig. 4.2. Eric Fraser's drawing for the 1940 *Seven against Thebes* (*Radio Times*, 23 August 1940, 11). Reproduced by kind permission of the Fraser family.

Persians at Plataea foretold, did not go unnoticed amongst critics or listeners: 'the one point which must have struck all', commented the reviewer in *The Listener*, 'was that, intentionally or not, the play was vividly topical. It was about an autocrat who, wishing to make himself master of the world, attacked a free and democratic people and then wished he hadn't done it.'[36] Furthermore, the immediacy of the radio production inspired the Buskins of Worcester College, Oxford to give the stage première of Murray's translation in June that year: Murray gladly advised on the production and permitted the group to rehearse from the galley proofs.[37]

Burnham turned again to Aeschylus for what appears to be the first wartime Greek drama on the new Home Service in August 1940, during the Battle of Britain (see Figure 4.2). The *Radio Times* on its cover announced the production of *Seven against Thebes* (which again featured a short introductory article by Murray) as 'a Greek tragedy with topical significance'.[38] Writing within the magazine, 'W. T. R.' noted in an accompanying article that, although 'It is a far cry from Britain in 1940 to ancient Greece', the play 'has particular point at the present time'. The writer continues: 'We have more in common with [ancient Greeks] than we have with many peoples less far

---

[36] Purbeck 1939.
[37] Letter from GM to BB, 5 May 1939 (GM/S). On this production see Wrigley 2011*b*, 112–13. In a letter to Burnham, Murray reports that he had received a number of letters which indicate that the production was 'greatly appreciated' (dated 20 April 1939, in GM/S).
[38] *Radio Times*, 23 August 1940, cover. In *Aeschylus: The Creator of Tragedy* Murray describes these as Aeschylean 'war plays' (Murray 1940, 111).

removed from us in time; certainly more than we have with the Nazis of our own day. [...] Their ideals of freedom lie at the root of the whole tradition of European civilization, which we are now fighting to defend.' More pertinently, notes the writer, the play is particularly topical because it tells the story of a siege: 'you will find much in it that is of more interest to us now than it would have been a year ago, before we too were fighting to defend our homes'.[39]

As noted above, in 1942 thirty minutes of scenes from Euripides' *Medea*, starring Thorndike and Casson from the Old Vic Company, were broadcast in the series *From the Theatre in Wartime*. This programme attracted what may appear to be a massive 10.6 per cent of the adult population, although the Listener Research Report states that this was 'not a very large audience for a play at a peak hour' (9.30 p.m.), the average audience for the previous five programmes in the series being 13.3 per cent. More than 60 per cent of the listening sample of 189 people were said to be unfamiliar with the play, 30 per cent quite familiar, and less than 10 per cent very familiar. Seventy per cent of the sample considered that it was a good choice for the series; those who disagreed considered it to be 'too highbrow', lacking in 'popular appeal', 'sordid', 'morbid', 'schoolish', and needing to be 'seen as well as heard to be appreciated'. Most of the criticism of the acting was directed at Thorndike's portrayal of Medea: 'her words were frequently indistinguishable'; 'she gained pace at the expense of clarity of diction'; 'over-dramatic'; 'the contrast between her lowered voice and the loud was really too much to enjoy in an ordinary room'; and there were also a number of complaints about 'ranting and wailing'. These comments echo earlier criticisms of her radio performance in Greek plays by both ordinary listeners and professional critics. A quarter of the sample liked the play very much, a third quite liked it, and another third disliked it. A Library Assistant considered that 'The murders were so extravagant and so far removed from anything that could happen nowadays that instead of being harrowed I thought the whole story rather ridiculous'. Several informed listeners considered that the choice of scenes did not do the play justice. One wrote:

> I don't think the selection of scenes really did Euripides justice. Inclusion of Medea's soliloquy before the murder of the children would have

[39] 'W. T. R.' 1940.

given us more of the value of the play as a psychological study. As it stood, it seemed little more than a picture of injured selfish pride verging on sadism. Euripides did better than that.[40]

The autumn following the end of the Second World War saw the inauguration of a new, once-monthly *World Theatre* series which was broadcast on Monday evenings on the Home Service. The aim of the series was to 'give listeners an opportunity to hear [...] a play which for one reason or another has become part of the dramatic heritage of the civilised world'.[41] It is interesting to note that the very first production in the series—which itself was a direct response of the Drama Department to the wartime expansion of the audience for radio plays— was of a Greek play, especially given the near coincidence of this inaugural *World Theatre* production of Euripides' *Hippolytus* (in Murray's translation, of course) on 1 October 1945 with the launch of the 'highbrow' Third Programme, on which much of the Greek output would subsequently be broadcast, just two days earlier.[42] This shift of most of the ancient Greek programming to the more erudite Third is, perhaps, symbolized by the fact that a recorded repeat of the Home Service *Hippolytus* was actually broadcast as the first Greek tragedy on the Third Programme a year later on 13 October 1946,[43] although the *World Theatre* series must be credited for bringing several more Greek dramas (most, it should be noted, in Murray's translations) to the attention of the Home Service audience: such productions include Euripides' *Trojan Women* (1946), Aristophanes' *Frogs* and Sophocles' *Antigone* (both 1947), Euripides' *Electra* (1948 and 1953), *Medea* (1949), *Alcestis* (1950), *Frogs* (1951), and *Agamemnon* (1953).

Val Gielgud himself produced the 1945 *Hippolytus*, and the incidental music—which included overtures from Gluck's *Alceste* and *Iphigenia in Aulis* and part of Mozart's *Adagio and Fugue in C Minor*—was selected by Edward Sackville-West (who had, with

---

[40] BBC WAC LR/858.
[41] Quoted in Anon. 1946c, an article which discusses the prevalence of Greek plays in this series.
[42] Other early productions included Chekhov's *The Seagull* and Ibsen's *Hedda Gabler*.
[43] Gielgud reports that following the Home production 'many listeners have asked us when they were to have another opportunity of hearing this production' (letter from VG to GM, 6 September 1946, in GM/S). See Chapter 7 for discussion of the first *new* production of a Greek drama on the Third, MacNeice's translation of *Agamemnon*.

Britten, created *The Rescue*, a version of the *Odyssey*, two years earlier: see Section 6.1). The response to the Home Service production was summarized in the Listener Research Report as follows: 'Considering the play's remoteness from the experience, not to say understanding, of the majority of listeners, this result [an Appreciation Index of 73] is not discouraging. It was clear from comments that those who had previously seen or read the play, or had, at least, some familiarity with the classical tradition, got a great deal more out of the broadcast than the others.' Many found 'dignity' and 'majesty' in the story and the listening experience 'exalting and unique'. For most this was generated by 'the beauty of the verse and the way in which it was spoken':

> To think I have lived and listened for 29 years without ever hearing any of Murray's Euripides before! When are we going to get the others? (Housewife)
>
> I listened to this play mostly out of curiosity because on the few previous occasions when I have heard Greek dramas I have found it very dull and heavy. Also I do not like poetry as a rule, but this was so beautiful that, as I listened, it seemed to flow over me like grand music. While there was nothing in it to shock a modern audience, yet one could feel all through the depth of passion and suffering. But for the goddesses it might have been written yesterday. (Comptometer Operator)[44]

MacNeice's introductory article in the *Radio Times* is an interesting and succinct study which refers to Freud, Shakespeare, and the Old Testament in its discussion of the play as a 'Sex Triangle' governed more by cosmic than social morality and a 'dialectical' drama with Euripides' sympathies balanced between Phaedra and Hippolytus.[45] It seems, however, that MacNeice's opening statement that *Hippolytus*, 'unlike some ancient Greek plays, is immediately intelligible to a modern audience' did not hold for a significant number of the listening panel. In fact, his article assumes a working knowledge of the play and it was found by a significant proportion of the listeners to be almost useless as an introduction and, consequently, a recurrent criticism was that the action of the play had been too difficult to follow. 'There was insufficient preparation in relating the background of the story and the personal relationships of the people involved, and

---

[44] BBC WAC LR/3796. For Murray's generally favourable opinion of the production, and some criticisms, see his letter to VG, 14 October 1946 (GM/S).
[45] MacNeice 1945b.

no indication of where or wherefore or why the characters appeared when they did. The need for some kind of introduction to the play, besides Louis MacNeice's article in the *Radio Times*, was strongly felt by this small group':

> A very short synopsis would have made it much easier to follow. I cannot understand why you do not give one for this type of play. I had mugged up the story beforehand so understood it, but my wife, who hadn't, could make little of it. (Civil Engineer)
>
> I could not get the hang of it after listening carefully for nearly an hour. I missed the point, so gave up. I did enjoy the verse and would like another chance of listening to one of the Greek plays. (Housewife)

Other typical complaints were concerned with the remoteness of the characters or the style of delivery:

> It had no interest for ordinary listeners at all. I tried hard to listen and for a time the beautiful speech of the actors held me, but I found I was quite uninterested in Hippolytus, Artemis, the chorus of the Troezenian women. I would be much more interested in the doings of ordinary everyday people. (Profession unknown)
>
> According to all the highbrow critics I ought to have been enraptured by this play. In truth I stuck it for twenty minutes and then found myself bored and beaten. Monotonous dialogue mouthed in dreary tones resembling a well conducted funeral finished me. (Produce Merchant)[46]

The sixth play in the *World Theatre* series was another Greek tragedy—Euripides' *Trojan Women*—which had immediate resonances with the recent experiences of wartime Britain. As well as supplying the translation, Murray contributed an introductory *Radio Times* article, entitled 'A Post-War Drama of 415 BC', the purpose of which was to drive home the modernity and topicality of the ancient play, referencing the German invasion of neutral Holland in 1940 and the atomic bombing of Hiroshima in 1945 before offering the interpretation that *Trojan Women* was Euripides' response to the Athenian seizure of Melos in 416 BC in which all adult males were killed and women and children enslaved.[47] What is also

---

[46] BBC WAC LR/3796.
[47] For an excellent discussion of this controversial interpretation see Goff 2009, 27–35. It is noteworthy that a 1958 BBC Television production of *Trojan Women*, which happens to be the first Greek play ever produced on British television, also references nuclear war at the start: see Wrigley 2016a.

important about this article is that, having first established the topicality of the play, Murray goes on to give the detailed background of the Trojan War, an engaging description of the focus of the play ('the living drama for Euripides lay in the conquered women. It was they who suffered most, who understood best what war and conquest really meant in terms of human life'), and an introduction to the main characters and action. He concludes with a paragraph acknowledging the difficulty posed by the tendency of Greek plays to use more than one name for mortal and divine characters, people, and places, thus striving to mitigate any possible confusion.[48]

An extant recording of this production informs that the performance was prefaced by a spoken introduction which first sets forth the play as 'the noblest expression in words of the brutality and the beastliness of war. It tells the universal story of the defeated, the captured, the helpless at their enemies' mercy. The story of all persons displaced', and then (in a different male voice) offers some words of scene-setting ('Troy [. . .] the walls of which, partially ruined, glimmer through the mists of early dawn. Before them are some low huts, dark, silent, containing those of the captive women who have been specially set apart for the chief Greek warriors. [. . .] It is just before dawn and a hush is over everything [. . .] as the day breaks the lost colour ebbs back to the sails of the Greek ships by the beaches'), followed by a description of some of the characters the listeners will shortly be introduced to (for example, 'Hecuba, the old white-haired queen of Troy, is lying on the ground asleep, by the dead bodies of armed men' and 'Suddenly the figure of the god Poseidon is dimly seen beneath the walls to be followed by another divine presence, the goddess Pallas Athene').

The critic Philip Hope-Wallace (1911–79), writing in *The Listener*, noted that the problem in producing this play lies in 'providing sufficient contrast and relief in what is in the main non-stop ululation', considering that 'Murray's translation is not as helpful as it might be in this matter, for it tends to give the same note to all the mourners'.[49] Both Hope-Wallace and the critic in *The Manchester Guardian*, however, singled out Rita Vale who as Andromache managed to strike a personal note in her beautifully delivered lines.[50] It is worth bearing in mind quite how formal Murray's verse translations of

---

[48] Murray 1946. [49] Hope-Wallace 1946c. [50] Anon. 1946b.

tragedy were, in order to appreciate what seems to have been increasingly noted as a lack of vitality, or old-fashionedness, as the 1940s went on and other translations, and translators, came into vogue:

> HECUBA Who am I that sit
> Here at a Greek king's door,
> Yea, in the dust of it?
> A slave that men drive before?
> A woman that hath no home,
> Weeping alone for her dead;
> A low and bruisèd head,
> And the glory struck therefrom.[51]

Hope-Wallace found fault with Murray yet again, praising the actors in the 1947 *World Theatre* production of Sophocles' *Antigone* for their 'valiant, audible efforts' to combat the 'monotony'.[52] Yet most listeners enjoyed the production to some extent, finding the language beautiful or parts of the play 'intensely moving'; a minority (9 per cent, most of whom were unfamiliar with Greek mythology) disliked it, complaining about the 'morbid' theme or perceived 'lack of action'.[53] The following year, Hope-Wallace again wonders about these regular productions of Murray's translations in his review of the *World Theatre* production of Euripides' *Electra*: 'The Gilbert Murray translations and the style of declaiming which (I think rightly) the drama department favours for it combines to project a most powerful "atmosphere". Whether it is quite the right one is another matter. Let us be grateful for small mercies. The amount of great drama which is transmissible and which thus seizes the imagination is little enough.'[54] However, an appreciable number of listeners found something of value in the production: the Listener Research Report attests that 19 per cent of the audience (which it considers to be 'a small minority') had read *Electra* before, and that the play was 'greatly appealing' to about half of the listening sample, with another third liking it 'moderately'. Sixteen per cent disliked the play, some finding in it too much 'murder, hate and vengeance'; others had

---

[51] Murray 1910*b*, 18.
[52] Hope-Wallace 1947*a*. These actors included, unusually, the producer Val Gielgud who stepped in when the actor due to take the part of Creon fell ill. Murray first sent in his *Antigone* script in 1940, but it is not certain that it was performed before 1947 (see correspondence between GM and BB in GM/S).
[53] BBC WAC LR/47/1811.   [54] Hope-Wallace 1948*b*.

difficulty following it, thus finding it boring.[55] Interestingly, Gielgud asked Murray to write some 'explanatory commentary' to be delivered by a narrator during the performance of this play, an innovation which, Murray felt, enabled some of the people who he knew had struggled with *Antigone* to follow *Electra* 'with ease'.[56]

Murray's translation of *Frogs*, discussed below, may in 1947 have been the first full production of Aristophanes broadcast on British radio,[57] but it was not, in fact, the very first Greek *comedy* to be produced. That honour rests with a 1942 production of Murray's unpublished translation and reconstruction of Menander's *Perikeiromene*, titled *The Rape of the Locks*. The fifty-minute radio première of Murray's text was broadcast at the late hour of 10.30 p.m. on a Saturday evening.[58] Little evidence survives for the wartime production process but the Listener Research Report reveals a typical mixture of response to Greek comedy on the radio. Perhaps predictably for a wartime broadcast of a modern reconstruction of an incomplete Menandrian play, the audience was already favourably disposed to the drama of ancient Greece: 60 per cent of the 136 listeners who responded to the post-production questionnaire had some familiarity with Greek plays and 80 per cent of them stated that they would welcome more of them on the radio. Twenty per cent found it hard going, with names being unfamiliar and entrances and exits confusing. A housewife wrote: 'My difficulty in this play was to really get acquainted with the players. Their names were so difficult to remember and seemed out of tune with the rather modern dialogue.' This sort of complaint suggests the bind that the Drama Department often found itself in with regard to Greek plays at this time: it concerned itself with broadcasting the 'classics' of the dramatic canon, but sometimes the scripts did not make the necessary leap of translation from the stage to the purely aural medium. Many did like the production, of course: 'I had looked

---

[55] BBC WAC LR/48/252.

[56] Correspondence between VG and GM, 24 November 1947–10 February 1948 (GM/S).

[57] In 1928, Archibald Young Campbell had focused on the play in one of his *Greek Plays for Modern Listeners*, as did the thirtieth episode of the *Readings from Classical Literature* series in 1933. Around fifty lines from W. J. Hickie's translation of the play appeared in *Hellas*, a half-hour programme to mark the occasion of Greek Independence Day at 8.00 p.m. on Tuesday, 25 March 1941 (on which see Section 5.2).

[58] Illness prevented Murray from travelling to London to record his introductory talk (memo from BB to E. Boughen, 6 March 1942, in GM/T2).

forward to this broadcast as an antiquarian, and enjoyed it much more than I expected to' said an Examiner; but an Accountant wondered, 'Is antiquity sufficient passport to production? [. . .] as a prototype or museum piece I think the broadcast worth while but only just.'[59]

This kind of response may have dissuaded the programme planners from accepting Murray's translation and partial reconstruction of Menander's *Arbitration* when he sent it along for consideration in 1944 (it was rejected once again for being 'bookish' and 'out-of-the-way' in 1949–50 but was produced, finally, in 1952), but radio in this period often did have time for some of the more unusual cultural offerings.[60] The 1947 *Frogs*, for example, is a noteworthy example of collaboration between the worlds of radio, scholarship, and the amateur academic stage. Immediately after the radio production of the play, listeners had the opportunity to hear J. T. Sheppard introduce a thirty-minute programme of scenes from the play given in ancient Greek by members of the University who had, earlier in the year, staged *Frogs* as the Cambridge Greek Play.[61] (Indeed, it says much about the Third's ambitions that its Controller George Barnes thought the audience may be able to 'take the whole play in Greek'.[62]) These two adjacent programmes were broadcast on the Third, but what is interesting is that the English-language radio production of *Frogs* had actually premièred a few months earlier, in February 1947, in the *World Theatre* series on the Home Service where, instead of being followed by scenes performed in ancient Greek, the production was prefaced by an introduction and synopsis of the action by Gilbert Murray himself (see Figure 4.3). It is with *this*, broader Home Service audience in mind that the following anxieties on the part of translator and producer about putting Aristophanes on the air must be read.

Val Gielgud had approached Gilbert Murray in April 1946 about writing a 'special version' of his 1902 rhyming verse translation of *Frogs*

---

[59] BBC WAC LR/722.
[60] Correspondence between GM and BB, July and November 1944; memo from E. J. King-Bull, 23 November 1949; memo from Controller, Third Programme [Harman Grisewood], 24 October 1950 (all in GM/S). Murray's *Arbitration*, adapted by Helena Wood, was later produced in 1952 (Home).
[61] The recording of scenes from the play, accompanied by Walter Leigh's score, was made in the Arts Theatre, Cambridge, where the production ran from 18 to 22 February 1947 (letter from the BBC Outside Broadcasting Manager to Norman Higgins, 17 December 1946).
[62] Memo from George Barnes to Mr Amyot, 22 October 1946 (S452/11/1).

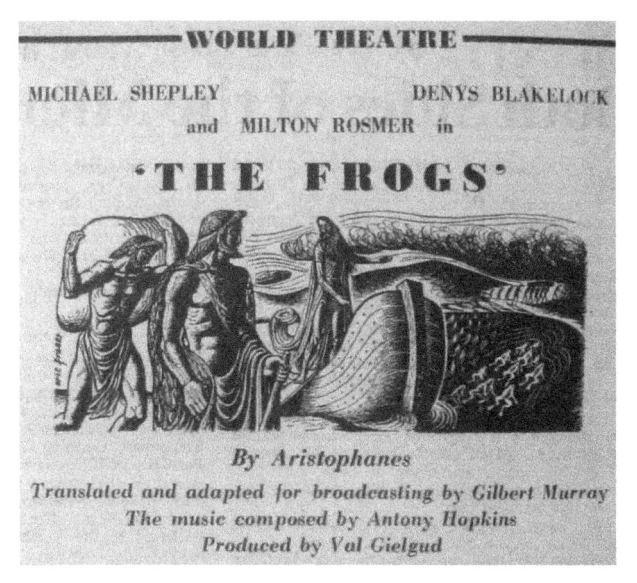

Fig. 4.3. The 1947 Home Service production of *Frogs*, illustrated by Eric Fraser (*Radio Times*, 31 January 1947, 10). Reproduced by kind permission of the Fraser family.

for radio.[63] From the start, the focus of their correspondence was on making the play both comprehensible and funny for the mass radio audience. 'The problem', as Gielgud wrote to Murray, 'is one of making the humour intelligible to an audience for the most part lamentably lacking in classical background. [...] I have little doubt that you would be able to make certain adjustments and possible additions to the script which would be of the greatest possible value.'[64] Gielgud was not the only one to be concerned about 'translating' Aristophanes to radio: 'You know my doubts whether our audience will appreciate the finer points, or even the broader points of Aeschylus + Euripides, but you persuade me that this difficulty can be overcome by special presentation. I'm sure that we need to make a quite special effort to help listeners with Aristophanes.'[65] Murray attempted to rise to this challenge:

---

[63] Published alongside his translations of Euripides' *Bacchae* and *Hippolytus*: Murray 1902.
[64] Letter from VG to GM, 3 April 1946 (GM/S).
[65] Handwritten note from Lindsay Wellington [Head of Home Service] to VG, 29 March 1946 at the foot of a typescript memo from the latter dated 12 March (GM/S).

I have been engaged for some days in trying to make the *Frogs* intelligible to the plain man. [...] I have tried,
(1) to cut out topical allusions, though of course they are (or were) part of the fun,
(2) to deal with some of the visual points, e.g. to write a slightly different opening showing who Dionysus is and that he is disguised as Hercules, with lion-skin and club. Also a line here and there to explain the entrance of new persons.[66]

A few months later, Murray wrote: 'I send you herewith a text of the *Frogs* roughly cut down to about the required length and modernised here and there so as to be intelligible to an average audience; e.g. putting Bacchus for Dionysus and Jove for Zeus and things like coupons for obols or oil-flasks. The beginning is unfortunately all visual, depending on the absurd appearance of Dionysus dressed as Heracles. I have therefore written a page to take the place of the first two or three pages of text.'[67] On hearing the broadcast, however, Murray was quite disheartened:

the difficulties of doing a Greek Comedy on the radio were greater than I realised. I listened in the company of a quite intelligent though not very nimble-witted lady, and found that she could hardly understand a word of it. It was a blow, but so it was.
I think for one thing that a comedy depends more on sight than a tragedy (Greek). There are more speakers, more movement &c. It was often hard to tell who was speaking. Then, though I tried to get rid of some of the topical allusions, I did not quite realise how many were left. I wonder if it would be better to have a Commentator such as they have for the Trollope novels.
It also struck me that a comedy in a theatre depends a great deal on the 'laughs' of the audience. A joke received in silence is very depressing.[68]

Here Murray is, perhaps unwittingly, gesturing towards some of the inherent difficulties in the Drama Department's traditional approach to presenting stage plays on the air in the 1940s. The level of adaptation permitted by the culturally conservative Department head Gielgud, who produced *Frogs*, was minimal. What Murray perfectly realizes is that they require specific kinds of intervention, or *adaptation*, to make them work well. Gielgud was frequently scornful about listeners (often ruder than Murray is, above, of his

---
[66] Letter from GM to VG, 25 April 1946 (GM/S).
[67] Letter from GM to VG, 13 September 1946 (GM/S).
[68] Letter from GM to VG, 5 February 1947 (GM/S).

listening companion) and often blames problems arising from the nature of the medium or a particular production on listeners' imaginative abilities and practical energies to engage, rather than daring to traverse the boundaries of his cultural traditionalism and let stage-plays be freely adapted so they work better on air. He responds to Murray as follows:

> I am sorry that your companion should have been so apparently flummoxed, but I think a good deal depends on whether she happened to be a fairly regular listener to plays broadcast or not. The audience inured to the convention of the broadcasting of plays, with all the limitations that that convention implies, has grown so astonishingly during recent years that I feel that the obscurities may have been, in practice, more apparent than real as far as the majority of listeners was concerned.[69]

Following his own initial unhappiness with the broadcast, Murray received a lot of unsolicited correspondence expressing appreciation and praise.[70] After a repeat on the Third he reported to Gielgud that some local children 'listened in and I hear they were delighted, and they say they understood most of it'.[71] A dominant note in the press criticism, which echoes the initial concerns of Murray and Gielgud, is what individual members of the audience at large may have made of it. The critic in *The Observer* considered that

> while there is much in *The Frogs* which the modern listener can apply to the foibles and mannerisms of our own time, there is also much which baffles him unless he enjoys a close knowledge of the local and topical objects of Aristophanes' satire. Yet I daresay that most listeners, despite their occasional bewilderment, persevered with the programme, because enough clues and allusions kept arising in the nick of time.

The writer concludes that 'A paraphrase by Louis MacNeice might have brought *The Frogs* nearer home to us, for the Gilbert Murray translation, despite its fluency and resourcefulness, is sometimes a little too formal to convey the pungency of Aristophanes'.[72] The reference here, of course, is to MacNeice's *Enemy of Cant*, which had been broadcast on the Third the previous year. Hope-Wallace

---

[69] Letter from VG to GM, 7 February 1947 (GM/S).
[70] Letter from GM to VG, 7 February 1947 (GM/S).
[71] Letter from GM to VG, 29 April 1947 (GM/S), in which he mistakenly refers to the Light Programme rather than the Third.
[72] W. E. Williams 1947.

makes a similar point in *The Listener*, noting that the 'Swinburnian surge and swing' of Murray's verse, although still passably 'period' in Greek tragedy, is of no advantage at all in comedy.[73]

Yet some domestic listeners were persuaded of the *modernity* of Murray's radio adaptation, even in response to a new *World Theatre* production of Murray's *Frogs* in 1951, by which time Murray himself feared that his post-war replacement of 'oil-pots' with 'coupons' was now out-of-date. Katharine Chapman, the wife of Robert William Chapman (1881–1960), the Secretary to the Delegates of Oxford University Press, 1920–42, wrote enthusiastically to him as follows:

> What a wonderful evening's entertainment that was! How amusing in all the best ways,—how clever, how witty, how rhythmic, how riotously funny in places, how interesting & how beautiful in others—& above all how up to date (right up to the moment), & how YOUNG it all was—in short, how <u>symbolic</u> of its second begetter![74]

Murray's translations, especially of Greek tragedy, were a staple in the Drama Department's repertoire into the 1950s, their performance life as full productions on air therefore exceeding by some decades their already very long life on the stage and, indeed, on the page. Inevitably, these verse translations did not suit all tastes and they increasingly seemed to fall out of vogue both with critics and BBC staff. Thus was one critic irritated by the 'declamatory style' of the 1948 production of Euripides' *Electra* and left wondering whether Murray's translation had become 'less acceptable on the air than in the study', especially since 'better clues for restoring these ancient monuments of literature' had been 'so brilliantly discovered' by others, such as MacNeice, who had recently impressed with his *Agamemnon* and his Aristophanic *Enemy of Cant* (on which see Chapters 7 and 8 respectively).[75] This sea-change in taste was voiced within the BBC, too: in an internal memorandum written in 1954 Helena Wood considers that Murray's translation of Aeschylus' *Suppliant Women* possessed 'the usual monotony of rhymed couplets, and over-romantic charm and liveliness' which utterly failed to convey the 'primitive, sculptural feeling of Greek drama' which she

---

[73] Hope-Wallace 1947*b*.
[74] Postcard from 'K.M.C.' to GM, 4 December 1951 (GM/S; the author is identified by Murray in a letter from GM to VG, 6 December 1951, in the same file).
[75] W. E. Williams 1948.

sought.[76] From another perspective, a 1950 production of Ford Madox Ford's adaptation of Euripides' *Alcestis* was introduced by the producer Frank Hauser in the *Radio Times* as a version which 'will shock those who were brought up on Gilbert Murray'.[77] Many more examples of tastes changing in the 1950s could be listed.

In 1956, the year before his death, the Third broadcast a fitting tribute to Murray's extensive and impressive career as 'radio Hellenist' in the form of a Menandrian feast. This included an introductory programme by Murray and, on the evenings following, productions of his versions of *Epitrepontes* and *Perikeiromene* (under the titles *The Arbitration* and *The Rape of the Locks*), plus *The Beauty from Samos*, Joanna Richardson (1925–2008) and Patric Dickinson's English translation of Charles Cordier's reconstruction of *Samia* in French.[78] Murray had lived an extremely rich life by the time he died in 1957 at the age of 91 and for the previous three decades radio had played an important role in his life's work. Indeed, he was involved in broadcasting almost to the very end, continuing to contribute regular introductions to productions of his translations of Greek drama as well as an impressively wide range of talks, as will be seen in the following section.

4.2. TALKS ON CLASSICS AND INTERNATIONAL POLITICS

> Murray was quite literally, to millions of radio listeners, the voice of classical learning.[79]

Gilbert Murray's contribution to what we may think of as 'ancient Greece on the radio' can be measured not merely by the large number of his Greek play translations which were produced by the Drama Department and his many and frequent introductory talks and

---

[76] Memo from Helena Wood to Script Editor, Sound [Barbara Bray], 29 June 1954 (GM/S).
[77] On the other hand, it is an 'impressive' play 'which needs no previous familiarity with Greek drama to prove itself as absorbing and enjoyable as any written for a modern audience' (Hauser 1950).
[78] The Drama Department commissioned this translation from Dickinson, who suggested the collaboration with the biographer and translator Richardson who was at the time undertaking her DPhil at Oxford (PD/S2a).
[79] Morris 2007, 294.

articles in the *Radio Times* and *The Listener*, but also by the even greater number of more general talks on classical subjects and his political broadcasts, many of which themselves drew on ideas from ancient Greece, and were aired both at home and overseas. As is well known, in addition to his work as a classical scholar Murray was an active participant in international politics, taking, for example, a leading role in the foundation of the League of Nations.[80] It naturally followed that this enthusiastic radio broadcaster should be a prolific contributor of radio talks on both classical and political topics— sometimes both together—and indeed many of his broadcasts during the Second World War take a clear political stance, being described at the time as 'propagandist' and 'morale-boosting'.[81] This group of talks stand alongside MacNeice's scripts (on which see the following chapter) as important contributions to the war effort.

The task of compiling a full catalogue of Murray's prodigious amount and range of radio work is—as Mick Morris acknowledges in his excellent overview essay of Murray's work for the BBC—truly a herculean (and, as yet, unfinished) task.[82] Morris offers a good summary listing which is far more suggestive of the breadth of Murray's radio talks than anything that had previously been published, but Murray's BBC WAC Scriptwriter and Talks files alone, not to mention the other archival sources at the BBC and elsewhere, offer many more tantalizing clues to the bigger picture. It is not the task of this chapter to offer anything approaching an exhaustive account of Murray's radio talks but, rather, simply to gesture towards the various ways in which Murray functioned as a kind of 'radio Hellenist', or even 'public classicist', through the mass medium of radio and how this function, or standing, may have gained particular force in combination with his interest and active participation in matters of international politics.

In the previous section, it was established how frequently and enthusiastically Murray wrote and delivered talks which were

---

[80] On Murray's political work and internationalism see Ceadel 2007 and P. Wilson 2007.

[81] See Briggs 1970, 6 ff. and Nicholas 1996 on radio propaganda in the Second World War. The *BBC Year Book 1946* stated that in the 'war of words' across Europe, 'certain good principles in broadcasting have defeated the worst possible principles' (British Broadcasting Corporation 1946, 7).

[82] Morris 2007, an essay which was published as my own doctoral thesis, which independently covered some of the same ground, was in preparation.

designed to elucidate radio productions of his own translations of Greek drama. There is no evidence to suggest that the radio productions of *Iphigenia in Tauris*, *Medea*, and *Rhesus* in 1925-6 were accompanied by this kind of talk, but it is fascinating to learn that one of the early approaches made to Murray about writing and delivering a broadcast talk was an invitation by J. C. Stobart to give the 'annual Shakespeare talk' in 1926. Murray, perhaps sensibly, replied, 'I do not think Shakespeare is my subject', although he noted that he 'would gladly broadcast some day'.[83] Murray had, in fact, already had some experience of broadcasting: on 1 December 1925 he had appeared alongside the social reformer Henrietta Barnett (1851-1936) on the topic of 'Matters that Matter' in a programme broadcast from London,[84] and he would very soon find himself on the air again, addressing the nation as the General Strike was coming to an end. Morris tells of how Reith himself asked Murray, as a respected public figure known for his work for international peace, to speak to the nation to try to 'bind wounds'.[85] Subsequent invitations followed to speak on the anniversary of the outbreak of the First World War and on the topic of 'Masters of Literature', but Murray was unable to take up all of these owing to other commitments.[86] In these early years of broadcasting his talk contributions seem to have been more on the political than the classical side, and sometimes they were considered to be potentially controversial: in 1926, for example, a nervous Foreign Office demanded to see his script 'The League or Chaos' on the topic of the League of Nations before it was broadcast.[87] In 1930 he gave the talk 'On Intellectual Cooperation' which opened the *International Co-operation and What It Means* series.[88] This series of talks, as many were around this time, was accompanied by the publication of an Aids to Study pamphlet which summarized each talk and offered illustrations, facts, and figures and a full

[83] Letters between J. C. Stobart and GM, 19 and 20 March 1926 (GM/T1).
[84] *Radio Times*, 27 November 1925, 444.
[85] Morris 2007, 298 (who dates the talk to 13 May 1926). See McKibbin 2000, 461 on how the BBC is perceived to have taken the government's side in the General Strike.
[86] Unsigned letter to GM, 28 June 1926 (GM/T1).
[87] See letters to C. W. Reith and GM, dated 6 and 8 September 1926 respectively (GM/T1).
[88] Broadcast at 7.25 p.m., Wednesday, 5 March 1930. Later programmes, delivered by other prominent speakers, covered topics such as economics, labour, and health.

bibliography for further reading.[89] Such pamphlets (which cost 1d. or 2d.) were designed to have 'independent value' of the associated series and it was believed that 'listeners tend to pay a good deal of attention to lecturers' advice [...] and Libraries like a full bibliography so that they may have a range of choice in their supply to readers'.[90] Furthermore, these very programmes and pamphlets made up the 'curriculum' studied by the increasing number of Listening Groups being formed at educational institutes and settlements up and down the country, a phenomenon which was discussed in Section 3.1.[91] Talks such as these, and associated print resources on subjects far removed from Aeschylus and Euripides, must be considered when evaluating Murray's contribution to the educational life of the nation. He was, as Morris has noted, 'to millions of radio listeners, the voice of classical learning' but also of *much* more besides.[92]

Towards the end of the decade Murray seems to have broadcast an increasing number of talks on classical topics. In 1937 he contributed a twenty-minute talk entitled 'Euripides' in a series of *Talks for Sixth Forms* (which also included talks on Shakespeare by J. Dover Wilson (1881–1969), foreign literature in translation by Alexander Gray (1882–1968), and modern poetry by Michael Roberts (1902–48)).[93] After reading some reports on the talk from schools sent to him by the BBC, Murray concluded that 'I am afraid Euripides was not a subject at first sight attractive to most schools',[94] but his colleagues at the BBC were not concerned by any lukewarm reaction, and neither was he discouraged from broadcasting the Greeks. In fact, just months later he began preparing a series of six fifteen-minute talks on 'the value of ancient Greek civilisation to the modern world', under the title *Why Greek?*, for broadcast on the Empire Service in the summer of 1938. No evidence suggests that these were repeated on the National network, but slightly shortened versions of the talks were printed in *The Listener* for the home audience.[95] The first talk,

---

[89] Anon. 1930, 405.
[90] Letter from Charles Siepmann to GM, 20 November 1929 (GM/T1).
[91] Siepmann anticipates that many new groups 'will be formed to hear this series' (letter to GM, 22 January 1930, in GM/T1).
[92] Morris 2007, 294.
[93] Broadcast at 3.35 p.m., Friday, 8 October 1937. Morris 2007, 300–2 offers a partial transcript.
[94] Letter from GM to F. N. Lloyd Williams, 25 October 1937 (GM/T1).
[95] Murray 1938*a* and 1938*b*.

'The Genius of the Greeks', argues that the ancient Greeks had a 'quality of genius' which has a 'stationary and eternal value' which makes them still relevant today. The second, 'Hellenism', addresses what made the Greeks different to other, ancient civilizations. The remaining talks discuss epic poetry, drama, history, and, finally, philosophy, and the printed versions are lavishly illustrated by photographs of ancient objects (such as sculpture, reliefs, vase-paintings). Murray throughout gestures to the continuing relevance and indeed importance of the ancient world: at the end of the final talk, with some ring composition, he brings the listener/reader back to one of his opening points, that ancient Greece refreshingly offers us other qualities to value than the 'dollars and miles and horse-power' of the 'complex material civilisation' of the twentieth century, a claim which doubtless springs from the general fear that the West had been, for some time, facing a crisis of civilization.[96] He also gestures towards current international unrest when he recalls that at the beginning of the First World War passages from Pericles' *Funeral Oration* (as reported by the Greek historian Thucydides) appeared on posters on London buses 'to remind us of the ideals which we had to defend'.[97]

A number of Murray's political broadcasts in the Second World War drew on ideas, and ideals, deriving from ancient Greece. Writing to him in April 1940 with an idea for talks under the title *The Glory that was Greece*, Val Gielgud considered that 'it is an excellent time now to remind people of the obvious parallel between the Persian Wars and to-day, and incidentally a shortened version of *The Persians* might well come into the series'; Murray was happy to cooperate, but thought the title was one that 'rather irritates or bores people'.[98] It is not certain whether this particular idea got off the ground, or whether it somehow fed into MacNeice's *The Glory that is Greece* in 1941 (on which see the next chapter), but Murray certainly participated in several broadcasts focused on the plight of modern Greece in the Second World War in the months following. At the beginning of December 1940, for example, when Greek forces were labouring to drive back the Italian armies, the Overseas News Editor wrote to Murray, inviting him to write a short script on the 'spirit of Greece'

---

[96] Murray 1938*a*, 373 and 1938*b*, 434.   [97] Murray 1938*b*, 433.
[98] Letter from VG to GM, 4 April 1940, and GM's reply, 6 April 1940 (GM/S).

and enclosing 'a note indicating the propaganda points that we are anxious to bring out', for translation and almost immediate broadcast to Germany on 14 December. Murray readily agreed, submitting a script which re-worked one of his recent talks on the topic of 'Greece's Contribution to Civilisation' which had been broadcast in the *In My Opinion* series in November.[99]

Also, in December 1940, Murray broadcast 'Greece and her Tradition' for Home Service listeners, a talk which describes Greece as bravely standing up 'against the giants' in its current battles (p. 81).[100] He considers that 'the thing called Hellenism—I apologise for the rather highbrow word—almost covers the cause we are now fighting for' (p. 81), gesturing towards the greatness of ancient Greek architecture, literature, science, and military campaigns as a prelude to thinking about 'what sort of society, what attempt at a better world, we can dare aim at after the war' (p. 82). He aligns notions of ancient Greek freedoms with the 'freedom for which we are now fighting':

> freedom against the claims of despots who are above the law, like the Roman Emperors who were worshipped as gods. There was never in Greece a superhuman semi-divine Great King [...]. The Greeks had kings and leaders—some good, some bad—but they are always sharply warned that they are not superhuman and will only get into trouble if they think they are. [...] 'Among the barbarians', said the Greek proverb, 'all are slaves but one'. That is the system against which the Greeks fought, and against which we are fighting to-day. (pp. 83–4)

Murray considers what this kind of freedom meant for ancient Greek society and what it means for Europe in 1940:

> How is this insistence on freedom, free speech, equality before the law, connected with the great achievements of the Greeks in art, thought and literature? We can see at least this connection, that if freedom does not of itself necessarily produce great art or thought, the absence of freedom makes great art and thought impossible. It is not for nothing that the tyrants of Germany and Italy to-day have driven out their great writers and men of science and are taking the trouble to murder university students. In fighting for freedom the Greeks fought not merely for the right to be unpersecuted in their daily lives; they fought for the right to

---

[99] On wartime broadcasts to Germany see Briggs 1970, 386–94. See Overy 2009 on the crisis of civilization of this and the previous decade.

[100] Page references in this paragraph are to Murray 1947a.

think and to speak, to write poems and plays and books on philosophy and to build temples like the Parthenon. And so do we. (pp. 84–5)

Murray continued to be an active contributor of a wide variety of talks throughout the war: for example, to name just a few, he gave a talk on Socrates (1941), delivered a seven-minute 'Message to Greece' (European News, 1941), contributed to the Home Service *Talks for Sixth Forms* series with 'Equipping Ourselves to Understand: An International Problem' (27 March 1942), offered his thoughts on oppression in Poland for broadcast on both the Home and Overseas Services in June 1942, and delivered a short lecture on 'Classical Humanism' (Home Service, 1943). The *Talks for Sixth Forms* series was considered by the BBC to be a contribution to 16- and 17-year-old pupils' 'general education in the widest sense'. Richmond Postgate, Director of Schools Broadcasting, wrote to Gilbert Murray as follows:

> We have long felt that broadcasts on classical subjects would be welcomed by schools, but we have been conscious of the difficulties of presenting scholarly material to young people who have little or no classical background. The theme of the broadcasts which we are planning for the Spring Term 1948, however, is the relevance of Greek and Roman thought to the problems of our own time, and the debt of our own civilisation to the civilisations of Greece and Rome. These talks are addressed to the mixed sixth form, with only a sprinkling of classical specialists; in fact, most of the pupils have no knowledge of Greek and only an elementary knowledge of Latin. Nevertheless, we believe that lack of linguistic knowledge should not be allowed to debar these young people from an understanding of the living thought of the ancient world. [...] the classical contribution of a liberal education was never more important than in an age of competing specialisms.[101]

Murray was, characteristically, only too happy to contribute to such a series, which had the potential to widen the audience for classical topics.

He also regularly approached the BBC with his own ideas for talks or series. In 1952 he offered English versions of a series of talks he had written for Radiodiffusion Française Universitaire, titled *Les Apports Grecs dans la Civilisation Contemporaine*, in which, he explains, 'I tried to show not merely the great extent to which our thinking is

---

[101] Letter from Richmond Postgate to GM, 8 September 1947 (GM/T3a).

influence[d] by Greek thoughts, but also how curiously similar the history of the last 50 years has been to that of Greek civilisation'.[102] Internal staff opinion on these talks was mixed and points to a diminishing appetite for Murray's brand of popular Hellenism. There were, for example, concerns that 'the hackneyed analogy with Hellenism' was already familiar to 'every sixth form child' and there was also the opinion that 'those who will enjoy hearing him have already worshipped at this shrine, and that those who will not, cannot, because of the gap between the present and the age of Murray'; yet there was also an acknowledgement that the talks offered 'really good teaching of its kind', and the fact that this 'teaching' was considered to be more to the taste of the larger Home Service audience than the Third would, one imagines, have pleased Murray greatly.[103] Thus *Hellenism and the Modern World*, comprising six fifteen-minute talks, was broadcast on the Home in 1953 with illustrated versions of the talks—which were also published as a book in the same year—appearing in *The Listener*.[104] Murray takes his audience through Rome and Jerusalem, he explains ideas such as the *polis* (city-state), aligns the ideal of ancient Athens with his cherished Liberalism, and explains its demise in terms of 'lust for power' (p. 42).[105] In the sixth and final talk the focus shifts to the modern world and, specifically, the 'continent of Europe', which is 'our modern Hellas': 'her separate nations have been the independent Cities, and their wars her ruin, as the wars of Athens and Sparta were the ruin of Hellas' (p. 52). He praises the good done by the empires of Europe, laments how the two world wars have led to a diminishing of continental strength and security, expresses concern over the political development of China, and worries over the spread of independence amongst former colonized nations ('backward peoples', p. 59). Such sentiments laid bare what the BBC had feared was the 'gap between the present and the age of Murray', but within the awkwardness of Murray's idealized notions of ancient Hellas and modern Europe-Hellas lies a long lifetime's quest for peace between nations, albeit one

---

[102] Letter from GM to Alexander Cadogan, 17 October 1952 (GM/T3a).
[103] Memo from John Green [Chief Assistant, Talks, Home Sound Broadcasting] to 'G.S.W.', 30 October 1952; memo from Michael Stephens [Talks Producer] to John Green, 14 November 1952 (GM/T3a).
[104] The book is Murray 1953. Page references in this paragraph are to this volume.
[105] On the Hellenic foundations of Murray's Liberalism see Ceadel 2007.

that is clearly tinged with nostalgia, and perhaps even sourness, in the face of the increasingly rapid changes and disturbances of recent history.[106]

From the birth of the BBC in 1922, Murray believed that broadcasting had had 'an immense effect on the life of mankind. It made an epoch. It did more to make the whole world one than any previous invention.'[107] Other classicists in the first three decades of British radio made contributions to the intellectual life of the nation, through series of talks, educational broadcasts, and dramatic entertainments. Murray, however, because of the public persona he had already achieved through his high-profile work for the League of Nations, collaborations with the professional stage and, also, the sustained popularity over several decades of his verse translations of Greek drama, was uniquely placed to make hugely effective use of radio to share his enthusiastic passion for Greek drama as poetry and in performance, his political ideals, which were rooted in an ideological marriage between Hellenism and Liberalism, and his pursuit of harmony on the international stage.[108] Occasionally in the 1920s and 1930s, and increasingly over the 1940s and 1950s (as will be demonstrated in the following chapters), styles of translation of Greek plays which differed from Murray's 'Swinburnian' verse were introduced to satisfy new tastes, and much more imaginative forms of adapting ancient texts for radio performance were developed in order to engage the listener. Murray, however, managed to maintain his position as, we might say, 'public Hellenist' over an impressive three decades through his energetic desire to communicate his ideas, and his ideals, to a wide public through an unceasing catalogue of accessible radio broadcasts and magazine articles, right up to the penultimate year of his life.[109]

---

[106] Memo from Michael Stephens to John Green, 14 November 1952. See Ceadel 2007, 237 on the rightwards political shift in the last years of his life.

[107] Murray 1947b, 839.

[108] To take just one example, his translation of Euripides' *Electra* was reprinted fourteen times between its first appearance in 1905 and 1931 (Murray 1905).

[109] No trace of any radio work survives from 1957, the last year of his life.

5

Greek History in the Wartime Propaganda of Louis MacNeice

Louis MacNeice worked for the BBC for over twenty years, from 1941 to his death in 1963, writing at least one hundred and sixty scripts for broadcast on a wide variety of subjects in programmes for which he was also in most cases the producer.[1] Given MacNeice's background as a classicist and the frequent use of Greek and Roman themes in his poetry it is not surprising to find that he often engaged creatively with the history and literature of Greece and Rome in his work for radio, which includes substantial re-workings of authors such as Homer, Thucydides, Aristophanes, Xenophon, Petronius, Apuleius, and Horace in programmes designed for, and heard by, a broad, non-specialist audience.[2] This particular seam in his work has interesting implications, since these were concerted attempts to make accessible texts and ideas from the classical world to a wide public, and the resulting works were not merely translations but adaptations and re-workings which were deliberately unfusty and accessible. Of course, MacNeice's use of antiquity is by no means the only important or interesting theme in his radio or other creative writings, but it is a dominant one which—given the quantity and diversity of the material under discussion—invites further study.[3] This chapter

---

[1] This figure is taken from Holme 1981, 46. Smith 1974 estimates that he has handled at least 150 scripts in the BBC's collections alone. Heuser and McDonald 1993, p. xi put the figure at 'more than 120'. Titles of around 130 scripts are included in the appendix to Wrigley and Harrison 2013, a volume which publishes the scripts of eleven of MacNeice's works for radio which draw on Greek and Roman themes, with individual introductions and explanatory notes.

[2] On classical themes in his poetry see, for example, Arkins 2000 and P. McDonald 1998.

[3] See the introductions in Wrigley and Harrison 2013.

considers, first, his multi-layered career as poet, classicist, radio writer, and radio producer, before examining some of his early scripts which respond to the contemporary international situation during the Second World War. Chapters 6, 7, and 8 consider his later work on an Odyssean radio series, the radio life of his translation of Aeschylus' *Agamemnon*, and the Aristophanic *Enemy of Cant* to give a fuller profile of his later radio engagements with ancient Greece.

5.1. POET AND CLASSICIST, RADIO WRITER AND PRODUCER

MacNeice was born in Belfast in 1907; two years later the family moved to Carrickfergus, also in Northern Ireland, where his father (who was later bishop of Down, Connor, and Dromore, near Belfast) had been appointed the new rector of St Nicholas. At 10 he was sent to the preparatory department of the independent boys' boarding school Sherborne in Dorset, from where he went to Marlborough on a scholarship. He read classics at Merton College, Oxford where he got a first in both Honours Moderations and Greats.[4] At the end of his Oxford days he married Mary Ezra, the stepdaughter of the Oxford classical archaeologist Professor J. D. Beazley. They moved to Birmingham in 1930 where he served as assistant lecturer in classics at the university until 1936 when he moved to London (Mary had left him and his son in 1935) where he took up a lectureship in Greek at Bedford College for Women. During his time at Birmingham he had worked on a book on humour in Latin literature. The book was never finished, but his work on it certainly fed into his radio plays, which drew on Roman themes such as *The Golden Ass* and *Cupid and Psyche* (both 1944), *A Roman Holiday* (1945), and *Trimalchio's Feast* (1948).[5]

---

[4] On MacNeice's classical education see Arkins 2000, 1–10.
[5] Dodds 1974, 36. A draft of this book, with accompanying notebooks, exists in box 34, Louis MacNeice Papers, Bodleian Library; parts are also held by the Harry Ransom Center, University of Texas at Austin. Publication was discussed with Faber but never achieved. Wrigley and Harrison 2013 publish for the first time the four named scripts and several others.

MacNeice's biographer, Jon Stallworthy, notes that he had not enjoyed 'the way in which Latin and Greek language and literature were taught [at Oxford]. He grew to hate the precedence given to language over literature, the "niggling over textual commentary", the memorization of emendations proposed by scholars.'[6] As a consequence, he considers, MacNeice was not the most inspirational of lecturers at Birmingham and Bedford College (where he stayed until 1939). Mrs F. Wilkinson, senior lecturer in classics at Bedford, reported that MacNeice's 'colleagues [...] had the impression that he did not find "either the classics in themselves, or the teaching of them, particularly absorbing". They were half right: he did not enjoy teaching the ancient texts, but never ceased to enjoy reading them.'[7] His classical education had, however, left him with a love for ancient literature and a rich mine on which he frequently drew in his creative writing, and, when presented with the opportunity to refashion ancient texts and subjects for the most modern of mass media, he intuitively understood how best to bring them alive for an audience who were likely to be, in the main, unschooled in Greek and Latin.

MacNeice was primarily a poet; his first substantial collection had appeared under the title *Poems* in 1935.[8] Around this time he also wrote a translation of Aeschylus' *Agamemnon* specifically for production, with music by Britten, by London's Group Theatre in 1936.[9] This translation was, as discussed in Chapter 7, the first new production of a Greek tragedy performed on the newly established Third Programme in 1946. Around this time he also worked on a translation of Euripides' *Hippolytus* for the Group Theatre, but this was never completed.[10] After Bedford's spring term ended, he went on a lecture tour of American universities—as a poet rather than a classicist.[11] He returned for the summer term and successfully applied for a

---

[6] Stallworthy 1995, 114.
[7] Ibid. 206. For further discussion see Arkins 2000, 10–12.
[8] For MacNeice's poetic career see, for example, Brown 2009 and P. McDonald 1991.
[9] Sidnell 1986, 326 and Sidnell 1984, especially ch. 10.
[10] His friend and former Birmingham colleague Professor E. R. Dodds commented on a draft as follows: 'it is usually adequate and actable and sometimes brilliant' (undated letter from ERD to LM, in box 43, folder ii, Louis MacNeice Papers, Bodleian Library; the *Hippolytus* typescript is also in this folder). See Nelson 2000 for discussion and partial publication.
[11] Stallworthy 1995, 243.

year's leave of absence for 1939–40; by September he wrote to his American lover Eleanor Clark that 'for some time now I have ceased from my academic vocation'.[12] Subsequently there was no further progress on his Roman humour book or *Hippolytus*. By this time, he was well regarded as a poet and part of the London literary scene. In 1939 his long autobiographical poem 'Autumn Journal', which sets his personal story against the oncoming war, was published and he began working on a book on Yeats (which appeared as *The Poetry of W. B. Yeats* in 1941). From February to May 1940 he held a Special Lectureship in Poetry at Cornell University but received orders from the British government to return. In correspondence with friends he wonders how he will be occupied in wartime Britain: 'What do you think they'll make me do? By this stage I am on for doing anything—cleaning sewers or feeding machine guns, but preferably nothing too intelligent.'[13]

Having been declared physically unfit for any strenuous war work, MacNeice thought of 'trying to crash in on the BBC'.[14] He had recently

Fig. 5.1. Louis MacNeice in rehearsal, script and pencil in hand. © BBC. Reproduced by kind permission of the BBC Photo Library.

---

[12] Ibid. 261.
[13] Letter from LM to ERD, 18 August 1940, reprinted in MacNeice 2010, 400.
[14] Letter from LM to John Frederick and Georgina Beatrice MacNeice, 16 December 1940, reprinted in MacNeice 2010, 416.

remembered a family connection with Sir Frederick W. Ogilvie, the Director-General of the BBC: 'I just remembered the other day that the present chief of the BBC [. . .] is a great fan of mine & a pal of my old man's, so maybe I shall cash in on that.'[15] Within weeks of returning from America he wrote to Ogilvie offering some writing for programmes broadcast to America.[16] And so began his first steps towards a career in radio writing and producing.

As noted in Chapter 2, in March 1940 the BBC wrote to MacNeice asking whether 'some aspect of Nazism and its influence or its victims would appeal to you as the theme of a radio programme. [. . .] We in this country have not yet been able to secure a first class poet for such radio programmes and I feel convinced that your lines would speak well.'[17] On the face of things, MacNeice jumped at this chance to earn a living and do something usefully connected with the war effort. From his personal correspondence, however, it is clear that he had decidedly mixed feelings about penning these wartime scripts for the BBC:

> I am probably going officially soon on to the staff of the BBC. It's a v. 2nd rate institution & Christ, the things they do to one's work (just chop it & sugar it & cut out the points & write in their own bloody crudities) but the choice of occupations here now [. . .] is just a choice of evils & the BBC, though deplorable, does leave some loophole for intelligence & individual decisions—which is more than can be said of most. [. . .] When I'm not doing more or less hackwork I don't do any work at all.[18]

A number of years later, MacNeice's position seems to have softened. He admits that 'Before I joined the BBC I was, like most of the intelligentsia, prejudiced not only against that institution but against

---

[15] Letter from LM to Mary MacNeice, 28 October 1940, reprinted in MacNeice 2010, 413–14. Ogilvie had been Vice-Chancellor of Queen's University, Belfast from 1934 to 1938, during which time Louis's father John Frederick MacNeice (1866–1942) was bishop of Down, Connor, and Dromore, near Belfast.

[16] Coulton 1980, 15.

[17] Letter from T. Rowland Hughes to LM, 7 March 1940, quoted by Stallworthy 1995, 287. See Havers 2007 on the BBC as a source of information and propaganda during the war.

[18] Letter from LM to Eleanor Clark, 20 April 1941, reprinted in MacNeice 2010, 429. At this time he had a particular aversion to the BBC, 'a frightful institution to have to spend yr [sic] days in', as he wrote in a letter to the wife of ERD on 10 February 1941 (reprinted in MacNeice 2010, 421).

broadcasting in general'.[19] Furthermore, although some of his radio writing may be 'hackwork', parts of it are not:

> Broadcasting is plastic; while it can ape the Press, it can also emulate the arts. Yes, people will say, that is theoretically true but in practice you will never get art—or anything like it—out of a large public institution, encumbered with administrators, which by its nature must play for safety and to the gallery. [...] I would maintain that in this country such an institution cannot be really authoritarian; with ingenuity and a little luck a creative person can persuade (or fool) at least some of the administrators some of the time.[20]

The distinction here seems to be between the more routine writing which he is required to do as part of his job and the more creative, enjoyable work which it is also possible to do alongside. MacNeice was employed as a scriptwriter for the Features Department to write and produce, ostensibly, feature programmes, yet much of the work he subsequently created may be more adequately described as radio plays. MacNeice also describes the radio writer and producer's task as 'a matter of craftsmanship', noting how rare it is for a band of creative writers (playwrights excluded) to be concerned with matters of performance.[21] Despite this emergent respect for the medium and its artistic possibilities, MacNeice identified an inherent tension in writing creative works for radio which simply did not exist for him when writing as a poet and which may been a contributing factor in his occasionally expressed sense of frustration with the medium:

> All the arts, to varying degrees, involve some kind of a compromise. This being so, how far need the radio dramatist go to meet the public without losing sight of himself and his own standards of value? He obviously cannot aspire to the freedom of lyric poetry written for the page; he must work to the limitations [...] imposed both by medium and audience.[22]

MacNeice, at the time of writing this essay, was also in the process of learning how to work skilfully within these bounds to produce radio plays of exceptional quality.

---

[19] MacNeice 1947b, 11. Rodger 1982, 5–8 discusses the intellectual bias against the medium and radio drama in particular.
[20] MacNeice 1947b, 13–14. In a note following the essay from which this quotation is taken, he says that since the Third Programme came into being in 1946 'there is less question than ever of playing "for safety and to the gallery"' (ibid. 17).
[21] Ibid. 14 and 15.   [22] MacNeice 1944, 10.

5.2. THE MARCH OF THE 10,000, THE GLORY THAT IS GREECE, AND PERICLES

During the war many writers and scholars had been employed by the BBC to lend their talents to the creation of propagandist, or morale-boosting, feature programmes. Writing after the war of this propaganda work, MacNeice notes that he considered the work to have been 'necessary' and that he did it 'as well—and that also means as truthfully—as I could'.[23] In wartime, the BBC was responsible for delivering to listeners at home and overseas entertainment as well as information and propaganda. The wartime policy for drama and features was (as discussed in Section 2.1) 'to supply first a "contribution to the preservation of civilised culture in time of war" and second "implicit or explicit propagandistic contributions to national wartime activity"',[24] objectives which to some extent overlapped both in practice and ideology. The employment by MacNeice of canonical works deriving from ancient Greece in order to comment on the plight of modern Greece, for example, is especially interesting in light of the broadcast of such material across Europe during wartime, and such BBC broadcasts worked to counter similar mass media projects which were designed to sustain Fascist and Nazi ideologies. The BBC's cultural propaganda can, therefore, be understood as an active weapon in the 'war of words', garnering support for the Allied cause and boosting morale through an appeal to a shared European cultural tradition.

A typical offering along these lines was *Hellas*, a half-hour programme broadcast on the Home and Overseas Services on 25 March 1941 to mark the occasion of Greek Independence Day, honouring the day in 1821 when the Greeks began their revolt against the Ottoman Empire; it was also used for the Ministry of Information's Transcription Scheme.[25] It was written and produced by Denis Johnston (1901–84) and it included a little from Homer, Pausanias, and Aristophanes' *Frogs* alongside modern authors such as Byron, Shelley, and Wilde; it was preceded earlier in the evening by a 'commemorative' musical programme, including Granville Bantock's *Sappho*.[26] The evening's

---

[23] MacNeice 1947c, 28.
[24] Internal BBC memo, quoted by Briggs 1970, 113.
[25] Memo from E. M. Haynes to Denis Johnston, 25 March 1941 (R19/457).
[26] *Radio Times*, 21 March 1941, 14.

entertainment strove to 'paint a picture of Greece as seen through the eyes of some of the many British writers who have visited and loved her', yet the illustration of the *Radio Times* listing with a photograph of a soldier 'in the full-dress uniform of the Evzones, the crack Greek regiment which has led the heroic advance against the Italians in Albania', ensured that the listener did not fail to recall the current plight of Greece.[27]

The following year, MacNeice's *Salute to Greece* was broadcast on the Home Service and (as *Salutation to Greece*) on several overseas services to mark Greek independence. This propagandistic feature highlights the suffering of Greeks at the hands of the Axis forces: the Greeks are starving and desperate—one old man pushes a decrepit pram which holds the corpse of a child who died from starvation—yet some have the strength to engage in acts of resistance, pulling down the swastika flag from the Parthenon, stealing a lorry of German Army petrol, and printing a secret newspaper. When the Germans come to take away the young Greek character Yannis, he declares that 'My death will become a voice, one of the many voices they cannot silence [. . .] another voice for freedom'. It concludes with 'Long Live Greece' spoken in English and Greek, and the Greek national anthem.

Another of MacNeice's early scripts for the BBC Features Department was *The March of the 10,000*, a fifteen-minute version of Xenophon's *Anabasis* which was broadcast on the Overseas Service in mid-April 1941 during the Axis invasion of Greece. This was among the first in a series of feature programmes by MacNeice which were sympathetic to the plight of Greece and which used aspects of Greek military history to shore up popular support for the plight of Greece in the Second World War. MacNeice is said to have written the script in March of that year when Greece was under attack by Italy.[28] This failed invasion is considered to be the first Allied land victory of the war; on 6 April, however, Germany invaded Greece on another front, overwhelming Greek and British Commonwealth forces. A week or two later—on 16, 17, and 18 April—*The March of the 10,000* was transmitted on the Eastern,

---

[27] 'Billing', 7 March 1941, typescript in R19/457; *Radio Times*, 21 March 1941, 13.
[28] Coulton 1980, 48 notes that MacNeice wrote the script in the dining-room of Ernest Stahl's flat in Oriel Square, Oxford. Stahl (1902–92) was then a lecturer in German at the University; he and MacNeice had both been at Birmingham in the 1930s.

Pacific, and North American Services. Athens fell on 27 April and the rest of Greece by the beginning of June. The shift in the political situation of Greece between the time of writing and the time of broadcast means that the feature can be interpreted both as a stirring paean to the courage and resilience of Greece in repelling the Italian invaders and also as a poignant metaphor for the long period of occupation that may lie ahead.

That this feature was broadcast on overseas services and not broadcast at home suggests that it may well have been intended to serve as vigorous international propaganda for the perilous situation of Greece. The following exchange between characters described as 'Common Soldiers' clearly illustrates this focus:

C.S. 2 I'm getting back to Greece. This sort of place is no good to me. We come from a free country and nothing else is good enough for me.
C.S. 3 What freedom is there in Greece?
C.S. 2 I'll tell you what freedom there is—freedom to say what you like and live the way you want to—that's what there is in Greece, and that's what I want.
C.S. 1 You're right, mate. And no bullying Great King is going to talk me out of getting back to Greece. (p. 6)[29]

Here Persian 'dictatorship' is allied with the might of the Axis forces and the Great King with Hitler or Mussolini. Freedom and also democracy (name-checked by a character named The Lady) are lauded and the piece becomes a British hymn to modern Greece, an effective piece of Anglo-Hellenic relationship-building (as *The Glory that is Greece* would be in October).

The action is set entirely in the ancient world: the ten thousand of the title are the Greek mercenaries who find themselves far from home in Mesopotamia, in the Persian Empire, and their 'march' is their long journey home via Mount Theches, where they catch sight of the sea and utter their famous shout '*Thalatta! Thalatta!*' ('The sea! The sea!'). The story is told in the *Anabasis* written by the Greek historian and philosopher Xenophon, who, as one of the generals in that very army, helped to lead the Greeks back home. MacNeice's

---

[29] Page references are to the copy of the script available in BBC WAC SL. This feature is not listed in the *Radio Times* (which did not cover overseas transmissions), nor does any information on it, beyond the existence of the script, seem to exist in the BBC WAC.

feature ends on the ecstatic note achieved when the Greeks glimpse the sea for the first time, but the march, and the *Anabasis*, did not end on this high: the army eventually returned to Greece but on crossing the Bosporus they found political uncertainty and isolation. MacNeice was not the first, nor the last, to focus attention in his re-telling on the high point of the Greeks' long march home: from the nineteenth century writers have drawn on the *Anabasis* as an archetypal adventure story, with the famous cry of '*Thalatta! Thalatta!*' being the moment of reward for the adventurers' endurance and courage.[30]

In *The March of the 10,000* MacNeice uses what would become the familiar technique of narration interspersed with dramatic flashbacks which take the audience into various pertinent points of an ancient story. Strikingly, perhaps, for a feature drawing on the male-dominated military history of Greece, the narrator figure here is a woman, a flute-girl who was the former girlfriend of the Spartan general Clearchus. Her narration emphasizes the often unvoiced female perspective in much ancient Greek literature and her chatty and colloquial speech provides an interesting and accessible framework for the dramatic portions in this ancient narrative:

> THE LADY   We had a good meal that night and lots of that palm-date wine—we all had heads the next morning. That very morning Clearchus and our other generals [...] went round to this Persian's tent for a conference. They went into that tent and they never came out again. I missed Clearchus—you don't meet men like that nowadays. A real brute but he knew his stuff.
>
> Well, there we were—in the back of beyond and without any generals. You can say what you like about us Greeks but we don't give up a thing easy, never have, never will. (p. 6)

The character of The Lady foreshadows the central importance that the female voice would have in MacNeice's later radio features: in *The Glory that is Greece*, for example, we hear the contrasting thoughts of modern-day Italian and Greek women; the character of Aristophanes

---

[30] Rood 2004 is an eloquent account of a wide range of fascinating engagements, in novels, film, and newspaper editorials, with the famous shout uttered by the Greeks in Xenophon's *Anabasis*. His account of *The March of the 10,000* is well worth reading: for example, he perceptively notes that the Greeks' arrival at the sea in this radio feature offers a potent echo of the retreat of the British Expeditionary Force to Dunkirk the previous year. Rood also catalogues moments in MacNeice's other writings and poetry which evoke Xenophon (see, for example, 168–9 and 175–6).

converses with his lover Sepia and his slave Thratta in *Enemy of Cant*; and the protagonist's wife in *Carpe Diem* has a central, supportive dramatic role. Perhaps because of the nature of the ancient material with which MacNeice was working, female characters are more often than not cast in subsidiary and supportive roles, but their voices usually carry energetic political purpose.

The Glory that is Greece was broadcast, both on the Home Service and on the North American Service (under the title *Greece Lives*), a few months later on 28 October 1941, which was the first anniversary of the Greek dictator Ioannis Metaxas's emphatic 'No!' to Mussolini, upon which began the Greek defence against the Fascist invasion on the Albanian front, leading to a land victory and invasion of Albania.[31] By the time of this broadcast, Greece was suffering many hardships. The *Radio Times* listing for the production, which describes it as a 'programme to celebrate the spirit of the Greek Army and the Greek people on the first anniversary of the entry of Greece into the war', further emphasizes the thrust of the programme to potential listeners: 'Louis MacNeice, through the mouths of Greek soldiers of today, and through those of the Greek soldiers who held Thermopylae against the Persians, has drawn a picture of this spirit and what it has meant to Greece. [...] Such a spirit still prevails among a people who have for the time being lost their independence only in name to Hitler's panzer divisions.'[32]

The Glory that is Greece is presented entirely as a play, moving back and forth between ancient and modern military history, opening with an Italian family talking about Greece and listening to the words of Mussolini broadcast on a loudspeaker ('We shall enter Greece and we shall conquer. *Noi vinceremo! Vinceremo!*', p. 3). The action then shifts to Greece, with a blast of the Greek national anthem heralding Metaxas's stirring words: 'The moment has come to fight for the independence of Greece ... to fight for our honour as a nation. Cheers. It is up to us to prove ourselves worthy of our ancestors,

---

[31] It is still today known as *ochi* day ('no' day) in Greece. The title recalls J. C. Stobart's 1911 book *The Glory that was Greece: A Survey of Hellenic Culture and Civilisation*. Stobart was the BBC's first Director of Education who worked for the Corporation until his death in 1933.
[32] *Radio Times*, 24 October 1941, 10–11. Hitler's *Panzerdivisionen* were self-contained units of several hundred tanks and other military forces which were set up to function as an independent army.

worthy of the liberty our forefathers won for us' (pp. 3-4).[33] But Metaxas's own tendency towards fascistic control of society is briefly touched on by a Greek couple next heard in conversation:

STAVROS   Maria, you know I've always been against Metaxas. He sent my best friends to prison. He banned the publication of my pamphlets. Nevertheless...
MARIA   Nevertheless?
STAVROS   Nevertheless I support him now... The whole nation will rise as one man! He's damn right it will. *Nun luper* [sic] *panton agon*.
MARIA   *Nun luper* [sic] *panton*... The final struggle. Who was it said that?
STAVROS   You should know. The poet Aeschylus... over two thousand years ago. He put it into the mouths of our ancestors... when they went in to the kill at the battle of Salamis.
MARIA   Salamis? Yes.
STAVROS   'Sons of Greece, go to it. Free your country, free your wives and children, the temples of your gods and the tombs of your fathers. *Nun nuper* [sic] *panton agon*'.[34] (p. 4)

Here, this quotation from Aeschylus' *Persians* 402-5 foreshadows the political thrust of the feature, for later in the play, when telling his fellow fighters about the wars of the ancient Greeks ('College or no college, a Greek should know his history', p. 7), the character Stavros suggests an equivalence between Italian expansionism of 1940-1 and the Persian Wars of 490 and 480-479 BC: 'The set-up's much the same. The bloated tyrant who thinks he can walk in and take us. They get the idea that Greece is easy pickings. Musso thinks so now. Darius thought so then. So did Xerxes' (p. 8).[35] The suggested equivalence is

---

[33] Page numbers refer to the copy of the script in the BBC WAC SL. The original typescript of a longer, unannotated version exists in R19/456; the fact that it is longer (36 pages to 31) and without any handwritten changes suggests that it was an earlier draft. It is, however, possible that the shorter SL script (despite being titled *The Glory that is Greece*) may have been the 30-minute version broadcast on the North American Service under the title *Greece Lives* and the longer typescript version may have been (perhaps an early version of?) the Home Service broadcast, but there is no evidence to support this suggestion.

[34] The words '*puper*', '*luper*', and '*nuper*' in the script (for '*huper*', the transliteration of the ancient Greek *hyper*) are likely to be typing errors.

[35] Van Steen 2007, 137 and 127-8 demonstrates how this quotation 'was enlisted to fulfil specific military or propagandistic purposes by parties ranging from the reactionary Right to left-wing partisans' in twentieth-century Greece, including via a popular 1940s 'resistance hit' as first sung by Sophia Vembo in the revue *La bella Grecia*. See also Van Steen's introduction to *The Glory that is Greece* in Wrigley and Harrison 2013.

reinforced with a flashback scene which introduces the ancient figures of Xerxes and Mardonius discussing the invasion of Greece (with the line 'Hail, O King! Hail! Hail! Hail!' (p. 8), delivered by multiple voices, being evocative of mass chanting of the Nazi salute). Stavros reads a report of a message from Winston Churchill to Metaxas in a newspaper which ends 'This recalls the classic age' (p. 17), serving as a re-entry into the ancient world and the Battle of Thermopylae, with dialogue between Xerxes and a Persian scout who had observed the Spartans exercising and combing their hair (Herodotus 7. 209). Cutting back to the present, we hear how Stavros fears the strength of Germany, telling his friend Kosta about the Battle of Thermopylae and warning him that 'We must be prepared for another Thermopylae. Another apparent defeat' (p. 22). The play ends with the women at home reiterating this theme:

MARIA   We are still in the stage of Thermopylae.
ANGELICE But some day we shall have a Salamis. (p. 28)

This follows some explicit Anglo-Greek friendliness:

VOICE OF GREEKS   Goodbye, Tommies, goodbye... Good luck.
VOICE OF BRITISH SOLDIERS Goodbye and good luck yourselves.
GREEKS   Come back soon.
BRITISH   We'll come back.
GREEKS   Send over your bombers. Don't mind us.
                         Bomb the Axis out of Greece. (p. 27)

In this series of wartime pro-Greece feature programmes MacNeice drew on ancient Greek military history to shore up popular support for the plight of Greece in the Second World War. Given the nature of these broadcasts there is not a great deal of evidence for how listeners responded to them but there are occasional glimpses in the archives. Writing two years later with modern Greek poetry suggestions for *Greece Fights On*, MacNeice's 25 March 1943 programme to mark Greek Independence Day, an unnamed person wrote to him as follows:

> This anniversary means so much to a Greek that only a poet like you can do the occasion justice. How grateful I am when I remember the beautiful and inspiring pathos, the richness, the mobility and that moving restraint of your the *Glory that is Greece*.[36]

---

[36] Letter from an unnamed writer to LM, 25 February 1943 (R19/457).

Greece Fights On was billed as 'A programme in homage to the Greek people who in spite of the terrible sufferings inflicted on them by the Axis still continue the fight—both at home and overseas as units in the forces of the United Nations'.[37] In this programme the Greek characters hark back to past glories, calling up the memory of the Sacred Bands of ancient Thebes and of the 1821 revolution, and quoting from Aeschylus, but it is bang up-to-date: the character of a classics professor, suspected of lecturing on 'The malignant growth of Fascism' and 'Nazi racial theory', is executed.[38] The Listener Research Report for *Long Live Greece* (as the Home Service broadcast of *Greece Fights On* was titled[39]) was extremely positive: the broadcast aroused strong sympathy and admiration for the 'steadfast and indestructible Greeks'. One listener offered the following spontaneous tribute: 'This was a beautifully written and acted programme. Its poignancy was sincere, unforced, terribly natural. One could not enjoy such a play—it was too real, but one was absorbed entirely.'[40]

MacNeice's wartime use of ideals of ancient Greek freedom and democracy was developed further in a programme entitled *Pericles*, the first of six fifteen-minute programmes in *The Four Freedoms* series which was broadcast on the Home Service on Sunday evenings in February and March 1943, immediately before the 9 o'clock news. All six programmes—*Pericles, The Early Christians*,[41] *The Renaissance, John Milton*,[42] *The French Revolution*, and *What Now?*—were written by MacNeice and all were produced by him except for *The Renaissance*, which was produced by Walter Rilla (1894–1980), a prominent actor of partial Jewish descent who moved his family

---

[37] Memo from LM to several recipients, 16 February 1943 (ibid.).

[38] In January 1944, MacNeice wrote and produced *The Sacred Band*, billed as 'a tribute to fighting Greece' which used dramatization and earlier models of 'the sacred band' active during the Greek War of Independence in 1821 and in Thebes of the fourth century BC to laud the Greek commando unit currently fighting in North Africa.

[39] *Greece Fights On*, overseas services, 22–6 March 1941; a slightly different version of the script, performed by the same actors, went out on the Home, 25 March 1943.

[40] BBC WAC LR/1647 (R19/457).

[41] The first scene of *The Early Christians* was once again Athens, but five hundred years or so after the death of Pericles. MacNeice's intention here was to use early Christianity (which, he considers, first took root 'in the oppressed and unprivileged sections of society') as a contrast to Periclean Athens, 'a "democracy" founded on slave labour' (LM, 'Freedoms Programmes' typescript, p. 1, in R19/393).

[42] MacNeice considered Milton to be 'one of our greatest Puritans, who—paradoxically—made the finest defence in our language of the freedom of the press' (memo from LM to the Editor of the *Radio Times* et al., 1 March 1943, ibid.).

from Berlin to London when Hitler came to power in 1934.[43] MacNeice's early plan had been also to include a programme focused on Lenin, stressing 'his hatred of suffering' and discussing the idea of 'Freedom from Want'.[44] All other programme ideas for the series were given the green light, but after consulting with 'the Board', Laurence Gilliam of the Features Department decreed that 'Lenin is out', presumably for being too politically controversial.[45]

MacNeice had a clear idea of how these various kinds of freedom should be presented:

> My suggestion is that none of these subjects should be whitewashed and that it should be made clear implicitly in the separate programmes and explicitly in the concluding one, that the theory and practice of particular kinds of freedom in each case were conditioned by circumstances and so inevitably limited. On the other hand, each programme should attempt to crystalise in as hard and clear a form as possible the essential and permanent value of whatever species of freedom was the concern of its protagonists. This will be made easier by a vivid presentation in each case of the particular enemies at the time concerned of the particular freedom that was being fought for.[46]

He considered that fifth-century Athens was 'a sitting target because of the beautifully clear-cut contrast between the Free-City-State Athens and the Totalitarian-City-State Sparta'—ideas which made it into the billing for *The Early Christians* in the *Radio Times*.[47] MacNeice wanted to show Pericles as the leader of people whose 'characteristics were free thinking, free argument, cultural experiment and tolerance'.[48] As we shall see, he was not, however, blind to the fact that in some important respects ancient Athens could not possibly be considered a haven of freedom in all senses.

In *Pericles*, which featured music by Britten, MacNeice draws on speeches allegedly spoken by the Athenian statesman Pericles (*c*.495–429 BC) as reported by the fifth-century Athenian historian Thucydides

---

[43] This follows the billing in the *Radio Times*; Rilla had earlier been on track to produce three programmes (memo from Olive Harding to LM, 22 February 1943, ibid.).
[44] Memo from LM to LG, 28 December 1942 (ibid.).
[45] Memo from LG to LM, 15 January 1943 (ibid.).
[46] LM, 'Freedoms Programmes' typescript, p. 1 (ibid.).
[47] Ibid.; *Radio Times*, 26 February 1943, 6.
[48] LM, 'Freedoms Programmes' typescript, p. 1 (in R19/393).

in his *History of the Peloponnesian War*.[49] At the start of the play the Compere suggests that ancient Athens may not have been so dissimilar from the modern world (from the British/Allied perspective, at least): 'If you went back there you'd find it all very strange... Would you?' (p. 1).[50] MacNeice lays emphasis on this question by immediately introducing Xenos, one of the central characters (whose name means 'guest', 'stranger', or 'foreigner' in ancient Greek), who wonders whether he should perhaps call himself a refugee since he intends to stay in Athens, if permitted. Xenos declares that he is out of sympathy with his own country: 'I am by nature a democrat. Where I come from I couldn't lead my own life. I couldn't even raise my voice. There was no such thing as free speech' (p. 1). In lines that were struck out of the script by hand (indicating that they were probably not spoken in the programme), the Citizen says that Athenians consider that 'if [refugees] come here, they come for some very good reason' (p. 1), lines which would have had great potency in wartime Britain with its not insignificant number of refugees from other European countries. The time is shortly before the outbreak of the Peloponnesian War in 431 BC, of which the Citizen says: 'It's been coming on us for years. What can you expect when you have two Powers so strong and so different in outlook? Why, all our interests conflict. Here we have a democracy; over there—well, you know what they have. A regime of blood and blindness. They want war anyway. And a very odd war it will be. They're a land-power, we're a sea-power' (p. 2). The Home Service audience would surely not have failed to pick up these strong resonances with the current (overwhelmingly naval) war in which Britain was engaged.

The Citizen takes Xenos to the Assembly to hear Pericles address the citizen body and the morale-boosting undercurrents of continuing resistance of the Axis powers are strong: 'We must never yield to Sparta nor to her satellites. [...] If you yield to them now on a matter however small, they will think that you are afraid. [...] Either we resist Sparta or we give up all that we value—we cease to be great, we cease to be free, and we cease to be Athens' (pp. 3-4). Yet, typical of MacNeice's honest approach to tricky concepts and topics (note his

---

[49] On Britten's conscientious objection see Section 6.1.

[50] Page references are to the annotated typescript in BBC WAC, Louis MacNeice Scripts, Box 1. This script has MacNeice's name written at the top in blue pencil, suggesting that it may have been his own copy.

desire not to 'whitewash', above), the Citizen follows with the self-reflective comment, which seems presciently to point to the limits of empire, that 'Maybe it's Athens herself that's getting too big. Too big for the rest of the world' (p. 4). MacNeice did not, at least in his first draft of this script, shy away from matters which were all too close to home: now the Spartans are gathering, preparing to invade, and the Athenians must evacuate the countryside and huddle within the city walls. Pericles declares that they must be prepared 'to give their lives for freedom' (p. 5), and the following scene is the public funeral for those who fell in the first year of the war, the setting for Pericles' famous Funeral Oration.

The suggested polarity between democratic Athens and 'totalitarian' Sparta—drawn more in terms of Athens' democracy than Sparta's 'totalitarianism'—admits *no* discussion of the nature of ancient Greek democracy, and how it falls short—in terms of inequalities with regard to, for example, women and slaves—of the modern concept. That this is laid bare in *Pericles* and—as we shall see—discussed openly by characters in the sixth programme in *The Four Freedoms* series indicates MacNeice's typically serious attempt to avoid 'whitewashing' problematic concepts, but, as Golphin has eloquently argued, it may also suggest MacNeice's literary response to perceived weaknesses of British democracy, a democracy in which the public had not been able to vote for eight years.[51]

In *What Now?*, the concluding part of the series, which was broadcast on 28 March, four 'real-life' characters discuss their reactions to the previous five programmes. The characters include a Mr Higgs, who remembered the First World War, his neighbour Miss Emmet (whose name was changed by hand to Evelyn on the script), who had served as a nurse in that war, her brother Robert, and the 'foreign gentleman' Dr Halden, a German refugee who had spent time in three internment camps (p. 1).[52] Their conversation implicitly and explicitly critiques the earlier notions of freedom presented in the series and touches on more modern-day concerns. Evelyn states that one 'definite gain' of the 1914–18 war was the 'emancipation of women' (p. 2). Higgs is shocked and, when he goes to answer the

---

[51] Golphin 2012, ch. 5.
[52] Page references are to the annotated typescript in BBC WAC, Louis MacNeice Scripts, Box 1. The fact that it has MacNeice's name written at the top suggests that it was his own copy.

door, she says: 'Poor Mr Higgs, he's quite flabbergasted. "One of them there blinking suffragettes!" Well, I'm proud that I was. The good old WSPU![53] In Nineteen Twelve I thought it was the only cause in the world' (p. 2).

Robert arrives and tinkers with the broken wireless set so that they can listen to the last programme in *The Four Freedoms* series (in which, complicatedly, they are the characters—a neat bit of writing on MacNeice's part which, of course, comes over perfectly understandably on radio). Meanwhile, they talk. 'All very nice and simplified', is how Robert remembers the Periclean Athens programme: 'You heard a great deal about Free Speech and you heard old Pericles himself saying his bit from Thucydides [...] But they didn't point out the snags in Athenian democracy—slave-labour at home and imperialism abroad. The BBC just left that out of the picture. [...] I think they're afraid that, if they put in the shadows, their public will get all confused. Why, take our own democracy—' (pp. 3–4).

Following this clever critique of his own series by a fictional listener who thereby demonstrates his capacity for free thinking, MacNeice offers a philosophical discussion between Evelyn, Robert, and Dr Halden on the nature(s) of freedom whilst Mr Higgs takes apart the wireless in the hope of fixing it. The fuse blows, leaving them in darkness. Evelyn recites lines from A. E. Housman's 'The Laws of God, the Laws of Man' (*Last Poems* XII) and Dr Halden extols the freedoms that can be achieved through internationalism ('You know why Goethe was a great German?', he asks. Because he was 'more than German. Because he was international', p. 7) and the powers of the heart and mind. Having missed the broadcast of the last programme in the series, the group settle down to the news, which, they note, 'these days [...] has to do with freedom', and some 'great music' which 'makes you believe [...] in humanity' (p. 8). The programme ends with Evelyn's recitation of some poetry which begins with Housman's line 'I, a stranger and afraid', discusses the uncertainty of life, eulogizes the 'great and good [...] brave and true', and ends by equating freedom with human rights (pp. 8–9). As Golphin notes, this programme presents 'an interesting tonal contrast' with MacNeice's earlier, more uncompromising propaganda pieces; yet the Listener Research Report for *What Now?* records the

---

[53] The Women's Social and Political Union was the leading organization campaigning for women's suffrage.

general unpopularity of the series.[54] The programme which had been heard by the largest audience and appreciated the most had been *Pericles*, while the conversational *What Now?* was the least popular amongst those who responded to the questionnaire: 'listeners could not discern what it was driving at, and found little connection between it and earlier broadcasts'.[55]

Certainly, the complications introduced by *What Now?*, both in terms of the subject matter and the narrative, may have been more challenging for the broad, national audience than some of the propaganda talks and dramatizations offered by the BBC in wartime. MacNeice wrote over seventy scripts for radio over the course of the war, and one or two more creative works such as *Christopher Columbus*, the first of his radio writings which can properly be considered to be a radio play.[56] This piece was commissioned in 1942 to celebrate the 450th anniversary of Columbus's 'discovery' of America but also, of course, to acknowledge the United States' recent entry into the war. Towards the end of the war there is a notable shift in the nature of MacNeice's radio output, from current affairs and propaganda items to creative works which made a significant contribution to the still developing form of radio drama. These included the study of Chekhov, *Sunbeams in his Hat* (1944), the Russian folk story *The Nosebag* (1944), and two related plays, broadcast in November 1944, which derived their stories from the second-century BC Roman writer Apuleius (whose *Golden Ass or Metamorphoses* was one of MacNeice's 'sacred books' at Marlborough).[57] These Apuleian adaptations mark a new chapter in MacNeice's radio writing—a turn to Roman comic themes which drew on his earlier academic research for his book on humour in Latin literature and which continued with *A Roman Holiday* (1945) and *Trimalchio's Feast* (1948).

Around this time MacNeice continued his collaboration with the pioneer producer of film, television, and radio Dallas Bower, with whom he had worked on the radio productions *Alexander Nevsky* (1941) and *Christopher Columbus* (1942).[58] Together they wrote an

---

[54] Golphin 2012 discusses *What Now?* at length.
[55] BBC WAC LR/1662 (in R19/393).
[56] Holme 1981, 39.   [57] MacNeice 1965, 98.
[58] I am very grateful to Tony Keen for his excellent, unpublished assessment of *Pax Futura* which is drawn on here. Keen dates the piece as follows: 'Internal evidence indicates that the script must have been written in late 1944 or possibly early 1945' (source: personal correspondence). It is subtitled 'A film fantasy on the future of

unrealized film script titled *Pax Futura*, set in a peaceful world in 1995 which—as in H. G. Wells's film *Things to Come*—is dominated by air travel. This thriller concerns a terrorist plot to kill the leader of the peace movement and destroy world peace. The use of a Latin title and classical names for the characters (Galba, Flavius, and Xanthias, with the beautiful heroine Helen recalling Helen of Troy) hint at the superficial level of classical association in this science fiction piece, although the use of a Roman fort in the final scene and the phrase Pax Aeria, which recalls the Pax Romana (the long period of relative peace in the Roman Empire from 27 BC to 180 AD), suggest the potential for a closer engagement with antiquity which—had the project progressed—may have been developed in a later draft.

In January 1946 one of MacNeice's most acclaimed works for radio, *The Dark Tower*, was first broadcast. This 'radio parable play' features a quest reminiscent of Odysseus's long journey home from the Trojan War but also has echoes of the Telemachy, the first four books of the *Odyssey* in which Odysseus's son Telemachus goes off on his own search for news of his father.[59] The protagonist of *The Dark Tower* is the young Roland, a reluctant hero sent off by his mother on a quest which he does not comprehend and does not take up readily, his father and brothers having before him set out on the same quest never to return.[60] This play, written and produced at the end of the Second World War, offers much food for thought on notions of authority, duty, and free will whilst also attempting to do 'justice to the world's complexity': 'I have my beliefs and they permeate *The Dark Tower*. But do not ask me what Ism it illustrates or what Solution it offers. You do not normally ask for such things in the single-plane work; why should they be forced upon something much more complex?'[61]

On 29 October 1946, MacNeice's 1936 translation of *Agamemnon* was produced on the Third Programme as was, three months later, his *Enemy of Cant*. As discussed in Section 8.1, *Enemy of Cant* offers fresh translations of substantial extracts from eight of Aristophanes'

---

aviation' (page 1 of the photocopy of the first draft of the *Pax Futura* typescript in box 54, Louis MacNeice Papers, Bodleian Library).

[59] The description is from MacNeice 1947b, 19. For a good evaluation of the play, see Holme 1981, 58–61.

[60] Rodger 1982, 79 considers that Roland 'is tempted like Ulysses by Neaera'.

[61] MacNeice 1947b, 21 and 22.

comedies which emerge from the 'real-life' situation of the playwright as he, over the years, converses about contemporary affairs with characters such as his lover, his slave, mask-makers, and fellow playwrights. The context is therefore made integral to the plays rather than standing apart from it, as it often did in BBC Drama Department productions in the form of a preparatory lecture, introductory talk, or advance *Radio Times* articles. The response from the listeners suggests that MacNeice was largely successful in his aim to 'to introduce Aristophanes to a public which can perfectly well appreciate him once he is divorced from pedantry'.[62]

In 1950–1 MacNeice was given leave of absence from his position at the BBC to take up an eighteen-month directorship of the British Institute in Athens.[63] One of the outcomes of his time there were several radio features, including one on Delphi and another named *Portrait of Athens*, a companion piece to his programme on Rome broadcast a couple of years earlier. The feature, which went out on the Home Service in November 1951, was introduced by MacNeice, who set out his approach as follows:

> In writing *A Portrait of Athens* I have attempted—rather impressionistically—to give a panorama of its present. But I have also brought in its past because I sincerely think that there is a continuity. [...] there are also social and political factors which seem to me to recur. Athenian democracy—and Athenian imperialism—flourished in the fifth century B.C. but through most of ancient history Athens was neither imperial nor democratic. And in the Christian era she was for long a mere provincial town first in the Roman and then in the Byzantine Empire, after which she was a vassal first of Western adventurers [...] and then of the Turks. After the liberation of Greece she became the capital of a kingdom that was too small to support itself.[64]

The feature begins, 'So this is Athens. A nagging bell and a glaring sky. A box on the ear. A smack in the eye. Crude as a poster. Hard as nails. Yes, this is Athens—not what I expected.'[65] Through word and sound he paints a picture which contrasts glaringly with imagined ideals of ancient Athens, but he brings in the character of Socrates

---

[62] Memo from LM to LG, 12 July 1946 (R19/307).
[63] See Andrews 1974 for thoughts on MacNeice's time in Athens (during which the Institute merged with the British Council: Coulton 1980, 115).
[64] LM, 'Introduction to *Portrait of Athens*' (typescript in R19/947).
[65] A recording is available via the BLSA.

himself who notes that surface appearances can be deceptive (which echoes the sentiments from 'Autumn Journal' discussed in the Conclusion).[66]

In these various ways MacNeice's educational background in literary classics and interest in modern as well as ancient Greek societies combined with his skill as a writer and his talent for exploring radio's potential for creative work to result in programmes which not only made the ancient world imaginatively accessible to the huge, non-specialist audience but could also at the same time (and increasingly, it seems, throughout his radio career) work to turn certain assumptions about classics (inaccessible, to be revered) and ancient Greece specifically (the 'paragons' of his 'Autumn Journal') on their head.

[66] On the poetic inspiration MacNeice found in Greece, see Coulton 1980, 118 ff.

6

The Poetry and Drama of Homeric Epic, 1943–1969

Homer's epic poems have been a rich source of material for radio presentation. These works, which were orally composed for performance around the eighth century BC, offer much that is worth re-telling, including many intrinsically 'dramatic' episodes; furthermore, a large proportion of each poem is delivered in direct speech which makes the task of adapting them for radio performance fairly straight forward.[1] As the radio producer Beaty Rubens has put it, 'if mime is the least suited to radio of all art forms, then oral poetry must be the best. So Homer's *Odyssey* makes an ideal basis for creative radio.'[2]

Because of their length, no attempt seems to have been made to deliver the Homeric poems on radio in anything approaching their entirety.[3] The epics are cut, adapted, and often 'radio dramatized', meaning that certain dramatic aspects are teased out and developed in interesting ways, with the text delivered by different actors playing the various characters, rather than one performer taking the responsibility of delivering all. There does, nonetheless, seem to be something of an affinity between the radio actor and the ancient performer of Homeric epic: both must capture and hold the imagination of the audience in the telling of an event or story which is not itself physically enacted or visually illustrated. (Although the radio actor is, of

---

[1] Approximately 45 per cent of the *Iliad* and 67 per cent of the *Odyssey* (figures from Schmid and Stählin 1929, 92 quoted by Griffin 2004, 156). On conversation in Homer see Beck 2005.
[2] Rubens 1989, 25. Graziosi and Greenwood 2007 offers a rich range of essays on (especially literary) engagements with Homer in the twentieth century; see Hall 2008*b* on re-tellings of the *Odyssey*.
[3] The *Iliad* is around 15,600 lines long, and the *Odyssey* 12,000.

course, prevented from using powerful aspects of his or her physicality which the ancient, unmasked performer may have utilized—for example, facial expression, eye contact, and gesture.[4]) Crucially, however, in both cases the action is realized in the imagination of the listener. Furthermore, music is often vital to radio productions of the Homeric epics (as we shall see, for example, with regard to *The Rescue* in the next section), just as it was important in their ancient performances.

Given the concern in the early years of broadcasting that the medium should function as a channel for the nation's cultural heritage, a concern which seems to have resulted in a fidelity to original performance forms, it is not surprising that early radio programmes drawing on Homer seem to have been delivered *as* oral poetry, in one voice, as if the listener were seated before a rhapsode. In the first years of broadcasting, then, we find that extracts from the epics were often delivered as part of poetry series. Early in 1928 a half-hour programme entitled 'Epic Poetry: the *Iliad* and the *Odyssey*' was given as part of a series on narrative poetry produced by J. C. Stobart and Mary Somerville (1897–1963) of the BBC Education Department for broadcast to schools on Wednesday afternoons.[5] The following week this *Stories in Poetry* series turned to Virgil's *Aeneid* and subsequent programmes covered Chaucer, Spenser's *The Faerie Queene*, Milton's *Paradise Lost*, and Victorian poetry. Programmes for schools such as this were 'designed to help teachers to illustrate their lessons and to give the school children a few sweets in addition to the meat of the school syllabus'; referring specifically to *Stories in Poetry*, the same writer continues, 'although these lectures are designed for children, adults listen to them with great pleasure'.[6]

Five years later, from January 1933, the London Regional network offered the *Readings from Classical Literature* series at tea-time on Sundays. The purpose of this series of half-hour programmes was 'to review the whole field of classical literature from the Greeks to the present day [. . .] passing from Greece and Rome to the Renaissance

---

[4] Nagy 1992, 24 and 25 states that the term oral poetry to describe Homeric epic 'may not fully capture the concept behind it', reminding the reader of 'the centrality of *performance* to the concept of oral poetry' (original emphasis).

[5] Days before the Homeric programme was broadcast, Monteverdi's *The Return of Ulysses* was broadcast twice on 16 and 18 January. *Stories in Poetry* may have been a repeat or development of an identically titled series broadcast in 1924.

[6] Stranger 1928, 8–9.

and through the seventeenth and eighteenth centuries in England to our own time [. . .] for the greater part of this year, the Greeks will be our background'.[7] The series began, naturally, with Homer. The first and second episodes covered the death of Hector and recovery of his corpse by Priam from *Iliad* XXII and XXIV. Next was offered John Masefield's re-telling of the Trojan horse episode from his *A Tale of Troy*, published the previous year. Episode four covered Odysseus's meeting with Nausicaa—T. E. Lawrence's (1888–1935) translation of passages from *Odyssey* V and VI (published the previous year under his pseudonym T. E. Shaw). Alexander Pope's (1688–1744) translation of the parts of the *Odyssey* dealing with the Cyclops and the slaying of the suitors occupied the fifth and sixth episodes of the series. The seventh episode traced Homeric echoes in Marlowe, Shakespeare, Rupert Brooke, and Tennyson.

The first dramatization drawing on Homer that has come to light is *Beware the Gods*, a forty-minute play written especially for radio by George Dunning-Gribble in 1938. Little information about this early production is available, but the reviewer in *The Times* considered Barbara Burnham's production to be 'a well-contrived glib entertainment entirely lacking in subtlety' which told the story of the American millionaire Ulysses B. Tucker who gets away with smuggling an ancient statue of Poseidon out of Naples via his yacht, despite run-ins with Odyssean diversions such as the Sirens (who he thinks are 'on the wireless' or 'Movie girls from another yacht having a lark with him'). The review concludes that although this production has merit it does not prove the case that the radio play is a special genre.[8]

The case for radio drama as a form of writing and performance distinct from any other genre was made persuasively in 1943 by the première of Sackville-West and Britten's *The Rescue*, an enduring 'radio classic' that enjoyed a succession of new productions over some decades. The next section in this chapter discusses how their collaboration on this version of the *Odyssey* made a distinctive exploration of the dramatic potential of radio, and also examines how the close association of words and music suggest a reflective awareness of *The Rescue*'s relationship with ancient epic performance, especially through the character of the bard Phemius. Furthermore, the narrative resonated with the contemporary international situation and

---

[7] *Radio Times*, 13 January 1933, 73.
[8] Anon. 1938. See also Grenfell 1938.

makes a strong case for the humanizing potential of aesthetic experience. These interrelated aspects make *The Rescue* a particularly significant subject for study and its exceptional status as a thoughtful meditation on the relationship between ancient epic performance and radio as a dramatic and storytelling form has played a useful part in the thinking behind the argument in Section 3.2.

In 1949 Odysseus's arrival in Ithaca received another dramatic retelling when Mary Garrett's 'light satire' of the *Odyssey*, titled *Twenty Years is a Long Time*, was broadcast on the Home Service. In this four-act play, which the *Radio Times* described as 'a neatly and wittily disrespectful version',[9] the character Ulysses (not, in this play, Odysseus) finds his old domestic life dull after his long and adventurous journey home from the Trojan War and his family are equally unimpressed by the tales of his adventures: this hero '[bores] the family rather with his tales of the Cyclops and the sirens'.[10] The play opens with Telemachus visiting Menelaus to ask whether he has any news of his father. There are occasional close references to the *Iliad*, but the story is re-imagined and the tone everyday and colloquial. For example, Garrett's re-working of the Homeric simile of a doe making a nest for her newborn fawns in the lair of a lion, which is used by Menelaus to describe the suitors who may have taken up residence in Ulysses' palace but who will suffer grievously on his return (IV.335 ff.), is undercut by Telemachus' prosaic response:

MENELAUS   Thus, in the absence of a terrible lion, a thoughtless doe leaves her fawns in the den of the king of the forests? But the lion shall come back and tear the fawns in pieces! The whole brood shall be overtaken by a swift death!
TELEMACHUS (practical) Well, that's what I've been hoping... something of that sort, anyway. (p. 2)[11]

Garrett has Helen tell Telemachus that, unlike her husband Menelaus, she already knows about the suitors clamouring for Penelope's hand in marriage. Helen, described as 'the first great feminist', asks 'Has it never occurred to you, Telemachus, that your mother was probably terribly bored?' (p. 4). She wonders whether Penelope's nightly sorrow may have been for 'her lost youth, her wasted life' rather than her absent husband, suggesting that it may have been the

---

[9] S. Williams 1949.   [10] Anon. 1949.
[11] Page references are to the script for the 1949 production in the BBC WAC SL.

arrival of the suitors that 'brought her the first taste of life and excitement after many years of bleakness and boredom' (p. 5). The second act opens after the return of Ulysses and is full of domestic disillusionment. The great hero scoffs at the 'feast' Penelope has carefully prepared for him, rejecting their local goats' milk, and he misremembers how old Telemachus was when he left for war. The refrain, often repeated, is 'twenty years is a long time, after all' (p. 13). Penelope disabuses him of his belief that life remained comfortably the same for his family whilst he was away, lending support to Helen's view of the difficulties of her life in her husband's absence:

PENELOPE	[...] our whole way of life had to change considerably, you know.
ULYSSES	In what way?
PENELOPE	Well, everybody had to work, for one thing...
ULYSSES	By 'everybody' you mean...?
PENELOPE	(smiling) Just... everybody.
ULYSSES	But... you, for instance. You had plenty of slaves. You don't mean to say that you worked, for example?
PENELOPE	Of course I did. And Telemachus there did his three hours a day from the age of seven like everybody else's children. (pp. 15–16)

Penelope tells of how Telemachus has specialized in goat-breeding and she herself turned farmer, converting fields to wheat crops to save Ithacans from starvation (p. 16) and managing food rations for the entire population. She asks her husband whether, during his 'long camping holiday outside Troy', he ever considered 'the economic dislocation you had caused us at home here by your removal of the fleet? Merchant ships, naval ships and even most of the fishing-boats went along with you' (p. 17). She tells him that the number of war casualties at Troy was matched by the number of deaths at home 'from privation and fatigue and chills due to exposure' since Ulysses had taken so many crucial supplies with him. Ulysses is astonished, and not at all happy with many of the changes. As months pass, domestic disharmony increases: Penelope berates him for 'squandering everything' that they had so carefully built up in his absence and he accuses his son of being 'terribly insular', encouraging him to explore the world beyond this 'poor barren little place' (p. 22); Telemachus in turn questions why it took his father so long to return home, pointing to discrepancies in his account of why, for example, he stayed so long with Circe, pointedly asking 'how many illegitimate brothers have I got strewn about the Mediterranean?' (p. 24), and being devastated when Odysseus admits to 'one... as far as I know' (p. 25).

There's no doubt that this lighthearted radio play on the Odyssean theme is at points meant to raise a laugh but at many other moments the attempts of the war hero to assimilate into his old and not-so-familiar environment is painful for both him and his family, and it doubtless also struck a chord with the personal experience of many who had served both in battle and on the home front in the Second World War, which, of course, had ended just four years earlier. The playwright's sympathy, however, lies mainly with the family, especially Telemachus, whose 'coming of age' in this re-telling is emotionally distressing: 'What sort of father has he ever been to me? And what sort of a husband to my mother? All the years we needed him he stayed away amusing himself and now that he is tired he comes back to assert his rights' (p. 31). Penelope, too, is disappointed:

> PENELOPE (faltering) I've tried hard, Ulysses, honestly I have. After all my dreaming and longing... that it should turn out like this ... I'd never have believed that it could be so difficult... (desperate) I must say it now I have got so far... Ulysses, I want a legal separation. (p. 33)

Ulysses wonders whether she wants to marry another, but no, she says, 'I don't want a husband at all!' (p. 34). She manages his disappointment and disillusionment well and soon he announces publicly to friends and family that he must set off on another journey (neatly picking up Odysseus's hint of future travels at *Odyssey* XXIII. 248–53), breaking it to Telemachus that the time has come for him to become king. The ever-resourceful Ulysses comes up with a plan for the future: 'I shall start to build up a merchant marine and start shipping the produce of your fertile kingdom to all the isles of Greece' (p. 47). Garrett considered that her play was 'faithful to Homer' but also 'topical in that it takes the line of the prisoner of war isolated [...] + returning home long after all other ex-prisoners to a land where there has been a social + economic upheaval,—where all is strange to him,— + to which he cannot [ad]apt himself. This I make the explanation for his second departure.'[12]

---

[12] Letter from Mary Garrett to VG, 21 March 1948 (MG/S1). This was a shortened version of her stage play *Penelope was Perfect*, first performed at the Alexandra Theatre, Birmingham (memo from Lance Sieveking to 'H. D.', 15 March 1949 (MG/S1).

Dramatic retellings of the Homeric poems continued to be broadcast, as will be seen in Section 6.2 which focuses on a prize-winning dramatization of Robert Graves's *The Anger of Achilles* of 1965; in the late 1960s, too, Cavander introduced school-age listeners to both epic poems through his eleven twenty-minute dramatizations from Homer's *Iliad* and *Odyssey* for broadcast in the *Living Language* series of BBC Schools Radio.[13] (See Section 3.1 for a selection of comments from teachers on their pupils' responses to the programmes, which give a valuable, albeit second-hand, snapshot of how they were experienced.)

However, from the late 1950s, there was a concerted effort to broadcast the Homeric poems once again as poetry, but re-told afresh in the voice of contemporary poets. A hybrid form of radio Homer at this time is suggested by two works by the poet and playwright Patric Dickinson, who, like MacNeice, joined the BBC in wartime after an early, brief career as a prep-school teacher and then being invalided out of the war in 1940.[14] He achieved a great deal in his short, six-year career in radio, transforming the broadcasting of verse in his role as Poetry Editor for the Third and writing a number of acclaimed dramatic programmes which drew on the ancient world, including *The Wall of Troy* (1946) and the *Death of Hector* (1953).[15] On receiving an Atlantic Award for Literature in 1948 he resigned his post at the BBC but, as will be seen in Section 8.2, for many years he continued to do much work for the Corporation on a freelance basis, including writing several translations of Greek and Roman comedy for broadcast from the early 1950s. His first documented interest in writing for radio takes the form of a manuscript entitled 'The Return of Odysseus' which was, poignantly, submitted in 1941 whilst he was recovering from injuries sustained in war.[16] This work was based on Books XIX–XXII of Homer's *Odyssey*: the theme of the returning hero was naturally 'in the air' at this time, and indeed Sackville-West and Britten's *The Rescue* would shortly receive its first broadcast. There is no indication that Dickinson's Odyssean re-writing attracted

---

[13] The plays were first broadcast in 1966 and 1968, with a repeat of the *Odyssey* in 1969. See Cavander 1969 for expanded versions of these scripts.

[14] See Dickinson 1965, 177 ff. and Mole 1994.

[15] Dickinson 1965, 208 ff. explains that Poetry Editor was the primary role he fulfilled, but that he was officially a Producer in the Drama Department. On the fate of poetry on the Third following his departure see Whitehead 1989, 152 ff.

[16] Letter from PD to the BBC, 20 April 1941 (PD/S1a).

serious interest; nevertheless he soon returned to the *Iliad*, the inspiration behind his twelve-line poem 'War', published in *The Observer* in November 1940.[17] As many poets and writers before and since, Dickinson believed that 'there are many pieces from Homer that would prove ideal for broadcasting as the poem was written for being spoken aloud and the events described particularly for the mind's eye'.[18]

His 1946 radio play *The Wall of Troy*, which draws on *Iliad* III (in which Paris and Menelaus meet in combat whilst Helen watches from the wall above), opens with a Voice narrating his poem 'War' to music composed by Lennox Berkeley. The poem laments the young soldiers who had died in battle whilst observing that Helen, the cause of the Trojan war, continues to thrive: it ends, 'Stone and bone lie still. | Helen turns in bed'. The rest of the play is a thoughtful meditation on the Trojan war from a multiplicity of perspectives, including two Trojan boys who reflect the views of their elders, Greek and Trojan foot soldiers, and Helen. Their thoughts are all offered in dialogue, thus permitting a close psychological examination of motivation and character. The play, produced by Val Gielgud, was generally well received: 'There was so much in it, and as a presentation of a Homeric episode it was so interesting that two hearings would be none too much to get a thorough impression of it'; although this anonymous reviewer in *The Guardian* wondered whether something 'vital' may actually be lost by bringing all the characters to the microphone in such a realistic way.[19] Of the ninety-seven respondents to the listener questionnaire, half thought the play good, with the remainder left quite indifferent; those who were unfamiliar with the narrative of the *Iliad* would have appreciated some introductory background information and Berkeley's music was not generally thought to be effective.[20]

The 1950s and the 1960s were an extremely rich decade for Homer on the radio and many programmes warrant close examination in a more in-depth study than is possible here. Before moving on to the two case studies of *The Rescue* and *The Anger of Achilles*, it is worth mentioning briefly the *Odyssey* of 1960, a twelve-part series of re-tellings of sequences from the *Odyssey* which MacNeice and fellow poet Anthony Thwaite had commissioned from contemporary poets

---

[17] Dickinson 1940.   [18] Letter from PD to the BBC, 20 April 1941 (PD/S1a).
[19] Anon. 1946d.   [20] BBC WAC LR/6751.

The Poetry and Drama of Homeric Epic 181

for individual broadcast on the Third Programme: 'The idea, as we see it,' wrote Thwaite to Dickinson, 'is not to present slavishly accurate versions, but to give a number of contemporary poets (who need not necessarily have Greek) the chance to try their hand at an extended piece of verse, not departing widely or wilfully from Homer, but at the same time speaking with an individual voice.'[21] This ambition echoes the drive behind a similar series of twelve half-hour programmes of readings of crucial scenes from the *Iliad*, translated by a variety of modern poets, broadcast two years earlier under the guardianship of D. S. Carne-Ross (1921–2010) of the Talks Department (who has recently been described as 'the finest critic of classical literature in English translation after Arnold').[22] In that series the variety of styles of poetic translation was 'intended to reflect the varieties of approach possible at the present time to a great traditional poem. The translations are, so far as possible, poets' translations rather than dons' translations.'[23] As part of this series, Christopher Logue's poem 'From Book XXI of Homer's *Iliad*' (his account of Achilles' fight with the river Scamander, *Iliad* XXI. 184–382) was broadcast, and soon after he was commissioned by Carne-Ross to write more Homer for radio, the result, of course, being *Patrocleia*, drawing on *Iliad* XVI, the first of Logue's several accounts of parts of the *Iliad*.[24]

MacNeice and Thwaite's 1960 *Odyssey* presented the story in Books IX–XII, V–VII, XIV, and XVII–XXIV, as follows:

I   'The Cyclops', Hugh Gordon Porteus
II 'Circe', Ian Fletcher
III 'Hades', Louis MacNeice
IV 'The Sirens' and 'Scylla and Charybdis', C. A. Trypanis
    'The Oxen of the Sun', Patric Dickinson

---

[21] Letter from Anthony Thwaite to PD, 18 July 1960 (PD/S3b). Twenty years later Thwaite worked with Roloff Beny on the book *Odyssey: Mirror of the Mediterranean* which juxtaposed poetry and philosophical writings with photographs of the art, architecture, and scenery of the lands surrounding the Mediterranean (Thwaite and Beny 1981).
[22] Letter from DSCR to RG, 30 December 1957 (RG/S1); Kenneth Haynes, in Carne-Ross 2010, 13.
[23] Letter from DSCR to RG, 30 December 1957 (RG/S1).
[24] MacNeice 1987, 236 and n. 10. Carne-Ross assisted Logue with ancient Greek language and culture. See Greenwood 2007, 145 on what she terms Logue's 'cinematic narrative techniques', discussed briefly in Section 3.2.

V	'Calypso', Alistair Elliot
VI	'The Storm', Ted Hughes
	'Nausicaa', Peter Green
VII	'The Palace of Alcinous', James Michie
	'Return to Ithaca', Rex Warner
VIII	'The Swineherd', Donald Davie
	'Odysseus Meets Telemachus', Patric Dickinson
IX	'Odysseus at his Palace' and 'Irus', Terence Tiller
	'Penelope', Rex Warner
X	'Eurycleia', Donald Davie
	'Preliminaries to Battle' and 'The Bow', Anthony Thwaite
XI	'The Bow', Anthony Thwaite (continued)
	'Beginning of Battle', Alistair Elliot
XII	'The Killing of the Wooers', Hugh Gordon Porteus
	'Recognition by Penelope', Peter Green

This was not the first time that MacNeice had had the idea of putting Homer on the radio. In 1952 he had been commissioned by the Third Programme to produce a translation of the *Iliad* for broadcasting two years later, although at some point, before progressing very far with the project, he decided not to continue.[25] His reasons for abandoning the project are not stated in the archival sources, although a reasonable conjecture would be that it proved to be simply too big a task to achieve 'in his spare time' alongside his other scriptwriting and producing duties at the BBC.[26] His Homeric preference may also be relevant: he wrote 'give me the *Odyssey* every time as against the *Iliad*' in an article in *The Times*.[27] When he returned to the idea of putting Homer on air, perhaps it simply made more sense to choose the *Odyssey* (especially in light of Carne-Ross's recent *Iliad* series) and also to spread the labour of translation amongst his fellow poets.

There is a certain poignancy in MacNeice's own choice to contribute a piece focusing on Odysseus's journey to Hades (in *Odyssey* XI) to consult with the deceased prophet Teiresias, for

---

[25] See memos from Stella Hillier to A. C. Ent., 10 July 1952, and to Administrative Officer, Entertainment [F. L. Hetley], 3 September, year unknown (LM/C).
[26] Memo from Stella Hillier to A. C. Ent., 10 July 1952 (LM/C).
[27] MacNeice 1961.

in Hades the hero also meets (amongst others) his long-dead mother Anticleia.[28] MacNeice lost his own mother when he was a young boy; his early memories of her are as a great comfort, but she 'kept being ill and at last was ill all the time [...] and at last she went away; the last I can remember of her at home was her walking up and down the bottom path of the garden, the path under the hedge that was always in shadow, talking to my sister and weeping'.[29] The Homeric lines in which the hero strives three times to embrace the ghost of his mother only to remain frustrated in his attempts would doubtless have resonated with MacNeice's sense of loss. His 'biting grief' and 'wintry lamentation' are indeed phrases from the heart:

> So she spoke and I was caught in two minds and wished
> To embrace the shade of my mother long since dead;
> Three times I rushed to clasp her just as my spirit urged me
> And three times forth from my arms like a shadow or rather a dream
> She was flown away while the biting grief in my heart kept growing.
> And I spoke to her and addressed her with winged words:
> 'My mother, cannot you wait for me when I am yearning to clasp you
> So that even in Hades, throwing our arms round each other,
> We two might take our fill of wintry lamentation? [...]'

The series was a critical success. Indeed, two years later one critic clearly remained impressed: 'we may still be grateful for the Third Programme *Odyssey*, commissioned from a series of translators'.[30] It was also warmly appreciated by listeners, even if the audience was too small to be estimated in numbers in the Listener Research Reports.[31] The few reports that exist in the BBC WAC for some of the programmes illustrate how enjoyable listeners found the series: 'I loved every minute of it!', 'I am devoted to this series', 'These *Odyssey* readings are an unfailing delight' (considered a Biochemist), and 'I think this is the nicest way of getting to know the *Odyssey*. I love comparing these translations with the one I possess, and find my

---

[28] MacNeice also includes Odysseus's meeting with his former comrades Agamemnon and Achilles; this may have resonated with his memories of his good friend Graham Shepard, whom he had known since Marlborough and who had died during active service in 1943.
[29] MacNeice 1965, 37 and 42. On this, see his poem 'Autobiography'.
[30] Anon. 1962.
[31] BBC WAC LR/60/1669, LR/60/1878, LR/60/1987 and LR/60/2190.

interest is raised enormously' (wrote one 'Housewife, formerly Draughtsman').[32] Criticism of the series as a whole was rare, although a few listeners, perhaps inevitably, found 'the variation of [poetic] style from week to week rather disturbing'.[33] It is valuable to note that, in their responses to later programmes, some listeners referred back to MacNeice's 'Hades' as having been the best so far:

> [The fifth programme was] The second best of the translations I have heard in this series—(I've heard all but one)—the best being Louis MacNeice's. [. . .] The great merit of MacNeice's translation was that it reminded one so strongly of the rhythm of the original, and also the hieratic through humorous tone. (Author)
>
> So far I think Louis MacNeice's 'Book of the Dead' was the best—better, on the whole, than Rieu.[34]

6.1. EDWARD SACKVILLE-WEST AND BENJAMIN BRITTEN'S *THE RESCUE* (1943)

> Although the story is as familiar as a nursery rhyme, I found it just as gripping and exciting as if it were a first hearing [. . .] in fact, I found myself sitting on the edge of my chair, waiting for the next word, though I knew perfectly well what it would be. (Shorthand-Typist)[35]

The Rescue and the *Odyssey*

It is with what appears to be not only the first substantial creative engagement with Homeric epic on BBC Radio, but also the most enduring, that this first case study is concerned. *The Rescue* was first broadcast during the Second World War and the 1943 première of this dramatic feature programme was followed by new productions in 1948, 1951, 1956, 1962, 1973, and 1988. *The Rescue*—subtitled *A Melodrama*

---

[32] BBC WAC LR/60/1878.   [33] Ibid.

[34] This and the previous quotation are taken from BBC WAC LR/60/1878, the report for programme five. E. V. Rieu's translation of the *Odyssey* appeared in 1946 as the first volume in the Penguin Classics series, of which he was editor, 1944–64.

[35] BBC WAC LR/62/413. This comment, made in response to the 1962 production of *The Rescue*, seems to imply familiarity with earlier productions of the play and perhaps with the script published in 1945.

for Broadcasting Based on Homer's Odyssey—was written by the novelist and music critic Edward Sackville-West (1901–65) and for it Benjamin Britten (1913–76) provided a substantial, integrated score.

This study considers two interrelated aspects of this particular radio *Odyssey*. First, it demonstrates how the collaboration of Sackville-West and Britten made a distinctive and, for the time, significant development in the exploration of the dramatic potential of radio. Second, it argues that the close association of words and music in *The Rescue* suggests a reflective awareness of the relationship of radio to the ancient performance of epic poetry, especially through the character of the bard Phemius. Furthermore, the creative combination of words and music serves to encourage a deep level of interpretative understanding on the part of the radio audience, especially during the scene in which Phemius gives Telemachus a tutorial on how to recognize the presence of the gods. In the Epilogue, Phemius implores the radio audience to 'Forget the poem I made; but remember | The purer voice you hear behind my words', distilling one of the central themes of the play which encourages characters (and listeners) to look carefully for the meaning and value of things. Thus, and in other ways, did *The Rescue* resonate with the contemporary international situation and make a strong case for the humanizing potential of aesthetic experience.

The Rescue is not a translation of the *Odyssey*, nor is it a straightforward dramatization. While it largely follows the Homeric model, the plot has been cut and the characters altered substantially. The adventures of Odysseus on his journey home to Ithaca are referred to only in passing, first by his wife Penelope, who has imagined and dreamed them (pp. 32–3) and by Odysseus in conversation with his son Telemachus (pp. 66–7).[36] Phemius's prologue is followed by a long speech by the goddess Athene, not unlike the divine prologues of Euripidean tragedy, which serves to set the background of both the Trojan War and the Ithacans' despair at the continuing absence of their leader Odysseus (pp. 17–19).

The action of the play falls on two days, weeks apart: on the first day (Part One of the play), Telemachus leaves Ithaca to seek information about his long absent father and Odysseus arrives home; on the second day (Part Two), Telemachus returns and Odysseus kills

---

[36] Throughout Section 6.1, page references are to Sackville-West 1945.

Penelope's suitors (see Figure 6.1). Part One also establishes the desperation of the people of Ithaca and the suitors' discovery of Penelope's delaying tactic. Part Two opens with another speech by Athene and with Odysseus in disguise at the swineherd Eumaeus's house, where Telemachus, with Athene's help, recognizes his father. Father and son travel to the palace where Phemius and the old nurse

Fig. 6.1. 'The Death of the Suitors' by Henry Moore (HMF 2305, printed in Sackville-West 1945). Reproduced by kind permission of the Henry Moore Foundation.

Euryclea in turn recognize Odysseus, who slaughters the suitors. At the conclusion, husband and wife are reunited and the gods contrive to soothe the bewildered people of Ithaca.

At first, Sackville-West intended to include as much of the *Odyssey* as possible: 'so much of it seems to me to be astonishingly well adapted to make a continuously exciting radio drama'.[37] His enthusiasm was, however, curtailed by Laurence Gilliam, Assistant Director of Features, who considered that this would place 'a considerable strain on the listening audience to whom the story was very largely unfamiliar'.[38] In his modestly titled Preamble to a version of the script published in 1945, Sackville-West records that the focus of *The Rescue* was therefore tightened 'to extract the maximum of dramatic interest from certain characters in the story', presenting them as 'people in whose emotions and actions it is possible for the men and women of our time to be interested' (pp. 11–12). 'It seemed to me', he continued, 'more worth while to try to present Penelope as a real woman, with the mind and problems common to many middle-aged women as well as those that were special to her own case, than to leave her in the over-emphatic chiaroscuro of legend' (p. 12). He was, therefore, very much concerned to create Odyssean characters with whom listeners might sympathize: 'If this process of revitalisation has the effect of making the drama seem incredibly topical, I can only suggest that history, and the fictions that arise from it, tend to repeat themselves.'[39]

The Rescue and the Second World War

Edward Sackville-West was first inspired to write *The Rescue* on learning that the composer Arthur Bliss (1891–1975), Director of Music at the BBC for three years during the war, had hopes of working on an opera based on the *Odyssey*.[40] In July 1942 Sackville-West wrote to Val Gielgud with the following proposal:

> a dramatic composition on the Return of Odysseus, designed to bring out the parallel between the position in Ithaca then and that in Greece

---

[37] Memo from ESW to VG, 4 August 1942 (R19/1026).
[38] Memo from LG to ESW, 14 August 1942 (ibid.).
[39] Sackville-West 1943.
[40] Memo from ESW to VG, 9 July 1942 (R19/1026).

generally now—Penelope (the symbol of Greece) surrounded by Quislings, invading generals, etc, Odysseus returning as the leader of a sort of Commando. The action would begin roughly at this point in the story; but I should use flash-backs to include a good deal of the earlier part of the *Odyssey* as well. [...] The method employed would have the advantage [...] of making the chief characters [...] very much more credible and interesting to modern minds that the rather 'flat' figures of Homer; and the topical value should please the Planners![41]

Sackville-West intended the contemporary political resonances of *The Rescue*—which was written and broadcast in wartime—to shine through. The 'rescue' of the title is, of course, the rescue of Penelope, the palace, and Ithaca from the grip of the suitors, who are described in such terms as the 'oppressor' (p. 18), 'invaders' (p. 22), and 'the enemy' (p. 70). As Odysseus declares, whilst waiting outside the palace for the right moment to enter: 'After the enslavement | The rescue!' (p. 74). Ithaca is portrayed as dilapidated, with its vitality ebbing away: the son of the fisherman Halitherses observes that his nets are 'as rotten as everything else in this island' (p. 24) and dejectedly complains that, in any case, 'What's the use of good nets, when fish won't come into them? [...] the fish have forsaken the sea round Ithaca [...] the waters all about us have grown slow and sluggish' (p. 25). Athene tells Odysseus that Penelope 'trusted your neighbours, whom she thought friends. They pretended to be so, encroached on your land; gradually—little by very little—they tightened their hold on Ithaca and on its men and women and children.' 'Possession of Ithaca', she continues, 'would mean that these arrogant men had defeated the gods themselves. The submission of Penelope would darken Olympus and shame high Zeus himself' (p. 52).

The domestic focus of the play works on more than one level when considered against the backdrop of the Second World War. It is personal, concerning the long-awaited return home of the soldier to his family and his war-ravaged land, where people are dying of starvation and young women are forced to service the sexual and other needs of the occupying forces (p. 22). So, it is *also* global: Sackville-West intended Penelope, and by extension other Ithacans, to stand as a symbol for modern Greece, which in 1942 was under Nazi occupation, with Odysseus representing the Allied forces.[42]

[41] Ibid.   [42] Mitchinson 2007, 5.

Sackville-West considered that his portrayal of the suitors was 'semi-comic [. . .] because gangsters, Fascists, and other childish persons are, when looked at by themselves, essentially figures of farce' (p. 12). 'For the startling parallel between the story, as I have told it', he continues, 'and the present state of Greece, I make no apology. It was too obvious to require underlining, but its continual presence in my own mind did, I believe, contribute something both to the character-drawing and to the balance of the action' (pp. 12–13). The analogy asserts that the submission of modern Greece to the occupying forces would be morally wrong and that it would dishonour the ancient history of that land. After Odysseus kills the suitors, Ithacans gather at the palace, uncertain and confused. Telemachus urges Odysseus to reassure them that his arrival will be better for them than Penelope taking a new husband would have been:

> Now look here, Father, I don't think you quite appreciate the position. The people are not ungrateful: they are simply bewildered and uncertain. [. . .] the people of Ithaca [. . .] have suffered [. . .] lost homes and goods and lands and even their children and relations—through starvation and ill-treatment. [. . .] they have learnt to suspect everybody and everything—even the high gods themselves. You will have to show them that they stand to gain more by your return than they would have gained if my mother had given in. (pp. 92–3)

Odysseus wants to postpone his responsibility as ruler until the next day, but Telemachus steps in, telling his father that 'To-morrow is already to-day' (p. 93). Odysseus invokes Athene's help, speaking of what needs to be done as 'my last ordeal' (p. 93). 'Unleash at last the dawn', he cries: 'Let it shine into the hearts of these island men | And reveal the truth of their rescue' (p. 94), upon which the four divinities Hermes, Artemis, Apollo, and Athene sing verses encouraging each other to engender in the Ithacans hope, belief, and peace.

Emerging from the musical climax are Penelope's words, 'What a long, long kiss!' (p. 94), thus shifting the focus back to the domestic situation and the very real concerns of spouses long separated by war. Penelope worries over the fact that 'you left me a young girl; you find me a middle-aged woman'; and, when Odysseus informs her that 'Just as I had to return here, so I shall go back again' (p. 95), they quarrel slightly. The domesticity is reinforced when Odysseus entreats his wife to 'Take my hand. Come to the window. It is getting light.' His next comment—'Those stupid fellows seem to have gone home.

I suppose Telemachus sent them packing' (p. 96)—reminds us of his initial reluctance immediately to re-establish his authority as ruler of the Ithacans by acknowledging their suffering and reassuring them about the future. Odysseus's characterization here stands in sharp contrast with his son's perceptive and sympathetic understanding of what is needed. This has been interpreted as a critique of the

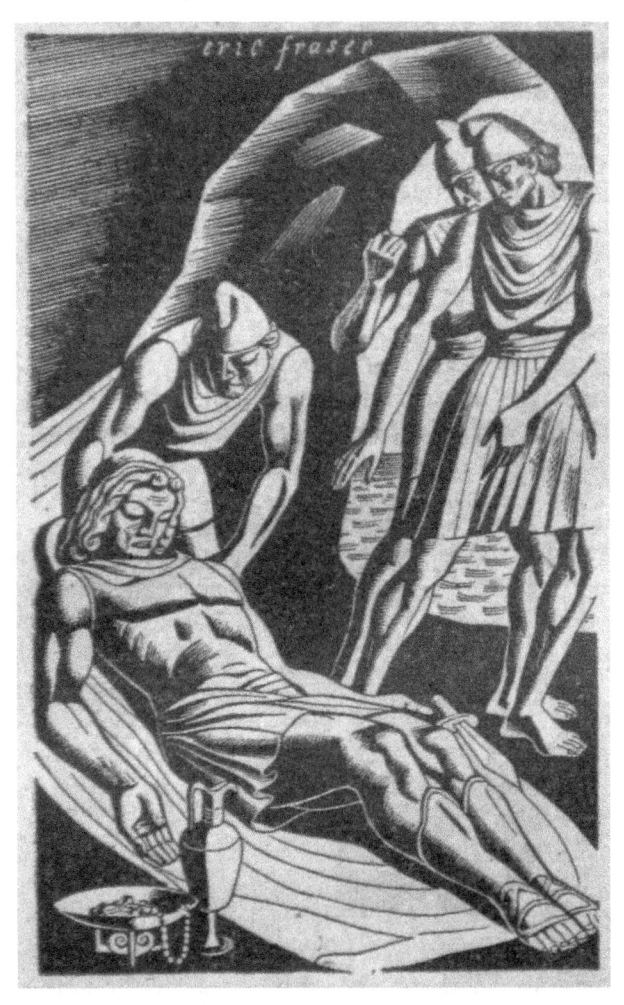

Fig. 6.2. 'The sleeping Odysseus is laid ashore on the island of Ithaca': Eric Fraser's drawing for Edward Sackville-West's article 'The *Odyssey* in Terms of Modern Radio' (*Radio Times*, 19 November 1943, 4). Reproduced by kind permission of the Fraser family.

'upper-class Odysseus' by Edith Hall, who concludes that *The Rescue* 'not only addressed the class tension that was to prove explosive at the general election two years later, but became a call to its British listeners *across* the class spectrum to take arms and assume responsibility for liberating all the lands threatened by Nazi "suitors"'.[43] Sackville-West (in his early forties) may have intended the generational tension between the father-hero and his newly matured son to represent burgeoning class tensions in Britain, but there seems to be no evidence to support this reading in his published writings or personal correspondence on *The Rescue*. However, the dominant themes of the play suggest that any vacillation on Odysseus' part serves to represent what Sackville-West sees as the Allied forces' obligation not merely to liberate occupied countries such as Greece but also to seize some responsibility for making sense of the past (and indeed the wartime present) and pointing the way to the future. Odysseus takes up his responsibility with the encouragement of his son and the help of the gods; Sackville-West seems to suggest that the parallel responsibilities on the part of the Allied forces might be fulfilled through what was felt to be the humanizing potential of the arts—a point which receives further discussion below.

'Warp and weft, verse and music': Sackville-West and Britten

The war also had an impact on the production process. Britten had been in America at the outbreak of war; he returned in April 1942. In July, the BBC wrote in support of his conscientious objection to active service, stating that 'Mr Britten has been commissioned by us to write music for a series of important broadcast programmes designed to explain this country to listeners in America';[44] indeed, he had already been contributing to the war effort by writing music for Louis MacNeice's propaganda programmes *Pericles* (1943), on which see Section 5.2, and *An American in England* and *Britain to America* (both 1942). Yet Britten's pacifism seems to have led to considerable hostility amongst some members of the BBC Music Department. When his music for *The Rescue* neared completion in 1943, confusion

---

[43] Hall 2008*b*, 41–2 (original emphasis); also in Hall 2008*a*, 517.
[44] Quoted in Foreman 1988, 30.

arose over who would conduct the BBC Symphony Orchestra during rehearsals and in performance. Britten had been informally invited to conduct but, before a contract was signed, the Music Department—apparently unaware of the informal arrangement—worked to secure the services of another conductor.[45] Bliss records that Adrian Boult (1889–1983) was first approached but refused, declaring himself 'antagonistic to the composer and his work'. Clarence Raybould (1866–1972) was of the same mind, but was persuaded to take it on by Bliss, who felt strongly that the orchestra should be led by a staff conductor over the unusually long eight-day rehearsal schedule.[46]

Britten wrote to Bliss to say that the reasons he had been given as to why he should not be allowed to conduct were 'entirely unsatisfactory' and to protest about 'the breaking of an implied contract', but also that he had decided, 'out of friendship' for Sackville-West, to complete the score; though he would take 'no further part in the production'.[47] This left the production team in difficulty. John Burrell (1910–72), who worked as a radio producer for the BBC during the war, complained that not only would there be a distinct disadvantage in Britten not taking the piano rehearsals and conducting the orchestra but also that Raybould did not have the necessary experience for this type of programme: 'I do not think that either Bliss or Raybould have any conception of the difficulties of this script.'[48] Several possible solutions were discussed, but Britten claims that while he was considering these his agent had received a letter from Raybould saying that 'he objected to Britten as a conscientious objector and was only conducting the music for *The Rescue* under protest'.[49]

---

[45] 'We are only committed by a personal note from Stephen Potter in which he said that Britten would be asked to conduct' (memo from VG to John Burrell, 2 October 1943, R19/1026).
[46] Memo from AB to Assistant Controller, Programmes [R. J. F. Howgill], 25 October 1943 (ibid.). The creative team comprised thirty musicians and actors; the performing forces included two flutes, two oboes, two clarinets, two bassoons, one alto saxophone, four horns, three trumpets, three trombones, one tuba, three percussion players, one harp, one piano, and unspecified strings (typescript entitled '*The Rescue*', ibid.).
[47] Letter from Benjamin Britten to AB, 27 October 1943 (ibid.).
[48] Memo from John Burrell to Assistant Director, Features [LG], 28 October 1943 (ibid.).
[49] Memo from LG to R. J. F. Howgill, 1 November 1943 (ibid.).

The collaboration between Sackville-West and Britten was fraught with no such tension. In fact, as already noted, it was out of friendship for Sackville-West that Britten decided to finish the score and, indeed, to pay and train a pianist who would attend rehearsals in his place, alongside Raybould.[50] Britten had been writing specially commissioned scores for the BBC since 1937, with a three-year hiatus while he was in America.[51] For music, Sackville-West had first approached Bliss (whose idea for an *Odyssey* opera had first kindled the idea for *The Rescue*).[52] Bliss declined to write the score on this occasion and before long Sackville-West became convinced that Britten was 'the only composer available who possesses both the technique and imagination equal to so large and varied a task'.[53]

Sackville-West explains his use of the word 'melodrama' in the subtitle of *The Rescue* with reference to the *Oxford English Dictionary* definition: 'a play, usually romantic and sensational in plot and incident, in which songs are interspersed and in which the action is accompanied by orchestral music appropriate to the situations' (p. 8). Sackville-West, 'one of the most widely read and respected music critics of his generation', hoped that it would be an example of something more than the customary radio play with 'backing' music (p. 8).[54] One contemporary critic considered that Britten's music was 'part of the texture of the play, warp and weft, verse and music, neither complete without the other'.[55] Sackville-West observed in radio 'possibilities of an operatic nature hitherto almost unexplored',[56] and *The Rescue* has been described as 'a kind of spoken opera'.[57] Just as the text is written in a variety of styles, from colloquial speech to high poetry, so the music exists and operates in different modes which contribute vividly to the sound drama. The four divine characters (Athena, Hermes, Apollo, and Artemis), whose presence in the play echoes that of a Greek tragic chorus, mostly sing. When soliloquy is accompanied by 'orchestral commentary', Sackville-West considered that the result was 'a new kind of *aria*' (p. 14; original emphasis). The music adds emotional depth to the words: for example, it suggests the keening of women at the death of their children. It assists in the construction of character, with the presence of individuals

---

[50] Ibid. [51] See Reed 1989, 325–6 for details.
[52] Memo from ESW to AB, 27 July 1942 (R19/1026).
[53] Foreman 1988, 31. [54] De-la-Noy 2004. [55] Crozier 1948, 167.
[56] Typescript entitled '*The Rescue*' (R19/1026). [57] Rodger 1982, 84.

underscored by the use of particular instruments and signature motifs. The sax is Penelope's signature instrument, for example, and the script states that Irus is accompanied by a 'wooden rattle', played on a xylophone. This rattle is used cleverly in conjunction with dialogue to indicate movement and gesture. The music also suggests the movement of characters, such as Phemius rushing down the steps from the watch tower. It structures the drama in a traditional way, effecting transitions between scenes or a shift in perspective from, for example, characters who are watching Halitherses from a distance to the man himself, whose words are heard in 'close-up'. Finally, it also renders basic sound effects: for example, the musical representation of thunder is highly effective (and innovative, since sound effects were at this time more usually articulated by non-musical sounds). Britten's music is thoughtful, illuminating, and innovative for British radio drama in the early 1940s. '*The Rescue* is not simply a play with incidental music stuffed into the joints or used to add colour to a speech here and there,' considered Sackville-West, 'but an attempt, however imperfect, in the direction of radio opera.'[58]

Phemius, 'the Poet'

Telemachus describes Phemius to a stranger (actually his father in disguise) as 'our local poet [...] A good chap too—taught me a lot about life' (p. 63). Later, Telemachus is relieved to hear that Phemius was not killed along with the suitors: 'I thank the gods for it. He was a good friend to me' (p. 92). Phemius in *The Rescue* is much enlarged from the Odyssean character, with one subtle difference being that he is not so unwilling a performer of poetry as he is in the *Odyssey*: He admits to some shame at profiting from the suitors while other Ithacans suffer but he is pragmatic, candidly admitting that he butters them up with false praise so that he can feed his family in difficult times. Furthermore, he notes:

> But it is not as simple for me as for some of you.
> I have a special talent: some day it will be needed,
> To celebrate 'his' home-coming;
> Meanwhile, there are certain things I can do. (p. 22)

---

[58] Typescript entitled '*The Rescue*' (R19/1026). For a fuller treatment of the music see Foreman 1988.

His 'special talent' is that of a poet and he longs to put it to use in celebration of Odysseus's homecoming. But other 'special talents' are hinted at in the words 'Meanwhile, there are certain things I can do'. As the play proceeds he is shown to have insight and knowledge deeper than that of other characters: he intuitively knows that the beggar is Odysseus in disguise (p. 76) and he has an ability beyond

Fig. 6.3. 'Phemius and Telemachus' by Henry Moore (HMF 2300, printed in Sackville-West 1945). Reproduced by kind permission of the Henry Moore Foundation.

that of the priest to notice and also interpret divine omens such as a pair of eagles ripping at each other's necks (pp. 27–8). He is keenly aware of the presence of the gods and strives to enable divine–human communication.

In an important scene, which is entirely Sackville-West's invention, Phemius teaches Telemachus how to recognize the presence of individual gods and hear 'Above all, | The voices of the gods' (p. 38). The dialogue in this 'tutorial' is reproduced below and is illustrated by Henry Moore's drawing of this scene in the 1945 publication of the script (see Figure 6.3):

TELEMACHUS   Snapped again, curse it! What's the good of you, Phemius, if you can't find me some better twine than this hopeless stuff? Euryclea wouldn't use it to darn a hole in my shirt. Here! Take hold of the haft a moment, will you? No, the haft, I said, not the blade, stupid!
PHEMIUS   Poets, Telemachus, are not supposed to know one end of a spear from the other.
TELEMACHUS   What are they supposed to know, then?
PHEMIUS   The heart's affections, and the strivings of men;
The forms of Destiny;
The beauty of faces, of limbs, of the folds in the chlamys you are wearing,
Of the waves in hair, and in water,
And in that standing corn over there beyond the wall.
The true end of courage
And endurance; the love of
Home.
High-hearted resignation to what is and what may come.
Above all,
The voices of the gods
When they pierce the breast as easily and painlessly
As the wind in your hair.
                                                                    (*Mutter of thunder.*)
TELEMACHUS   A god spoke then, but I could not tell his meaning. (*Fearfully.*) It's getting darker. The sky is of burnished copper—like a shield.
Phemius, tell me (you are so wise) how may I know a god, when one is near?
                                                                    (*Thunder again, nearer.*)
PHEMIUS   By his voice, Telemachus. When the gods are really near to you, they speak to you in words.
At other times you may hear or see, but never touch them.

	A poplar rustles in the breeze: it is Artemis.
	A lazy wave tumbles forward on the shore: Poseidon muttering in his sleep. You look into the heart of a blazing fire and there—suddenly—is the face of Apollo. Look again and the fair god is gone, leaving only a burning log.
	Even as in the bubbles on the surface of a newly poured goblet of wine you may trace the features of Dionysus.
TELEMACHUS	Show me, Phemius! Show me!
	(*Thunder again, nearer still.*)
PHEMIUS	Look then at my lyre... I put it up there on that ledge of stone just now. Watch its outline against the copper shield of the sky.
	See how it glows! The face of Apollo...
	(*Harp to background.*)
TELEMACHUS	(*doubtfully*). Yes... Yes...
PHEMIUS	Now look at the crack which runs down that wall, over there by the first olive tree. Slant-eyed Hermes regards you, Telemachus.
	(*A flute adds itself to the harp.*)
	Look there now—quick!—a quail aslant the evening! Artemis is here!
	(*An oboe wheedles into the harmony.*)
TELEMACHUS	Too late! I was too late.
PHEMIUS	Look over there, then—at that ear of bearded wheat which weeps over the low wall: Demeter lamenting Persephone.
	(*Add solo violin. The four instruments play in quiet counter-point, then fade out behind dialogue.*)
TELEMACHUS	Phemius, you have given me eyes!
PHEMIUS	Eyes, perhaps; but it is ears you need most.
	Not you only, but all men. Every man could be a poet, if only he would listen instead of talking.
	The eye deceives, the ear never.
TELEMACHUS	But I do listen—
PPHEMIUS	Not with all your ears. Yet I tell you listening is the only true means to *know* a thing. (pp. 38–9; original emphasis)

The words on the page inform us that the presence of the gods can be recognized through visual as well as auditory clues, but Britten's musical contribution to this scene in performance plays a trick on the imagination, so that we seem to 'see' the presence of the gods aurally. The violin helps us appreciate how the ear of wheat droops in the breeze with the sorrow of Demeter. As the classicist Barbara Graziosi notes, human characters in the *Odyssey* regularly recognize when a god has intervened in events but rarely can they pinpoint which god it was; poets, however, because of their special connection with the Muses, 'can see and reveal to ordinary mortals how each god is and how he or she relates to others'.[59]

Throughout *The Rescue* the senses of hearing and touch, and the act of memory, are privileged over the sense of sight: for example, the old nurse Euryclea recognizes Odysseus's scar by touch alone, as they stand in the shadow of a pillar (p. 88). Furthermore, at their reunion, Odysseus tells Penelope that he can see her better with his eyes closed: 'For years I have held your image engraved on my eyelids. [. . .] Your own face is less real to me' (p. 95), a scene which is reminiscent of how Homer's disguised Odysseus tells Penelope that he has a picture of her husband in his mind's eye.[60] At the beginning of Part Two, Athene describes how she watches with sadness Odysseus sitting by Eumaeus's house, plaiting garlic as he gazes in the direction of home; but when Odysseus himself, in a long soliloquy, tells of the ways in which he is 'disconsolate, | Inconsolable' (p. 57), the listener feels the pain of his sorrow more acutely. As Phemius says to Telemachus: 'The eye deceives, the ear never. [. . .] listening is the only true means to *know* a thing' (p. 39). The emphasis in this radio *Odyssey* on listening over seeing privileges the position of the radio audience in their ability only to listen. Telemachus's tutorial on how to sense the presence of the gods may also function as a tutorial for the listener on how to appreciate the cooperation of music and words in the construction of dramatic meaning.

As in the *Odyssey*, both words and visual reports in *The Rescue* can be unreliable and not what they seem on first appearance. Phemius in particular is an elusive, shape-shifty character: his presence is twice mistaken for that of others; and he is also slippery, inventing stories and false praise in order to flatter the suitors. For the listener, Phemius defies concrete categorization. For as well as being a character within the drama, he also stands outside of it, delivering a Prologue and an Epilogue. Sackville-West insists that there is no narrator in *The Rescue*, not even Athene, who opens the two parts of the play with a long scene-setting speech very like the divine prologues of Greek tragedy. Phemius's position outside the drama, reminiscent of the invocations to the Muses in the Homeric epics,

---

[59] Graziosi 2002, 6.   [60] Homer, *Odyssey* XIX. 224.

seems to suggest an equivalence with a narrator or poet figure. Indeed Sackville-West states that he stands for '*the* Poet, rather than any particular one, [...] I have tried to invest him with something of the mysterious timelessness, the knife-edge balance between being and not-being, which only the poetic imagination seems able to achieve' (p. 13; my emphasis). The Prologue and Epilogue do accordingly offer brief meditations on the art and function of poetry. Poetry connects the past with the future (which are described in the Prologue in terms suggestive of both archaeological ruins and neo-classical architecture: 'yesterday of ruined, friable stone'; 'to-morrow of the perfected arch') by bringing knowledge and experience to bear on the 'eternal present' (p. 17). Consider the very end of the Epilogue, and the play:

> PHEMIUS   Men seldom know me when they see me.
> I am here and not here; I am
> The captured shadow; the intersection
> Of Past and Future;
> The moment of death;
> The mysterious blood of sleep; the eyes
> Of the statue whose gaze is inwards.
> Victory and defeat have in me their resolution, in that
> Ever future voice beyond the interval
> Where joy and grief are one.
>   (*Music to background and hold.*)
> Think of my face, all you who listen.
> Look into my eyes, before they fade into your night.
> Forget the poem I made; but remember
> The purer voice you hear behind my words.
>   (*Music up to end.*) (p. 96)

Sackville-West's designation of Phemius as 'the Poet', rather than any particular one, seems to invest him with the power and the function of poetry itself—to move, to interpret human experience, and to capture the imagination. In the final lines of the play Phemius implores the listener to 'Forget the poem I made; but remember | The purer voice you hear behind my words'. This sentiment is foreshadowed earlier in the play when Athene encourages Telemachus to recognize his father: 'Look not behind you at the stranger! Watch the shadow of his head and hand!' (p. 65; illustrated by Moore in Figure 6.4). The play thus seems to encourage a deep level of interpretative understanding on the part of the radio audience. Hear not just the story, but listen also to its meaning. Similarly, do not just hear the music but *listen* to what it is saying.

Phemius's 'special talents', which include interpreting omens and communicating with the divine realm, seem to hint at a more than ordinary human dimension to his character. In this regard it may be worth mentioning that, whereas Athene appears in the guise of

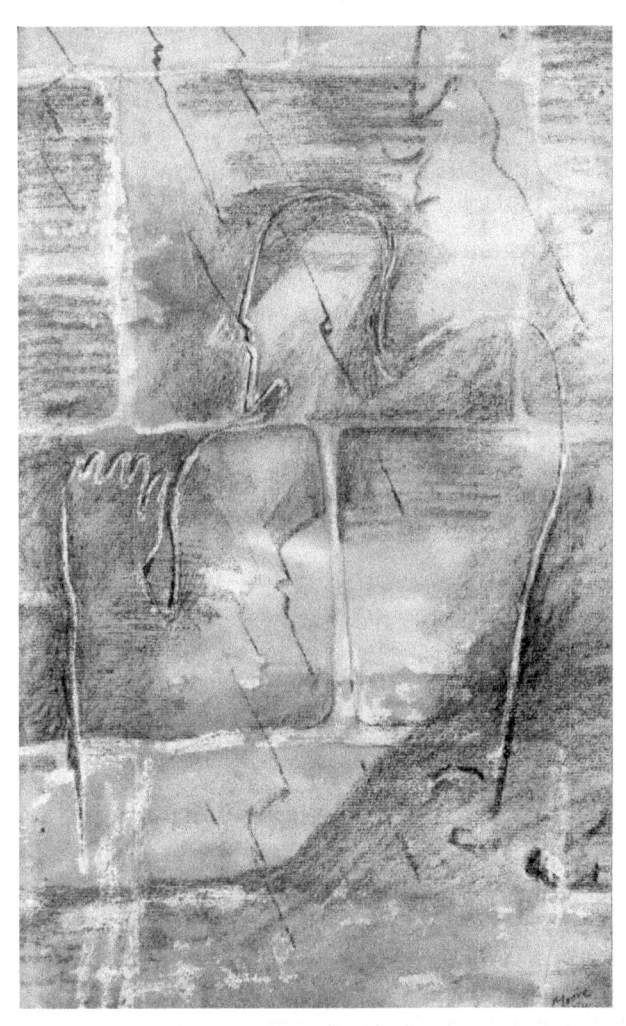

Fig. 6.4. 'The Shadow on the Wall' by Henry Moore (HMF 2304, printed in Sackville-West 1945). Reproduced by kind permission of the Henry Moore Foundation.

Mentor in the *Odyssey*, in *The Rescue* Odysseus thinks he sees Mentor, but it is actually Phemius about to deliver his closing Epilogue. Perhaps Phemius can be understood as representing in *The Rescue* various strands of knowledge and storytelling which are apparent in the *Odyssey*—he is both the loyal and trusted household poet, and also the type of lying 'impostor' (in buttering up the suitors) that Alcinous refers to in Book XI.[61] In the context of the Second World War may we also hear in the imperative to 'remember | The purer voice you hear behind my words' a claim for what was felt to be the humanizing potential of the arts? This was, after all, the ideal behind the BBC's contribution to the cultural life of the nation—especially in wartime— and it was embodied in a very practical way in the activities of the Entertainments National Service Association (ENSA) and CEMA, both of which, like radio, engaged huge and responsive audiences.

The response of listeners to the 1943 première and later productions

The Listener Research Report for the 1943 production estimates that 10.5 per cent of the adult civilian population (something in the region of 3½ million people) tuned in to Part One, broadcast on 25 November 1943, and 8.7 per cent to the second part, broadcast on the following evening.[62] These figures were considered to be 'very satisfactory', especially in light of the fact that both parts 'had to compete with powerful attractions from the Forces Programme'. From the 209 questionnaires returned, the Appreciation Index for those who listened to both parts was calculated to be a high 80. A large proportion (38 per cent) already knew the *Odyssey* story and most of these thought that Sackville-West's version was successful. Half of the sample liked the broadcast very much, although the chief criticism even amongst these was that, at three hours in total, it was too long. The names of minor characters were strange to many and also, because of their number, confusing. Only a few disliked the play because 'its story seemed remote from our times or fantastic' or

---

[61] On how the figure of 'the poet' is represented in ancient Greek poetry, see Goldhill 1991. On poetic appeals to the Muses in the Homeric epics see Minchin 1995 and bibliography there.
[62] BBC WAC LR/2235.

'were deterred by the style of the writing'. A sample of reactions from the 1943 audience captures something of the variety of listener experience:

> I <u>wanted</u> to like this production, [...] I was ready to see the best in the production. But I found the hour and a half at that time of night far too long, and where there was so much declamation and music, I nearly fell asleep. (Journalist)
>
> I did not expect to like this play at all, I thought classics were nothing in my line, but this broadcast has made me want to hear more plays of this type. This beautiful broadcast has aroused my interest, and made me realise that I am missing something worthwhile. (Housewife)
>
> Lovely, lovely, lovely! Of all the joys wireless has given me this was the greatest. [...] The words were so fine I was afraid to breathe for fear of losing any. The images, so effortlessly invoked, flooded one's mind with vivid pictures. (Civil Servant)

This last comment typifies the way in which the evocative and powerful combination of words and music in *The Rescue* left many listeners feeling that their imaginative experience had had a visual dimension. The Listener Research Report for a subsequent production in 1948 records that the music seemed to encourage this dimension: listeners 'seemed to find it helpful in picturing the scene'.[63] In Section 3.2 I argue that this kind of response to *The Rescue* may be interpreted as the active collaboration of the radio play (comprising not just words but also music and other sounds) with the listener's imagination.

Britten's music was not to the taste of all in 1943 (for some it was 'too loud when the actors were speaking'; for others there were 'too many short bursts of music punctuating the dialogue'), but the majority enjoyed it, finding it very appropriate. Indeed, a considerable number 'praised the music very enthusiastically, saying that "it fitted like a glove" and that they "wouldn't have enjoyed the play so much without it"'. The following are a sample of enthusiastic comments:

> True background music of [the] highest type, that became an integral part of the play. It matched, and often set, the mood of the dialogue, pointed it sharply and greatly heightened the interest often. PS I'm not a Britten [fan,] most of his music is beyond me. (Retired Bank Cashier)

---

[63] BBC WAC LR/48/399.

I have so often criticised and deplored the use, or rather misuse, of music [in] straight plays that it gives me great pleasure to record this appreciation. The instrument and the music used for Irus was superb [...] an essential part of the characterisation. (Electrical Engineer)

It was not only a perfect accompaniment, but it thrilled in itself and provided inspiring variety of tempo. (Elocution Teacher)[64]

The Rescue was also a critical success. In *The Listener* Herbert Farjeon (1887–1945) wrote: 'I was sufficiently affected to be left wondering why I had frittered away so much of my life thinking about anything but the Greek gods and heroes.'[65] *The Manchester Guardian* thought that the second production of *The Rescue* in 1948 confirmed it as being

> at the head of all work of this kind written specially for broadcasting. It has beauty of word, beauty of sound, and a strong, massive architecture. It paints a series of pictures of the happenings on Ithaca most skilfully; it has movingly dramatic moments such as the recognition of Odysseus by Telemachus and later by Penelope; it has, too, some spurts of sardonic humour, and it conveys a wonderful sense both of the purposes of the Grecian gods and of the greatness of the enduring heart of man.[66]

Commenting on the 1951 production, *The Times* considered that 'Britten composed music rich in evocative effect, but strongly integrated into the atmosphere and structure of the work'; and *The Manchester Guardian* in 1956 acknowledged that *The Rescue* 'must still be considered [...] as the most completely satisfactory combination of words and music'.[67]

The music in particular was abidingly enjoyed by listeners: in 1951, the Listener Research Report asked the panel whether the music was appropriate and almost all respondents agreed that it was, with some commenting that 'the music was the play, and several said that Benjamin Britten was closer to the essence of the *Odyssey* than Sackville West [sic]'; only a few found it 'inarticulate or mere noise'. In 1951, a listener identified as an Independent Lady, wrote that 'the music made the play, which, without it, would, to my thinking, have been commonplace';[68] more than a decade later, in 1962, another listener considered the score 'not merely a background to the play,

---

[64] BBC WAC LR/2235. [65] Farjeon 1943b. [66] Anon. 1948.
[67] Anon. 1951; Anon. 1956b. [68] BBC WAC LR/51/2025.

but its very backbone'.[69] Although the reviewer in *The Times* in 1951 noted that the topicality of 'a drama which present events had made gripping and actual in wartime' had passed, *The Rescue* still showed 'the immediacy of the eternal tale'.[70] Sackville-West's desire that the audience appreciate the deeper application of the work's meaning seems to have been fulfilled:

> I thought the play most able, exciting and moving. The old, old story is told with flexible and sustained force that both reveal[s] its beauties as a deep and ancient story and convince one of its universality. (Psychiatric Social Worker)[71]

In 1956, a new production on the Home Service, offered as part of a *Festival of Radio Drama*, fared less well in terms of overall audience response than the previous high-scoring productions on the Third Programme in 1948 and 1951, achieving just the average Appreciation Index for Home Service plays. A considerable number thought that Val Gielgud's production—which stretched from 7.40 p.m. to 10.40 p.m. with a fifteen-minute break—was far too long. Furthermore, one considered it to be 'trash which should have been on the Third Programme'; another thought it 'a pretentious, untidy, incompetent handling of what remains a basically good story' (which may suggest a traditionalism amongst the Home Service audience with regard to canonical works). While some found the language to be 'stilted and old-fashioned', for others it was 'too modern in idiom and phraseology'. Despite some strong negative responses, the majority of the listening panel 'welcomed this broadcast with enthusiasm' and the following positive comments were noted:

> An exciting modern version of this evergreen classic. It was excellently done. The story lost nothing in the retelling but if anything gained in reality. It was full of life and vigour. (Retired Headmistress)
>
> The language is beautiful, the music exciting, the dramatisation superb, and the imagery magnificent. What more can I say? (Housewife)
>
> It was indeed a first-class play, and fine entertainment, brilliantly based on a well known but almost limitless story. (Printer and Stationer)[72]

---

[69] BBC WAC LR/62/413. [70] Anon. 1951.
[71] BBC WAC LR/51/2025.
[72] BBC WAC LR/56/847. The later life of *The Rescue* includes the two-hour 1973 Radio 3 production which 'misguidedly concentrated on the "play" at the expense of

Listeners also made comments which reflected their awareness that the act of listening to Homer via radio had a close affinity with the ancient experience of listening to Homer's epic poems in performance:

> It reminded one, too, that Homer's epics were first said or sung in ancient Greece, and that in *The Rescue* the *Odyssey* had come full circle to be spoken, with music, in modern England. (*The Manchester Guardian*)
> I hardly noticed the play took almost three hours; it held my attention from start to finish. Short of hearing the *Odyssey* in the original this was the next best thing. (Sociologist)[73]

Postscript: Henry Moore and *The Rescue*

There is an interesting history to be written about the relationship between radio broadcasting and the publication of the associated translations, poems, radio dramatic scripts, or other textual versions of programmes. It was also not unusual for the texts of successful radio broadcasts to find their way into print, especially in the 1940s and the 1950s, thus enduring in another form for original or new audiences, and also attaining a degree of permanence not offered by the ephemeral radio medium. In this way, Edward Sackville-West's script was published by Secker and Warburg in July 1945, nearly two years after the first broadcast. Words are accompanied by musical cues (for example, '*Distant sound of four Naiads singing*', p. 46) and cues for sound effects ('*Hubbub. Banging and thumping.* [...] *whip cracks and screams of women*', p. 35). The volume is also, rather unexpectedly, illustrated by six drawings made by

---

Britten's music, cutting most of the vocal numbers without making clear that this had been done' (Foreman 1988, 30). Fresh attention, however, was paid to Britten's score from 1988 following a new Radio 3 production by Chris De Souza and Ian Cotterell which featured a five-minute 'interval' reading from a new autobiography of Sackville-West (De-la-Noy 1988) and was immediately followed by Britten's Serenade (Opus 31), composed in 1943 and dedicated to Sackville-West (A. Porter 1995). Stimulated by his work on this production, De Souza compiled a 35-minute concert version of Britten's score for *The Rescue* (for narrator, soprano, mezzo-soprano, tenor and baritone soloists with orchestra) which retained Athene as a narrator. This new work, *The Rescue of Penelope*, premièred at Snape Maltings, Aldeburgh on 23 October 1993, fifty years after the first radio broadcast of *The Rescue*; in 1995 a recording was issued by Warner Elatus.

[73] 'M. C.' 1945; BBC WAC LR/62/413.

Henry Moore in 1944, three of which are given here as Figures 6.1, 6.3, and 6.4.[74]

That Moore should have provided the illustrations is unexpected for two reasons: first, he was primarily a sculptor and, second, he is known to have been deliberately resistant to classical influences. These six drawings, together with others from his sketchbook for *The Rescue*, were shown alongside his drawings for an illustrated edition of André Gide's *Prométhée* in the 2007 exhibition on 'Moore and Mythology' at the Henry Moore Foundation, Perry Green. The exhibition catalogue's introductory essay discusses Moore's avoidance of classical and ancient mythological material and relates his comment, made in 1960, that 'there was a period when I tried to avoid looking at Greek—and Renaissance—sculpture of any kind: when I thought that [they] were the enemy and that one had to throw all that over and start again from the beginning of primitive art'.[75] His work on the drawings took place at a time when he 'had only just returned to sculpture after being forced temporarily to abandon it during the Second World War' and they carry echoes of his three-dimensional works: see especially, of those reprinted here, Figure 6.1.[76]

A fusion of 'primitive' and 'classical' elements seems to exemplify Moore's approach to this commission. In addition to the six published drawings, Moore made studies of other scenes in the play such as 'Phemius on the Watch Tower' (HMF 2296), in which he evidently drew inspiration from photographs from the ethnologist and archaeologist Leo Frobenius's cultural studies of Africa: African storage towers appear in a rolling landscape, with a classical temple nestling in the hills behind.[77] 'Odysseus in the Naiads' Cave' (HMF 2302) echoes Moore's famous 'Shelter Drawings' but the influence is reported not to be underground, wartime London but cave formations in Zimbabwe, again as depicted by Frobenius, and Frobenius's depictions of Algerian and Libyan rock drawings inspired 'The Shadow on the Wall' (Figure 6.4).

---

[74] The three not reproduced here are 'Penelope and Eurynome' (HMF 2301), 'Odysseus in the Naiads' Cave' (HMF 2302), and 'Odysseus, the Beggar' (HMF 2303).
[75] Moore's comment, made in an interview with Donald Hall (published in *Horizon*, November 1960, 114) is quoted in Mitchinson 2007, 4. The 'Moore and Mythology' exhibition at the Henry Moore Foundation, Perry Green travelled to the Musée Bourdelle, Paris in 2008.
[76] Mitchinson 2007, 10.   [77] Ibid. 9–10.

6.2. ROBERT GRAVES'S *THE ANGER OF ACHILLES* (1965)

It was quite by chance we heard that Robert Graves would be interested in making a broadcasting adaptation of his own racy, vivid translation [of Homer's *Iliad*]—he wanted to do this as a first step to making a dramatisation for the stage, for television, and the films.[78]

In the early 1960s the poet and novelist Robert Graves (1895–1985) was talking to the film and theatre director Sam Wanamaker (1919–93) about making, first, a stage dramatization and, later, a film of *The Anger of Achilles*, his version of Homer's *Iliad* which had first been published in 1959 by Doubleday in the United States.[79] Wanamaker testified to much interest in America for this idea. A letter to Graves states that he wanted 'to mount your Trojan War using all sorts of film + projection techniques'.[80] He was in conversation with the Lincoln Center in New York about a production which was likely to cost half a million dollars.[81] By 1967, little progress towards these goals had been made, but the idea was still considered to be a live project. The designs which the Czech set designer Josef Svoboda (1920–2002) presented to the Lincoln Center for this production were considered by Wanamaker to form 'a staggeringly exciting concept which surpasses every expectation and hope that I have had'.[82] In 1968, however, the Lincoln Center decided not to proceed with the project, largely because of the enormous budget.[83] Wanamaker began to write to a variety of other theatres and foundations for support, and was still writing to Graves as late as 1972 about his efforts to launch a big professional theatre production of *The Anger of Achilles*.[84] In the meantime—whilst this big idea for a theatre and film

---

[78] Raikes 1966.
[79] Graves 1959. It was subsequently reprinted many times, most recently by Penguin as Graves 2009.
[80] Letter from Beverley Cross to RG, 7 January 1963 (RGA).
[81] Letter from Sam Wanamaker to RG, 17 July 1967 (RGA).
[82] Letter from Sam Wanamaker to Beverley Cross, 21 November 1967 (RGA).
[83] Letter from Schuyler G. Chapin (Vice-President, Programming, Lincoln Center for the Performing Arts) to Sam Wanamaker, 23 January 1968 (RGA).
[84] For example: 'I am pushing the *Iliad* with the Kennedy Centre as hard as I can' (letter from Sam Wanamaker to RG, 28 May 1972 (RGA)). The almost decade-long attempt to stage and film Graves's version of the *Iliad*—although ultimately unsuccessful—prefigures the stage and small-screen production of his 1934 novel *I,*

Iliad seemed continually to falter, and whilst other film versions of Homer's epic poem proved themselves to be more successful in making it to the big screen[85]—a performed version of Graves's translation reached something in the region of several hundred thousand people via the radio medium. Not only did this radio adaptation of *The Anger of Achilles* prove to be continually popular with listeners in its revivals but it was also deemed to be an artistic success, winning the Prix Italia in 1965.

Graves had often been approached to write for radio. In 1946, for example, producer of features Rayner Heppenstall (1911–81) invited him to contribute a script for the *Imaginary Conversations* series (drawn from authors such as Plato, Erasmus, and Boswell) to be broadcast on the Third Programme, the new network which would be launched later that year.[86] Graves's response to this invitation starkly demonstrates his ambivalent feelings towards the Corporation at this time:

> Nothing that I have ever been asked to do for the BBC has prospered: there has always been some technical reason for turning it down if it is a script; and when I recorded a broadcast in German they told me it was too slow for use and when I did a Brains Trust I was rude to Joad + never asked again. And as I never listen to the BBC except News + Tommy Handley I must conclude that the radio + I are not in sympathy. But thanks very much all the same.[87]

One can easily understand the frustration of the writer, who, as he claimed, had 'been paid three times for scripts which were never used, never for one which was used'.[88]

Heppenstall persisted in his wooing of Graves, addressing his anxious feelings about 'not being one of the boys' by saying that 'I am sure cliques do form, but one of the virtues of the BBC is that it's so large that it can never fall into the hands of a single clique. What is

---

Claudius which was staged in 1972 and achieved major success as a BBC Television serial later in the 1970s.

[85] For example, *Helen of Troy*, dir. Robert Wise, 1956 and *L'ira di Achille* [*The Fury of Achilles*], dir. Marino Girolami, 1962. See Paul 2013.

[86] Letter from RH to RG, 25 April 1946 (RG/S1).

[87] Letter from RG to RH, undated, but stamped 29 April 1946 (RG/S1). From 1940 to 1948 the philosopher C. E. M. Joad (1891–1953) presented the very popular radio discussion programme *The Brains Trust* (on which see McKibbin 2000, 469–70).

[88] Letter from RG to RH, undated, but stamped 29 April 1946 (RG/S1).

certain is that your prose work is particularly up the street of this department (Features), because of its factual and speculative nature.'[89] In 1952 he wrote to him again about a new series of *Imaginary Conversations* and by now Graves had become more favourable to the idea of writing for radio, offering a thirty-minute talk on 'The Argonauts' for the Third Programme.[90] Some months later, an internal memo written by Douglas Cleverdon (1903–87), Heppenstall's colleague in the Features Department, notes that 'we should like to recommend very strongly that Robert Graves be commissioned to undertake a major work for the Third Programme. [. . .] it appears that Graves would be very willing to write something within the range of a work of creative imagination like *The Dark Tower* [Louis MacNeice's radio masterpiece] [. . .]. We should prefer to leave the precise form and subject to Graves' choice.'[91] Accordingly the Third offered Graves a commission for 'a new and major work of some kind—preferably, but not necessarily in verse, and if possible, dramatic or semi-dramatic in form. [. . .] I know this is all extremely vague; but that vagueness was really part of Third's intention. They are too eager to broadcast a new work of yours to try laying down the law about its nature.'[92]

The BBC was enthusiastic about persuading authors of standing to write new work for radio, but when the material produced was not fit for broadcasting—either in terms of length, style, or content—much internal hand-wringing accompanied the decision on whether or not to turn the script into a broadcast. In 1956, for example, Graves proposed a series of three talks on *Why I Hate the Romans*, one of which was focused on the Etruscans and another on Nero. An independent reader of the scripts offered the following advice to P. H. Newby (1918–97), the Chief Assistant for Talks:

> Robert Graves as the child at large in the world of scholarship is now such a well known public character that nobody I think would take

---

[89] Letter from RH to RG, 10 February 1948 (RG/S1).
[90] Letter from RH to RG, 12 February 1952 (RG/S1); letter from RG to P. H. Newby, 2 June 1952; and Talks Booking Requisition, 24 June 1952 (RG/T1). Newby accepted the offer, on the condition that it be twenty minutes long; it was broadcast as *The Geography of the Golden Fleece Legend* on 28 November 1952 (letter from Gilbert Phelps to RG, in RG/T1).
[91] Internal memo from Douglas Cleverdon to the Assistant Controller of the Third Programme, 13 October 1952 (RG/S1).
[92] Letter from [illegible name] to RG, 19 December 1952 (RG/S1).

these pieces seriously if we put them on. The question is, would they entertain? Of the two, the more outrageous from a scholar's or historian's point of view, + so the more frivolously amusing, perhaps, is that on the Etruscans. If we let it go out, we should have to make it clear to the uninitiated, I suppose, that we were not offering it seriously as historical research but possibly Graves's reputation would do that well enough for us.[93]

Newby writes to Graves with his concerns and a lively correspondence ensued on such matters as the likelihood that the average Third Programme listener has read Suetonius. Graves insisted that the talks were well researched and must go out pretty much as they are since he had no time to recast them; Graves wins the battle but Newby still privately hopes that he can be encouraged to edit the scripts before broadcast.[94] The three talks, which were broadcast on the Third Programme in 1956 under the title 'The Cultured Romans', generated some anger amongst scholars. The Acting Controller of Talks, J. C. Thornton, relates a conversation he had with the furious Otto Skutsch (1906–90), Professor of Latin at University College London: 'I told him that we had not imagined that Robert Graves was making a serious contribution to classical scholarship and that we had put on this talk rather as a *jeu d'esprit*. He said he appreciated this point but nevertheless he had found some of his students were taking it seriously and he did think it bad to broadcast a talk which contained errors of fact which could have been corrected.'[95] Another outraged listener, R. D. Greenaway, wrote a long and strong letter to *The Listener* to pick up on several points in the talk which he considered 'in many ways inaccurate and misleading', concluding that 'Mr Graves would do better to stick to poetry'.[96]

As it happens, in 1957, the following year, the BBC invited Graves to provide a poetic translation of the scene between Thetis and Achilles in *Iliad* XVIII. 1–147 for one of twelve half-hour programmes of readings of key scenes from the epic poem, as translated by a variety

---

[93] Letter from [M. C. H.?] to Mr [P. H.] Newby, 5 April 1956 (RG/T1).
[94] See correspondence in RG/T1.
[95] Letter from J. C. Thornton to P. H. Newby, 26 February 1957 (RG/T1).
[96] Typescript copy of letter from R. D. Greenaway for publication in *The Listener*, 7 March 1957 (RG/T1). These negative responses to Graves's somewhat controversial talks did not, it must be noted, prevent the BBC from repeating the talks in June of the same year.

of modern poets, for broadcast in 1958.[97] In his letter to Graves, Carne-Ross notes that the variety of styles of translation offered by the series 'is intended to reflect the varieties of approach possible at the present time to a great traditional poem. The translations are, so far as possible, poets' translations rather than dons' translations.'[98] The idea appealed to Graves, but he replied that he would be prevented from accepting the commission by the backlog of work he had to tackle before embarking on an American lecture tour.[99] In reply Carne-Ross wrote: 'Indeed, what a pity! It would have been immensely interesting to have seen you at grips with Homer.'[100]

In truth, Graves was already very much 'at grips with Homer', writing *The Anger of Achilles*, which would be published by Doubleday in 1959. It can have been no coincidence, then, that soon after this correspondence with Carne-Ross, Graves's literary agent W. P. Wyatt wrote to the BBC to inform them of Graves's forthcoming translation, suggesting that the Third Programme might be interested in broadcasting readings from it.[101] In the light of the already planned series, however, Carne-Ross's response to this suggestion could perhaps have been anticipated: 'it does not seem likely that we will be able to place readings from it in the Third Programme since we have just finished a series of twelve readings devoted to new translations of the same poem'.[102] It was as a result of his conversations with Wanamaker that Graves had been struck with the idea of trying out the script on radio as the best approach to lay the ground for his ambitious theatre and film project.[103] The radio idea may not have had legs in 1958, but in 1961 the University of Oxford elected Graves to the prestigious Professorship of Poetry and in late 1962—the year in which W. H. Auden described Graves as England's 'greatest living poet'—his idea to put *The Anger of Achilles* on air, made via his agent, was accepted by the BBC.[104]

---

[97] Letter from DSCR to RG, 30 December 1957 (RG/S1).
[98] DSCR to RG, 30 December 1957 (RG/S1).
[99] Letter from RG to DSCR, 8 January 1958 (RG/S1).
[100] Letter from DSCR to RG, 14 January 1958 (RG/S1).
[101] Letter from W. P. Watt to the Director of Talks, Third Programme, 18 May 1958 (RG/S1).
[102] Letter from DSCR to W. P. Watt, 21 May 1958 (RG/S1).
[103] Letter from Peter Watt to Martin Esslin, 11 December 1962 (RG/T1).
[104] Memo from Martin Esslin to Peggy Wells, 9 January 1963 (RG/S2).

It is interesting to note that—at this point in Graves's career, perhaps—it did not seem to matter to the BBC that the publication of *The Anger of Achilles* had received a mixed reception from scholars. The volume was illustrated by lively and humorous drawings by Ronald Searle (1920–2011), cartoonist for *Punch*, *The New Yorker*, and *Le Monde*,[105] which capture well the flavour of the sentiments expressed on the flyleaf:

> Known the world over as a great epic and a literary classic, the *Iliad* was composed primarily to amuse and is filled with great comedy and biting satire. In *The Anger of Achilles*, Robert Graves has translated the narrative into sharp, clear prose, interpolating the songs into exquisite lyric poetry, and has caught all the rich humor lacking in the usual solemn, pedantic versions of the *Iliad*.[106]

The flyleaf records that Searle's fourteen cartoons within the book are intended to highlight 'the satire accented in this fresh, new rendering of Homer's epic'. The flyleaf also anticipates that the translation 'may shock some scholars'. Indeed, the certainty and confidence with which the first two sentences of the Introduction state what are offered as the 'facts' of the *Iliad*'s composition and early performance left some Homeric scholars and students aggrieved:

> The *Homeridae* ('Sons of Homer'), a family guild of Ionian bards based in Chios, enlarged their ancestor's first short draft of the *Iliad* to twenty-four books, and became comprehensively known as 'Homer'. They earned their livelihood by providing good popular entertainment for such festivals as the All-Ionian at Mount Mycale in Lydia, the All-Athenian at Athens, and the four-yearly homage to their patron Apollo at Delos; also, it seems, by going on circuit to various small royal courts where Greek was spoken, from Asia Minor to Sicily, and perhaps even visiting Spain and Western Morocco.[107]

Graves goes on to set forth some theories on the interpretation of the *Iliad* which are so controversial that one scholar—who is otherwise favourable in his review of the translation itself—suggests 'that the reader ignore completely Graves' introduction'.[108] Where Graves

---

[105] McNay 2012. [106] Flyleaf to the first edition: Graves 1959.
[107] Ibid. 13. For a concise summary of the issues of composition and transmission which continue to be discussed under the banner of the 'Homeric question', see Rutherford 1996, 9 ff.
[108] Rexine 1962, 281.

may be more in line with scholarship is in his emphasis on entertainment as a function of Homer's epic poetry. The Homeric epics, he declares, need to be 'rescued from the classroom curse which has lain heavily on them throughout the past twenty-six centuries, and become entertainment once more'.[109] Further along in his Introduction, Graves pays homage to the recent translation of the *Iliad* by Richmond Lattimore (1906–84), published in 1951, but he describes it merely as a 'crib', a close translation for the use of students. Translations such as his, Graves considers, 'are made for the general, non-Classical public, yet their authors seldom consider what will be immediately intelligible, and therefore readable, and what will not'.[110] It is this perceived failure that Graves seeks to rectify with his own translation of the *Iliad*, which is written in prose with frequent short passages of verse—which he describes as song—'where prose will not suffice' (for example, addresses to gods and Homeric similes).[111] He appoints himself as rescuer of the *Iliad* for readers who wish thoroughly to enjoy it in English translation. Some reviewers considered that this was a much needed mission in which Graves succeeds. For example, the literary scholar and critic F. W. Bateson (1901–78), writing in *The Observer*, considers that, whereas the fortunes of Homer's *Odyssey* have gone 'up and up', 'The *Iliad* has become more than sophisticated modern flesh can bear [...] A modern translation of the *Iliad* is, therefore, primarily a rescue operation.'[112]

Raymond Raikes was in charge of producing the première for the Drama Department for broadcast in three one-hour parts on the Home Service. As noted in Section 2.2, Raikes was a producer for whom radio dramatic sense was of the utmost importance, and it certainly was not curtailed by his academic background in classics.[113] In his first letter to Graves about *The Anger of Achilles*, he accordingly displays his confidence in both adapting scripts for the

---

[109] Graves 1959, 13.   [110] Ibid. 33.
[111] Ibid. 35. Notably, Steiner 2004 leaves Graves out of his survey of Homeric translations.
[112] Bateson 1960. See Wrigley 2015 for detailed discussion of reviews of *The Anger of Achilles*.
[113] Perhaps this was in recognition of the debates in the press on the seemingly limited appeal of the Third Programme's subject coverage. In his obituary of Raikes, Tydeman 1998 refers to this tendency. He produced at least twenty Greek and Roman plays over his thirty-year career.

comprehension of the listener and understanding where musical and radiophonic sounds are required:

> I have timed the scripts and, finding that they were quite a bit short of the hour, I have extended them, working direct from your translation of the ILIAD (you will notice I have even used a phrase at the start of each from page xii of your introduction). Again, learning that the BBC Home Service hopes to broadcast the three parts at <u>weekly</u> intervals, I have tried to make each script self-contained so that a listener should he have missed part 1 and/or part 2 can still enjoy part 3. I have also, as you will see, prepared the scripts for my radio production and have inserted cues for music, both orchestral and radiophonic.[114]

Music was an important part of this production: each of the three hour-long parts was to include between twenty-five to thirty minutes of musical accompaniment specially composed by Roberto Gerhard (1896–1970) for a sizeable orchestra. The score was later described as an 'orchestral-cum-radiophonic score' because of the composer's collaboration with the BBC Radiophonic Workshop: the ensuing 'radiophonic music' was used specifically to accompany scenes involving Athene, Thetis, Aphrodite, and Zeus in order to emphasize their divinity.[115]

The Anger of Achilles was first broadcast as *The Sunday Play* on the Home Service on three consecutive Sunday afternoons in 1964, billed in the *Radio Times* as 'An Epic for Radio by Robert Graves from his translation of the *Iliad*'. The first part covers Agamemnon's seizure of Achilles' war-prize Briseis and Achilles' subsequent withdrawal from battle; parts two and three cover the Greeks' reversal, the intervention of the gods, the death of Patroclus at the hands of the Trojan Hector, the subsequent death of Hector at the hands of Achilles, and Achilles' reconciliation with Hector's father, Priam.

Following the première, Raikes devised a 'shortened and tautened' script for a single 95-minute broadcast on the Third Programme in 1965 which was submitted as the BBC's entry for the prestigious Prix Italia.[116] The script for this begins with a '<u>SHORT, EVOCATIVE, ORCHESTRAL OPENING</u>' after which a narrator briefly sets the scene: 'Two thousand six hundred years ago in a royal courtyard in

---

[114] Letter from RR to RG, 17 June 1963 (RG/T1).
[115] 'Radiophonic Music in *The Anger of Achilles*', typescript notes (ibid.).
[116] Raikes 1966.

The Poetry and Drama of Homeric Epic 215

Greece... an audience, relaxing with wine-cups at their elbows, sat waiting for one of Homer's story-telling sons.'[117] An unspecified 'King' welcomes the bard Phemias (played by Denis Quilley)—whose name clearly owes a substantial debt to the Phemios of the *Odyssey*, the bard of Odysseus's household—upon his arrival from Delos. The script begins with Graves's invocation of the Muse (renamed 'Mountain Goddess') which is spoken by Phemias, who goes on to narrate, over music, the background of the Trojan War, bringing the listener to the moment when Chryses, the priest of Apollo whose daughter Chryseis had been taken by Agamemnon, approaches him to request her return. This structuring technique is used throughout the play—short scenes are interspersed with 'narration over music' by Phemias—thus lending a great economy to the radio storytelling. The dialogue, too, is shortened to give the drama of the tale a fast pace and vivid feel. For example, Graves's published translation of the angry confrontation between Agamemnon and Achilles in Book I begins with Achilles addressing Agamemnon thus:

> Son of Atreus, you are the greediest man in the Assembly, as well as the noblest-born! Why should these princes give you a prize of honour [as compensation if he were to return Chryseis to her father]? They have no common stock of booty upon which to draw. What we took from captured cities has already been distributed; and it would not be decent were a particular award withdrawn and made over to you. Send back the girl, as Apollo demands, and later, if Zeus lets us sack some other Trojan fortress, we will vote you three or four times her value.

After a further page of increasingly heated discussion between the two heroes, Agamemnon concludes: 'Yet, let me inform you that, since Apollo insists on robbing me of Chryseis, my own ship and crew will carry her back; and that I shall then visit your hut and compensate myself with your prize of honour, the beautiful Briseis.'[118] In the shortened, prize-winning radio script, this dialogue is rendered much more concisely as:

> ACHILLES (In harsh tones) King Agamemnon, you are the greediest man alive!
> AGAMEMNON (Stung) What. Achilles!

---

[117] A copy of the script is held in RGA.
[118] Graves 1959, 42 and 43, his translation of lines from *Iliad* I.

ACHILLES   Send back the girl, as Apollo demands.
AGAMEMNON   (More furious still) So I must surrender Chryseis, and expect no compensation—is that it? You, I suppose, are to keep your prize of honour and leave me chafing empty-handed? No, indeed! I shall visit your hut and recoup my loss with your prize of honour, the beautiful Briseis of Lyrnessus.

It was this abridged radio version of *The Anger of Achilles* which in 1965 won the Prix Italia for best literary and dramatic work for radio; furthermore, Raymond Raikes's production of *The Foundling* by Peter Gurney (the pen-name of Dr Andrew M. Wilkinson), with music by Humphrey Searle (1915–82), won the prize for stereophonic radio work.[119] This was the first time since the mid-1950s that the BBC had come away with two prizes in one year, and it was the first time ever that any country had won two prizes for works produced by the same man.[120] Graves had not been able to attend the ceremony himself, but he celebrated the news of the win with a bottle of champagne, poignantly remembering that 'This time 50 years ago I was dining at the Montmorency Château Béthune watching my fellow officers who were [...] going to be killed at Loos next day'.[121] On returning from Florence with his record-breaking two prizes, Raikes wrote to the composer Gerhard as follows: 'I shall be going to a Third Programme meeting on Monday and hope to persuade them to give a further "airing" to the 55 minutes version of *The Anger of Achilles* which I devised specifically for the Italia Prize.'[122]

---

[119] Gurney had also written *The Guilt of Polycrates*, a radio play in verse drawn from Herodotus III and broadcast on the Third in 1960, telling the story of Polycrates, King of Samos, who met an unhappy end after a remarkable run of luck in life. The play neatly re-works Herodotean narrative technique, re-casting the story in radio dramatic terms: Herodotus appears as a narrator, briefly introducing the three acts; a chorus of unidentified individual 'voices' adds dramatic depth and poetic texture throughout; moments in the ancient model, such as when the fisherman lands the fish, are expanded and dramatized; and Amasis's first letter to Polycrates is given verbatim but presented in radiophonic terms (an Ambassador announces the letter; fade to Polycrates reading it aloud; finally, fade to Amasis's voice reading the words which gives the neat and intimate effect for the listener of Polycrates 'hearing' the voice of his ally in his mind as he reads).
[120] 'Italia Prize Double for BBC Producer from Bromley', BBC Press Service, 12 October 1965 (S452/S4/1).
[121] Letter from RG to Isla Cameron, 24 September 1965 (RGC, Gr 3: 1–49).
[122] Letter from RR to Roberto Gerhard, 8 October 1965 (S452/48/1).

The Radio Times listing for this 1966 repeat production is illustrated by an elaborate drawing titled 'Radio Italiana Prize 1965' and accompanied by an appealing and informative article by Raikes:

> How did we set about making this 'epic for radio' which won the Radio Italiana Prize in A.D. 1965? It was quite by chance we heard that Robert Graves would be interested in making a broadcasting adaptation of his own racy, vivid translation—he wanted to do this as a first step to making a dramatisation for the stage, for television, and the films. [. . .] And then another letter arrived from Robert Graves: 'Homer should be grateful for our having let him have his story without any clever embellishments. I feel that this performance is going to bring us good luck!' His words were prophetically true: originally serialised on three hot Sunday afternoons in May 1964, I shortened and tautened it for the revival as one programme in the Third (June 1965), and the version you will hear tonight was awarded the prize in the Palazzo Vecchio in Florence last September.[123]

The 1966 broadcast of the abridged version was heard by an estimated 150,000 Home Service listeners.[124] The choice of network is interesting. The 1964 première had also been broadcast on the Home in one-hour chunks over three Sundays. In 1965, however, the newly abridged version appeared on the Third Programme, a network which from its foundation in 1946 had sought to appeal to an already educated and cultured listenership and on which what we thought of as 'highbrow' cultural works—a definition which came to include a great deal of the Greek material subsequently broadcast—were naturally at home. Following the award of the Prix Italia, however, it was revived on the Home Service, which served a much broader audience in terms of 'brow', and this no doubt testifies to its perceived, and actual, wide appeal.[125] As the critic (and later author) Paul Ferris noted in *The Observer* in response to the 1966 broadcast: 'Poetry and poetry-programmes rarely get further than the Third (a notable exception last week was Robert Graves's *The Anger of Achilles* on the Home Service, a radio spectacular from his translation of the *Iliad*, which won the 1965 Radio Italiana Prize).' Ferris concludes that

---

[123] Raikes 1966.
[124] 'BBC Audience Research Barometer of Listening, Thursday, Week 11, 17 March 1966' (WAC).
[125] On radio networks, audiences, and perceptions of cultural 'brow', especially with regard to works drawing on Greek antiquity, see Section 2.1.

'Programmes like [...] *The Anger of Achilles* are still among the best things that radio has to offer'.[126]

In August 1964, Richard Imison, Script Editor for the Drama Department for nearly thirty years, wrote to Graves's agent to press for a radio adaptation of *I Claudius* and *Claudius the God* to be written either by Graves himself or 'another adaptor of high standing':

> If [the film people] really aren't going to do anything with it and are merely jealously guarding their rights, could you possibly put to them the point of view that a radio production would in no way prejudice any future plans for a film, and could even be very useful publicity in bringing the books back into the public eye?[127]

Following some further communication between the two men, another letter from Imison followed in which he expressed a wish to commission 'an original work from Mr Graves for Third Programme [...] One idea in particular occurred to us and that was that radio might prove an ideal medium for a new work about Nero [...] We were enormously pleased with *The Anger of Achilles* and it was extremely popular with the audience.'[128] This fascinating private correspondence bring us back to the fact that, whatever Graves's standing amongst scholars (past and present) and however many feathers he ruffled with his interpretations of the ancient world, his ancient stories held enormous popular appeal. Audiences for these works—and these not only included readers and viewers but also hundreds of thousands of *listeners*—may not in the main have been schooled in classics but their experience of the ancient world was made memorable by Graves, who had a remarkable ability to make ancient stories come alive. As an unidentified reader for the BBC put it to P. H. Newby, when considering the radio potential of Graves's *The Cultured Romans* scripts: 'The question is, would they entertain?'[129] Entertain they clearly did, but they also made a significant contribution to the life of the ancient world in the public imagination. A *New York Times* review of the 1959 publication of *The Anger of*

---

[126] Ferris 1966.
[127] Letter from Richard Imison to Peter Watt, 12 August 1964 (RG/S2).
[128] Letter from Richard Imison to Peter Watt, 19 August 1964 (ibid.).
[129] Letter from [M. C. H.?] to Mr [P. H.] Newby, 5 April 1956 (RG/T1).

Achilles by Dudley Fitts nicely captured the paradox surrounding Graves's writings on the ancient world:

> Classical scholars do not automatically jump for joy when the name of Robert Graves is mentioned. His excursions into their territory are raids, not pilgrimages—gay assaults, hit-and-run, 'unprofessional', popularizing, irreverent to the point of impudence. Clearly he is not a Classical Scholar: the man can take an ancient text—Apuleius, Suetonius and now Homer—and make it live again in an English as fresh and as pure and as compelling as a morning gale.[130]

---

[130] Fitts 1959.

7

Greek Tragedy: The Case of Aeschylus' *Agamemnon*, 1946–1976

Agamemnon, whether performed alone or as part of Aeschylus' *Oresteia* trilogy, is an interesting case for study. Regarded by theatre directors and radio producers as one of the greatest dramatic challenges, with its powerful, complex language and good range of voices, it has, perhaps unsurprisingly, been one of the most popular tragedies for radio broadcast. This section examines the production history of Aeschylus' *Agamemnon* on BBC Radio from the inaugural Greek tragedy on the Third Programme in 1946 (the first known BBC production of the play) to a landmark experimental production of Gabriel Josipovici's *Ag* on Radio 3 thirty years later. It presents a variety of engagements with the ancient text, often achieved through a collaboration of producers with translators/writers, with the recurrent phrase 'adapted for broadcasting and produced by' signalling a new and significant function of the radio producer in the radio dramatization process.[1]

Louis MacNeice's *Agamemnon* on the Third Programme

MacNeice's translation of *Agamemnon* was written for the 1936 Group Theatre production in London for which Britten composed the music.[2] For the stage production MacNeice notably tacked onto the end of the play the first chorus of the *Choephoroi*, giving the

---

[1] On the producer as textual editor see Rodger 1982, 120.

[2] Hugh Lloyd-Jones considered MacNeice's translation to be 'the most successful version of any Greek tragedy that anyone in this country has yet produced' (Dodds 1977, 116).

production 'a grim note of foreboding that was no less pertinent to the Europe of 1936 than to the house of Atreus'.[3] In his Preface to the published translation, MacNeice wrote: 'I have consciously sacrificed certain things in the original—notably the liturgical flavour of the diction and the metrical complexity of the choruses. It is my hope that the play emerges as a play and not as a museum piece.'[4] Philip Hope-Wallace, writing in *The Listener* of its first radio production in 1946 (see Figure 7.1), admired its modernity and clear imagery but considered that it lacked power in this medium: 'better perhaps a successful Victorian pageant, all inaccurate sentiment, fustian and purple patches, than... well nothing at all in the way of drama'. He perceives that the actors seemed to agree, 'throbbing and sighing through the lines as if they had been concocted by Swinburne at his wildest'.[5] In contrast, the reviewer in *The Times* considered that the new clarity afforded by MacNeice's translation rendered the play 'twice as effective': 'imagine nations, instead of these petty and barbaric chiefs, caught in a net of crime and retaliation, and the tragedy becomes curiously timeless'.[6]

The Listener Research Report confirms that the 29 October 1946 broadcast was heard by 2 per cent of the adult civilian population; in other words, around three-quarters of a million individuals tuned in to the Third Programme's first new production of a Greek tragedy.[7] Listeners were introduced to the themes of the play by MacNeice himself in a lucid *Radio Times* article and the magazine's listing for the production was illustrated by a remarkable line drawing by Eric Fraser which shows the domineering Clytemnestra resting on her double-edged axe, with the netted Agamemnon and the despairing Cassandra to the left, and three cowed Elders to the right (see

---

[3] Sidnell 1986, 326. On the 1936 production see Sidnell 1984, especially ch. 10.
[4] MacNeice 1936, 8.
[5] Hope-Wallace 1946b. Cf. Heuser 1998, 136 who asserts that 'MacNeice in fact invariably requested his actors to avoid "the poetry voice"' which, 'with its polished elocution and exquisite pronunciation, seemed mannered and affected' (Scannell and Cardiff 1991, 162).
[6] Anon. 1946a.
[7] BBC WAC LR/6566. At the time of publishing an earlier version of this *Agamemnon* case study, not knowing about the existence of Listener Research Reports, I followed Carpenter 1997, 48 in stating that 'audience figures for these early Third Programme drama broadcasts suggest that there could have been an astonishing 1½–2½ million listeners for this its first new production of a Greek tragedy' (Wrigley 2006, 224).

Fig. 7.1. 'To me this hour was dreamed of long ago': Eric Fraser's drawing for *Agamemnon* in 1946 (*Radio Times*, 25 October 1946, 12). Reproduced by kind permission of the Fraser family.

Figure 7.1).[8] No sound recording of this production is available through the BLSA, but it is clear from an internal memo that Britten's music for the 1936 stage production was not used; only drum rolls and trumpets augmented the sound of the voices, with a few seconds of music from Josef Suk's 'V nový život' and Handel's 'The Great Elopement'.[9] The production, directed by Val Gielgud, starred leading radio actors of the day who offered voices which were 'distinguishable, and full of colour', with the 'awful transports' of Olive Gregg's Cassandra earning her the palm for performance.[10]

One hundred and seventeen listeners (representing 3 per cent of the listening panel) completed questionnaires on this production. The overall Appreciation Index was 68, which was considered to be 'very good'; it was five points higher than the figure for the Home Service *Trojan Women* broadcast in April. Fifty-eight per cent of those who were already familiar with the play were impressed with MacNeice's translation and 42 per cent liked it moderately: 'Inevitably there were some comparisons with the well known Murray translations, but listeners' comments were mainly enthusiastic, several praising what a housewife described as MacNeice's "powerful, lucid and poetic

---

[8] MacNeice 1946*b*.
[9] 'The Third Programme: Tuesday 29.10.1946' typescript (BBC WAC).
[10] Anon. 1946*a*.

writing"'. A handful found the themes of the play 'distasteful', the speeches 'boring', and the 'declamatory style' of acting 'out of date':

> I dislike intensely the way actors in this type of play nearly always 'elocute'. They never talk naturally—they always shout and hurl their voices out. It is unconvincing and, after a time, irritating. I can't see why they do it. (Teacher)

But the vast majority, it seems, 'were moved by the grandeur and universality of the drama'. For example:

> The whole thing gave me a feeling of being in the presence of something great. It was full of eternal truth and a particularly apt picture of post-war disillusionment. (Housewife)
>
> A new and thrilling experience. Sometimes very moving. (Advt. Clerk)

A small minority were vociferously critical of the production. Even amongst those who were familiar with the play there was some difficulty 'distinguishing the voices and following the action [...] the general feeling seemed to be that the difficulty would best have been met by a synopsis before the actual broadcast, or a fuller account in the *Radio Times*': a Research Chemist considered that 'It was difficult to refrain from switching off during the first ten minutes or so because, to a person little acquainted with the details of the story, the play seemed to be most incomprehensible'.[11] This was not, of course, the first time that MacNeice's *Radio Times* articles had failed to hit the spot for those looking for a first, general introduction to the plot of a Greek play: his article introducing the previous year's production of Murray's translation of *Hippolytus* on the Home Service, for example, had been considered by many to be inadequate in communicating the basics (as discussed in Section 4.1).

MacNeice's translation was given in a new production on the Third on 12 July 1950, just two days after a broadcast of Gluck's opera *Iphigénie en Aulide*. Raymond Raikes is credited both with arranging the translation for broadcasting and producing, and the BLSA recording of this production offers a useful insight to his priorities in producing a Greek tragedy on radio. He makes judicious cuts designed to sharpen the impact of long choral odes and confidently transposes lines for clarity and dramatic effect. A startling

[11] BBC WAC LR/6566.

example of the transposition of lines takes place in Clytemnestra's dialogue with the chorus immediately after the murders: the passionately delivered lines referring to her husband's infidelity have been brought almost to the beginning of her first passage of speech, placing the husband's faithlessness uppermost in the wife's mind, notably long before her words on his sacrifice of their daughter. This suggests that the cut from the parodos of the second half of the graphic description of Iphigenia's sacrifice might have been made to suit Raikes's dramatic interpretation of the play rather than to avoid upsetting audience taste. He also makes liberal use of what may be described as dramatized 'stage directions', interpolations spoken by the characters to indicate the location and movement of the characters in the mind's eye of the audience: for example, the additional words 'But now already the day is dawning and below in the courtyard the Elders of Argos assemble. I take my news to the Queen!' stage-manage the Watchman's 'exit' early in the play and prepare the way for the 'entrance' of the Chorus. Furthermore, at almost every opportunity nouns take the place of pronouns, acting as clear signposts which ensure that the audience follow the dramatic action. As discussed earlier, Raikes was no academic purist, despite having studied classics at Uppingham School and Oxford. He was well known for his tendency to cut, re-structure, and re-write dramatic texts to make them work as accessibly as possible on radio, perhaps in recognition of the debates in the press on the seemingly limited appeal of the Third Programme's subject coverage.[12]

Hope-Wallace found more to his liking in this production of MacNeice's *Agamemnon* but he reiterated his view that this 'carefully un-fustian' modern translation would have more impact if it were delivered on stage by actors attired in the neo-classical style immortalized in Frederic Leighton's paintings; for him, MacNeice's text was simply not grand enough to convey the power of Aeschylus in this 'sightless' medium and he particularly deplores un-Greek characterizations such as the 'local yokel' Watchman.[13] The recording informs us that the actors largely deliver their lines in speech, with musical phrases illustrating their words at key points. Performances are

---

[12] Tydeman 1998.
[13] Hope-Wallace 1950. Regional accents had only begun to emerge on BBC Radio during the war (and on the reaction to the Yorkshireman Wilfred Pickles reading the news see McKibbin 2000, 469).

strong, with Sonia Dresdel and Diana Maddox acting the parts of Clytemnestra and Cassandra with particular verve. The Chorus sometimes speak in unison, but more often individually, sharing sentences with the speaker changing every phrase or few lines. Song is interwoven into the choral odes in significant ways: it is used to round off sections of spoken text, to emphasize key lines (for example, the refrain beginning '*Ailinon, ailinon*' at *Agamemnon* 121, 139, and 159), and to deliver the words of Calchas and Agamemnon in direct speech (or, rather, direct song) in the first choral ode. Musical refrains established early on in the drama reappear later and in this way the music, specially composed by John Hotchkis for strings (including a harp), woodwind, and trumpet, adds texture to this tapestry of song and speech delivered by multiple and single voices. With reference to the sung and musical elements of the play, Hope-Wallace recognizes how the emerging conventions of radio drama differ from those of staged plays: 'Oratorio, opera? We had better not start beating the bounds again on that vexed no-man's-land which divides opera and radio play.'[14] One angry listener wrote to Raikes the next day to question whether the ancient Greeks would have performed *Agamemnon* in an operatic style: 'I had looked forward to this programme immensely and was forced to switch off in disgust after about ten minutes—ten minutes during which I had heard nothing but background noises and moaning singing.' Raikes patiently responds by explaining the sung and danced element of Greek tragedy, and why he chose to apply song and music to the choruses in this way: 'to sing the entirety of these lengthy choral odes would be more than the modern ear could assimilate and comprehend; and so I tried to strike a mean, having certain phrases sung and the remainder spoken to the accompaniment of music'.[15]

Raikes produced MacNeice's translation of the play for a second time just three years later in June 1953, but this time for the *World Theatre* series on the Home Service.[16] The Home Service drama

[14] Hope-Wallace 1950.
[15] Postcard from A. Mackenzie-Smith to RR, 13 July 1950 and Raikes's letter in response, 21 July 1950 (S452/29/1).
[16] As mentioned above, the Home had in 1953 broadcast Murray's six talks on *Hellenism and the Modern World*; and in 1955 an 8½-minute extract from MacNeice's translation of *Agamemnon* was used as dramatic illustration in *Mycenae's Second Glory*, a programme on archaeological discoveries written and produced by Leonard Cottrell for the Home.

policy was to broadcast popular plays on Saturdays and less popular plays on Mondays, with every fourth Monday seeing the broadcast of a work of recognized distinction for the *World Theatre* series. That Raikes should produce this play again so soon afterwards, and on this much more populist network, is a strong indication of the perceived success of the 1950 production. The listing in the *Radio Times*, illustrated by Eric Fraser's drawing first used in 1946, is accompanied by a longer than usual introductory article by MacNeice which also features a helpful diagram of the family tree of the House of Atreus.[17] The production was, perhaps tellingly, passed over in the review of radio drama in the following issue of *The Listener*, despite the entirely new cast and fresh recording of music by Hotchkis: this omission may owe something to the play's re-appearance on the Home Service rather than the more esoteric Third.[18]

In 1953 a BBC survey of Third Programme listeners reported that the audience on an average winter evening had shrunk to 90,000, but also that far fewer of those who might be expected to be listening—on the basis of education and tastes—were doing so, and that many outside of this bracket were in fact tuning in.[19] From the start the press had been critical of the Programme's choice of subject matter: just days before its first birthday the *Daily Express* complained that 'too many of the items smell of the dust of a don's study, and give the impression that they are broadcast because they are highbrow and/or unusual, not because they are good'.[20] Yet it was not until the BBC began to experience financial difficulties in the early 1950s that suggestions began to be made that the Programme should be scrapped, or at least have its hours cut, on account of the disproportionate size of its budget in relation to its audience. In 1957, the year in which the *Radio Times* moved its television listings before those for radio, the Third Programme's air-time was indeed cut by 40 per cent, resulting in the time for major theatrical items—including Greek drama—being reduced by more than half.[21] This cut was part of a wider raft of changes in sound broadcasting responding to the fact that BBC Radio no longer held the broadcasting monopoly in Britain. The *Radio Times* reassured listeners that the Third Programme would

---

[17] MacNeice 1953. The family tree drawing exists amongs the BBC Transciption Service materials in S452/29/1.
[18] Published on 2 July 1953. [19] Carpenter 1997, 109.
[20] Hallam 1947. [21] Carpenter 1997, 185.

still broadcast one opera, play, and feature, on average, per week, but the response from the arts world was unforgiving.[22] The night before the controversial reduction in hours came into effect, the Sound Broadcasting Society, led by the Cambridge historian and freelance BBC producer Peter Laslett (1915–2001), marked the eleventh birthday of the Programme with a mock funeral at the Royal Court at which the Allegri Quartet, Peggy Ashcroft, Cecil Day-Lewis, T. S. Eliot (via a pre-recorded speech), and John Gielgud offered music, dramatic recitations, and speeches. Now the press enjoyed the role of staunch defender, with *The Times* asking, 'must a Third Programme die again before we may mix our media so boldly and so successfully?'[23]

Towards the Greek tragic climax of Val Gielgud's career

On Sunday, 27 May 1956, during the period of uncertainty and discontent before the shortening of the Third's air-time, its audience was faced with the challenge of a 3¾-hour production of the *Oresteia*. The production, together with its 'interval music'—*Agamemnon* was followed by music by Quantz, Handel, de Falla, and Hindemith and an overture from Gluck's *Iphigénie en Aulide* was played between *Choephori* and *Eumenides*—actually took up almost five hours of air-time. Perhaps echoing one possible popular reaction to such Third Programme broadcasts, the critic J. C. Trewin (1908–90) reported that he had suffered 'a rain of blows on the head rather than a piercing of heart, a shaking of soul', laying the blame firmly at the feet of the translator Philip Vellacott.[24] Vellacott was a teacher of classics at

---

[22] *Radio Times*, 27 September 1957, 5. In this issue the BBC published a defence of the changes affecting the Home, Third, and Light networks (Wellington 1957). It also introduced the new service Network Three: the shorter Third, rather than lower the 'brow' of its output, would have its nightly three hours preceded by two hours of what was considered to be a more 'middlebrow' mix of programmes on hobbies, families, and further education, the wide unpopularity of which suggested that it had been an ill-conceived substitute for Third broadcasts. With programmes on subjects such as record collecting, exotic cats, and astronomy, the new service became known as the 'fretwork network', the emergence of which alongside the Third provoked concern that 'highbrow' culture was widely considered to be little more than another minority hobby. There was also a suspicion that the Third might have disappeared altogether were it not for the intellectual and political power of many of its high-profile supporters.

[23] Anon. 1957d.   [24] Trewin 1956, 733.

Dulwich College, London who had introduced a wide public to Greek literature through his numerous translations in the Penguin Classics series.[25] Although Trewin considers the translation to have been 'hard work for the players' at points, any criticism of the decision to broadcast the entire trilogy on a single, 'exhaust[ing]' evening should surely have been better directed at the producer.[26] Raikes himself, in an introductory article in the *Radio Times*, wrote that he had in 1950 and 1953 produced MacNeice's translation of *Agamemnon* 'with a deep sense of its incompleteness. For it is but one act of a three-act play.'[27]

He devised a substantial educative exercise to accompany the lengthy 1956 *Oresteia*: an introductory talk by Vellacott was followed in subsequent weeks by talks on the theological and moral aspects of the trilogy by Hugh Lloyd-Jones (1922–2009), who was shortly to become Regius Professor of Greek at Oxford, a post he would hold from 1960 to 1989.[28] In addition, on the evening following the production, Elsa Vergi of the Greek National Theatre both read and sang extracts from the trilogy in Greek (eight in ancient Greek, and one in Ioannis Gryparis's modern Greek translation) which were interspersed with summaries in Vellacott's English translation given by Raikes himself. In his introduction to the programme Raikes warned that Vergi would pronounce ancient Greek 'in the way it is taught in the University of Athens', yet still his learned listeners wrote in suggesting variously that Reformed, Tonal, or Standard pronunciation would have been much better.[29] Indeed, as Trewin notes, 'in radio-drama, the word is in our ear, and when the word is that of the *Oresteia* we have to be in full training'.[30]

Something in the region of 35,000 listeners (0.1 per cent of the adult population) heard Vellacott's introductory talk, and most of the 59

---

[25] His *Oresteia* is dedicated to Raymond Raikes, who commissioned the translation for radio production (Vellacott 1956; see also Vellacott 1991).
[26] Trewin 1956, 733.   [27] Raikes 1956.
[28] I am grateful to Wolfgang Haase for the suggestion that these lectures may have been an early version of his *Classical Quarterly* article 'The Guilt of Agamemnon' (Lloyd-Jones 1962).
[29] 'Extracts from *The Oresteia* read in Greek by Elsa Vergi' (typescript in S452/29/1; see also correspondence between RR and Vergi in this file, and various letters from listeners to RR regarding the pronunciation). The extracts were recorded whilst Vergi was on holiday in England in the summer of 1955, the year after she had first appeared as Clytemnestra in Dimitris Rondiris's production of *Oresteia* for the Greek National Theatre.
[30] Trewin 1956, 733.

listeners who reported back to the BBC about it thought it to be 'just what was needed', with an Industrial Consultant considering it 'a first class introduction to Aeschylus, which will enable me to follow and enjoy tomorrow's broadcast'. A few considered it to be 'disappointingly elementary' and would have liked 'a more detailed discussion of the basic theological and moral ideas, or [...] of the difficulties of translation. But the bulk of the sample were evidently not such informed classicists, and definitely welcomed this kind of talk.'[31]

A similar number listened to the production itself and the Appreciation Index was calculated, from the 207 questionnaires sent in, to be 71, well above the average of 61 for Third Programme plays at this time. Most considered that hearing the entire trilogy over one evening had been 'a most worthwhile experience', even if some (echoing Trewin) admitted it had also been 'exhausting'. Amongst the sample of 'general reactions' recorded in the report are the following:

> There is no doubt, in spite of difficulties, that the plays gained much in point and significance by being given in one evening. I thought it was well worth the effort of setting aside the evening and devoting it to the trilogy. (Bank Manager)
>
> A superb entertainment, but an exhausting one. Very little to complain about—music good, acting good, production good, everywhere signs of intelligence and passion. Even choral speeches were well done. But it is exhausting to hold hard and listen, missing nothing—but so worth it. Now for the *Oedipus* and Theban groups! (Personal Assistant)
>
> The plays obviously gained a great deal by being acted so close together, so that small details hadn't time to fade from one's mind, and one could see the story as a whole. The music was excellent, and heightened the effect considerably. [...] I was glad to hear it will be repeated in a few months' time—but I hope there will be more than just one more chance of hearing it. (Shorthand-Typist)
>
> Glad to have heard it all. I still, after reading the trilogy in Greek several times, can't conceive what the Athenians made of it on one hearing, in the open air. Probably the direct effect of the poetry in the Greek accounts for most of the effect: and the translation used here (even more than MacNeice's of the *Agamemnon*) seemed to me as I compared it with the text, to convey very little of the poetry. Also the words of the choruses must surely have been clearly conveyed somehow to the original audience. The BBC's way of wrapping them up in more or

[31] BBC WAC LR/56/906.

less twentieth century musical orchestration, with counterpoint of voices even, is quite disastrous to intelligibility. Why not solo speech for the choruses next time? (Classics Teacher)

This classics teacher was not alone in disliking the setting of some of the choruses to Antony Hopkins's music. The report notes that one third of respondents 'had a good deal to say about the treatment of the choruses':

> This written response was almost equally divided for and against [. . .] On the one side, setting the choruses to music was thought a happy idea: the music itself harmonized with the play, was pleasant to listen to, and was effective in pointing action and dramatic climaxes. On the other hand, this 'semi-operatic' treatment was very much disliked, because it 'cluttered' the production, made it too complicated, and also because all-important words were lost by choruses which suggested 'now an oratorio, now a Puccini recitative'; the background music, 'too loud, too much and too insistent', did not help, either, they said.[32]

Such negative response to the musical aspects of the production may have irked the production team in light of the fact that a special application had had to be made to the Musicians' Union in order to record more than the permitted twenty minutes of incidental music in each play; permission was granted but at a cost of £4,100, which more than doubled the budget for the entire production (£3,206 had already been spent on other necessities such as the orchestra, copyright, and more than thirty actors and singers).[33]

Raikes received a remarkable amount of personal correspondence from listeners: some letters were written in praise, but many more offered strong criticism or suggestions for improvement. His responses are good-natured, even when defending against robust attack his musical interpretation of the choruses or his transposition of lines of Aeschylus for clarity and dramatic effect. Mild annoyance can be detected only once—in response to new undergraduates of Corpus Christi College, Cambridge, who had denounced his production as an 'unworthy travesty' of the Aeschylean play, suggesting that 'in future the BBC either seeks the advice of someone with an understanding of Greek Tragic drama, or else freely admits that

---

[32] BBC WAC LR/56/916.
[33] Memo from RR to C. J. Morris, Controller of the Third, 13 January 1956, and handwritten notes headed 'Actual Costs', both in S452/29/1.

their production is only remotely related to the original'. In response to their frustrated attempt to follow the play with a text, Raikes writes: 'I was concerned to express the play in terms of radio and to try to recreate something of its original impact on an Athenian audience; this audience would not have followed Aeschylus' words from writing but would have been content only to listen. I was not concerned to offer a "play-reading", for this, with the text readily available in a Penguin translation, would be a redundancy.'[34] 'What a pleasure, and excitement, it was to hear the *Oresteia*', wrote another: 'I'm an *Agamemnon* man myself, and I rather thought I'd have had enough with the first play. But I heard every word of the three, and the big thing came over well—hearty congratulations.'[35] The writer, Francis Richard Dale (1883–1976), headmaster of the City of London School and writer of books on the teaching of Latin language and literature, was not the only one to persevere through the entire production. The wife of a radio actor living in the Essex countryside writes, somewhat condescendingly, in *The Times* of how the listening tastes of the local tradesmen and their wives changed once they discovered a radio actor living nearby:

> Last summer George [their occasional gardener] and Lulu his wife— Lulu 'obliges' in the house—listened to the *whole* of the *Oresteia— Agamemnon, Choephori, Eumenides* and all! Which is more than we did. Lulu thought the music was lovely, and assured us most earnestly that they really enjoyed it, 'Right to the end'. But so far George has not been able to put into words his personal reactions to the really rather strange doings of that unhappy family at Mycenae, so very many years ago. And we too still wonder about it. What's Orestes to him? Or he to Orestes?[36]

The review in *The Times* is typical of its time with its concern over the translation (both its faithfulness to the original and its dramatic impact) and the expressiveness of the acting voices in 'getting across' the drama. Critical of the translation, it nevertheless awarded full

---

[34] Letter from D. D. Galloway and David E. [Soulsby?] to RR, 22 November 1956, and RR's response, 27 November 1956 (S452/29/1). To a similar criticism made by a reader of ancient Greek outside academia, Raikes is notably more patient in his response (see correspondence between James Toplis and RR, May–June 1956 in S452/29/1).

[35] Letter from Francis Richard Dale to RR, 28 May 1956 (S452/29/1).

[36] Anon. 1957a.

marks to the actors: 'the undertones of a wisdom born of sorrow and experience in Mr Quartermaine's voice, the lurking murder in the treacherous greeting of her husband by Miss Margaret Rawlings's Clytemnestra, and a remarkable suppleness of speech in Mr Peter Wyngarde's Orestes were among the most striking qualities of individual performances'.[37] Leon Quartermaine, the leader of the spoken choruses, had been urged by Raikes to imagine himself as Aeschylus when delivering the more philosophical of the choral passages.[38] The soprano Mary Rowland wrote to Raikes after performing in the sung choruses: 'I feel I was there—in Greece 500 BC.'[39] Vellacott, too, was pleased with the production. Writing to Raikes, he said: 'Looking back on all we heard, it is possible to emerge at last from the detail [...] to the scope + architecture of the whole performance. [...] You have achieved a dynamic success; + I hope it will be universally recognized.'[40] The production appears to have been submitted to the BBC's Transcription Service which distributed materials for overseas broadcasts of programmes—further testament to its perceived success.

In 1958 Raymond Postgate's prose translation of *Agamemnon* was produced on the Third by Frederick Bradnum (1920–2002), who was himself a prolific radio dramatist. Postgate ends his introductory talk with some useful 'scene-setting', focusing the listener's attention on the character of the Watchman: 'Facing you are the great doors, and on either side is a statue, one of Zeus and one of Apollo. You cannot as yet see them, for it is dark, but by straining your eyes you can make out the figure of a guard or watchman pacing up and down on the flat roof of the palace.' The play opens as follows:

WATCHMAN   God's the only person I can ask to get quit of this job; I've been watching here for a full year now. All the time I've been sleeping like a dog in the corner of the Atrid's roof. By now I know by heart the patterns the stars make at night. I can pick out too the bright strong lights in the sky, the ones that bring us Winter and Summer. I'm still watching for a signal from a beacon. It'll be a flash of fire that brings news

---

[37] Anon. 1956a.
[38] Letter from RR to Leon Quartermaine, 30 January 1956 (S452/29/1).
[39] Letter from Mary Rowland to RR, 9 May 1956 (ibid.).
[40] Letter from PV to RR, 10 May 1956 (ibid.).

from Troy and tells us it has fallen. That is what I have been told by the Queen; she's optimistic and very masterful.[41]

In his talk, Postgate had said, 'What I lose in poetry I hope to gain in clarity', and the radio dramatist and critic Ian Rodger approved of this 'sharp' translation in *The Listener*: 'no longer hypnotized by the ritual or modern renderings of Aeschylus's poetry I felt that I could come nearer to understanding'.[42] Two years later, in 1960, no such praise was forthcoming for Val Gielgud's Third Programme production of a 'puritanically unpoetic' version of *Agamemnon* by William Alfred (1922–99), the American playwright and Harvard Professor of the Humanities who had been a protégé of the poet Archibald MacLeish.[43] The critics of *The Listener* and *The Times* were polarized on the language of Alfred's version—which the *Radio Times* listing describes as 'an original verse play on the legendary Greek theme'— with the former considering it 'drab' and the latter eloquent and dignified at points.[44] The critics agree that acting was of a high standard, with Judy Bailey (Cassandra), Malcolm Keen (Agamemnon), and Mary Wimbush (Clytemnestra) deserving particular mention.

In his autobiography, Gielgud explains that he had always felt there to be 'magnificent microphone material' in Greek drama but that, in his own radio productions, the 'chorus-speaking had always left much to be desired, and available translations had always seemed either too dully academic or too lusciously free'.[45] That was the case, he goes on to say, until he struck up a particularly fruitful working relationship with Constantine Trypanis, the poet and Professor of Medieval and Modern Greek at Oxford, and the undergraduate producer Colette King, an association which led to a series of Greek tragedies in Gielgud's last few years at the BBC before retirement. Gielgud first met Trypanis early in 1957, when invited to Oxford to see his translation of Sophocles' *Oedipus Tyrannus* staged by the University's Poetry Society. He was impressed and immediately set

---

[41] No recording exists in the archives but the BBC WAC has the script. The translation is published as Postgate 1969.

[42] Rodger 1958.

[43] Laws 1960, 727. Alfred's adaptation of the play was popular on American college campuses: the APGRD Database records a number of stagings from 1947 onwards, and in 1951 Alfred gave a reading at Harvard which was recorded for later broadcast by the radio station WGBH.

[44] *Radio Times*, 8 April 1960, 31; Laws 1960, 727; Anon. 1960a.

[45] Gielgud 1965, 183.

Fig. 7.2. Brothers John and Val Gielgud rehearsing *Oedipus at Colonus* in 1959. © BBC. Reproduced by kind permission of the BBC Photo Library.

about arranging a radio production of the translation which was broadcast later that year. Gielgud produced several more translations of Greek tragedies in Trypanis's translation: Aeschylus' *Persians* in 1958; Sophocles' *Oedipus at Colonus* (with Val's brother John Gielgud (1904–2000) in the title role: see Figure 7.2) and *Antigone* in 1959; the *Oresteia* trilogy in 1962; and Sophocles' *Electra* in 1963. It was not until 1959, with *Oedipus at Colonus*, that Colette King came on board to direct the choruses in these productions. She had greatly impressed Trypanis when producing his translation of *Oedipus at Colonus* for a private OUDS production in 1958,[46] and it was doubtless on his suggestion that Gielgud invited her to direct the choruses in the 1959 radio production of the same play.[47]

---

[46] OUDS did not grant full membership to women until 1964; King was made an associate member for the purposes of the 1958 production and was thus the first female undergraduate to produce for the Society. She went on to teach at the Central School of Speech and Drama and to establish the four-year theatre degree course at Dartington College of Arts.

[47] In his autobiography, Gielgud remembers it differently: 'I saw an amateur performance of the *Hippolytus* in which I was immensely impressed by the handling of the Chorus and the simple accuracy and unpretentiousness of the translation. I found that the latter had been made by Professor Trypanis of Exeter College who had been helped in the production by a Miss Colette King, who had specialised in the unison speaking of verse' (Gielgud 1965, 183). But Trypanis did not translate *Hippolytus* for performance, nor did King produce it. Cavander's translation of

King was still an undergraduate reading English at Somerville College, Oxford when she began work on the radio productions, but she was not daunted by the prospect of working with established BBC actors, nor did she fail to impress Gielgud: 'Miss King tackled [. . .] the choruses with an indefatigable enthusiasm which began by frightening her actors almost to death, went on by driving them almost to the pitch of nervous exhaustion, and ended by infecting them with her own perfectionist vitality.'[48] Trypanis was aware that the uncluttered simplicity of his translation of the *Oresteia*—designed to appeal to what he called the 'present feeling in poetry'—failed to convey the grandiloquence of Aeschylus.[49] He had pared Aeschylus down, but retaining the order and imagery of the original; Gielgud made no cuts and no additions in the way of dramatized 'stage directions'. Of the presentation of the choruses, Trypanis writes:

> Choruses, because of their long static character, have always been the stumbling-block in any sound or other production of ancient Greek drama. The music which accompanied them in antiquity having been lost, a spoken and not a sung chorus is all we can ask for today, as the words are bound to be obscured if set to modern music, however successful that may be. [. . .] Colette King, by introducing a variety in the tempo and the grouping of the voices, has shown a way out of the difficulties and has contributed to a lively and artistic effect.[50]

The Aeschylean trilogy was presented on the Third on three separate evenings in 1962 (see Figure 7.3).[51] The music, composed by John Hotchkis for harp and flute, accompanies the actors' spoken and sung lines much less than in the 1950 production of *Agamemnon*. With its

---

Hippolytus had been produced by Casper Wrede as OUDS' 100th major production in 1955; on the strength of seeing *this* production, Gielgud produced Cavander's *Hippolytus* on radio (see Wrigley 2011b, 117–20). The Trypanis/King production which led to their radio collaboration with Gielgud was certainly the 1958 OUDS *Oedipus at Colonus*, despite the fact that Gielgud was not actually in the audience. He had intended to be but, owing to commitments at the BBC, he sent a colleague in his place. A couple of weeks afterwards, however, Trypanis wrote to Gielgud: 'I told Mis [sic] Colette King about your suggestion that she should train the *Oedipus* chorus, and she was delighted, and will with pleasure do so. I think you will find her very good indeed' (letter dated 28 November 1958 in CAT/S1, a file which contains much Gielgud/Trypanis correspondence from these years).

   [48] Gielgud 1965, 183–4.   [49] Trypanis 1962.   [50] Ibid.
   [51] The APGRD has a reel-to-reel recording of the production, deposited by Pete Hartley.

Fig. 7.3. Eric Fraser's illustration for an article introducing the 1962 *Oresteia* in the *Radio Times*, 25 January 1962, 26. Reproduced by kind permission of the Fraser family.

strict adherence to the text, its lack of dramatic clues as to the movement of actors in time and space, and its paucity of music to add greater depth, texture, and emotional register to the voices, the production may strike the modern ear as a professional and highly polished *reading* of a Greek tragedy. It was King's energy, craft, and precision that enabled Gielgud to realize his ideal of a perfectly delivered choral ode. As he wrote to her in 1959, 'ever since I handled a Greek play on the air I have been concerned with and baffled by the problem of the Chorus. On Wednesday, in the *Antigone*, for the first time the ship came home.'[52] This series of Greek plays at the culmination of Gielgud's long radio career was for him something 'of which the Third Programme could justifiably be proud, and [...] for which, if for anything, I should like to be remembered'.[53] Indeed, it was selected at the BBC's annual review as a 'Gielgud Classic Production'.

---

[52] Letter from VG to Colette King, 27 November 1959 (APGRD).
[53] Gielgud 1965, 184.

Gabriel Josipovici's 're-textured' *Ag*

Almost a decade and a half passed between Gielgud's 1962 *Oresteia* and the next dramatic presentation from the Aeschylean trilogy on BBC Radio. The intervening years saw the close of the Third Programme in April 1970 and the birth of Radio 3. The air-time given to music on the Third Programme had gradually increased throughout the 1960s as the spoken word programmes offered by the Features, Talks, and Drama Departments became, in the judgement of P. H. Newby, who was Controller of the Third from 1958, not sufficiently compelling; and in 1964 the BBC introduced the daytime Music Programme, principally to prevent any future commercial channels from occupying the frequency during those hours.[54] This is not to say that there was no drama of value produced on the Third Programme in the 1960s; indeed, much that was broadcast exhibited innovation and distinction. Under Martin Esslin, who replaced Gielgud as Head of Drama in 1963, the Department became more supportive of contemporary playwrights such as Beckett and Orton. It is, however, noteworthy that approximately half the number of Greek tragedies broadcast in the 1950s were aired in the 1960s; and beyond the 1962 *Oresteia* there seems to have been only one Aeschylean play (*Persians* in 1965) produced in that decade.[55]

On 30 September 1967 the popular music network, Radio 1, came on air; the Light Programme and the Home Service were renamed Radio 2 and Radio 4 respectively; and the Third Network umbrella title for various programmes including the Third Programme became Radio 3 (the labels the networks still have today). The new Director-General Charles Curran informed the press that whereas hitherto the emphasis had been on excellence, henceforth the BBC would become more business-minded;[56] indeed, a report conducted by the

---

[54] Carpenter 1997, 223 ff.

[55] Havergal Brian's operatic *Agamemnon*, which draws on Aeschylus, was composed in 1957 as an introduction to Strauss's *Elektra*. Its first concert performance in 1971 was following by a 16 June 1973 Radio 3 broadcast of a recording of its first staged performance (Richard Armstrong conducted the BBC Northern Singers and Symphony Orchestra, Manchester Town Hall, March 1973). The libretto was adapted from J. S. Blackie's nineteenth-century translation. A recording of the broadcast introduction to the play, available in the BLSA, states that Brian stripped the play down to its essentials, subordinating character in favour of action in order to stress the brutality of fate.

[56] Carpenter 1997, 247.

management consultants McKinsey & Company proposed the dropping of the Third Programme name and concept. In September 1969, the distinguished membership of arts practitioners and intellectuals of the Campaign for Better Broadcasting (whose CBB logo parodied the BBC's) began publishing its concerns, fearing a mere 'token airspace for drama, poetry and the arts'.[57] In October, three thousand BBC staff went on strike to protest about lack of consultation, and on 14 February 1970 more than one hundred broke the terms of their employment by writing a letter to *The Times*. On the front page of that very newspaper, however, the BBC declared that it would pay no heed to their complaints, and on 3 April 1970 the Third Programme broadcast for the last time.[58] The increasing music output of the Third Programme, together with the Music Programme, had paved the way for Radio 3 to become primarily a forum for classical music. Radio 4 took on much of the Third Programme's speech output, although drama would be broadcast on Radio 3 on Friday and Sunday evenings. The CBB had asked in January 1970, 'What is left of speech on Radio 3? Only drama that demands a special interest or knowledge, or that is too long or too difficult for Radio 4. [. . .] speech on Radio 3 becomes what it has never been before—an area confined to difficult, demanding, "really heavy esoteric stuff"'.[59]

There is a huge leap—in dramatic and stylistic terms—from Gielgud's 1962 *Oresteia* to the next dramatic production of *Agamemnon*. The simply titled *Ag*, described as a 're-texturing' of Richmond Lattimore's translation by the writer and critic Gabriel Josipovici which featured music composed by Christos Pittas, was produced by John Theocharis and broadcast on Radio 3 on 14 November 1976. It was chosen by the BBC to be entered for the Prix Italia the following year, which it might well have won if there had not been an objection that it was an adaptation and not an original radio play.[60] *Ag* has the feel of abstract impressionism when compared with the textual fidelity of many of the productions discussed above,

---

[57] John Donat, 'Campaign for Better Broadcasting', September 1969, page 2 of attached report (R101/323/1).

[58] On the end of the Third, see Carpenter 1997, 247–58.

[59] Campaign for Better Broadcasting, 'Statement Following the New Radio Schedules', 1970 (R101/323/1).

[60] Karpf 1977 reviews the quality of entries in the 1977 competition, including the 'remarkable' *Ag*.

and, indeed, Josipovici has described the modernist element in his writing as analogous to that of Picasso's art. Of *Ag*, Theocharis writes:

> Of course, the creative treatment of the Aeschylus/Lattimore text is the work of my old friend Gabriel Josipovici, as indeed is the general concept. *AG* wouldn't have existed without Gabriel. But the most complete and accomplished literary or dramatic text is only the blueprint for the aural/imaginative listening experience that genuine radio is all about. In this case I found myself having to try to realise in terms of sound what I interpreted as Gabriel's intentions.[61]

Josipovici had first become interested in staging *Agamemnon* when collaborating with the Australian composer Peter Sculthorpe on an operatic commission to mark the opening of the Sydney Opera House. Josipovici explored ideas with Sculthorpe—who had already rejected several librettists in his search for the right subject—for a large-scale music-theatre piece, rather than a conventional opera. Sculthorpe had been interested in Aeschylus' *Prometheus Bound* but Josipovici suggested that *Agamemnon* would be better: with Javanese shadow puppets in mind, he envisaged 'eight-foot puppets, a vast Klytemnestra throwing the net or robe over an enormous Agamemnon, and then hacking him to death. Perhaps we could also have a tiny, electrically controlled version of them, moving very fast and jerkily over the stage and perhaps through the auditorium. Agamemnon's nightmare of a futile bid to escape his avenging wife.'[62] Sculthorpe would later reject Greek tragedy as a source of ideas for his commission but Josipovici's interest in *Agamemnon* had been stimulated.[63] The production he envisaged was 'on rather a grand scale [...] formally extremely adventurous and totally apolitical', thus not something which he felt would easily find a large and well-resourced stage in early 1970s Britain.[64] He decided, therefore, to write the script for production on radio: 'there would be a loss, of course, but there might even be some sort of gain'.[65]

---

[61] Letter from John Theocharis to AW, 7 February 2004.

[62] Josipovici 1989, 71. Josipovici has written on the relationship between *Agamemnon* and T. S. Eliot's poem 'Sweeney Among the Nightingales': Josipovici 1999, 258–61.

[63] His *Rites of Passage* premièred in Sydney, although it was completed too late to open the Opera House.

[64] Josipovici 1989, 73.

[65] Ibid. Here he explains that the work was not commissioned by the BBC; instead he wrote it and then sent it for consideration, having already had some radio plays and

The recording of *Ag* available through the BLSA is well worth hearing for the really inventive scope of imagination that lies behind its reconfiguration of the ancient play for radio form. The structure of the drama is centred on the stichomythia between husband and wife leading up to the moment of Agamemnon's death. *Ag* is not a relatively simple composition of dialogue, narration, music, and 'sound-signs', as the two recordings discussed above might be described. It is a more complex and suggestive tapestry of fragmentary dialogue, scenes, and symbols. Three 'ways in' to this complexity are offered at the start of the drama: first, a narrator offers an interpretation of the play which links Agamemnon with the sun, with his death in the bath-tub symbolizing the daily and seasonal cycles of light and dark; secondly, a clear and short synopsis of the action of the Aeschylean play is offered by another voice; and, thirdly, the less immediately comprehensible 'introduction' to the drama is heralded by Clytemnestra's chillingly triumphant wail '*Eleleleleu!*', and manifests itself as a rich and evocative collage of significant words and phrases which set the scene for the action to follow. Words and phrases such as 'mortal light blossoming black splendours SUN! clusters birth *threnon* sing sorrow Father! with griefless heart *oikos*' offered by many different voices clearly outline the significant themes and symbols of the play. The Herald, Agamemnon, Clytemnestra, and Cassandra all deliver the lines of their big speeches closely following the Aeschylean model. The Chorus offer a substantial contribution in song and speech, but their lines are less anchored in Aeschylus.

The play pivots around the moment of Agamemnon's entry into the palace to face his death. The stichomythia between husband and wife leading up to his treading on the purple cloth is replayed three times. The first time it is briskly cut short by a leisurely game of table tennis. It begins again, with the sound becoming increasingly distorted until it expands and seemingly explodes at the moment when Agamemnon takes off his sandals. Strange snatches of dialogue follow: two girls at the zoo giggling at a splashing hippopotamus; a man reeling off a catalogue of Greek masks ('scanty white hair, considerable beard, hooked nose') against a backdrop of Ella Fitzgerald crooning; a serious narration of the story of the House of Atreus from the quarrel between Atreus and Thyestes to the revenge of Orestes. The stichomythia is then heard for a third and final time,

adaptations of his novels broadcast. Richard Imison, Script Editor in the Drama Department, was 'immediately intrigued' by it (letter to GJ, 13 November 1974, GJ/S3).

but the voices this time are strained and drawn out. This third time Agamemnon's words as he crushes the purple fabric with his feet are heard and the drama moves on out of this loop towards Clytemnestra's final speech before she enters the house and the subsequent prophetic visions of Cassandra. After the murders, Clytemnestra returns, with a harsh tone to her words, followed by some minutes of the comfortable heavy breathing and gentle snoring of the hippopotamus/Agamemnon. A second collage of words and phrases heard in tandem with this snoring leads the listener out of the drama, with an academic voice explaining the peculiarity of the death of Agamemnon, how 'if some of the sources are to be believed' with one foot on the ground he died neither in the sea, nor in dry land. The voice goes on to draw connections between the hippopotamus (literally, in Greek, the 'river horse'), who spends the day dozing in the water and the night grazing on land, and Agamemnon, the sun-king, whose death in the bath tub symbolizes the cycles of light and dark, summer and winter; he also likens Clytemnestra to the 'Egyptian sea-dragon or hippopotamus, which daily swallows the sun and daily spews him up again'.[66] The academic musings die out leaving the listener gently hypnotized by the continuing deep sleep-breathing of the hippopotamus, until this, and the play, ends on a final, and surprising, intake of breath. Josipovici has written that 'to try to enter the mind of the hero is, in Schiller's terms, [...] to import both pathos and a false ethical judgement into an art which asks us rather to see human life and death as part of a larger rhythm'.[67] The implication is therefore that Agamemnon, the 'sun-king' whose death is merely temporary in some sense, is resurrected on this final, life-affirming intake of breath. If Josipovici has taken the Aeschylean play as a model for the inevitable advancement of an individual towards death, then the ending suggests the irrepressibility of life and the continuity of humanity on a larger scale.

The 'sound signs' used in the production are masterful: a game of table tennis, first introduced at a point when it seems to illustrate the leisure of the Greeks waiting to set sail from Aulis, continues

---

[66] In ancient Egyptian myth the female hippopotamus was associated with Taweret, goddess of childbirth and the protection of the young; the bull hippopotamus was generally associated with destruction. Pinch 2002, 142 adds that the hippopotamus goddess could be 'thought of as giving birth to the creator sun god'.
[67] Josipovici 1999, 37.

alongside the description of the sacrifice of Iphigenia; and it is replayed at several key points, as a reminder of the sacrifice, as resonant of the rhythm of stichomythia, and developing into a symbol of the 'game' of death avenging death in the House of Atreus. Wolf-whistles sometimes accompany the mention of Clytemnestra by the chorus; the sound of her high heels walking rather alarmingly closer to the microphone, football stadium-sized cheers upon the fall of Troy, and the lyric 'Soon, our little ship will come sailing home' from Gershwin's 'Soon' are heard. Another Gershwin song, 'I've Got a Crush On You' as sung by Ella Fitzgerald, serves as a dominant motif of the play, appearing for example within Clytemnestra's opening speech, as the backdrop to the evocation of Agamemnon walking towards the gentle lapping of his bath, and again after his death:

> Could you coo, could you care
> For a cunning cottage we could share
> The world will pardon my mush
> 'Cause I've got a crush, my baby, on you.

Although he had enjoyed working on the project, Josipovici felt that the music specially composed by Pittas—although good—did not suit his play: 'there was a Brittenish flavour to it, and the choruses were treated with such operatic gusto that the peculiar feel of my piece was destroyed'.[68] Theocharis, however, considers that Pittas's music provided a masculine, heroic, and military counterpoint to the female represented by Ella singing Gershwin. Of the musical clips and other sound effects, Josipovici has said: 'I find it difficult to explain the logic behind these intrusions. At times I have tried to persuade myself that the play is really set in Agamemnon's head, as he returns to what he knows awaits him in Argos. But I am not sure this is entirely right. I think the problem may be similar to that encountered by Eliot in accounting for much of *The Waste Land*: is it going on in Tiresias's head? In that of the Sybil [sic]? Or merely in that of the reader?'[69] The interventions into the action of the drama by narrators and academic figures provide a comic subversion of the earlier Third Programme

---

[68] Josipovici 1989, 73. Notably, in his next adaptation of Aeschylus for radio, *The Seven* (produced by Theocharis in 1981), there was no music or singing but just the spoken voice and its electronic transformation. He also wrote *Vergil Dying* (Radio 3, 1979), a monologue about the Roman poet as he looks back on his life from its end point, drawing on the *Eclogues*, *Georgics*, and *Aeneid*. On both see GJ/S3.

[69] Josipovici 1989, 73.

productions which were, as noted above, often actually accompanied by introductory talks from translators and/or academics. No longer, it seems, were 'difficult' plays even given introductory articles in the *Radio Times*. The listing for *Ag* simply introduces the play with the briefest of synopses and the following general statement: 'it is presented, in radio terms, from inside out; it is broken down into fragments of sounds and words, in order to explore the tragic image of Man advancing towards inevitable death'.[70]

The critic in *The Listener* is enthused, and almost surprised, that such a patchwork of sounds and words sometimes so removed from the text of Aeschylus should work so well in conveying the drama: 'the components of the patterns of sound were too numerous. Only if we had been truly gods would we have known the occasion and meaning of every sound used. Some noises were merely comic, but it was the total effect that mattered, and that was extraordinarily impressive.' However, his interpretation of the sound which was intended to suggest a game of table tennis as 'an infuriating tick tock, as of a man with two wooden legs walking on marble' does, however, serve to illustrate the difficulty of correctly hearing, or interpreting, such experimental and symbolic use of sound in radio drama.[71] Listening to such an experimental production requires both a reasonable amount of concentration—otherwise the 'action' becomes lost in the sound collage—and also a certain amount of passivity, in order that the suggestive nature of the sound collage lend its texture and depth to the 'action' and the movement of the drama. The freedom from the line-by-line rendition of the original, translated text together with an inventive and rich soundscape effectively conveys the essence of the Aeschylean drama.

Concluding remarks

In 1976, some years after Greek tragedy had lost its prominent presence on BBC Radio, Theocharis hoped his production of *Ag* would stand alone independently of Aeschylus: indeed it needed to, since no introduction to the play was either printed or broadcast; instead several ways into the play were woven into the fabric of the production itself. Theocharis writes that most of the actors in *Ag*

[70] *Radio Times*, 14 November 1976, 33.   [71] F. Dillon 1976.

knew nothing of the Aeschylean model, and that he expected the ancient Greek play to be largely unknown amongst his audience also. This gave him 'one more strong reason for the new piece to generate its <u>own</u> tension, "frisson", poetry etc; echoing the original, but not always depending on it'.[72] The production achieves something remarkable, and perhaps something not thought possible in the earlier decades of broadcast drama: a 'classic' play made entirely radiogenic, a version of Aeschylus' *Agamemnon* which simply could not exist in another medium. With this production, it can be seen that the 'theatre of the home' that Gielgud envisaged in the 1930s has truly evolved into the 'theatre of the mind'. Yet *Ag* is a 'difficult' presentation of what might be considered to be a 'difficult' play: it stands apart from the Aeschylean prototype as a distinct dramatic work, but it necessarily draws more strongly on the mythological background of the House of Atreus than the earlier productions, through such devices as the parodic academic exposition.

Several of the productions discussed above involved the collaboration of the translator or adaptor with the radio producer, but what is clear from the extant recordings is that the dramatic preference of the radio producer is key to the nature of the production: the text is simply—to borrow Theocharis's term—the 'blueprint' for the aural experience of the listener. The notion that Greek tragedy might be best done on radio, voiced by Val Gielgud as late as 1957, rejects the challenges posed by the 'live' performance of a play which has been inherited from a different time and culture. At the same time it perhaps elevates the text—the translated words of the ancient playwright—to a position of greater importance than its performance in dramatic terms. Many critics of productions discussed here support this perspective, their two central questions in reviews being how good the English translation is in conveying Aeschylus, and how effective the acting voices are in 'getting across' the drama. Gielgud is acknowledged as a pioneer in his field, and indeed his considerable achievements over three decades as Head of Drama must not be dismissed; his conservative, almost reverential, approach to Greek tragedy did not allow him, however, to explore the possibilities of the medium for the fullest expression of the drama. The recording of Gielgud's 1962 production shows that he left the

[72] Letter from John Theocharis to AW, 7 February 2004.

translation virtually untouched from the page on which it was printed, and consequently the performance comes across as little more than a highly polished, professional play-reading. In contrast, Raikes had no such desire to preserve the text intact on the air. His production displays a realistic understanding of the need to manipulate the text for performance in the listener's imagination. As noted above, he firmly declared that it was not his intention to produce a play-reading. His confidence as a textual editor (something lacking from Gielgud's professional 'tool-box') displays an intelligent and sensitive conception of both the medium and its audience.

The *Oresteia*s produced by Raikes in 1956 and Gielgud in 1962 both illuminate aspects of the Third Programme which would contribute to its demise. The marathon 1956 production and its series of accompanying programmes were (at least 'higher') educational in aspiration, although there is no indication that they were marketed to a wider audience than usual. There was a high degree of confidence in serving up such a feast for 'highbrows' (and 'aspirants') in the face of severe cuts and strong criticism of the Programme's narrow appeal. The production stands as a rather ostentatious flourish before the cuts of 1957, representing the kind of expensive, lavish fare the wide value of which critics of the Third Programme doubted. Six years later came Gielgud's stately production which conformed more closely to the dry, academic output for which the Third Programme was often berated. It is perhaps not insignificant that the only *Agamemnon* to be broadcast between the 1962 and 1976 productions, the period during which the Third Programme was absorbed into the classical-music-focused Radio 3, was Havergal Brian's opera.[73] Music—both that specially composed by Pittas and the Gershwin—was also, of course, important in the 1976 production.

---

[73] The first serious attempt to televise the *Oresteia* came in 1979 with *The Serpent Son* (translation by Frederic Raphael and Kenneth McLeish). Directed by Bill Hays (1938–2006) with music by Humphrey Searle, it was broadcast on BBC2 over three days. The cast included Denis Quilley (Agamemnon), Diana Rigg (Klytemnestra), Helen Mirren (Kassandra), Claire Bloom, Billie Whitelaw, and Siân Phillips. Much earlier in 1965 came 'The Myth Makers', the comic retelling of the Trojan War story written by Donald Cotton for the third season (four episodes) of the BBC television series *Doctor Who*, which had originally been intended as an educational programme for children but the science fiction elements of which would later prove most popular. On these and many other British televisual engagements with ancient Greece see Wrigley 2016a.

8

Post-War Greek Comedy

The comic humour in Aristophanic drama on the stage lies in both the text—the words and verse forms—of the plays and also the concomitant use by actors of gesture, movement, props, and stage machinery. As with much comedy to the present day, it therefore relies on a highly visual performance for a large part of its effect.[1] This chapter considers representations of Aristophanic plays in the notoriously 'blind', or invisible, medium of radio. It therefore builds on the discussion of Gilbert Murray's Aristophanic translations on radio in the 1940s (Section 4.1) in order to explore other approaches that have been taken in response to the challenge of rendering a very visual comic form in purely aural and imaginative terms and of making intelligible and understandable to the mass audience works from the unfamiliar and sometimes obscure genre of Old Comedy. The chapter also picks up some themes which have already arisen in this volume, such as the symbiotic relationship between radio and the spheres of education, publishing, and the stage, highlighting some important points of contact between classicists and writers, on the one hand, and creative professionals in radio, on the other; furthermore, it throws light on some of the tensions involved in rendering certain aspects of Aristophanic drama in the mass medium of radio, such as the question of propriety in this very public sphere.

The study of *Ag* with which the previous chapter closed prepares the ground for a detailed exploration of one approach taken by the Features Department towards the radio representation of Greek comedy thirty years earlier: Louis MacNeice's *Enemy of Cant* (1946) offers fresh translations of scenes from most of Aristophanes' plays which

---

[1] See Wrigley 2007*a* (reprinted in Wrigley 2011*b*) for the importance of music and 'stage business' in a 1892 Oxford production of *Frogs*.

emerge from the 'real-life' situation of the playwright as he, over the years, converses about contemporary affairs with characters such as his lover, his slave, mask-makers, and fellow playwrights. These fictional interludes function—simply and brilliantly—to provide social and political context for the scenes from the plays. In contrast with some of the Drama Department productions of *Agamemnon* discussed in the previous chapter, the writing is strikingly fresh and the dramatic presentation energetic. The Aristophanic translations and radio adaptations commissioned from Patric Dickinson by the BBC in the 1950s are the subject of the second section of this chapter, with a particular focus on his *Lysistrata*, which was produced on radio in 1957 and on television in 1964.

As with tragedy, there are many more radio productions of Greek comedy to be explored than those which are mentioned in this chapter. In 1957, for example, the discovery of the first complete play of Menander—*Dyskolos*—made the front page of *The Manchester Guardian*,[2] and within a couple of years the Third Programme broadcast a talk on this newly discovered play by Hugh Lloyd-Jones whose edition of the Greek text was being prepared for publication by Oxford University Press.[3] His talk, which was reprinted in *The Listener*, persuaded at least one critic that the play 'certainly sounded as if it would be an engaging, high-spirited affair'.[4] Indeed a Third Programme production of the play six months later struck another as being of 'a current dramatic work rather than [...] a piece of scholarship'; furthermore, it was noted that it was 'a curious experience to listen to a 2,000-year-old comedy which contained many situations that we commonly believe to be the invention of present or nearly contemporary script writers and music-hall gagsters'.[5] The creative process which led to the translation of the Menandrian text into English and the adaptation of this to the air was not, however, without its problems. Philip Vellacott was commissioned to translate Hugh Lloyd-Jones's Greek edition of the text for radio performance and it was at this point that a wrinkle emerges within the creative team: Lloyd-Jones wrote to Raymond Raikes, the producer for whom he had agreed to serve as textual adviser on the English-language script, to say that, on reflection, he would prefer not to collaborate in this way after all. He had offered several names who he considered

---

[2] Anon. 1957e.   [3] Lloyd-Jones 1960.
[4] D. Paul 1959. Lloyd-Jones 1959.   [5] Rodger 1959, 799 and 798.

would make a good job of the translation (for example, Kenneth Cavander, and even his then wife, Frances Hedley, who had studied classics at Newnham College, Cambridge and was a poet); he did not approve of Raikes's final choice: 'I know nothing of Mr Vellacott personally; but I know his work', and based on this he predicts that 'I shall find any form of collaboration with him extremely difficult'.[6] Raikes expertly deals with this potential crisis, gently reminding him of his earlier commitment. Lloyd-Jones relents, despite his continuing doubt that 'Mr Vellacott was the kin[d] of translator who cared enough about the meaning of the text to make that sort of thing worth doing'.[7]

The rest of their correspondence is worth reading for its elucidation of the collaborative nature of the radio production team and the reciprocal influence radio work could have on scholarship. Lloyd-Jones was undoubtedly the expert where the Greek text was concerned, but Raikes—true to his style as a producer—did not flinch from adapting Vellacott's translation to the needs of radio performance: 'You will also notice', he writes to Lloyd-Jones, 'that I have brought back Simice at the end of the play: this I find a great help as, otherwise, the speeches thereabout simply do not fit the characters of the Head Slave and the drunken Sugar-Cook! Sometimes these sort of dramatic instincts of mine have proved not unhelpful and I shall be particularly interested to hear from you whether you think that this return of Simice can be justified textually.' To this, Lloyd-Jones responds very positively:

> Your suggestion about Simice interests me very much indeed. The tone of the speeches you give her [...] certainly suit her character better; and in a wireless version I feel quite sure it is a perfectly reasonable liberty to take. I do not think one can be sure; just at the vital point, four lines are almost blank; but I have discovered a concrete argument in

---

[6] Letters from HLJ to RR, 29 April and 17 July 1959 (S452/36/1).
[7] Letter from HLJ to RR, and RR's response, 27 and 31 July 1959 (ibid.). After the broadcast his attitude softened: Raikes told Vellacott that 'he was most keen to keep in touch with you; that he knew your translation was to be published by Oxford University Press and was most anxious that it should incorporate his latest researches into the text' (letter from RR to PV, 28 October 1959, ibid.). The translation, published as Vellacott 1960, included some of Raikes's revisions for broadcast (letter from PV to RR, 1 November 1959, ibid.). RR was delighted, as he was with Vellacott's earlier radio commissions being printed by Penguin (see Section 3.1), considering that it offered 'a sense of permanency for our far too ephemeral radio productions' (letter from RR to PV, 19 January 1960, ibid.).

your support. The account of what is happening at the party would suit a person who has just come from that party; and Getas and Sicon have for some time been with Cnemon. This is not decisive, as they might be supposed to have spent some time at the party before going off to bait Cnemon. But it amounts to something. I shall continue to think hard about this from the point of view of my edition. People who edit ancient plays ought to have the opportunity of discussing their text with experienced producers![8]

8.1. LOUIS MACNEICE'S *ENEMY OF CANT* (1946)

At the time when Gilbert Murray's translations were the popular choice for Greek play productions by the Drama Department, Louis MacNeice's feature programme *Enemy of Cant: A Panorama of Aristophanic Comedy* demonstrated how radio could make the ancient world imaginatively accessible to a large and diverse audience in a more vibrant and striking way than these traditional productions. It was at one of the early Features Department meetings to discuss their plans for the new Third Programme that MacNeice put forward an idea for a 'satirical fantasy' which became *Enemy of Cant: A Panorama of Aristophanic Comedy*.[9] This dramatic feast did not present just one Aristophanic play (as a production by the Drama Department might have done) but scenes from all of them except *Ekklesiazousai*, *Wealth*, and *Thesmophoriazusae*. MacNeice's translations of these dramatic extracts were considered by one critic to be 'examples of translation at its best, translation in the widest sense of the word. Here was Ancient Athens in terms of our own day, in terms of our own sense of humour moreover.'[10] Writing to T. S. Eliot, MacNeice describes his translation technique as 'continuously free and sometimes somewhat condensed as I omitted various jokes and topical allusions which would be caviar to a modern'.[11] The extracts were arranged in the chronological order of their first production, except for *Birds*, which is alluded to at the appropriate point, but which, as an 'escape fantasy', MacNeice considered more appropriate

[8] Letter from RR to HLJ, and HLJ's response, 7 and 10 October 1959 (ibid.).
[9] Memo from LM to Director of Features [LG], 21 May 1946 (R19/307).
[10] Hope-Wallace 1946a.
[11] Letter from LM to TSE, 26 March 1952 (reprinted in MacNeice 2010, 549–50).

for the end of the production, with its 'nice fly-away final scene' being 'the wish-fulfilment of a war-weary generation'.[12]

What makes this potpourri work so well is that the scenes from the different plays are interspersed with conversations between Aristophanes and other characters such as his mistress Sepia, his slave Thratta, the theatrical producer Callistratus, fellow playwright Cratinus, and his son Araros. The life and times of Aristophanes the man (historical detail dressed up with fictional context) is therefore—simply and brilliantly—served up as the framework for understanding the plays. By contrast with the Drama Department's practice of having a short talk before a production of an ancient play, to provide mythological and historical context and explain ancient dramatic conventions, in this feature programme MacNeice deftly makes the social and political culture and context integral to the piece rather than standing apart from it, situating the plays within the playwright's lifetime, and thus Aristophanic comedy within the sociopolitical concerns of the day.[13]

Indeed, as MacNeice wrote in the *Radio Times*, 'All Aristophanes's best work was produced during this struggle [with Sparta] and it reflects consistently a clear perception of the futilities of war and a bitter opposition to the militaristic demagogues, of whom the most notorious was Cleon.'[14] The resonances of the ancient plays with recent military history in Britain and contemporary post-war privations are strong, giving the production a firm footing in the imagination of the listening public. But there were other 'contemporary analogies' that MacNeice found in Aristophanes which had first aroused his interest in putting him on radio, namely 'the burlesques

---

[12] Memos from LM to the Director of Features [LG], 21 May 1946 and 12 July 1946 (R19/307). MacNeice was aware that this made for an 'enormously long' script and he requested permission to over-run the allocated transmission time if needed (memo from LM to Leslie Stokes, 27 November 1946, ibid.).

[13] When offering *Enemy of Cant* to T. S. Eliot for publication with Faber in 1952, MacNeice says that he would like to *rewrite* these linking scenes: 'if it were published I should wish to cut all the invented dialogue between Aristophanes and his friends and write new linking material (in fairly formal, but concentrated prose)'. He would also have liked to rename the play: 'What about calling it *Brekekekex*, plus a clarifying sub-title?' (letter from LM to TSE, 26 March 1952, reprinted in MacNeice 2010, 549–50). Faber did not publish *Enemy of Cant*; for its first publication see Wrigley and Harrison 2013.

[14] MacNeice 1946a.

of power politicians, the New Thought, literary cliques, and managerial women'.[15]

MacNeice's friend and fellow poet Dylan Thomas was cast in the role of Aristophanes, and also Dikaiopolis in the extract from *Acharnians*.[16] But he didn't approve of how much he was to be paid for *Enemy of Cant*:

> There are 3 whole days' rehearsals, plus one rehearsal from 2 p.m. onwards, *plus* two one-hour-&-a-half performances. Thus four whole days (minus one morning) are to be spent on this show. Living in London for four days will cost me at least five pounds. Add to this my railway fare, & it works out that for four whole days' work, including two live performances, I am offered about £14: £7 for each long feature performance, in which I am the principal character.[17]

Thomas had some considerable skill for the job. After his death MacNeice wrote: 'as a producer I realized that he was a god-send to radio. His famous "organ-voice" was already well known in straightforward readings of verse, but the same voice, combined with his sense of character, could be used for all sorts of strange purposes. I cast him (and was never disappointed) in a variety of dramatic parts.'[18] The Listener Research Report described his performance in *Enemy of Cant* as 'outstanding',[19] and the recording held by the BLSA proves him to be a skilful and commanding radio presence.[20]

---

[15] Memo from LM to Director of Features [LG], 21 May 1946 (R19/307).

[16] Thomas did a great amount of work for radio at this time, as an actor, a reader of poetry, and a script writer: see Rodger 1982, 72–3. His *Under Milk Wood*, originally written for radio, is considered by Lewis 1981a, 72 (and many others) to be 'easily the most celebrated full-length play for radio, or "play for voices" as [he] designated it, that the BBC has produced in more than fifty years of broadcasting, and it is for many people the outstanding example of the genre, an unsurpassed and virtually unsurpassable achievement'.

[17] Letter from Dylan Thomas to Jean Leroy of Highams (his literary agents), 6 November 1946, reproduced in Thomas 1985, 605. A letter to his wife Caitlin, written during the second rehearsal in the Maida Vale Studio, refers to *Enemy of Cant* as 'Louis's *endless* play' (ibid. 607).

[18] MacNeice 1954b, 196. The radio producer Douglas Cleverdon (1903–97) confirms that Thomas was an exuberant deliverer of lines who was able to get across the 'subtlest shades of intonation', pulling 'the full value out of every word' ('Voice of Dylan Thomas', Radio 3, 19 August 1971; accessible in the BLSA, reference T327R; this radio programme includes an extract from *Enemy of Cant*).

[19] BBC WAC LR/6842 (in R19/307).

[20] A recording of the 4 December 1946 broadcast is available through the BLSA.

Before the production the Announcer explains that it is the comic playwright Aristophanes who is the enemy of cant of the title: 'we offer a sketch of him with paraphrases from eight of his plays. We mean thereby to pay homage to an author of infinite fantasy, a lover of slapstick and beauty, a good hater and a hard hitter, a live man, an Enemy of Cant.' This is followed by a 'solemn chord, then raspberry, on orchestra' (p. 1).[21] The script then has a short scene in which an Oxford don attempts to elaborate on the manuscript tradition of Aristophanes, but is severely hindered by fits of coughing ('must be the dust in this lecture-room', p. 2). This scene did not make it into the broadcast performance; instead we hear an incandescent Cleon, who threatens to prosecute Aristophanes, having evidently just emerged from the performance of *Babylonians* in which (as the scholium on *Acharnians* 378 suggests) he received a sharp attack at the hands of the playwright. This cuts to cheering and Aristophanes' producer Callistratus congratulating him on having escaped prosecution in the ensuing legal and political battle with Cleon. Aristophanes— to Callistratus' astonishment—proceeds to narrate his idea for a new play, 'a plea for peace' (p. 3). Callistratus reminds him that most people take the war in which Athens has been embroiled for six years rather seriously, to which Aristophanes responds:

> I take it one hundred per cent seriously. Look, Callistratus. What good's this war done anyone? This city's cluttered up with evacuees on the one hand and political informers on the other. Think of the plague. Think what it's done to agriculture. Think what it's done to the national character, man. Everyone's turning nasty. Well, I've had enough of it. The hero of my new play is a dear old man from the country. Name Dicaiopolis. (p. 3)

Aristophanes says that he has 'roughed out' the bit where Dicaiopolis sets up his private market (p. 5), and the following five and a half pages of script paraphrase *Acharnians* 719–928. The sense follows that of the Greek closely, with obvious omissions being the puns on

---

[21] Page references are to the microfiche copy of the script held in the BBC WAC SL. A recording of the 4 December 1946 broadcast is available at the BLSA (reference T28123). The recording confirms that the microfiche copy is almost precisely the script-as-broadcast (and this is the basis for the version published for the first time in Wrigley and Harrison 2013). The microfiche copy contains handwritten additions and emendations which make it not identical to the two original typescripts held in the two boxes of Louis MacNeice Scripts at the BBC WAC.

genitalia and the choral ode between the appearances of the Megarian (who is played with a Scottish accent) and the Boeotian (Irish). This opening extract is likely to have struck a chord with an audience who were suffering the privations of post-war life such as ration books, and who at the mention of 'evacuees' and 'plague' (p. 3) might easily think of the recent end of the government's evacuation scheme and recall the flu which took so many lives at the end of the First World War. The long war between democratic Athens and oligarchic Sparta had an all-too-obvious parallel in 1946 (and, later on, George Owen, the actor playing the Spartan, speaks with a German accent when he says, 'Athenians, these are the terms of your surrender. Sign here please', p. 68).

Following a fanfare on the award of first prize to Aristophanes for *Acharnians*, the playwright talks with a mask-maker (played by Alan McClelland with his native Northern Irish accent):

MASK-MAKER   How can you have the nerve, Aristophanes sir? Cleon was always powerful enough—but today! Now that he's captured Pylos and proved himself a general—
ARISTOPHANES   He's no more a general than I am.
MASK-MAKER   Hsh! Hsh! Well, general or no general, I'm not going to make no portrait of Cleon for you, sir.
ARISTOPHANES   But, damn it, you're a mask-maker.
MASK-MAKER   Yes—but I'm not a suicide.
ARISTOPHANES   Alright then but, mask or no mask, the Braggadocian—that's Cleon—is going to appear in my play.
MASK-MAKER   I'll do all the other masks for the *Knights*, sir.
ARISTOPHANES   Big-hearted of you, I'm sure. Mind you do a good job on the Sausage-seller. Grotesque as you can make it. The Maestro's playing the part.
MASK-MAKER   Ah, there's an actor, sir. I see from this synopsis you sent me as how this Sausage-seller appears in answer to a prophecy. (pp. 11–12)

This short scene not only performs a narrative function, filling in some of the historical context (namely that Cleon had obtained the Spartans' surrender at Pylos in 425 BC) and paving the way for the next extract, from *Knights*, but it also touches on ancient staging conventions, the political weight of comic theatre in ancient Athens, and the potential danger of being too critical within drama. Following the scene from *Knights*, an 'Intellectual' questions Aristophanes on his motive for writing comedy, an exchange which prompts the playwright to make Socrates the subject of his next play: 'The *Clouds* it will be called. It's an attack on the new education, on the sophists' (p. 17).

INTELLECTUAL But Socrates isn't a sophist. At least, if he is, he's not like any of the others.
ARISTOPHANES My dear boy, I'm quite aware of that.
INTELLECTUAL But in that case what you'll be doing is telling a lie.
ARISTOPHANES I suppose so. I often do. Not always, you know; I told no lies about Cleon. But Socrates is a godsend; he's so funny anyway. (p. 18)

In the extract from *Clouds*, Strepsiades is himself resolved to 'matriculate' (p. 21) having failed to persuade his son to enter the 'Thinkory [...] the laboratory of intellect' (p. 20); but his resolve is undermined with comic intent by his difficulty in articulating the letter 'r' throughout the scene. Words such as 'matriculate', together with 'hearties' and 'professors', could not fail to evoke modern British academic life. *Clouds* is awarded third place to Cratinus' *Wine-bottle* and Ameipsias' *Connos*: the victorious elder playwright, gruff and a little drunk, advises Aristophanes that he would do better to 'give 'em something familiar. Give 'em the well-worn gags; don't bother about the meaning' (p. 29). Aristophanes ignores Cratinus' advice, and a paraphrase of much of the plot of *Wasps* opens with Xanthias (played by Basil Jones in a Welsh accent). The following explosive choral ode, which is sung to musical accompaniment in the recorded version, is a paraphrase of *Wasps* 403–14. MacNeice wrote to the composer Hopkins with suggestions for this lyric passage: 'the trio should be very angry—and the orchestration suggestive of nasty insects. Put in as many "buzzes" as you like; the cast, I should think, could buzz too.'[22]

MALE WASPS Why do we linger, why do we linger to discharge our famous bile
Which we turn on all who beard the wasp within his nest?
Buzz—zz—zz—zz. Buzz—zz. Buzz—zz.
Now's the time, now's the time
To advance our bitterly sharp—
Buzz—zz! Buzz—zz!
To advance our punitive sharp—

---

[22] Notes accompanying letter from LM to Antony Hopkins, 19 November 1946 (R19/307).

> Buzz—zz. Buzz—zz. Buzz—zz. Buzz—zz.
> To advance our malevolent sharp—
> > Buzz! Buzz! Buzz! Buzz! Buzz! Buzz! Buzz! Buzz!
> > STING!
> Off with you now, you slaves, to Cleon; run as fast as you can,
> Bawl our SOS in his ear, warn him about this poisonous man;
> > Let him come, let him vent his fury
> > On this god-damn chiselling quisling[23]
> > Who proposes the abolition
> > Of—can you believe it—trial by jury! (pp. 31–2)

After an extract from *Peace*, Aristophanes' slave Thratta brings the audience up to date with the political and military situation:

THRATTA   A couple of years and it's all started again. Whether it's the fault of that young chap Alcibiades—my master doesn't think much of him but I wouldn't know, I'm a slave—but we've only had two years peace and it's all started again.

ARISTOPHANES   [...] Have you heard what's just happened in Melos? [...] my government killed all the people of Melos. Melos was neutral. Rot my government, Thratta. [...]

CALLISTRATUS   Well, Aristophanes, my friend, what about a political satire?

ARISTOPHANES   Not this year. Let 'em have their Sicilian expedition! I'm expediting away from it. If I write anything it will be up in the air. Up in the air with the birds.
> O mortal men whose lives are in shadow, who grow and wither like leaves,
> You puppets, you frail homunculi, you weak generation of ghosts,
> Bound to the ground, things of a day, creatures resembling dreams,
> Attend to us now—to the birds who are godlike and live for ever. (pp. 48–9)

The escape fantasy of *Birds*—which was originally produced between *Peace* and *Lysistrata*—is here brought in with a paraphrase

---

[23] The collaboration of the Norwegian politician Vidkun Quisling with the Nazis during the Second World War made his name synonymous with traitor.

of some lines of chorus (685 ff.) but, since MacNeice wished to end the programme with a nostalgic look back to this play, after a brief musical interlude Aristophanes states that the worst he feared came to pass: 'The wages of our imperialism. Our whole expeditionary force lost in Sicily. Our allies revolting' (p. 51).[24] Thratta brings him wine, and consoles him with her belief that wartime is harder on women than on men. Her words inspire him to write *Lysistrata*:

THRATTA   Look at these free-born girls, these young Athenian ladies. Those that are maidens still can't find any men to marry; not of their own age anyway. And those that's married already—Pah!—the husband comes back from the war once in a strange moon—and he sleeps with her—and he's gone again. What sort of life is that for a girl whose blood is young? Ah if we women only had the say, we'd soon stop this war. [...] Master, if women only had the strength of will [...] to keep their bodies back—to what's the word—to blackmail their men with the bed, why then they could get whatever in the world they want. Once a man couldn't take his fun in bed for granted, he'd give anything for it. He'd become like potter's clay in his wife's hands. Aye, and if all us women were to get together—

ARISTOPHANES   Thratta! My writing tablets! (pp. 51–2)

In MacNeice's re-telling of *Lysistrata*, lines such as 'Thanks to conscription we sleep alone' and 'The returned ex-serviceman, grey or bald, can quickly pick up a maiden' (p. 57) are likely to have had a strong resonance with the listening public. Thratta berates her master for stealing her ideas for his play and tells him to go to bed, where his bedtime reading is a volume of plays by Euripides, 'Dead just the other day' (p. 59).

ARISTOPHANES   Poor old Euripides—I do admire him. But I am a critic of poetry—and now what else can I write about? They'll say it's bad taste but I codded him alive and—well, now he's died, he's handed me himself on a plate. Euripides in Hades! Gods, what a laugh! (p. 59)

---

[24] I am grateful to Stephen Harrison for the suggestion that these lines may have prompted listeners to think of the rebellion of the sailors of the British Indian Navy in February 1946.

The scene from *Frogs* unfolds with Dionysus knocking at Heracles' door. Some lines of Aristophanes, closely translated, offer nice touches of 'radio slapstick':

> DIONYSUS Pick up my hold-alls, Xanthias.
> XANTHIAS I've not put 'em down yet. (p. 61)

MacNeice's brilliantly clever and catchy lines from the Frog chorus are also worth reprinting:

> FROGS Stop it? No!
> Stronger let our music flow
> In the name of all the lays
> That we plugged in olden days
> When we still had games and fun
> Beside the bull-rush in the sun
> Revelling in our harmonies—
> Poly-high-dive polyphonics—
> Thonics—phonics—Brekekekex ko-ax!
> Or when God sent dirty weather
> We took cover all together
> At the bottom of the swamp
> Where with circumstance and pomp
> Out of tune and out of trouble
> In fortissimos of bubble
> Rose the song we ne'er relax
> Brekekekex, ko-ax, ko-ax!
> Brekekekex, ko-ax, ko-ax! (p. 64)

Following *Frogs* Aristophanes warns his son Araros, who wants to follow in his father's footsteps, that a writer's life is not what it used to be:

> When Cratinus and I used to compete for the ivy, there were two things that made our comedies possible. Public spirit and money. But now there's no money and as for public spirit! I don't want to frighten you, son, but even a boy should know it. This is a dead city. The only life remaining is nasty life. The next few years are going to be pretty unpleasant. You mark my words, there'll be witch-hunts and things like that. They've got to take it out on someone. (pp. 68–9)

Rather than end on this note of pessimism, with the reference to 'witch-hunts' seeming to anticipate McCarthyism (heightened fears of communist influence on American institutions and espionage by Soviet agents), MacNeice has Aristophanes begin to reminisce, looking back to the happy flourish of *Birds* ('That was escape! And what a production—we couldn't afford it now. All those feathers and Iris's huge hat—and didn't we use the machines! What a long time ago that was. And the writing—though I say it—the writing was pretty good too', pp. 69–70). He repeats the four lines which were spoken earlier (beginning 'O mortal men whose lives are in shadow', p. 49) which serve as introduction to a paraphrase of *Birds* 685–716 and 786–97. For example:

> ARISTOPHANES Now if anyone present in the listening public would like to throw in his lot with the birds
> And spend the rest of his life in pleasure—let him come over to us!
> For indeed a suit of feathers is the most becoming wear
> And, if you spectators had them, you need not have sat up there
> All the morning feeling empty while the tragics bored you so,
> You'd have slipped back home for lunch and still enjoyed the present show;
> Ditto with the public man whose bowels maybe are too loose—
> He could flit off unregarded and return with no abuse;
> Ditto with the jolly lecher with his eye upon a wench—
> None would mark him flying off or landing back upon his bench.
> Surely then, if you had wings,
> You would live the life of kings. (p. 71)

The script and the overall production were by MacNeice, but the production was of course a team effort. MacNeice's correspondence with Hopkins shows that the composer was given free rein to put his own imagination to work on this production: 'I am anxious that the essential bits of meaning should come over but apart from that please do what you like with these pieces, apportioning lines as you prefer among your different singers and working in any nice polyphonic convolutions that occur to you.'[25] And so he did: 'it seemed perfectly right when, to underline a parody of some bombast, Anthony [*sic*] Hopkins [...] should make a comic reference to Tchaikovsky',

---

[25] Letter from LM to Antony Hopkins, 19 November 1946 (R19/307).

considered the reviewer in *The Listener*.[26] Hopkins also received high praise in *The Observer*: 'There were moments in *Enemy of Cant* when he seemed to take over a mood or a situation which had baffled the ingenuity of MacNeice, and there were other occasions when he invented noises off so cunning as to send (I hope) the BBC sound-effects boys back to school to learn the ABC of aural-association.'[27]

Before considering the ways in which listeners engaged with *Enemy of Cant*, it may provide useful context to summarize what is known about stage productions of Aristophanes in Britain in the two decades before this radio broadcast. During this period, there were at least forty stage productions of Aristophanic plays in Britain almost all of which were staged in academic institutions (the Universities of Cambridge, Edinburgh, and Oxford; several public and grammar schools including Dulwich College and Lancing College; and, notably, a production of *Frogs* at the Sheffield Educational Settlement in 1945).[28] Many were in Greek, although several used translations by Gilbert Murray or Benjamin Bickley Rogers.[29] The few productions outside educational establishments include *Frogs* at the People's Theatre in Newcastle (1937) and musical versions of *Birds* (1928) and *Lysistrata* (1931) staged by Terence Gray's Cambridge Festival Theatre. It is worth reflecting on the relatively small number of people who would have seen these performances in light of the size of the audience for Aristophanes on radio, which at this date is likely to have been counted in the hundreds of thousands, if not millions. The BBC Listener Research Report for *Enemy of Cant* was based on eighty-six returned questionnaires, and it notes that the general reaction was very favourable, with the acting, music, production, use of dialect, and the script generally received very positively. The Appreciation Index was calculated to be 64, substantially higher than for MacNeice's recent broadcast works *The Dark Tower* and *Enter Caesar* which had received 55 and 46 respectively.[30]

The questions the listeners had been asked to respond to were as follows:[31]

---

[26] Hope-Wallace 1946a.   [27] W. E. Williams 1946.
[28] On the modern performance of Aristophanes see Hall and Wrigley 2007 and Van Steen 2000.
[29] For a bibliographical survey of published translations of Aristophanes from the fifteenth century to 1920 see Giannopoulou 2007.
[30] BBC WAC LR/6842 (R19/307).   [31] 'Questionnaire A6/49M' (ibid.).

1. What did you think of the acting as a whole?
   EXCELLENT / VERY GOOD / QUITE GOOD / POOR / VERY POOR
2. What did you think of the way this programme was produced, with special reference to the way the music was used?
   EXCELLENT / VERY GOOD / QUITE GOOD / POOR / VERY POOR
3. Do you think Anthony [sic] Hopkins' music fitted this programme?
   PERFECTLY / NOT ENTIRELY / NOT AT ALL / NO OPINION
4. What did you think of the script, i.e. the programme as written, apart from the way it was acted or produced?
   EXCELLENT / VERY GOOD / QUITE GOOD / POOR / VERY POOR
      What, if any, were the script's good points?
      What, if any, were the script's weak points?
5. Please sum up your feelings about this broadcast by ringing one of the following:
   A+   A   B   C   C-

A small proportion of the listeners responding to the questionnaire 'admitted no knowledge of the background and found it all rather confusing and incomprehensible'; and although the Report acknowledged that some had considered MacNeice's script rather 'arty', 'a bit of wimsy wamsy put on by the Senior Common Room', it stated that 'by far the greater part of comment was, however, extremely enthusiastic, listeners greatly appreciating the way in which the script of the original had been caught in the modern idiom, the people, the period and the humour had been brought to life, and the extracts from the plays wedded with the general context into a coherent whole'. To illustrate this positive summary of the reception of *Enemy of Cant* in the questionnaires, the Report prints quotations from five listeners:[32]

> As a free translation of Aristophanes the programme succeeded in combining the words of the dramatist and modern topical wit. [. . .] MacNeice has made [Aristophanes' jokes] come alive again. (Student)

---

[32] The possibility of partiality in the interpretation and quotation of listener feedback should, of course, be borne in mind; but with regard to these extremely positive quotations printed in the Report on *Enemy of Cant* it should also be noted that Reports almost as often provided negative comments as well, which suggests that, at least among the respondents, *Enemy of Cant* was generally very well received.

The really clever way Mr MacNeice strung together the various comedies into one scintillating whole [...] the amusing sophistication and biting satire of Aristophanes which his adaptation never lost. (Medical Practitioner)

You certainly succeeded in putting Aristophanes over as a person (not a classic!) (Civil Servant)

Amazingly 'up-to-date' and yet one felt one was hearing the real thing, and not a modern translation. (School Secretary)

This was really something, pulling down gods—swimming against the tide—using words that said what they meant and not glib mouthings. This is indeed my idea of satire, give us more, much more. Put this on the Home Programme at an early hour and let's have a great tearing of hair all round! (Fitter)

MacNeice's original idea for this programme had been 'to have a crack at the teaching of classics (and possibly teaching methods in general) in this country. I propose a series of unfortunate teachers ranging from hack school masters grinding little boys who have little Greek, to old-fashioned Oxford dons of the textual criticism cult. These, having made Aristophanes in their different ways as boring as possible, would be cut off by the irruption of bits of him sprung into life.'[33] Although MacNeice did not follow this train of thought in his production (as noted above, even the don who could not stop coughing with the dust in his lecture-room was struck out of the script), this privately expressed critique of traditional methods of teaching Greek and Roman texts may incline us to believe that he might have enjoyed reading the letters he received from a teacher at Malvern Girls' College. From 'an Old Girl working at the BBC', this teacher had obtained the unpublished script of *Enemy of Cant* 'to illustrate a class on Greek drama that I give to a large body of girls here who have never done Greek + have stopped Latin', and she later reported to him that 'it was received with great relish by a class of non-classical senior girls here—almost seventy of them who could scarcely believe that it was a version of what they are pleased to call a dead language'.[34] MacNeice therefore succeeded, at least in this well documented case, in his original aim 'to introduce Aristophanes to a public which can perfectly well appreciate him once he is divorced from pedantry',[35]

---

[33] Memo from LM to LG, 21 May 1946 (R19/307).
[34] Letters from Mary Warry to LM, 3 March 1948 and 29 June 1948 (ibid.).
[35] Memo from LM to LG, 12 July 1946 (ibid.).

and this example seems to encapsulate radio's potential to engage its audience in both practical and imaginative ways: not only did the teacher get 'immense pleasure out of it' but she was encouraged by what still may be perceived to be an implicit 'crack at the teaching of classics' to introduce—it seems with great success—this vibrant re-working of Aristophanic texts to the girls she taught.

8.2. PATRIC DICKINSON'S ARISTOPHANIC ADAPTATIONS

At the time when Patric Dickinson was displaying his considerable aptitude for making Homer work on radio (in his 1946 *The Wall of Troy* and 1952 *Death of Hector*), he wrote to Val Gielgud to say that 'I am very, very keen on translating G[ree]k + Roman Comedy': 'everyone seems to go on + on doing the tragedies + nobody cares for the comedies!'[36] His enthusiastic persistence in suggesting translations of comic playwrights led to his position as the leading translator of Aristophanes for radio in the 1950s. His regular supply of classical plays in translation began when he offered to translate Plautus's *Pseudolus*, a Roman comedy centred on buying the freedom of a prostitute from a brothel, for broadcast on the Third in 1949. E. A. Harding of the Third Programme encouraged him to aim for an 'entertaining radio show' rather than an academic exercise. Entertain it certainly did, as well as shock the more genteel Third Programme listener with a little 'Anglo-Saxon' here and there: 'How was Mr Dickinson to translate', asked Hope-Wallace in *The Listener*, 'save with the words used in every barrack-room or four-ale-bar—and the scene of this play is not any such respectable place but what I suppose I had better call a house of a certain kind?'[37] Many other ideas followed—a dramatic feature adapted from Thucydides' *History of the Peloponnesian War*, more Plautine comedies, and those of Terence and Aristophanes.[38]

---

[36] Letter from PD to VG, 14 May [1952] (PD/S1a).
[37] Letter from E. A. Harding to PD, 22 July 1949 (PD/S1a); Hope-Wallace 1949*b*.
[38] Letters from PD to Harman Grisewood, 14 March 1951, and from PD to E. A. Harding, n.d. (PD/S1a).

Harman Grisewood (1908–97), Controller of the Third from 1948 to 1952, did not, however, share Dickinson's enthusiasm for putting classical comedy on the air. In response to Dickinson's suggestion, made in 1952, that he might translate Aristophanes' *Wasps*, which he accompanied with two specimen scenes in translation and which he intended for production with the music that Vaughan Williams had composed for the 1909 Cambridge Greek Play, Grisewood wrote a lengthy internal memorandum expressing serious concerns. Grisewood considered that the only way to render Aristophanes in another language was to produce a 'crib' (a very close translation), believing that any attempt to convey the comic force of the plays in modern terms produces an adaptation which is 'estranged from the context of the original' and, although it may be funny, would no longer be Aristophanic:

> This sort of thing can be appreciated in the study but I cannot see how it is effective in performance except by what I would call illicit devices so that you are constructing comedy upon a broadly Aristophanic base but you are not constructing Aristophanic comedy. [...] It simply isn't Greek at all. It is just some kind of comic monster that can be made to perform tricks but they are not Hellenic ones.[39]

Grisewood therefore scotched the idea of *Wasps*, but—fortunately for Dickinson—he shortly left the post of Controller of the Third and, within a year or two, Dickinson's renewed suggestions for tackling Aristophanes received a much warmer welcome. In 1954 the Third Programme expressed great interest in his suggestion that he translate *Acharnians* for production, although by now there was an open acceptance that it would 'be more a question of making a "version" rather than a simple translation' in order to make the comedy work on air.[40] Dickinson loved the task: 'I can't tell you what a joy it's been to do. For ten years I've wanted to do this play',[41] and so successful was it that within three months he was commissioned to translate *Peace* and *Lysistrata* and further ancient comedies in years to come (Plautus's *Trinummus*, 1958 and Aristophanes' *Women in Power* (*Ekklesiasouzai*), 1970).

---

[39] Letter from Harman Grisewood to 'H. D.', 16 April 1952 (ibid.).
[40] Letter from Donald McWhinnie to PD, 29 November 1954 (ibid.).
[41] Letter from PD to Donald McWhinnie, date-stamped 22 April 1955 (PD/S2a).

Raymond Raikes, who, as noted above, had produced so many Greek and Roman plays for radio, was responsible for both the adaptation and production of *Acharnians*, and *Peace* and *Lysistrata* which were to follow. It may well have been Raikes's suggestion that *Acharnians* open with a sizeable prologue-like speech by the character of Aristophanes (played by Russell Napier) *before* the Announcer introduced the play. The technique draws something from the Aristophanic model provided by MacNeice's *Enemy of Cant*, although it lacks the lightness and integration of MacNeice's style. Aristophanes talks directly to the listener, explaining the military context of his comedies with modern terminology ('satellite' states) and a suggested parallel between the Greek pro-war politician Cleon and Hitler ('preaching a doctrine of mass terror—he had nearly succeeded in persuading Athens to put to death the whole adult male population of Mytilene'). Aristophanes concludes with a glance back to the Second World War and a parting shot about Britain's lack of a national theatre:

> Well, with that I'll leave you to listen to my 'war-time' Comedy written for an overcrowded city, full of evacuees and political informers, restless with war fever... but I have to laugh when I think what your war-time Censor might have done if he'd been confronted with a 'pacifist' play like this, putting the Enemy's point of view... Would it have reached your national theatre (if you had one!) as it reached ours—and won first prize?... (Laughs)

The Announcer then introduces the play and locates it in ancient time and space. The play proper opens with Dikaiopolis (played by Charles Leno) in the 'tones of one of the blither Cockney 'bus conductors'.[42] Here is a taste of the easy, colloquial translation from the opening scene:

> DIKAIOPOLIS [...] I sit alone, alone in the wide assembly,
> Alone I sit and wait; I groan and yawn and stretch,
> I fiddle, I doodle, I tweeze out bristles,
> I add up my savings, but always I gaze
> Out over the fields, craving for Peace,
> Hating this city, aching for my village
> Where the cry isn't always 'Buy, haggle and fleece'
> But where there is give and take and a living for all...

---

[42] Trewin 1955.

> So here I am ready to tackle these city speakers
> Shout 'em down, curse 'em, heckle 'em, if they debate
> About anything but Peace.
> (A buzz of noise)
> Ph! Here they come—our mid-day Deputies—
> What did I tell you?—just exactly that!
> And every man jack of them elbowing to the Front.
>
> CRIER (Stentorian guide's voice)
> Move up there! Move up! With-hin the 'allowed ground!
> The Deputies 'ave taken their seats—[43]

The critical reception of Dickinson's translation was extremely positive. Trewin, writing in *The Listener*, thought he preserved 'the spirit of Aristophanes [...] present[ing] colloquially the satire, the mischief, the inner urgency of it all [...] The zest, the happy malice, the fierce stinging of *The Acharnians* duly stung and quivered.'[44] The critic in *The Times* noted that Dickinson 'does not follow Mr Ezra Pound, who offered Sophocles in slang, or even Mr Dudley Fitts, who has a racy way with Aristophanes. But he certainly belongs to what another translator, Hookham Frere, called the class of spirited translators rather than the more academic faithful translators. He does not emasculate the bawdy, though he neatly avoids some four-letter words.'[45] Or, as Dickinson himself put it: 'the Greeks liked their Phallic jokes straight; we do not'.[46]

Having got wind of the further BBC commissions of *Peace* and *Lysistrata*, Oxford University Press approached Dickinson with the idea of publishing all three plays in a volume entitled *Aristophanes against War* dedicated to Raymond Raikes, whom Dickinson had found to be a 'meticulous and imaginative craftsm[a]n'.[47] The volume was published in 1957 alongside well received productions of *Peace* and *Lysistrata* on the Third.[48] This volume, a notable example of radio's interaction with other cultural and educational spheres, was

---

[43] Script for the 1955 production of *Acharnians*, 4–5 (BBC WAC SL).
[44] Trewin 1955.   [45] Anon. 1955.
[46] Quoted in Anon. 1957c.   [47] Dickinson 1965, 229.
[48] Letter from PD to VG, 8 August 1956 (PD/S2b). Oxford University Press hoped to time the publication to coincide with the radio productions (letter from John Bell, OUP to Donald McWhinnie, 19 March 1957, ibid.). This was not the first *Lysistrata* on the air: in 1947 Noel Iliff produced Reginald Beckwith and Andrew Cruickshank's adaptation (originally written for performance in the 1935-6 season of London's Gate Theatre: see Marshall 1947, 112–13) with Avice Landone in the title role.

considered by *The Times* to be 'a sporting effort and one well worth making', even if 'the inevitable bowdlerizing takes much of the wind out of the great sails'.[49] *The Listener* was even more positive: 'the dialogue keeps the snap and sparkle of the original, and the choral interludes in long sprawling lines are surprisingly successful. The dialect scenes are alive and entertaining, and the exuberant language, atrocious puns, and the speed and attack of the swiftly changing episodes are most skilfully reproduced and maintained.'[50]

The Listener's review of the 1957 production of *Lysistrata* points to the bind in which the BBC found itself when broadcasting an ancient Greek—and therefore canonical and, on the face of it, 'respectable'—play which turns out to be terrifically bawdy:

> Mr Dickinson is desperately determined not to sound half-hearted in his semi-seemly paraphrase of Aristophanes' jests about the upright men of war. He, and his producer Raymond Raikes, were so intent on insisting that the poet's purpose was serious that they made Miss [Googie] Withers start off as though the play was not a comedy at all. It soon got going, all the same, though there was at times the truly awe-inspiring sound of respectable British matrons conscientiously resolved to be heartily outspoken or die in the attempt, but definitely not amused.[51]

The solution to the problem of maintaining a level of propriety for the widely accessible medium of radio therefore seems to have been to have the actors deliver, in a serious and 'matronly' tone of voice, a condensed and diluted version of Aristophanic humour. Observe the nature of the sexual innuendo in the opening scene of the play:

KALONIKE	But, Lysistrata, what? Why've you called us? What's up?
LYSISTRATA	Something big.
KALONIKE	A stiff proposition?
LYSISTRATA	Stiff as it could be.
KALONIKE	Then why on earth isn't everybody here?
LYSISTRATA	Oh, it's not that—they'd come quick enough for that! No; it's an idea. Something I've thought of in bed— Alone... awake in the night, tossing and turning.
KALONIKE	It must be a teaser to keep you tossing and turning. (pp. 2–3)[52]

---

[49] Anon. 1957c.   [50] Anon. 1957b.   [51] Walker 1957.
[52] Page references are to the script for the 1957 radio production of *Lysistrata* (BBC WAC SL).

Like *Acharnians*, the radio production of *Lysistrata* was prefaced by a speech by the character of Aristophanes which, again, attempted to do a little of what MacNeice's *Enemy of Cant* did so fluently. Dickinson's historical contextualizing is a little more prosaic, however: 'After s<u>i</u>x years of war, in the Comedy called *The Acharnians* [. . .] Then, after t<u>e</u>n years of war, a Comedy called *The Peace* [. . .]' (p. 1). This prologue does, however, go on to offer a strikingly interesting interpretative context for the play: 'This period of despondency in Athens produced a spate of sexual licence and pleasure-seeking in the city, the sort of lust that in wartime so often accompanies the shedding of so much blood... But might not this very fever of licentiousness be made an instrument to save Athens from disaster, and to reconcile her with her enemy (yes, her great and noble enemy) Sparta?' (p. 1). The sexual content of the play, then, is set up as a mere temporary reaction to military and political disaster, rather than an exuberant perspective on natural bodily functions and sexual habits and tastes.

Seven years later, Dickinson's translation of *Lysistrata* was produced for BBC Television. *Lysistrata; or Women on Strike* (to give the television production its full title) was directed by Prudence FitzGerald for broadcast in 1964 as part of the *Festival* series. The critic in *The Listener* testified to having enjoyed the production more than any in the series 'partly because we all really enjoy an occasional dirty joke [. . .] The dirty jokes were on this occasion put over very coolly and unblushingly by most of the cast.'[53] Dickinson's translation had been adapted for television by Marc Brandel so that it 'did not offend the sensitive mass audience';[54] still, some viewers let the BBC know in no uncertain terms that they had found aspects of it 'disgusting and coarse'.[55] One Mr Stanton, an incensed viewer (who nevertheless seemed to have forced himself to watch to the very end), wrote a sternly worded letter to the Director of the Television Service, complaining in particular about *Lysistrata* but also more broadly about 'The pre-occupation with sex and infidelity which permeates the BBC'.[56] *Lysistrata* was clearly not, for some, the only bit of sauciness on television in the early 1960s. (This was, of course, the beginning of the era of Mary Whitehouse's 'Clean Up TV Campaign', the

---

[53] Taylor 1964.   [54] Anon. 1964.   [55] Quoted in VR/64/39 in T5/2160/1.
[56] Letter from Mr H. B. Stanton to 'The Director of Television Service', 16 January 1964 (ibid.).

manifesto of which made a direct appeal to the women of Britain in January 1964. One has to wonder what she made of this televised *Lysistrata*!)

Although some of the more explicit sexual and other potentially offensive references were cut, it is notable how *much* was left in, which begs the question of how these moments in the play were portrayed on screen, where very little can be left to the imagination. The *Daily Mirror*, for example, comments on 'the camera work picking up the expressions of the women when told they must resist bed and men'.[57] Following what is sometimes referred to as the 'striptease' scene between Myrrhine and Kinesias, the chorus comment on his painfully aroused state as follows:

LEADER	Poor old cock!
CHORUS ONE	You're in a bad way!
CHORUS TWO	You're distressed—
CHORUS THREE	We're sorry for you.
CHORUS FOUR	The pangs of unemployment.
CHORUS FIVE	Are more than a body can bear. (p. 60)[58]

When the Spartan Herald arrives in a similar state, the innuendo continues:

LEADER (ADMIRINGLY)	Look at him.
CHORUS ONE	A big one, isn't he?
SECOND MAN	Where did you spring from?
SPARTAN HERALD	From Sparta.
THIRD MAN	I see you're having the same trouble down your way.
FOURTH MAN	No! He's just stiff from the journey.
SPARTAN HERALD	I've got an urgent message to deliver to your senators.
FIFTH MAN	It's urgent all right.
LEADER	But it isn't a senator you need.
SPARTAN HERALD	It's a matter of public importance.
LEADER	Looks more like a private problem to me. (pp. 60–1)

The production makes visual references to ancient Greece with, for example, costumes consisting of robes, cloaks, and sandals, and the introduction of sacrificial goats.[59] The set also included strong

---

[57] Sear 1964.
[58] Page references are to the script of the 1964 television production (BBC WAC).
[59] A recording of the production does not, unfortunately, survive, but the T5/2160/1 file contains a wealth of information. Dickinson himself thought the BBC made a 'ghastly

Grecian references, with great columns suggestive of the buildings on the Athenian Acropolis. Did the producer stick with Aristophanic convention and portray the male actors with larger-than-life *phalli*, in accordance with these other gestures to ancient convention in the costume and set design? There were limits, of course, to nudity permitted on television, and one strongly suspects that the painfully erect phalli which are continually referred to in Aristophanes' play were left to the viewer's imagination in the televised *Lysistrata*—thus introducing a glaringly obvious and awkward tension between what was heard and what was seen.

In the earlier 1957 production of *Lysistrata* on radio, perhaps it was the *absence* of the visual dimension that made the comic force of this play work particularly well in the audience's imagination. Consider what the following review of a scene from the 1957 production suggests about what was effectively left to the imagination on radio and may well have received a far more modest portrayal on the screen: the actor playing Myrrhine, Janette Richer, it is said, 'really seemed to be having the time of her life in the strip-tease scene, which was therefore easily the funniest'.[60]

The Audience Research Report for the 1964 television production records that the 220 viewers from the Viewing Panel who responded to the production were evenly divided between those who 'very much enjoyed themselves watching it' and others who had very little good to say about it. For example, a clergyman 'liked the play immensely' and other enthusiasts found it 'a vastly entertaining affair, full of cheek, fun (at the expense of men, various housewives noted gleefully), and an unblushing broadness of expression that made "great stuff for adults"'. On the other hand, for half the audience 'it was no joke but everything that was disgusting and coarse, thoroughly embarrassing to watch in mixed or family company and, said certain older members of the sample[,] likely to have a harmful effect on young minds'.[61]

This audience response well illustrates the fact that it is impossible to please all of the people all of the time, especially in a mass medium. Audiences are so large and so immensely varied in terms of their previous educational experience and cultural expectations that a wide

---

mess' of it (letter from PD to RR and 'Jean', n.d., in PD/S3). See Wrigley 2016a for a full treatment of this and all other Greek plays produced on British television.

[60] Walker 1957.   [61] VR/64/39 in T5/2160/1.

spectrum of audience response is visible in most of the research reports available in the BBC archive. Such sources provide rich evidence for general social and cultural barometers regarding propriety and humour, as indeed do the translations themselves. Also evident in the translations in this period is the increasing shift to greater adaptation for the radio medium—both in terms of ensuring the audience can appreciate the play without a classical education and in terms of cuts and changes which make the play comprehensible without the visual element. The examples discussed throw light on the significant relationship of radio broadcasting with other spheres of educational and cultural activity, such that radio can be seen to work in productive symbiosis with them. Gilbert Murray's popularity on the stage made him the foremost translator of Greek plays for radio. The Cambridge Greek Play of 1947 had a partial radio performance. Louis MacNeice's *Enemy of Cant* stimulated amateur performances and was taught in the classroom. Patric Dickinson's translations were first commissioned by the BBC and then published by Oxford University Press as *Aristophanes against War* (1957), after which he was stimulated to publish translations of all Aristophanes' plays (some more of which were broadcast, and many of which were staged by amateurs) in 1970.[62] Listeners and viewers were interested, bored, and enraged; some felt themselves to have been educated by these productions, which is surely the greatest testament to the significance of mass media engagements for our full understanding of the reception of Aristophanes (and, of course, other Greek texts) in twentieth-century Britain.

---

[62] Dickinson reports that London's Attic Players staged *Acharnians* in 1958 and the Unity Theatre, Liverpool did *Lysistrata* in 1959 (letter from PD to 'Barbara', 29 October 1958, in PD/S3a). Dickinson 1970*a* and 1970*b*.

Conclusion:
Public Property; or, Classics for All

So the humanist in his room with Jacobean panels
    Chewing his pipe and looking on a lazy quad
Chops the Ancient World to turn a sermon
    To the greater glory of God.
But I can do nothing so useful or so simple;
    These dead are dead
And when I should remember the paragons of Hellas
    I think instead
Of the crooks, the adventurers, the opportunists,
    The careless athletes and the fancy boys,
The hair-splitters, the pedants, the hard-boiled sceptics
    And the Agora and the noise
Of the demagogues and the quacks; and the women pouring
    Libations over graves
And the trimmers at Delphi and the dummies at Sparta and lastly
    I think of the slaves.
And how one can imagine oneself among them
    I do not know;
It was all so unimaginably different
    And all so long ago.
        Extract from Louis MacNeice, 'Autumn Journal', IX.[1]

In 'Autumn Journal', comments Oliver Taplin, 'MacNeice explores with depth and wit his whole knotted relationship with the Greek and Roman world and with his classical education'.[2] Although in the above quotation MacNeice describes the ancient world as being 'all

---

[1] MacNeice 1939, 39.
[2] Taplin 2002, 8. For discussion see P. McDonald 1998.

so unimaginably different', in his creative writing for radio he clearly demonstrates that an attempt to 'imagine oneself among them' is not only possible but also worthwhile. The ancient Greeks may be incontrovertibly 'dead', but MacNeice's potted description of the ways in which they lived—beginning with 'crooks' and ending with 'slaves' eight lines later, with allusions to politics, love affairs, sports, and noise—energetically undercuts the assertion that it was 'all so unimaginably different'.[3] So too does work such as *Enemy of Cant* in which he makes a leap of imagination into the life and times of the ancient Greeks. MacNeice is not interested in the 'paragons of Hellas' which others have put to use. Indeed, he writes not for those 'who expect the ancient world to look like the Parthenon Frieze', as he stated in a *Radio Times* article prior to a 1944 broadcast of *The Golden Ass*, his version of the Apuleian story.[4]

The usefulness of MacNeice's attempt to represent the ancient world lies in the interpretation and fleshing out of texts and the giving of life to ancient characters (historical and fictional), paraphrasing and contextualizing as necessary in order to achieve what he considered to be the primary goal of the radio writer—the audience's entertainment.[5] To paraphrase a line spoken by Stavros in *The Glory that is Greece* ('College or no college, a Greek should know his history', p. 7), MacNeice's treatment of classical literary and historical subjects seems to suggest that his position might well have been 'College or no college, the listeners should enjoy their classics'. Not that they *should* enjoy their classics, but that his listeners should *enjoy* his broadcasts (and do so whatever the subject, for his work for radio was impressively wide-ranging). As was noted above, his hope for *Enemy of Cant* had been 'to introduce Aristophanes to a public which can perfectly well appreciate him once he is divorced from pedantry', but his primary goal was neither the education of the mass audience nor the promotion of classics.[6]

The correspondence between MacNeice and the listener Mr J. Kershaw of Poynton, Cheshire on the Apuleian adaptations *The Golden Ass* and *Cupid and Psyche* (both 1944) illustrates

---

[3] He was writing about 'the less fortunate and the deviant' as a 'modern social historian' would, considers Arkins 2000, 16.
[4] MacNeice 1945a.   [5] MacNeice 1947b, 9.
[6] Memo from LM to LG, 12 July 1946 (R19/307).

MacNeice's priorities in adapting classical subjects for radio performance.[7] Kershaw began his letter by saying that Apuleius was 'very dear and precious' to him, and that the broadcast had been a 'disappointment': for 'it is decidedly not a book for everyman—it needs a considerable amount of culture—if I dare use that much abused word—to appreciate it [...] No, you tried the impossible, there are some things that cannot be made "popular", and the Golden Asse [sic] is certainly one of them.'[8] MacNeice responded by saying that he had been incorrect to think that the purpose of the broadcast was to encourage people to read the original, and he went on to defend his radio adaptation as follows:

> I admit that in any modern dramatisation either for radio or in any other medium it is not possible to do full justice to Apuleius, but this does not seem to me a valid reason for refusing to make use of what is obviously very dramatic material [...]. I did rather regret not being able to suggest more forcibly some of the stylistic colour of the original, but in turning it all into dialogue I had naturally to beware of pedantry. Incidentally, when you say 'there are some things that cannot be made popular' I (a) very much doubt whether *The Golden Ass* would not sell very well if it were printed in the Penguin edition (especially if unexpurgated), and (b) am pleased to be able to inform you that this particular broadcast programme seems to have been very favourably received by a large variety of persons including my butcher.[9]

Or, as Hope-Wallace succinctly put it when reviewing *Enemy of Cant* for *The Listener*: 'Does one hear murmurs against foolin' about with the classics? Probably. But I think the risk of spoiling classics in this way is very much smaller than the approach which is so reverent that no listeners save a handful of highly educated cognoscenti, text in hand, can make head or tail of them.'[10]

Interestingly, Kershaw wrote back to say that 'evidently I misunderstood that the object of the broadcast was purely entertainment', having assumed that the BBC's cultural project was intended to turn listeners towards the original works. He admits,

---

[7] For the radio scripts and discussion of the productions see Wrigley and Harrison 2013.
[8] Letter from J. Kershaw to LM, 3 November 1944 (R19/440).
[9] Letter from LM to J. Kershaw, 14 November 1944 (ibid.). For a similar defence of his methods to another disgruntled listener to the December 1952 broadcast see his letter to Laurence A. Eveleigh, 14 January 1952, reprinted in MacNeice 2010, 547–8.
[10] Hope-Wallace 1946*b*.

though, that although it is difficult for him to be objective, having known and loved the original for over twenty years, his 13-year-old son 'listened to it with great enjoyment'. 'Now for a bouquet', he continues: 'We listened also to the broadcast of *Cupid and Psyche* and have nothing but praise for it. It gave us great delight + we listened entranced. Few things from the BBC have given us so much pleasure recently.'[11]

This kind of correspondence demonstrates that the audience for engagements with ancient Greece on the radio was composed of individuals across the full spectrum of knowledge of the ancient world, whether they were familiar with ancient texts in the original languages, had done some Latin and Greek at school, had read the works in English translation, or had not encountered the material or anything like it before. What seems particularly striking and important is that it was not only the listener who had some degree of acquaintance with the original texts or detailed knowledge of the ancient world who felt able to offer a firm viewpoint on how these things had been represented on radio. Much of the correspondence from listeners to those who involved in making the programmes suggests that radio was able to elicit a strong sense of 'ownership' of cultural broadcasts, through a combination of the lack of boundaries conditioning the reception of programmes broadcast into the personal, domestic sphere, and the psychologically intimate nature of the radio performance. For all programmes drawing on the ancient world there are likely to have been some (like Mr Kershaw) who believed that 'there are some things that cannot be made "popular"', and others who were pleased that the programme had been made, such as the housewife who did not know 'how close he stuck to the original', but who thought that 'the humour is ageless and the people one might meet anywhere'.[12] (It was not, of course, always the classically educated listener who was disappointed and the non-classically-educated who was pleased.)

Listeners such as Kershaw were not alone in worrying about what popularization through translation, adaptation, and transmission through mass media did to cultural works. Following the establishment of the Third Programme in 1946, some of MacNeice's own

[11] Letter from J. Kershaw to LM, 24 November 1944 (R19/440).
[12] BBC WAC LR/3015: Listener Research Report on the 1944 broadcast of *The Golden Ass*.

colleagues at the BBC also displayed much anxiety in internal correspondence over the extent to which 'crutches' were to be offered to the many eager listeners who requested more background information on cultural broadcasts so that they might get more out of their listening (requests which support the Reithian project of educative broadcasting), fearing what they imagined would be the 'dilution' of the work. Those in a position of authority (whether institutional, educational, critical, or otherwise cultural) tend to express such fears in terms of the damage they perceive to be done to the original work; but, of course, nothing *happens* to the original work—it is still there, on the shelf. A spectrum of engagements with modern presentations of ancient works by diverse groups of people might nowadays be embraced as a positive thing—not necessarily in Reithian terms of 'improvement', but as demonstration of the continuing imaginative appeal of the ancient world, which—and to a certain extent incidentally—cannot also but serve to give the still restricted academic subject of classics a more meaningful place within wider society. MacNeice, naturally, puts it more elegantly:

> It is so hard to imagine
> A world where the many would have their chance without
> A fall in the standard of intellectual living
> And nothing left that the highbrow cared about.
> Which fears must be suppressed. There is no reason for thinking
> That, if you give a chance to people to think or live,
> The arts of thought or life will suffer and become rougher
> And not return more than you could ever give.
>   From 'Autumn Journal', III.[13]

This book has sought to demonstrate that as a mass medium BBC Radio made the literature, history, and thought of ancient Greece practically accessible to a very large audience of listeners who were extremely diverse in terms of their prior educational and cultural experience; and as a new and distinctively evolving medium for the dissemination of cultural works, radio made the ancient Greek world come alive for the audience in a particularly striking way. In an important study on ancient Rome on film, Professor of Latin Maria Wyke argues that 'a certain kind of cinema can be truer to

---

[13] MacNeice 1939, 17–18.

the present fragmented condition of classical antiquity than more conventional historical scholarship', citing the Italian film director Federico Fellini, who considered that film enabled the ancient world to be evoked in a suggestive but fragmentary way and 'the characters and their adventures [to] live before our eyes as though caught unawares'. Wyke concludes that 'the question, for Fellini, would not be *whether* cinema should have a place in the classical tradition but *what else* could best capture the mysterious, obscure and ethereal quality of the ancient world today'.[14] The present book argues that visual representation is not, in fact, necessary to bring the characters and stories of the ancient world strikingly to life in the modern imagination and, indeed, that the *absence* of the visual dimension in radio engagements with ancient Greece may actually enable the listener to get more readily to the human dimension of ancient Greek stories, histories, and ideas. The ancient world undoubtedly remains 'mysterious, obscure and ethereal' and yet radio has for countless listeners made it far less mysterious and more real: one may, therefore, boldly ask whether *radio* is the performance medium which might be best suited to the task of capturing the still vital force of the ancient works, through culturally informative, educationally enriching, *and* imaginatively stimulating broadcasts.

[14] Wyke 1997, 192 (original emphasis).

APPENDIX

Production Chronology

The following production chronology lists BBC Radio programmes drawing on ancient Greek literature, history, and thought which have been the subject of some discussion in this volume. For reasons of space, not all programmes mentioned in passing have been included. This is not, therefore, a comprehensive listing of all programmes engaging with ancient Greek culture broadcast on radio in the period under discussion; as a very rough estimate, it lists one third of all such broadcasts. Radio programmes on Roman themes and television and stage productions drawing on ancient Greece which are referred to in the text do not appear here; neither do planned programmes which were cancelled before broadcast (such as *Prometheus the Engineer* in 1934).

It is important to bear in mind that very many of the programmes in this production chronology received more than one (and sometimes several) repeat broadcasts in the weeks, months, and sometimes years following their radio première, even though, for reasons of space, details of repeat broadcasts are not usually noted below. Standardization has not been imposed on the titles of programmes when they refer to an ancient work or the names of ancient historical figures or characters when performed by an actor; rather, they are given as they are listed in the most reliable source available. The discussion in the preceding chapters may, for example, refer to the July 1951 radio performance of Euripides' play *Iphigenia at Aulis*, but the title of the production itself is given as it was billed at the time, using the variant play title *Iphigeneia in Aulis*. Following the date of a programme are listed the network on which it was broadcast (with the abbreviations Home for the Home Service, National for the National Programme, Third for the Third Programme, etc.), the start time, and the duration of the programme, where this information is available. The title of the programme is given, together with an indication of the series in which it appeared, the author/writer, adaptor (where relevant: for example, in the case of translations of plays), producer, composer, and some actors (who are listed in alphabetical order of surname, followed by the role they took). Other pertinent information follows where applicable.

The most important institutions for the research which lies behind the compilation of this production chronology have been the BBC WAC, the

Appendix

BLSA, and the Bodleian Library's modern papers collections (especially the Papers of Gilbert Murray). The extremely helpful production catalogues maintained by the BBC WAC and the BLSA are, however, substantially incomplete. This information has been usefully augmented with archival research in, for example, the BBC's written archives. Where possible, programme information has been verified against several archival and documentary sources and listings such as the *Radio Times*. It should be noted that the *Radio Times*, printed as it was a couple of weeks before programmes were aired, does not always contain accurate data (for example, with regard to the names of performers).

Thursday, 15 May 1924 (broadcast from Glasgow, 7.35 p.m., 130 mins)
Antigone **by Sophocles.** Translator: John Harrower. Producer: A. Parry Gunn. Composer: Percy Gordon.

Thursday, 14 May 1925 (Belfast, 7.30 p.m., 150 mins, including orchestral music before and afterwards)
Iphigenia in Tauris **by Euripides.** Translator: Gilbert Murray. Producer: Tyrone Power (=Tyrone Guthrie). Actors: Arthur Malcolm (Orestes), Tyrone Power (=Tyrone Guthrie) (Pylades), Flora Robson (Iphigenia).

Sunday, 28 June 1925 (London, 4.15 p.m., 45 mins)
Medea **by Euripides.** Condensed version of Gilbert Murray's translation. 'The play rehearsed by' Lewis Casson. Actors: Lawrence Anderson (Jason), Lewis Casson (Creon/Messenger), Lilian Moubrey (Nurse), Sybil Thorndike (Medea).

Wednesday, 22 September 1926 (London, 8.00 p.m., 90 mins)
Rhesus **by Euripides.** Translator: Gilbert Murray. Producer: Henry Oscar. Composer: Victor Hely-Hutchinson. Actors: Douglas Burbidge (Æneas), Irene Rooke (Athena), Frank Vosper (Rhesus), Edmund Willard (Hector).

Wednesday, 1 February 1928 (London and Daventry, 3.00 p.m., 30 mins)
'Epic Poetry: the *Iliad* and the *Odyssey*', the second programme in the series *Stories in Poetry* by J. C. Stobart and Mary Somerville of the BBC Education Department for broadcast to schools.

Tuesday, 28 February 1928–Tuesday, 3 April 1928 (London, Daventry, Aberdeen, Liverpool, etc., usually broadcast at 7.25 p.m., 20 mins)
Greek Plays for Modern Listeners **by Archibald Young Campbell**, a six-week series covering (in order of broadcast) 'The General Character of a Greek Tragedy', 'Æschylus and his *Oresteia*', 'Sophocles and his *Œdipus at Colonus*', 'Euripides and his *Hippolytus*', 'Aristophanes and his *Frogs*', and 'Survivals and Influences'.

Appendix

Monday, 2 April 1928 (all stations except Manchester and 5GB, 9.35 p.m., 85 mins)
Speed: A Tragi-Comic Fantasy of Gods and Mortals by 'Charles Croker'. A play written for radio by a well-known (but unidentified) author for the stage; divine characters include Cronos and Zeus.

Thursday, 17 May 1928 (Daventry, 10.30 p.m., 15 mins)
After Euripides' Electra and *The Greek Vase* by Maurice Baring, accompanied by two other of his 'diminutive dramas'.

Wednesday, 5 December 1928 (Daventry, 9.30 p.m., 30 mins)
Alcestis by Euripides. Extracts translated and read by Gilbert Murray, with some commentary.

Tuesday, 22 January–Tuesday, 19 March 1929 (London and Daventry, 4.15 p.m., 15 mins)
Classics in Translation, a five-part series for schools, consisting of talks by J. Arbuthnot Nairn on translators from different ages, ancient and modern.

Tuesday, 19 February 1929 (London and Daventry, 9.40 p.m., *c.*30 mins)
X = O: A Night of the Trojan War, a poetic play by John Drinkwater.

Thursday, 28 February 1929 (Daventry, 10.15 p.m., 60 mins; repeated 22 May 1929 from London and Daventry)
Three Great Playwrights, a programme consisting of passages from *The Persae* by Aeschylus (translated by Lewis Campbell), *Ulysses* by Stephen Phillips and *Doctor Faustus* by Marlowe.

Tuesday, 5 March 1929 (London and Daventry, 7.25 p.m., 20 mins)
New Light on Ancient Greece, six weekly talks by Stanley Casson, drawing on his excavation work. The programmes focused on Sparta, Troy, Delphi, Mycenae, Corinth, and Olympia.

Tuesday, 16 July 1929 (Daventry, 8.15 p.m., 105 mins; repeated 17 July from London and Daventry)
Electra by Euripides. No. 11 in the *Great Plays* series. Translator: Gilbert Murray. 'Arranged for broadcasting' by Dulcima Glasby. Producer: Howard Rose. Actors: Douglas Burbidge (Orestes), Barbara Couper (Electra), May Saker (Clytemnestra).

Monday, 5 September 1932 (Belfast, 8.00 p.m., 100 mins)
King Oedipus by Sophocles. Translator: W. B. Yeats. Producer: S. A. Bulloch. Presented by the Abbey Players.

Sunday, 15 January 1933 (London Regional, 5.00 p.m., 30 mins)
The *Readings from Classical Literature* series broadcast a thirty-minute reading from Greek and Roman literature almost every Sunday from January 1933 until well into 1934. The first programme was 'Troy: The Slaying of

Hector', a translation from Homer's *Iliad* XXII; later programmes in the Greek half of the series included 'A Softer Strain. The Lyric Poets: Sappho, Simonides, Pindar, Sophocles, and others', 'The Messenger's Speech: The Greek Tragedians and Milton', 'The Greek Historians. Herodotus: The Battle of Salamis', and 'Greek Philosophy: Features in the Portrait of Socrates from the *Protagoras*, the *Phaedrus* and the *Symposium* of Plato'.

Thursday, 15 October 1936 (National Programme, 9.20 p.m., 20 mins)
'An Introduction to *The Hippolytus* of Euripides', written and delivered in part by Gilbert Murray.

Sunday, 18 October 1936 (National Programme, 5.35 p.m., 90 mins)
Hippolytus by Euripides. Translator: Gilbert Murray (who had given a 20-minute introductory talk on the play three days earlier). Producer: Barbara Burnham. Chorus direction: Elsie Fogerty. Chorus trainer: Gwynneth Thurburn. Actors: Hubert Gregg (Hippolytus), Hermione Hannen (Artemis), Lilian Harrison (Phaedra), Margaret Rawlings (Aphrodite), Gladys Young (Nurse). See Figure 4.1.

Monday, 30 November 1936 (Regional, 11.40 p.m., 20 mins)
'The Slaying of the Suitors', a reading from Homer's *Odyssey* arranged by C. R. Spencer.

Friday, 12 February 1937 (National, 3.35 p.m., 20 mins)
'Socrates', a talk by Richard Livingstone in the *Talks for Sixth Forms* series.

Sunday, 25 April 1937 (National, 6.15 p.m., 95 mins)
The Trojan Women by Euripides. Translator: Gilbert Murray. Producer: Barbara Burnham. Chorus direction: Elsie Fogerty. Chorus trainer: Gwynneth Thurburn. Actors: Belle Chrystall (Helen), Hubert Gregg (Talthybius), Lilian Harrison (Athena), Lillah McCarthy (Hecuba), Flora Robson (Cassandra), Edith Sharpe (Andromache), Ion Swinley (Menelaus).

Saturday, 11 September 1937 (all regions, 5.00 p.m., 30 mins)
Aesop's 'Frog Fable' told to music and songs devised by Henry Reed as part of *The Children's Hour*.

Friday, 8 October 1937 (National, 3.35 p.m., 20 mins)
'Euripides', a talk by Gilbert Murray in the *Talks for Sixth Forms* series.

Wednesday, 13 October 1937 (National, 2.05 p.m., 20 mins)
'Greece and Persia: Salamis', a dramatic interlude written by Hugh Ross Williamson for the series *For the Schools* under its 'World History' banner.

Friday, 15 October 1937 (National, 3.35 p.m., 20 mins)
'How Philosophy Began: Socrates and Plato', a talk by C. E. M. Joad, the first of three *Talks for Sixth Forms* on aspects of philosophy.

Appendix

Sunday, 14 November 1937 (Home, 6.30 p.m., 80 mins)
The Alcestis by **Euripides**. Translator: Dudley Fitts and Robert Fitzgerald (their translation had not yet been performed on stage). *World Theatre* series. Producer: Barbara Burnham. Composer: Allan Sly. Actors: Francis de Wolff (Heracles), Robert Speaight (Admetus), Veronica Turleigh (Alcestis, replacing Jean Forbes-Robertson).

Saturday, 11 December 1937 (all regions, 5.00 p.m., 30 mins)
Aesop's 'Fox Fable' told to music and songs devised by Henry Reed as part of *The Children's Hour*.

Thursday, 3 March 1938 (Regional, 7.55 p.m., 40 mins)
Beware the Gods by **George Dunning-Gribble**, a radio play drawing on Homer's *Odyssey*. Producer: Barbara Burnham.

Summer 1938 (Empire)
Why Greek? by **Gilbert Murray**, a series of six 15-minute talks on the value of ancient Greek civilization to the modern world.

Sunday, 16 April 1939 (National, 9.05 p.m., 70 mins)
The Persians by **Aeschylus**. Translator: Gilbert Murray. Producer: Barbara Burnham. Chorus direction: Elsie Fogerty. No. 1 in the *Great Plays* series. Actors: Ivan Brandt (Xerxes), William Devlin (Chorus Leader), Godfrey Kenton (Messenger), Sybil Thorndike (Atossa), Cecil Trouncer (Darius).

Saturday, 30 March 1940 (Home, 9.25 p.m., 65 mins)
Alcestis by **Euripides**. Translator: Gilbert Murray. Producer: Barbara Burnham.[1]

Sunday, 25 August 1940 (Home, 9.25 p.m., 45 mins)
The Seven against Thebes by **Aeschylus**, translated and introduced by Gilbert Murray. Producer: Barbara Burnham. Actors: Catherine Lacey (Leader of the Chorus), John Laurie (Scout), G. R. Schjelderup (Herald), Abraham Sofaer (Eteocles). See Figure 4.2.

Wednesday, 22 November 1940 (Overseas)
'Greece's Contribution to Civilisation', a talk by Gilbert Murray. *In My Opinion* series.

Saturday, 14 December 1940 (broadcast to Germany)
Gilbert Murray's November talk on **'Greece's Contribution to Civilisation'** re-worked for broadcast to Germany.

---

[1] Source: letter from BB to GM, 24 February 1940 (GM/S); not listed in the *Radio Times*.

Appendix

Tuesday, 25 March 1941 (Home, 8.00 p.m., 30 mins; also broadcast on Overseas)
Hellas, a half-hour programme broadcast to mark the occasion of Greek Independence Day, arranged and produced by Denis Johnston. It included extracts from Homer, Pausanias, and Aristophanes alongside modern authors such as Byron, Shelley, and Wilde, and was preceded earlier in the evening by a 'commemorative' musical programme, including Granville Bantock's *Sappho*.

Wednesday, 16–Friday, 18 April 1941 (Overseas, 15 mins)
The March of the 10,000 by Louis MacNeice, drawing on Xenophon's *Anabasis*. Producer: Royston Morley.

Thursday, 5 June 1941 (details not known)
'Socrates', a talk by Gilbert Murray. *In My Opinion* series.

Sunday, 12 October 1941 (for European News, 7 mins)
'Message to Greece' by Gilbert Murray.

Tuesday, 28 October 1941 (Home, 8.00 p.m., 45 mins; also on the North American Service as *Greece Lives*)
The Glory that is Greece by Lous MacNeice. Subtitled 'A programme to celebrate the spirit of the Greek Army and the Greek people on the first anniversary of the entry of Greece into the war'. Producer: Laurence Gilliam. Composer: George Walter (=Walter Goehr). Actors included Michael Cacoyannis, Hermione Hannen, Grizelda Hervey, Robert Speaight, Cecil Trouncer.

Saturday, 28 February 1942 (Home, 10.30 p.m., 60 mins)
The Rape of the Locks, Gilbert Murray's translation and partial reconstruction of Menander's *Perikeiromene*. Radio première of this as yet unpublished text. Producer: Barbara Burnham. Actors included Peggy Ashcroft, Felix Aylmer, Alec Guinness.

Sunday, 15 March 1942 (Home, 3.30 p.m., 75 mins)
The Cornerstones by Eric Linklater. Adapted for broadcasting by Edward Sackville-West. Producer: Val Gielgud.

Saturday, 22 March 1942 (Home, 8.45 p.m., 15 mins; repeated on Overseas, 25–26 March, as *Salutation to Greece*)
Salute to Greece by Louis MacNeice, a programme to mark Greek Independence Day. Producer: Malcolm Baker-Smith.

Wednesday, 15 April 1942 (Home, 9.30 p.m., 30 mins)
Medea by Euripides, extracts from Gilbert Murray's translation were given by the Old Vic Company as the sixth programme in the *From the Theatre in Wartime* series. Arranged for broadcasting by Frank Baker. Presented by

Barbara Burnham. Actors: Lewis Casson (Jason) and Sybil Thorndike (Medea).

Sunday, 11 October 1942 (Home, 9.30 p.m., 60 mins)
Socrates Asks Why, a play by Eric Linklater. Produced by Val Gielgud. Incidental music chosen by Edward Sackville-West. Actors included Felix Aylmer (Socrates).

Sunday, 21 February 1943 (Home, 8.45 p.m., 15 mins)
Pericles, written and produced by Louis MacNeice, the first programme in the six-part series *The Four Freedoms* (in which the second and sixth programmes, *The Early Christians* and *What Now?*, also referred to ancient Greece). Composer: Benjamin Britten. Actors: Laidman Browne (Citizen), Philip Cunningham (Xenos), Allan Jeayes (Rough), Tony Quinn (Councillor), Ronald Simpson (Friend), Cecil Trouncer (Pericles).

Thursday, 25 March 1943 (Home, 9.40 p.m., 30 mins; broadcast as *Greece Fights On* on Overseas, 22-26 March)
Long Live Greece written and produced by Louis MacNeice. A programme to mark Greek Independence Day.

Thursday, 25 and Friday, 26 November 1943 (Home, the two parts began at 9.40 p.m. and 9.35 p.m. respectively, 90 mins each)
The Rescue by Edward Sackville-West and Benjamin Britten, a radio dramatization from Homer's *Odyssey*. Première. Producer: John Burrell. Conductor: Clarence Raybould. Actors: Hedli Anderson (Athene), Dennis Arundell (Odysseus), John Byron (Telemachus), James McKechnie (Phemius), Cathleen Nesbitt (Penelope), Esmé Percy (Irus).

Sunday, 12 December 1943 (Home, 10.15 p.m., 15 mins)
'Classical Humanism', a talk by Gilbert Murray.

Friday, 7 January 1944 (Home, 8.15 p.m., 45 mins)
The Sacred Band, written and produced by Louis MacNeice. Subtitled 'A Tribute to Fighting Greece'.

Monday, 30 July 1945 (Home, 9.30 p.m., 60 mins)
Theseus and the Minotaur, a play in verse by Patric Dickinson. Produced by Barbara Burnham. Composer: Leighton Lucas. Actors: Pauline Letts (Ariadne), Stephen Murray (Theseus), Esmé Percy (Herald), Bryan Powley (Old Man), Julian Somers (Minotaur).

Monday, 1 October 1945 (Home, 9.30 p.m., 90 mins)
Hippolytus by Euripides. Translator: Gilbert Murray. First in the new *World Theatre* series. Producer: Val Gielgud. Music selected by Edward Sackville-West. Actors: Barry Morse (Hippolytus), Diana Wynyard (Phaedra), Gladys

Appendix

Young (Nurse). A recorded repeat of this production was broadcast as the first Greek tragedy on the Third Programme on 13 October 1946 (see below).

Monday, 4 March 1946 (Home, 9.15 p.m., 90 mins)
The Trojan Women by Euripides. Translator: Gilbert Murray. *World Theatre* series. Producer: Val Gielgud. Actors: Anne Cullen (Cassandra), Deryck Guyler (Talthybius), Grizelda Hervey (Athene), Margaret Leighton (Helen), Esmé Percy (Poseidon), Leon Quartermaine (Menelaus), Sybil Thorndike (Hecuba), Rita Vale (Andromache), Gladys Young (Chorus Leader).

Sunday, 13 October 1946 (Third, 9.30 p.m., 90 mins)
Hippolytus by Euripides. Translator: Gilbert Murray. Producer: Val Gielgud. Music selected by Edward Sackville-West. This was a recorded repeat of the Home Service production of 1 October 1945 (see above).

Friday, 18 October 1946 (Third, 9.45 p.m., 60 mins)
Phèdre by Racine, the first programme in the *International Drama: Comment and Action* series. Producer: Mary Hope Allen. Included Jean-Louis Barrault and Michel Saint-Denis discussing the difference between Racine and Euripides, Sarah Bernhardt and Marie Bell performing extracts in French, and David King-Wood (Hippolytus) and Margaret Rawlings (Phaedra) performing extracts from an English translation.

Tuesday, 29 October 1946 (Third, 8.30 p.m., 105 mins)
Agamemnon by Aeschylus. Translator: Louis MacNeice. Producer: Val Gielgud. Actors: Lewis Casson (Watchman), Raf de la Torre (Herald), Olive Gregg (Cassandra), Margaret Rawlings (Clytemnestra), Sydney Tafler (Aegisthus), Frederick Valk (Agamemnon). See Figure 7.1.

Thursday, 21 November 1946 (Third, 9.15 p.m., 60 mins)
The Wall of Troy by Patric Dickinson, a 'transcription' of Homer, *Iliad* III. Producer: Val Gielgud. Composer: Lennox Berkeley. Actors: Andrew Churchman (Idaios), Frank Cochrane (Priam), Raf de la Torre (Agamemnon), Francis de Wolff (Hector), Rachel Gurney (Laodice), Margaret Leighton (Helen), Ella Milne (Aphrodite), Lionel Stevens (Paris), William Trent (Odysseus), Richard Williams (Menelaus).

Sunday, 24 November 1946 (Third, 7.15 p.m., 40 mins)
Aristotle's Mother: An Argument in Athens by Herbert Read, the third programme in the *Imaginary Conversations* series. Actors: Anthony Jacobs (Narrator), Ivan Samson (Protogenes), Norman Shelley (Apelles), Alan Wheatley (Aristotle).

Tuesday, 3 December 1946 (Third, 9.45 p.m., 90 mins)

Enemy of Cant: A Panorama of Aristophanic Comedy written and produced by Louis MacNeice. Composer: Antony Hopkins. Actors included Dylan Thomas (Aristophanes/Dikaiopolis).

Monday, 3 February 1947 (Home, 9.15 p.m., 90 mins)
Frogs by Aristophanes. Translator: Gilbert Murray. *World Theatre* series. Producer: Val Gielgud. Composer: Antony Hopkins. Actors: Denys Blakelock (Euripides), Milton Rosmer (Aeschylus), Michael Shepley (Dionysus). Repeated on the Third on Sunday, 27 April when it was followed by a 30-minute programme of scenes from the play given in ancient Greek by members of the University of Cambridge and introduced by J. T. Sheppard. See Figure 4.3.

Monday, 18 August 1947 (Third, 8.55 p.m., 75 mins)
Philoctetes by Sophocles. Translator: Blair (=W. W. Blair-Fish). Producer: John Richmond. Actors: Baliol Holloway (Philoctetes), Alan Hood (Herakles), Roderick Lovell (Neoptolemus), Abraham Sofaer (Odysseus).

Monday, 1 September 1947 (Third, 7.35 p.m., 75 mins)
Lysistrata by Aristophanes, adapted by Reginald Beckwith and Andrew Cruickshank. Producer: Noel Illif. Composer: Leslie Bridgewater. Actors: Reginald Beckwith (Cinesias), Sheila Burrell (Myrrhine), Marjorie Clayton (Lampito), Andrew Cruickshank (Spartan Herald), Philip Cunningham (Magistrate), Robert Desmond (Narrator), Shelagh Fraser (Stratyllis), Sibell Gill (Corinthian Woman), Ursula Hanray (Calonice), Godfrey Kenton (Bobus), Avice Landone (Lysistrata), J. B. Powell-Jones (Athenian).

Tuesday, 14 October 1947 (Third, 9.55 p.m., 60 mins)
'The Apology and Crito', the first programme in *The Dialogues of Plato* series. Translator: Hugh Tredennick. Arranged for broadcasting and produced by Rayner Heppenstall. Actor: Arthur Young (Socrates). Later programmes in the series, which continued into 1948, included 'Phaedo', 'Protagoras and Phaedrus', 'The Republic', and 'The Laws' (in different translations).

Monday, 3 November 1947 (Home, 9.15 p.m., 85 mins)
Antigone by Sophocles. Translator: Gilbert Murray. *World Theatre* series. Producers: Val Gielgud and Rex Tucker. Actors: Robert Farquharson (Tiresias), William Fox (Haemon), Val Gielgud (Creon), Rachel Gurney (Ismene), Margaret Halstan (Eurydice), Valerie White (Antigone).

Monday, 9 February 1948 (Home, 9.15 p.m., 90 mins)
Electra by Euripides, translated and adapted by Gilbert Murray. *World Theatre* series. Producer: Val Gielgud. Composer: John Buckland. Actors: Maria Becker (Electra), Duncan Carse (Messenger), Ralph de Rohan

(Peasant), Baliol Holloway (Old Man), Martita Hunt (Clytemnestra), Barry Morse (Orestes), Leon Quartermaine (Castor), Rita Vale (Chorus Leader).

Wednesday, 3 March 1948 (Third, 7.40 p.m., 165 mins + interval)
The Rescue by Edward Sackville-West and Benjamin Britten, a radio dramatization from Homer's *Odyssey*. Producer: Val Gielgud. Conductor: Walter Goehr. Actors: John Byron (Telemachus), Clifford Evans (Odysseus), Leslie French (Irus), Rachel Gurney (Penelope), Leon Quartermaine (Phemius), Lydia Sherwood (Athene). Repeat: Thursday, 4 March 1948.

Sunday, 24 July 1949 (Third, 7.10 p.m., 90 mins)
Antigone by Jean Anouilh. Lewis Galantière's translation adapted for radio by Merlin Thomas and the producer Frank Hauser. Actors: Catherine Campbell (Ismene), Denholm Elliott (Haemon), Alec Guinness (Chorus), Mary Morris (Antigone), Peter Ustinov (Creon).

Sunday, 4 September 1949 (Third, 6.00 p.m., 105 mins)
Iphigeneia in Tauris by Euripides. Translator: Philip Vellacott. Producer: Raymond Raikes. Actors: Frederick Allen (Narrator), Hermione Hannen (Iphigeneia), Anthony Jacobs (Orestes). See following entry for an associated programme with excerpts spoken in Greek.

Sunday, 4 September 1949 (Third, 7.45 p.m., 15 mins)
'Excerpts in Greek from the *Iphigeneia in Tauris* of Euripides', compiled and introduced by Philip Vellacott. Producer: Raymond Raikes. Commentary by R. F. Willetts. Readers: Raf de la Torre, Hermione Hannen, Anthony Jacobs (all three of whom were in the preceding production), and Heather Brown.

Monday, 5 September 1949 (Home, 9.15 p.m., 80 mins)
Twenty Years is a Long Time by Mary Garrett, a dramatization from Homer's *Odyssey*. Producer: Noel Iliff. Actors: Peter Hoar (Peisistratus), Harry Hutchinson (Laertes), Avice Landone (Penelope), Barry Letts (Telemachus), Howard Marion-Crawford (Ulysses), Rita Vale (Helen), Wilfrid Walter (Menelaus).

Monday, 26 September 1949 (Home, 9.30 p.m., 75 mins)
Medea by Euripides. Translator: Gilbert Murray. *World Theatre* series. Producer: Val Gielgud. Actors: Clifford Evans (Jason), Eileen Herlie (Medea), Cathleen Nesbitt (Nurse).

Saturday, 18 March 1950 (Third, 7.10 p.m., 80 mins; repeated in the Home's *World Theatre* series on 17 July)
Alcestis adapted from Euripides by Ford Madox Ford. Producer: Frank Hauser. Composer: Antony Hopkins. Actors: Valentine Dyall (Hercules), Robert Farquharson (Pheres), Grizelda Hervey (Alcestis), André Morrell (Admetus), Robert Urquhart (Apollo).

Wednesday, 12 July 1950 (Third, 8.30 p.m., 100 mins)
Agamemnon **by Aeschylus.** Translator: Louis MacNeice. 'Arranged for broadcasting' and produced by Raymond Raikes. Composer: John Hotchkis. Actors: Franklyn Bellamy (Watchman), Laidman Browne (Agamemnon), Sonia Dresdel (Clytemnestra), Deryck Guyler (Herald), Carleton Hobbs (Chorus Leader), Godfrey Kenton (Aegisthus), Diana Maddox (Cassandra).

Sunday, 8 October 1950 (Third, 6.10 p.m., 85 mins; repeated on the Home's *World Theatre* series on 11 December)
Antigone **by Sophocles.** Translator: Dudley Fitts and Robert Fitzgerald. Radio adaptation and production by Raymond Raikes. Composer: John Hotchkis. Prefaced by a 10-minute introductory talk by Gilbert Murray. Actors: Angela Baddeley (Antigone), Deryck Guyler (Messenger), Carleton Hobbs (Chorus Leader), Baliol Holloway (Teiresias), Diana Maddox (Ismene), David Peel (Haemon), Basil Sydney (Creon), Marjorie Westbury (Eurydice).

Sunday, 6 May 1951 (Third, 8.25 p.m., 60 mins)
Oedipus, **translation of André Gide's** *Œdipe* by John Russell. Producer: Donald McWhinnie. Actors: Michael Goodliffe (Oedipus), Grizelda Hervey (Jocasta).

Sunday, 29 July 1951 (Third, 6.10 p.m., 125 mins)
Iphigeneia in Aulis **by Euripides.** Translated and produced by Raymond Raikes. Composer: Anthony Bernard. Actors: Vivienne Chatterton (Clytemnestra), Howard Marion Crawford (Menelaus), Hermione Hannen (Iphigeneia), Carleton Hobbs (Agamemnon), John Slater (Achilles). Preceded by a 10-minute introductory talk by D. L. Page.

Thursday, 13 September 1951 (Third, 7.30 p.m., 175 mins + interval; repeated 14 September)
The Rescue **by Edward Sackville-West and Benjamin Britten**, a radio dramatization from Homer's *Odyssey*. Producer: Raymond Raikes. Conductor: Clarence Raybould. Actors: Leslie French (Irus), Rachel Gurney (Penelope), James McKechnie (Odysseus), David Peel (Telemachus), Leon Quartermaine (Phemius), Catherine Salkeld (Athene).

Sunday, 18 November 1951 (Home, 9.45 p.m., 60 mins)
Portrait of Athens, **written and produced by Louis MacNeice.** Actors: Laidman Browne (Pericles), Grizelda Hervey (Pallas Athene), Duncan McIntryre (Socrates).

Monday, 3 December 1951 (Home, 9.15 p.m., 75 mins)
The Frogs **by Aristophanes.** Translator: Gilbert Murray. *World Theatre* series. Producer: Val Gielgud. Actors: Felix Felton (Dionysus), Baliol Holloway (Aeschylus), David Kossoff (Xanthias), Alan Wheatley (Euripides).

Sunday, 3 August 1952 (Home, 2.30 p.m., 75 mins)
The Arbitration by **Menander** [*Epitrepontes*]. Translated (and partially reconstructed) by Gilbert Murray. Adapted for broadcasting by Helena Wood. Producer: Wilfrid Grantham. Composer: Norman Demuth. *Monday Night Theatre* series. Actors: Philip Cunningham (Davus), John Gabriel (Syriscus), Anthony Jacobs (Chaerestratus), Kathleen Michael (Habrotonon), Winifred Oughton (Sophrone), Jill Raymond (Pamphile), John Ruddock (Smicrines), Richard Warner (Onesimus), Raymond Young (Charisius).

Sunday, 21 September 1952 (Third, 6.00 p.m., 90 mins)
Women of Troy by **Euripides**. Translator: Philip Vellacott. Producer: Raymond Raikes. Actors included Sybil Thorndike (Medea). The production was followed by a 15-minute programme in which Elsa Vergi read extracts from the play in ancient Greek.

Friday, 28 November 1952 (Third, 9.00 p.m., 25 mins)
The Geography of the Golden Fleece Legend, a talk by Robert Graves.

Tuesday, 7 April–Tuesday, 12 May 1953 (Home, 10.00 p.m., 15 mins)
Hellenism and the Modern World by **Gilbert Murray**, a series of six 15-minute talks on 'The Christian Tradition: Rome, Jerusalem, Athens', 'Historical Hellenism', 'The Logos', 'A "Liberal" Civilisation, Wrecked by War', 'The Hellenistic Age', 'Hellene and Barbarian'. (English versions of a series of talks, titled *Les Apports Grecs dans la Civilisation Contemporaine*, he had written for Radiodiffusion Française Universitaire.)

Monday, 13 April 1953 (Home, 9.15 p.m., 90 mins)
Electra by **Euripides**. Translator: Gilbert Murray. *World Theatre* series. Producer: Peter Watts. Composer: Dennis D. Arundell. Actors: Peter Coke (Orestes), Joan Hart (Electra), Catherine Salkeld (Clytemnestra).

Sunday, 26 April 1953 (Third, 6.40 p.m., 100 mins)
Hippolytus by **Euripides**. Translator: Philip Vellacott. Adapted and produced by Raymond Raikes. Composer: John Hotchkis. Actors: John Gabriel (Hippolytus), Rachel Gurney (Phaedra), Joan Hart (Artemis), Howard Marion-Crawford (Theseus), Audrey Mendes (Aphrodite), Gladys Young (Nurse).

Monday, 29 June 1953 (Home, 9.15 p.m., 90 mins)
Agamemnon by **Aeschylus**. Translator: Louis MacNeice. *Word Theatre* series. Arranged for broadcasting and produced by Raymond Raikes. Composer: John Hotchkis. Actors: Hugh Burden (Aegisthus), Francis de Wolff (Agamemnon), Maxwell Gardner (Herald), Anthony Jacobs (Chorus Leader), Allan Jeayes (Watchman), Catherine Lacey (Clytemnestra), Marjorie Westbury (Cassandra).

Appendix 291

Tuesday, 1 September 1953 (Third, 9.25 p.m., 50 mins)
The Death of Hector by Patric Dickinson, an adaptation from Homer, *Iliad* XXII. Producer: Val Gielgud. Composer: James Bernard. Actors: Marion Berry-Hart (Helen), David Enders (Paris), Joan Hart (Andromache), Trevor Martin (Achilles), Leon Quartermaine (Priam), Eileen Thorndike (Hecuba), Mary Wimbush (Cassandra).

Sunday, 10 January 1954 (Third, 3.20 p.m., 85 mins)
Helen by Euripides. Translator: Philip Vellacott. Adapted and produced by Raymond Raikes. Composer: John Hotchkis. Actors included Sonia Dresdel (Helen).

Sunday, 19 December 1954 (Third, 3.00 p.m., 95 mins)
Ion by Euripides. Translator: H. D. [Hilda Doolittle]. Adapted and produced by Raymond Raikes. Composer: Anthony Bernard. Actors: Jill Balcon (Voice), Francis de Woolf (Xouthos), John Forrest (Ion), John Gabriel (Hermes), Joan Hart (Athene), Carleton Hobbs (Old Man), Dorothy Holmes-Gore (Pythian Priestess), Margaret Rawlings (Kreousa).

Sunday, 7 August 1955 (Third, 6.35 p.m., 75 mins)
Acharnians by Aristophanes. Translator: Patric Dickinson. Adaptor and producer: Raymond Raikes. Composer: Christopher Whelen. Actors: Charles Leno (Dikaiopolis), Russell Napier (Aristophanes).

Sunday, 4 September 1955 (Home, 9.15 p.m., 60 mins)
Mycenae's Second Glory, a programme on archaeological discoveries written and produced by Leonard Cottrell.

Sunday, 18 September 1955 (Third, 6.20 p.m., 95 mins)
Hippolytus by Euripides. Translator: Kenneth Cavander. Producer: Michael Bakewell. A radio version of the recent OUDS production. Actors: Avril Elgar (Nurse), Dilys Hamlett (Phaedra), Jeffry Wickham (Hippolytus).

Sunday, 9 October 1955 (Third, 3.00 p.m., 85 mins)
The Beauty from Samos, an English translation by Joanna Richardson and Patric Dickinson of Charles Cordier's reconstruction of Menander's *Samia* in French. Producer: Charles Lefeaux. Composer: Antony Hopkins. Actors: Derek Hart (Moschion), Rolf Lefebvre (Narrator), Jean Lester (Kallinike), Miles Malleson (Parmenon), Milton Rosmer (Demeas), Elizabeth Sellars (Chrysis).

Wednesday, 16 May 1956 (Home, 7.40 p.m., 165 mins + interval)
The Rescue by Edward Sackville-West and Benjamin Britten, a radio dramatization from Homer's *Odyssey*. Produced as part of a *Festival of Radio Drama*. Producer: Val Gielgud. Conductor: John Hollingsworth.

292　　　　　　　　　　　Appendix

Actors: Denis Goacher (Telemachus), Stephen Murray (Odysseus), Leon Quartermaine (Phemius), Jeffrey Segal (Irus), Lydia Sherwood (Penelope).

Sunday, 27 May 1956 (Third, 6.00 p.m., 225 mins plus intervals between the three plays)
Oresteia by Aeschylus (comprising *Agamemnon, The Choephori,* and *The Eumenides*). Translator: Philip Vellacott. Producer: Raymond Raikes. Composer: Antony Hopkins. Actors: Nicolette Bernard (Electra), Beth Boyd (Cassandra), Joan Hart (Athene), Howard Marion-Crawford (Agamemnon), Leon Quartermaine (Chorus Leader), Margaret Rawlings (Clytemnestra), Cyril Shaps (Watchman), Peter Wyngarde (Orestes).

Monday, 28 May 1956 (Third, 10.10 p.m., 30 mins)
'Extracts from the *Oresteia*', a programme in which Elsa Vergi of the Greek National Theatre read and sang extracts from Aeschylus' *Oresteia* in ancient and modern Greek, interspersed with summaries in Vellacott's English translation given by Raymond Raikes.

Friday, 1 June 1956 (Third, 8.00 p.m., 15 mins)
'The Theology', the first talk in the two-part series *The Interpretation of the Oresteia* by Hugh Lloyd-Jones.

Thursday, 7 June 1956 (Third, 10.00 p.m., 20 mins)
'The Morality', the second talk in the two-part series *The Interpretation of the Oresteia* by Hugh Lloyd-Jones.

Sunday, 8 July 1956 (Third, 9.45 p.m., 20 mins)
'Menander' by Gilbert Murray, an introductory talk preceding the three Menandrian plays to be broadcast in the next few days.

Tuesday, 10 July 1956 (Third, 9.05 p.m., 85 mins)
The Beauty from Samos by **Menander** (a repeat of the 1955 production for the following week's three-play Menandrian festival).

Wednesday, 11 July 1956 (Third, 8.20 p.m., 90 mins)
The Arbitration by **Menander** [*Epitrepontes*], translated (and partially reconstructed) by Gilbert Murray. Producer: Charles Lefeaux. Composer: Antony Hopkins. Actors: Richard Bebb (Chaerestratus), Peter Copley (Onesimus), John Gabriel (Syriscus), James Hayter (Smicrines), Simon Lack (Charisius), Geraldine McEwan (Habrotonon), Miles Malleson (Davus), Sheila Shand Gibbs (Pamphile), Gladys Young (Sophrone).

Friday, 13 July 1956 (Third, 9.50 p.m., 80 mins)
The Rape of the Locks by **Menander** [*Perikeiromene*], translated (and partially reconstructed) by Gilbert Murray. Producer: Charles Lefeaux. Composer: Antony Hopkins. Actors: Richard Bebb (Moschio), Peter Coke (Polemo), Patricia Driscoll (Glycera), James Hayter (Sosias), Avice Landone (Myrrhine), Keith Pyott (Pataecus).

Appendix 293

Sunday, 26 May 1957 (Third, 6.25 p.m., 70 mins)
Peace by Aristophanes. Translator: Patric Dickinson. Adaptor and producer: Raymond Raikes. Composer: Christopher Whelen. Actors: Annette Kelly (Harvest), Hugh Manning (Hermes), Howard Marion-Crawford (War/Crest Maker/Helmet Seller), Ernest Milton (Hierocles), Russell Napier (Aristophanes), Frank Pettingell (Trygaeus), Janette Richer (Peace/Holiday), David Spenser (Tumult/Spear Burnisher), Frank Windsor (Sickle Maker).

Tuesday, 15 October 1957 (Third, 9.45 p.m., 70 mins)
Oedipus the King by Sophocles. Translator: C. A. Trypanis. Producer: Val Gielgud. Actors: Coral Browne (Jocasta), Stephen Murray (Oedipus), Leon Quartermaine (Tiresias).

Tuesday, 26 November 1957 (Third, 9.05 p.m., 70 mins)
Lysistrata by Aristophanes. Translator: Patric Dickinson. Adaptor and producer: Raymond Raikes. Composer: Christopher Whelen. Actors: Francis de Wolff (Magistrate), Mary Law (Kalonike), Hugh Manning (Kinesias), Russell Napier (Aristophanes, as Prologue), Janette Richer (Myrrhine), Googie Withers (Lysistrata).

Sunday, 29 December 1957 (Third, 9.50 p.m., 30 mins)
The first in a series of twelve weekly programmes offering passages from Homer's *Iliad* in new translations by different hands, arranged by Donald Carne-Ross. (Episodes two to twelve are not listed individually below.)

Tuesday, 8 July 1958 (Third, 9.20 p.m., 75 mins)
The Persians by Aeschylus. Translator: C. A. Trypanis. Producer: Val Gielgud. Composer: John Hotchkis. Actors: Gwen Ffrangcon-Davies (Atossa), Marius Goring (Messenger), Gabriel Woolf (Xerxes), Arthur Young (Ghost of Darius).

Friday, 24 October 1958 (Third, 8.50 p.m., 95 mins)
Agamemnon by Aeschylus. Translator: Raymond Postgate. Producer: Frederick Bradnum. Actors: Barbara Chilcott (Cassandra), Freda Jackson (Clytemnestra), Godfrey Kenton (Agamemnon), George Merritt (Watchman), Harold Young (Aegisthus).

Tuesday, 17 March 1959 (Third, 9.00 p.m., 90 mins)
Oedipus at Colonus by Sophocles. Translator: C. A. Trypanis. Producer: Val Gielgud. Composer: John Hotchkis. Chorus direction: Colette King. Actors: Judy Bailey (Ismene), William Devlin (Theseus), John Gielgud (Oedipus), Carleton Hobbs (Leader of the Chorus), Malcolm Keen (Creon), Joan Plowright (Antigone). See Figure 7.2.

Saturday, 25 April 1959 (Third, 8.40 p.m., 20 mins)
'Menander's *Misanthrope*' by Hugh Lloyd-Jones, a talk on the discovery of Menander's *Dyskolos*.

Friday, 30 October 1959 (Third, 9.35 p.m., 75 mins)
The Misanthrope by Menander [*Dyskolos*]. Translator: Philip Vellacott. Adapted and produced by Raymond Raikes. Composer: Thomas Eastwood. Textual Adviser: Hugh Lloyd-Jones. Actors: Laidman Browne (Cnemon), Sheila Grant (Myrrhine), John Humphrey (Sostratos).

Thursday, 17 December 1959 (Third, 9.30 p.m., 70 mins)
Antigone by Sophocles. Translator: C. A. Trypanis. Producer: Val Gielgud. Composer: John Hotchkis. Chorus direction: Colette King. Actors: Judy Bailey (Ismene), Carleton Hobbs (Leader of the Chorus), Brewster Mason (Creon), Joan Plowright (Antigone), Leon Quartermaine (Teiresias), Gabriel Woolf (Haemon).

Tuesday, 8 March 1960 (Third, 9.20 p.m., 60 mins)
The Guilt of Polycrates by Peter Gurney, a radio play drawing on Herodotus III. Producer: Raymond Raikes. Composer: Humphrey Searle. Actors: Michael Hordern (Polycrates), Leon Quartermaine (Amasis), Charles Simon (Herodotus).

Tuesday, 12 April 1960 (Third, 8.50 p.m., 100 mins)
Agamemnon, **a verse play on the Aeschylean theme by William Alfred.** Adapted for broadcasting by Cynthia Pughe. Producer: Val Gielgud. Actors: Judy Bailey (Cassandra), Denis Goacher (Aegisthus), Malcolm Keen (Agamemnon), Michael Turner (Narrator), Mary Wimbush (Clytemnestra).

Thursday, 6 October 1960 (Third, 10.10 p.m., 30 mins)
The first in a series of twelve weekly programmes offering passages from Homer's *Odyssey* in new translations by contemporary poets. Series devised by Louis MacNeice. Producer: Anthony Thwaite. (Episodes two to twelve are not listed individually below.)

Tuesday, 30 January, Wednesday, 31 January, and Friday, 2 February 1962 (Third, 8.55 p.m., 90 mins; 8.55 p.m., 65 mins; 9.00 p.m., 60 mins)
The Oresteia by Aeschylus (comprising *Agamemnon*, *The Choephoroe*, and *The Eumenides*). Translator: C. A. Trypanis. Producer: Val Gielgud. Chorus direction: Colette King. Composer: John Hotchkis. Actors: Nigel Anthony (Pylades), Gwen Ffrangcon-Davies (Athene), Michael Gough (Orestes), Malcolm Hayes (Aegisthus), Carleton Hobbs (Watchman), Brewster Mason (Agamemnon), June Tobin (Cassandra), Margaret Whiting (Electra), Mary Wimbush (Clytaemnestra), Gabriel Woolf (Apollo). See Figure 7.3.

Friday, 2 March 1962 (Third, 8.00 p.m., 170 mins)
The Rescue by Edward Sackville-West and Benjamin Britten, a radio dramatization from Homer's *Odyssey*. Producer: Val Gielgud. Conductor: John Hollingsworth. Actors: Hugh Dickson (Telemachus), Rachel Gurney

(Penelope), Pinkie Johnstone (Athene), Stephen Murray (Odysseus), Leon Quartermaine (Phemius), Jeffrey Segal (Irus).

Sunday, 25 March 1962 (Home, 10.10 p.m., 40 mins)
Odysseus Tells **by John Masefield**. Producer: Val Gielgud. Actors: William Eedle (Priam), Godfrey Kenton (Priest), Stephen Murray (Odysseus), Diana Olsson (Goddess Athene), Leslie Perrins (Agamemnon), June Tobin (Cassandra).

Friday, 18 May 1962 (Third, 8.50 p.m., 75 mins)
Medea **by Euripides**. Translator: Philip Vellacott. Arranged for broadcasting and produced by Raymond Raikes. Composer: Christopher Whelen. Actors: Stephen Murray (Jason), Leslie Perrins (Creon), Elsa Vergi (Medea). Followed by a 15-minute programme billed as 'Extracts from the *Medea* read in Greek by Elsa Verghis', arranged and introduced by Raymond Raikes. See Figure 2.1.

Friday, 1 March 1963 (Third, 8.00 p.m., 90 mins)
Philoctetes **by Sophocles**. Translator: Kenneth Cavander. Producer: CharlesLefeaux. Composer: Christopher Whelen. Actors: Anthony Jacobs (Odysseus), Barry Justice (Neoptolemus), Stephen Murray (Philoctetes). See Frontispiece.

Friday, 10 May 1963 (Third, 8.40 p.m., 80 mins)
Electra **by Sophocles**. Translator: C. A. Trypanis. Producer: Val Gielgud. Composer: John Hotchkis. Chorus direction: Colette King. Actors: Michael Gough (Orestes), Malcolm Hayes (Aegisthus), Margaret Whiting (Electra), Mary Wimbush (Clytemnestra).

Sundays, 17, 24, and 31 May 1964 (Home, 4.10 p.m., 4.15 p.m., and 4.10 p.m., 60 mins each)
The Anger of Achilles, **a version of the** *Iliad* **by Robert Graves**. Producer: Raymond Raikes. Composer: Roberto Gerhard. *The Sunday Play* series. Actors: Maurice Denham (Agamemnon), Robert Hardy (Achilles).

Friday, 5 June 1964 (Third, 8.35 p.m., 120 mins)
Bacchae **by Euripides**. Translator: Kenneth Cavander. Producer: Charles Lefeaux. Composer: Christopher Whelen. Actors: Robert Hardy (Dionysus), Beatrix Lehmann (Agave), Arthur Ridley (Teiresias), Cyril Shaps (Kadmos), Nigel Stock (Penthous).

Wednesday, 10 February 1965 (Third, 9.15 p.m., 45 mins)
The Tragedy of Phaethon, **a comedy by Donald Cotton**. Producer: Douglas Cleverdon. Composer: Alan Owen. Actors included Denis Quilley (Phaethon).

Thursday, 10 June 1965 (Third, 8.45 p.m., 95 mins)
The Anger of Achilles, a version of the *Iliad* by Robert Graves (and a shortened script from that broadcast in May 1964). Producer: Raymond Raikes. Composer: Roberto Gerhard. Won the Prix Italia. Actors: Maurice Denham (Agamemnon), Robert Hardy (Achilles).

Sunday, 25 July 1965 (Third, 9.00 p.m., 90 mins)
Persians by Aeschylus. Translator: David Rudkin. Producer: Richard Imison. Composer: John Buckland. Actors: John Justin (Xerxes), Mary Morris (Atossa), Donald Wolfit (Ghost of the Emperor Darius), Patrick Wymark (Messenger).

1966 (BBC Schools Radio)
Sections of Homer's *Iliad* and *Odyssey*, translated and dramatized by Kenneth Cavander, broadcast in eleven 20-minute programmes for BBC Schools *Living Language* series. All eleven programmes re-broadcast again in 1968, with a repeat of just the *Odyssey* programmes in 1969.

Tuesday, 3 March 1970 (Third, 8.00 p.m., 60 mins)
Women in Power by Aristophanes [*Ekklesiasouzai*]. Billed as 'An Aristophanic musical'. Translator: Patric Dickinson. Producer: Raymond Raikes. Composer: Stephen Dodgson. Actors included Marjorie Westbury (Praxagora).

Sunday, 22 July 1973 (Radio 3, 5.30 p.m., 120 mins; repeated 17 February 1974, 7.00 p.m.)
The Rescue by Edward Sackville-West and Benjamin Britten, a radio dramatization from Homer's *Odyssey*. Producer: Raymond Raikes. Conductor: Rae Jenkins. Actors: Jill Balcon (Athene), Hugh Dickson (Telemachus), Leslie French (Irus), Marius Goring (Phemius), Rachel Gurney (Penelope), Stephen Murray (Odysseus).

Sunday, 31 August 1975 (Radio 3, 6.10 p.m., 110 mins, including 'interlude')
Iphigeneia in Aulis by Euripides. Translator and producer: Raymond Raikes. *World Drama* series. Composer: Anthony Bernard. Actors: Denise Bryer (Iphigeneia), Carleton Hobbs (Agamemnon), Godfrey Kenton (Menelaus), John Shrapnel (Achilles), Marjorie Westbury (Clytemnestra).

Sunday, 14 November 1976 (Radio 3, 8.00 p.m., 60 mins)
Ag by Gabriel Josipovici, described as a 're-texturing' for stereo of Richmond Lattimore's translation of Aeschylus' *Agamemnon*. Producer: John Theocharis. Composer: Christos Pittas. Actors: Jill Balcon (Klytemnestra), Maureen O'Brien (Cassandra), Timothy West (Agamemnon).

Bibliography

Adam, Kenneth (1947), 'The Programme and its Critics', in British Broadcasting Corporation (1947b), 30-7.
Anderson, Benedict (2006), *Imagined Communities: Reflections on the Origin and Spread of Nationalism*. Rev. edn; first published 1983. London: Verso.
Andrews, Kevin (1974), 'Time and the Will Lie Sidestepped: Athens, the Interval', in Brown and Reid (1974), 103-9.
Anon. (1925a), 'Broadcasting: The Programmes', *The Times*, 29 June 1925, 7.
Anon. (1925b), 'Grecian Theatre near London', *The Daily Mirror*, 3 July 1925, 8.
Anon. (1925c), 'An Open-Air Theatre in London', *The Manchester Guardian*, 3 July 1925, 12.
Anon. (1928), 'Broadcast Talks: Speakers and their Subjects', *The Times*, 16 January 1928, 20.
Anon. (1929a), 'Celebrations of Empire Day', *The Times*, 25 May 1929, 7.
Anon. (1929b), 'Educational Talks for Students: Programme of the BBC', *The Times*, 15 January 1929, 23.
Anon. (1929c), 'How I Listen to Radio Drama. A Listener on the Part Played by Imagination', *Radio Times*, 1 March 1929, 504.
Anon. (1929d), 'The Twelve Great Plays', *The Listener*, 14 August 1929, 216.
Anon. (1930), 'Week by Week', *The Listener*, 5 March 1930, 404-5.
Anon. (1936), 'Greek Tragedy on the Radio: Success of Sunday's Performance', *The Manchester Guardian*, 21 October 1936, 10.
Anon. (1937a), 'Review of Broadcasting', *The Manchester Guardian*, 13 March 1937, 16.
Anon. (1937b), 'The Women Who Rule the Waves', *Radio Times*, 12 November 1937, 12-13.
Anon. (1938), '*Beware the Gods*', *The Times*, 5 March 1938, 18.
Anon. (1939), 'Review of Broadcasting: Professor Gilbert Murray's New Translation of *The Persians*', *The Manchester Guardian*, 19 April 1939, 10.
Anon. (1940), 'Broadcasting Review', *The Manchester Guardian*, 28 August 1940, 6.
Anon. (1945), 'Homeric "Melodrama"', *Radio Times*, 3 August 1945, 5.
Anon. (1946a), 'Broadcasting Drama: The *Agamemnon* of Aeschylus', *The Times*, 31 October 1946, 6.
Anon. (1946b), 'Broadcasting Review', *The Manchester Guardian*, 6 March 1946, 3.
Anon. (1946c), 'Broadcasting Review', *The Manchester Guardian*, 25 September 1946, 3.

Anon. (1946d), 'Broadcasting Review', *The Manchester Guardian*, 23 November 1946, 3.

Anon. (1946e), 'Broadcasting Review', *The Manchester Guardian*, 7 December 1946, 7.

Anon. (1948), 'Review of Broadcasting', *The Manchester Guardian*, 10 March 1948, 3.

Anon. (1949), 'War History Programmes: Ithaca Debunked', *The Manchester Guardian*, 7 September 1949, 3.

Anon. (1951), 'Melodrama Based on *The Odyssey*', *The Times*, 14 September 1951, 8.

Anon. (1952), 'The Classics as Best-Sellers: Influence of Radio on Public Demand', *The Times*, 29 December 1952, 2.

Anon. (1955), 'Private Treaty: *The Acharnians* Broadcast', *The Times*, 8 August 1955, 10.

Anon. (1956a), 'The *Oresteia* on the Air: Revelation of the Dramatic Values of the Trilogy', *The Times*, 28 May 1956, 5.

Anon. (1956b), 'Revival of Radio Triumph: *The Rescue*', *The Manchester Guardian*, 19 May 1956, 5.

Anon. (1957a), 'Aeschylus—and Others. How an Essex Village was Converted to the Drama', *The Times*, 31 January 1957, 10.

Anon. (1957b), '*Aristophanes against War: The Acharnians, The Peace, Lysistrata*, translated by Patric Dickinson', *The Listener*, 28 November 1957, 893.

Anon. (1957c), 'In the Classical Manner', *The Times*, 7 November 1957, 13.

Anon. (1957d), 'Lament for the Third: Mourners at the Royal Court Theatre', *The Times*, 30 September 1957, 3.

Anon. (1957e), 'Menander's *Dyskolos*: Discovery of Play MS', *The Manchester Guardian*, 14 September 1957, 1 and 10.

Anon. (1960a), 'A Myth Refurbished', *The Times*, 13 April 1960, 5.

Anon. (1960b), 'Sore Thumbs and Poetry Prizes: Mr Robert Graves at Foyle's', *The Guardian*, 4 March 1960, 3.

Anon. (1962), 'Bringing a Little Poetry into Life', *The Times*, 5 May 1962, 4.

Anon. (1964), 'Televised Aristophanes with a Nuclear Slant', *The Times*, 16 January 1964, 15.

Anon. (n.d.), 'A History of Penguin Classics', http://us.penguingroup.com/static/pages/classics/history.html (accessed 2 September 2012).

APGRD Productions Database, online at http://www.apgrd.ox.ac.uk/research-collections/performance-database/productions.

Arkins, Brian (2000), 'Athens No Longer Dies: Greek and Roman Themes in MacNeice', *Classics Ireland* 7, 1–24.

Armitage, Simon (2006), *Homer's Odyssey*. London: Faber.

Avery, Todd (2006), *Radio Modernism: Literature, Ethics, and the BBC, 1922–1938*. Aldershot: Ashgate.

Babington Smith, Constance (1985), *John Masefield: A Life*. First published 1978. London: Hamish Hamilton.

Backemeyer, Sylvia (1998), *Eric Fraser: Designer and Illustrator*. London: Lund Humphries.

Bailey, Michael (2009), 'New Ventures in Adult Education in Early Twentieth-Century Britain: Pastoral Government and the Pedagogical State', *CRESC Working Papers* 62, online at www.cresc.ac.uk/sites/default/files/wp62.pdf (accessed 2 September 2012).

Baker, Martin (2002), *Artists of Radio Times: A Golden Age of British Illustration*. Oxford: Ashmolean Museum.

Bakker, Egbert J. (1993), 'Discourse and Performance: Involvement, Visualization and "Presence" in Homeric Poetry', *Classical Antiquity* 12.1, 1–29.

Bateson, F. W. (1960), 'See the Great Achilles!', *The Observer*, 13 March 1960, 21.

Beck, Deborah (2005), *Homeric Conversation*. Washington: Center for Hellenic Studies.

Beckett, Samuel (1983), *Worstward Ho*. London: Calder.

Birch, I. C. (1910), 'The School Play. Iphigenia', *Oxford High School Magazine*, April 1910, 740–3.

Blanshard, Alastair and Shahabudin, Kim (2011), *Classics on Screen: Ancient Greece and Rome on Film*. London: Bristol Classical Press.

Blyth, Alan (1972), 'Elisabeth Lutyens', *The Times*, 24 February 1972, 15.

Bourdieu, Pierre (1985), 'The Market of Symbolic Goods' (an abbreviated translation of 'Le Marché des biens symboliques', 1971), *Poetics* 14.1–2, 13–44. Reprinted in Bourdieu (1993), 112–41.

Bourdieu, Pierre (1993), *The Field of Cultural Production: Essays on Art and Literature*, ed. Randal Johnson. Cambridge: Polity Press.

Bridges, Emma, Hall, Edith, and Rhodes, P. J., eds (2007), *Cultural Responses to the Persian Wars: Antiquity to the Third Millennium*. Oxford: Oxford University Press.

Bridson, D. G. (1971), *Prospero and Ariel: The Rise and Fall of Radio. A Personal Recollection*. London: Gollancz.

Briggs, Asa (1961), *The History of Broadcasting in the United Kingdom*, Vol. 1: *The Birth of Broadcasting*. Rev. edn published 1995. Oxford: Oxford University Press.

Briggs, Asa (1965), *The History of Broadcasting in the United Kingdom*, Vol. 2: *The Golden Age of Wireless*. Rev. edn published 1995. Oxford: Oxford University Press.

Briggs, Asa (1970), *The History of Broadcasting in the United Kingdom*, Vol. 3: *The War of Words*. Rev. edn published 1995. Oxford: Oxford University Press.

Briggs, Asa (1979), *The History of Broadcasting in the United Kingdom*, Vol. 4: *Sound and Vision*. Rev. edn published 1995. Oxford: Oxford University Press.

Briggs, Asa (1995), *The History of Broadcasting in the United Kingdom*, Vol. 5: *Competition*. Rev. edn. Oxford: Oxford University Press.
British Broadcasting Corporation (1928), *BBC Handbook 1928*. London: British Broadcasting Corporation.
British Broadcasting Corporation (1929), *The BBC Handbook 1929*. London: British Broadcasting Corporation.
British Broadcasting Corporation (1930), *The BBC Year-Book 1930*. London: British Broadcasting Corporation.
British Broadcasting Corporation (1931), *The BBC Year-Book 1931*. London: British Broadcasting Corporation.
British Broadcasting Corporation (1946), *BBC Year Book 1946*. London: British Broadcasting Corporation.
British Broadcasting Corporation (1947*a*), *BBC Year Book 1947*. London: British Broadcasting Corporation.
British Broadcasting Corporation (1947*b*), *The Third Programme: A Symposium of Opinions and Plans*. London: British Broadcasting Corporation.
British Broadcasting Corporation (1950), *BBC Year Book 1950*. London: British Broadcasting Corporation.
British Broadcasting Corporation (1959), *The Public and the Programmes: An Audience Research Report on Listeners and Viewers, The Time They Devote to Listening and Viewing, The Services they Patronize, Their Selectiveness and Their Tastes*. London: British Broadcasting Corporation.
British Broadcasting Corporation (1974), *The BBC and The Open University: An Introduction*. London: British Broadcasting Corporation.
Brown, Richard Danson (2009), *Louis MacNeice and the Poetry of the 1930s*. Tavistock: Northcote.
Brown, Terence and Reid, Alec, eds (1974), *Time was Away: The World of Louis MacNeice*. Dublin: Dolmen.
Calder, John (2006), 'Esslin, Martin Julius (1918–2002)', *Oxford Dictionary of National Biography*. Published online by Oxford University Press at http://www.oxforddnb.com/view/article/76703 (accessed 4 September 2012).
Carey, John (1992), *The Intellectuals and the Masses: Pride and Prejudice among the Literary Intelligentsia, 1880–1939*. London: Faber.
Carey, John (2005), *What Good are the Arts?* London: Faber.
Carne-Ross, D. S. (2010), *Classics and Translation: Essays by D. S. Carne-Ross*, ed. Kenneth Haynes. Cranbury, NJ: Associated University Presses.
Carney, Michael (1999), *Stoker: The Life of Hilda Matheson OBE, 1888–1940*. Llangynog: Michael Carney.
Carpenter, Humphrey (1997), *The Envy of the World: Fifty Years of the BBC Third Programme and Radio 3, 1946–1996*. London: Phoenix.
Cavander, Kenneth (1969), *The Iliad and Odyssey of Homer: Radio Plays*. London: British Broadcasting Corporation.

Bibliography

Ceadel, Martin (2007), 'Gilbert Murray and International Politics', in Stray (2007a), 217–37.
Chaston, Colleen (2010), *Tragic Props and Cognitive Function: Aspects of the Function of Images in Thinking*. Leiden/Boston: Brill.
Coulton, Barbara (1980), *Louis MacNeice in the BBC*. London: Faber.
Crook, Tim (1999), *Radio Drama: Theory and Practice*. London: Routledge.
Crozier, Mary (1948), 'Four Radio Plays', *The BBC Quarterly* 3.3, 165–70.
Crozier, Mary (1958), *Broadcasting (Sound and Television)*. London: Oxford University Press.
Currie, Gregory and Ravenscroft, Ian (2002), *Recreative Minds: Imagination in Philosophy and Psychology*. Oxford: Clarendon Press.
Darlington, W. A. (1929), 'The *Electra* of Euripides: The Play and its Author', *Radio Times*, 12 July 1929, 80–1.
Davin, D. M. (2004), 'MacNeice, (Frederick) Louis (1907–1963)', rev. by Jon Stallworthy, *Oxford Dictionary of National Biography*. Published online by Oxford University Press at http://www.oxforddnb.com/view/article/34808 (accessed 4 September 2012).
Davis, Alec (1974), *The Graphic Work of Eric Fraser*. Uffculme: Uffculme Press.
Davis, Robert (2013), 'Civilization and Savagery at the 1893 World's Columbian Exposition', in Hardwick and Harrison (2013), 105–17.
De-la-Noy, Michael (1988), *Eddy: The Life of Edward Sackville-West*. London: Bodley Head.
De-la-Noy, Michael (2004), 'West, Edward Charles Sackville-, fifth Baron Sackville (1901–1965)', *Oxford Dictionary of National Biography*. Published online by Oxford University Press at http://www.oxforddnb.com/view/article/35901 (accessed 11 July 2012).
Denselow, Robin (2004), 'MacColl, Ewan (1915–1989)', *Oxford Dictionary of National Biography*. Published online by Oxford University Press at http://www.oxforddnb.com/view/article/40664 (accessed 4 September 2012).
Devine, Kathleen and Peacock, Alan J., eds (1998), *Louis MacNeice and his Influence*. Gerrards Cross: Colin Smythe.
Dickinson, Patric (1940), 'War', *The Observer*, 3 November 1940, 3.
Dickinson, Patric (1957), *Aristophanes against War: The Acharnians, The Peace, Lysistrata*. Oxford: Oxford University Press.
Dickinson, Patric (1965), *The Good Minute: An Autobiographical Study*. London: Gollancz.
Dickinson, Patric (1970a), *Aristophanes: Plays I, Newly Translated into English Verse*. Oxford: Oxford University Press.
Dickinson, Patric (1970b), *Aristophanes: Plays II, Newly Translated into English Verse*. Oxford: Oxford University Press.
Dillon, Francis (1976), 'Stereo Sensation', *The Listener*, 2 December 1976, 724.

Dillon, Robert (2010), *History on British Television: Constructing Nation, Nationality and Collective Memory*. Manchester: Manchester University Press.

Dodds, E. R. (1974), 'Louis MacNeice at Birmingham', in Brown and Reid (1974), 35–8.

Dodds, E. R. (1977), *Missing Persons: An Autobiography*. Oxford: Clarendon Press.

Doherty, Lillian (1996), 'The Performance of Homeric Epic: Performance Dynamics and the Internal Audiences of the *Odyssey*', *Didaskalia* 3.3, published online at http://www.didaskalia.net/issues/vol3no3/doherty.html (accessed 4 September 2012).

Doherty, M. A. (2000), *Nazi Wireless Propaganda: Lord Haw-Haw and British Public Opinion in the Second World War*. Edinburgh: Edinburgh University Press.

Drakakis, John (1981a), 'The Essence That's Not Seen: Radio Adaptations of Stage Plays', in Lewis (1981), 111–33.

Drakakis, John (1981b), 'Introduction', in Drakakis (1981), 1–36.

Drakakis, John, ed. (1981), *British Radio Drama*. Cambridge: Cambridge University Press.

Driver, David, ed. (1981), *The Art of Radio Times: The First Sixty Years*, with Introduction by Asa Briggs. London: British Broadcasting Corporation.

Dunbar, Janet (1960), *Flora Robson*. London: Harrap.

Eagleton, Terry (2005), *The Idea of Culture*. First published 2000. Oxford: Blackwell.

Edwards, Russell, Hare, Steve, and Robinson, Jim, eds (2008), *Penguin Classics*. Exeter: Penguin Collectors Society.

Eliot, T. S. (1920), 'Euripides and Professor Murray', reprinted in T. S. Eliot (1986), *Selected Essays*, 59–64. 3rd edn. London: Faber.

Esslin, Martin (1971), 'The Mind as a Stage', *Theatre Quarterly* 1.3, 5–11.

Farjeon, Herbert (1943a), 'Broadcast Drama: Bax and Bridie', *The Listener*, 2 September 1943, 276.

Farjeon, Herbert (1943b), 'Broadcast Drama: *The Rescue*', *The Listener*, 2 December 1943, 648.

Felton, Felix (1949), *The Radio Play: Its Techniques and Possibilities*. London: Sylvan Press.

Ferris, Paul (1966), 'Prerecording Pitfalls Exposed', *The Observer*, 20 March 1966, 24.

Fink, Howard (1981), 'The Sponsor's v. the Nation's Choice: North American Radio Drama', in Lewis (1981), 185–243.

Fitts, Dudley (1959), 'Homer's *Iliad*, Retold in English', *The New York Times*, 8 November 1959.

Foreman, Lewis (1988), 'Benjamin Britten and *The Rescue*', *Tempo* 166, 28–33.

Bibliography 303

Forsyth, James (1977), 'Tyrone Guthrie: Pioneer in the Field of Radio Drama', in Lewis (1977), 121-35.

Fowler, Robert, ed. (2004), *The Cambridge Companion to Homer*. Cambridge: Cambridge University Press.

Frattarola, Angela (2009), 'The Modernist "Microphone Play": Listening in the Dark to the BBC', *Modern Drama* 52.4, 449-68.

Giannopoulou, Vasiliki (2007), 'Aristophanes in Translation before 1920', in Hall and Wrigley (2007), 309-42.

Gibson, A. G. G., ed. (2015), *Robert Graves and the Classical Tradition*. Oxford: Oxford University Press.

Gielgud, Val (1929), 'Leave the Stage Alone', *Radio Times*, 1 March 1929, 499 and 502.

Gielgud, Val (1934), 'Do You Listen to These Radio Plays? Or Do You Merely Switch on and Hear Them?', *The Daily Mirror*, 14 March 1934, 12.

Gielgud, Val (1945), 'Radio Drama During the Next Three Months', *Radio Times*, 9 February 1945, 3.

Gielgud, Val (1957), *British Radio Drama, 1922-1956: A Survey*. London: Harrap.

Gielgud, Val (1963), 'The *Electra* of Sophocles', *Radio Times*, 2 May 1963, 44.

Gielgud, Val (1965), *Years in a Mirror*. London: Bodley Head.

Gifford, Terry (2009), *Ted Hughes*. London: Routledge.

Gilliam, Laurence (1950), 'The Making of a Feature Programme', in Gilliam (ed.), *BBC Features*, 204-8. London: Evans.

Goff, Barbara, ed. (2005), *Classics and Colonialism*. London: Duckworth.

Goff, Barbara (2009), *Euripides: Trojan Women*. London: Duckworth.

Goldhill, Simon (1991), *The Poet's Voice: Essays on Poetics and Greek Literature*. Cambridge: Cambridge University Press.

Goldhill, Simon (2011), *Victorian Culture and Classical Antiquity: Art, Opera, Fiction and the Proclamation of Modernity*. Princeton: Princeton University Press.

Goldman, Lawrence (1995), *Dons and Workers: Oxford and Adult Education since 1850*. Oxford: Clarendon Press.

Golphin, Peter (2011), 'Encouraging America: Louis MacNeice and BBC Propaganda in 1941', *Symbiosis: A Journal of Anglo-American Literary Relations* 15.2, 1-15.

Golphin, Peter (2012), '"Ephemeral Work"?: Louis MacNeice, Broadcasting and Poetry', doctoral thesis submitted to The Open University.

Gordon, Charles (1940), 'Women behind the Mike: She Produced Plays in her Nursery', *News Chronicle*, 11 March 1940.

Graves, Robert (1959), *The Anger of Achilles: Homer's Iliad, Translated by Robert Graves, Illustrations by Ronald Searle*. New York: Doubleday.

Graves, Robert (2009), *The Anger of Achilles: The Iliad*. London: Penguin.

Gray, Frances (1981), 'The Nature of Radio Drama', in Lewis (1981), 48-77.

Gray, Frances and Bray, Janet (1985), 'The Mind as Theatre: Radio Drama since 1971', *New Theatre Quarterly* 1.3, 292–300.

Graziosi, Barbara (2002), 'Gods and Poets in the *Odyssey*', *Omnibus* 43, 4–6.

Graziosi, Barbara and Greenwood, Emily, eds (2007), *Homer in the Twentieth Century: Between World Literature and the Western Canon*. Oxford: Oxford University Press.

Greenhalgh, Susanne (2009), 'Listening to Shakespeare', in Terris, Oesterlen, and McKernan (2009), 74–93.

Greenwood, Emily (2007), 'Logue's Tele-Vision: Reading Homer from a Distance', in Graziosi and Greenwood (2007), 145–76.

Grenfell, Joyce (1938), 'Broadcasting: Sunday Afternoons', *The Observer*, 6 March 1938, 23.

Griffin, Jasper (2004), 'The Speeches', in Fowler (2004), 156–67.

Grigson, Geoffrey (1978), *The Fiesta and Other Poems*. London: Secker and Warburg.

Grigson, Geoffrey (1984), *Recollections: Mainly of Writers and Artists*. London: Chatto and Windus.

Guralnick, Elissa S. (1996), *Sight Unseen: Beckett, Pinter, Stoppard, and Other Contemporary Dramatists on Radio*. Athens: Ohio University Press.

Guthrie, Tyrone (1931*a*), 'Future of Broadcast Drama', in British Broadcasting Corporation (1931), 185–90.

Guthrie, Tyrone (1931*b*), *Squirrel's Cage and Two Other Microphone Plays*. London: Cobden-Sanderson.

Hague, René (1973), *The Death of Hector: A Version*. Wellingborough: Skelton.

Hajkowski, Thomas (2010), *The BBC and National Identity in Britain, 1922–53*. Manchester: Manchester University Press.

Haley, William J. (1945), 'The Two New Programmes', *Radio Times*, 27 July 1945, 1.

Haley, William J. (1947), 'The Next Five Years in Broadcasting', in British Broadcasting Corporation (1947*a*), 7–11.

Hall, Edith (2004), 'Introduction: Why Greek Tragedy in the Late Twentieth Century?', in Hall, Macintosh, and Wrigley (2004), 1–46.

Hall, Edith (2008*a*), 'Can the *Odyssey* Ever be Tragic? Historical Perspectives on the Theatrical Realization of Greek Epic', in Martin Revermann and Peter Wilson (eds), *Performance, Iconography, Reception: Studies in Honour of Oliver Taplin*, 499–523. Oxford: Oxford University Press.

Hall, Edith (2008*b*), *The Return of Ulysses: A Cultural History of Homer's Odyssey*. London: Tauris.

Hall, Edith and Harrop, Stephe, eds (2010), *Theorising Performance: Greek Drama, Cultural History and Critical Practice*. London: Duckworth.

Hall, Edith and Macintosh, Fiona (2005), *Greek Tragedy and the British Theatre, 1660–1914*. Oxford: Oxford University Press.

Hall, Edith, Macintosh, Fiona, and Taplin, Oliver, eds (2000), *Medea in Performance, 1500–2000*. Oxford: Legenda.

Hall, Edith, Macintosh, Fiona, and Wrigley, Amanda, eds (2004), *Dionysus since 69: Greek Tragedy at the Dawn of the Third Millennium*. Oxford: Oxford University Press.

Hall, Edith and Wrigley, Amanda, eds (2007), *Aristophanes in Performance, 421 BC–AD 2007: Peace, Birds, and Frogs*. Oxford: Legenda.

Hallam, Nicholas (1947), 'Advice to a One-Year Old...', *Daily Express*, 25 September 1947, 2.

Hardwick, Lorna (1999), 'The Theatrical Review as a Primary Source for the Modern Reception of Greek Drama—A Preliminary Evaluation', published online at http://www2.open.ac.uk/ClassicalStudies/GreekPlays/essays/Reviews.html (accessed 4 September 2012).

Hardwick, Lorna (2000), *Translating Words, Translating Cultures*. London: Duckworth.

Hardwick, Lorna (2001), 'Who Owns the Plays? Issues in the Translation and Performance of Greek Drama on the Modern Stage', *Eirene: Studia Graecia et Latina (Theatralia)* 37, 23–39.

Hardwick, Lorna (2003), *Reception Studies. Greece & Rome*: New Surveys in the Classics 33. Oxford: Oxford University Press.

Hardwick, Lorna and Harrison, Stephen, eds (2013), *Classics in the Modern World: A 'Democratic Turn'?* Oxford: Oxford University Press.

Hardwick, Lorna and Stray, Christopher, eds (2008), *A Companion to Classical Receptions*. Oxford: Blackwell.

Harrison, Tony (2008), *Fram*. London: Faber.

Hauser, Frank (1950), '"Translating" the *Alcestis*', *Radio Times*, 14 July 1950, 7.

Havers, Richard (2007), *Here is the News: The BBC and the Second World War*. Stroud: Sutton.

Hendy, David (2007), *Life on Air: A History of Radio Four*. Oxford: Oxford University Press.

Hendy, David (2009), 'Early Radio, Intellectuals, and Cultures of Listening', lecture given at the Centre for Research in the Arts, Social Sciences and Humanities, University of Cambridge, 12 March 2009. Podcast published online at www.crassh.cam.ac.uk/page/162/podcasts.htm (accessed 19 March 2009).

Hendy, David (2015), *Media and the Making of the Modern Mind*. Oxford: Oxford University Press.

Heuser, Alan (1998), 'Tracing MacNeice's Development in Drama: A Commentary on the Published and Unpublished Plays', in Devine and Peacock (1998), 133–55.

Heuser, Alan and McDonald, Peter (1993), 'Introduction', in MacNeice (1993), pp. xi–xv.

Hilmes, Michele (1997), *Radio Voices: American Broadcasting, 1922–1952.* Minneapolis: University of Minnesota Press.

Hinton, James (2008), '"The 'Class' Complex": Mass-Observation and Cultural Distinction in Pre-War Britain', *Past and Present* 199, 207–36.

Hobden, Fiona and Wrigley, Amanda, eds (2016, forthcoming), *Ancient Greece on British Television.* Edinburgh: Edinburgh University Press.

Hodkinson, Stephen (2010), 'Sparta and Nazi Germany in Mid-20th-Century British Liberal and Left-Wing Thought', in Anton Powell and Stephen Hodkinson (eds), *Sparta: The Body Politic.* Swansea: Classical Press of Wales.

Hogan, Robert and Burnham, Richard (1992), *The Years of O'Casey, 1921–1926: A Documentary History.* Gerrards Cross: Smythe.

Hoggart, Richard (1961a), 'Culture—Dead and Alive', *The Observer*, 14 May 1961, 30. Reprinted in Hoggart (1970), 131–4.

Hoggart, Richard (1961b), 'Mass Communications in Britain', in Hoggart (1970), 135–51. First published 1961 in B. Ford (ed.), *The Pelican Guide to English Literature*, vol. 7.

Hoggart, Richard (1970), *Speaking to Each Other: Essays*, Vol. 1: *About Society.* London: Chatto and Windus.

Holme, Christopher (1981), 'The Radio Drama of Louis MacNeice', in Drakakis (1981), 37–71.

Holub, Robert C. (1984), *Reception Theory: A Critical Introduction.* London: Methuen.

Honderich, Ted, ed. (1995), *The Oxford Companion to Philosophy.* Oxford: Oxford University Press.

Hope-Wallace, Philip (1945), 'Broadcast Drama: All in a Maze', *The Listener*, 9 August 1945, 164.

Hope-Wallace, Philip (1946a), 'Classical Capers', *The Listener*, 12 December 1946, 859.

Hope-Wallace, Philip (1946b), 'MacNaeschylus', *The Listener*, 7 November 1946, 647.

Hope-Wallace, Philip (1946c), 'What's Hecuba to Us?' *The Listener*, 7 March 1946, 316.

Hope-Wallace, Philip (1947a), 'The Ladies', *The Listener*, 6 November 1947, 831.

Hope-Wallace, Philip (1947b), 'Much-Croaking-in-the-Cistern', *The Listener*, 6 February 1947, 259.

Hope-Wallace, Philip (1948a), 'Music, Oh!', *The Listener*, 11 March 1948, 435.

Hope-Wallace, Philip (1948b), 'None So Blind . . . ', *The Listener*, 12 February 1948, 275.

Hope-Wallace, Philip (1949a), 'Memory Slam the Door!', *The Listener*, 15 September 1949, 464.

Bibliography

Hope-Wallace, Philip (1949b), 'Mouthing Becomes Medea', *The Listener*, 6 October 1949, 599.
Hope-Wallace, Philip (1949c), 'The Unities in Radio Drama', *The BBC Quarterly* 4.1, 21–5.
Hope-Wallace, Philip (1950), 'Greek, French and Mummerset', *The Listener*, 20 July 1950, 104.
Hopkins, Antony (1982), *Beating Time*. London: Joseph.
Horten, Gerd (2002), *Radio Goes to War: The Cultural Politics of Propaganda during World War II*. Berkeley: University of California Press.
Hughes, David (1952), 'Three Cheers for the Home, Three Beers for the Light but Three Tears for the Third Programme', *The Isis*, 12 November 1952, 21.
Hunter, Fred (1994), 'Hilda Matheson and the BBC, 1926–1940', in Sybil Oldfield (ed.), *This Working-Day World: Women's Lives and Culture(s) in Britain, 1914–1945*, 168–74. London: Taylor and Francis.
Hunter, Fred (2004), 'Matheson, Hilda (1888–1940)', *Oxford Dictionary of National Biography*. Published online by Oxford University Press at http://www.oxforddnb.com/view/article/49198 (accessed 4 September 2012).
Huxley, Aldous (1934), *Beyond the Mexique Bay*. London: Chatto and Windus.
Imison, Richard (2004), 'Gielgud, Val Henry (1900–1981)', *Oxford Dictionary of National Biography*. Published online by Oxford University Press at http://www.oxforddnb.com/view/article/31145 (accessed 23 August 2012).
Jacobus, Mary (1999), *Psychoanalysis and the Scene of Reading*. Oxford: Oxford University Press.
Jauss, Hans Robert (1982), *Toward an Aesthetic of Reception*. Translated by Timothy Bahti. Minneapolis: University of Minnesota Press.
Jennings, Hilda and Gill, Winifred (1939), *Broadcasting in Everyday Life: A Survey of the Social Effects of the Coming of Broadcasting, Conducted on Behalf of the BBC*. London: British Broadcasting Corporation.
Joicey, Nicholas (1993), 'A Paperback Guide to Progress', *Twentieth Century British History* 4.1, 25–56.
Josipovici, Gabriel (1989), 'Music and Literary Form', *Contemporary Music Review* 5, 65–75.
Josipovici, Gabriel (1999), *On Trust: Art and the Temptations of Suspicion*. New Haven: Yale University Press.
Karpf, Anne (1977), 'Junket in Venice', *The Observer*, 25 September 1977, 28.
Kris, Ernst and Speier, Hans (1944), *German Radio Propaganda: Report on Home Broadcasts during the War*. Oxford: Oxford University Press.
Laws, Frederick (1960), 'Understated Furies', *The Listener*, 21 April 1960, 727–8.
Leavis, F. R. (1930), *Mass Civilisation and Minority Culture*. Cambridge: Minority Press.
Leavis, F. R. and Thompson, Denys (1933), *Culture and Environment: The Training of Critical Awareness*. London: Chatto and Windus.

LeMahieu, D. L. (1988), *A Culture for Democracy: Mass Communication and the Cultivated Mind in Britain Between the Wars*. Oxford: Clarendon Press.

Lewis, Peter, ed. (1977), *Papers of the Radio Literature Conference, 1977*. 2 vols. Durham: University of Durham.

Lewis, Peter (1981a), 'Introduction', in Lewis (1981), 1–11.

Lewis, Peter (1981b), 'The Radio Road to Llareggub', in Drakakis (1981), 72–110.

Lewis, Peter, ed. (1981), *Radio Drama*. London: Longman.

Lewis, Peter (1995), 'Radio Drama', in Martin Banham (ed.) (1995), *The Cambridge Guide to Theatre*, 894–900. New edn. Cambridge: Cambridge University Press.

Lianeri, Alexandra and Zajko, Vanda, eds (2008), *Translation and the Classic: Identity as Change in the History of Culture*. Oxford: Oxford University Press.

Linklater, Eric (1942), *The Raft and Socrates Asks Why*. London: Macmillan.

Lloyd-Jones, Hugh (1959), 'A Greek Classic Rediscovered', *The Listener*, 14 May 1959, 837–8.

Lloyd-Jones, Hugh (1960), *Menandri Dyscolus*. Oxford: Clarendon Press.

Lloyd-Jones, Hugh (1962), 'The Guilt of Agamemnon', *Classical Quarterly* 12, 187–99.

Low, Donald A. (1977), 'Radio Adaptations of Literary Classics', in Lewis (1977), 39–44.

Low, Donald A. (1981), 'Classic Fiction by Radio', in Lewis (1981), 134–42.

Lowe, Dunstan and Shahabudin, Kim, eds (2009), *Classics For All: Reworking Antiquity in Mass Culture*. Newcastle upon Tyne: Cambridge Scholars Publishing.

Lucchesi, Joachim (1993), *Das Verhör in der Oper*. Berlin: BasisDruck.

McDonald, Marianne (2007), 'The Dramatic Legacy of Myth: Oedipus in Opera, Radio, Television and Film', in Marianne McDonald and J. Michael Walton (eds) (2007), *The Cambridge Companion to Greek and Roman Theatre*, 303–26. Cambridge: Cambridge University Press.

McDonald, Peter (1991), *Louis MacNeice: The Poet in his Contexts*. Oxford: Clarendon Press.

McDonald, Peter (1998), '"With Eyes Turned Down on the Past": MacNeice's Classicism', in Devine and Peacock (1998), 34–52.

Macintosh, Fiona (2000), 'Introduction: The Performer in Performance', in Hall, Macintosh, and Taplin (2000), 1–31.

Macintosh, Fiona (2008), 'Performance Histories', in Hardwick and Stray (2008), 247–58.

Macintosh, Fiona (2009), *Sophocles: Oedipus Tyrannus*. Cambridge: Cambridge University Press.

Macintosh, Fiona, Michelakis, Pantelis, Hall, Edith, and Taplin, Oliver, eds (2005), *Agamemnon in Performance, 458 BC to AD 2004*. Oxford: Oxford University Press.

Mackail, J. W. (1925), *Classical Studies*. London: Murray.

Mackenzie, Compton (1929), 'The Future of the Broadcast Play', *Radio Times*, 1 March 1929, 497–8.

McKibbin, Ross (2000), *Classes and Cultures: England, 1918–1951*. Paperback edn. First published 1998. Oxford: Oxford University Press.

Mackinnon, Kenneth (1986), *Greek Tragedy into Film*. London: Croom Helm.

McNay, Michael (2012), 'Ronald Searle Obituary', *The Guardian*, 3 January 2012; online at www.guardian.co.uk/books/2012/jan/03/ronald-searle (accessed 18 June 2012).

MacNeice, Louis (1936), *The Agamemnon of Aeschylus*. London: Faber.

MacNeice, Louis (1939), *Autumn Journal*. London: Faber.

MacNeice, Louis (1944), *Christopher Columbus: A Radio Play*. London: Faber.

MacNeice, Louis (1945a), '*The Golden Ass*, or *Metamorphoses* of Apuleius', *Radio Times*, 2 February 1945, 8.

MacNeice, Louis (1945b), 'The *Hippolytus* of Euripides', *Radio Times*, 28 September 1945, 4.

MacNeice, Louis (1946a), 'A Greek Satirist who is Still Topical', *Radio Times*, 29 November 1946, 5.

MacNeice, Louis (1946b), 'Sin and Divine Justice', *Radio Times*, 25 October 1946, 13.

MacNeice, Louis (1947a), *The Dark Tower*. London: Faber.

MacNeice, Louis (1947b), *The Dark Tower, and Other Radio Scripts*. London: Faber.

MacNeice, Louis (1947c), 'Scripts Wanted!', in British Broadcasting Corporation (1947a), 25–8.

MacNeice, Louis (1953), 'A Greek Story of a Family Curse', *Radio Times*, 26 June 1953, 21.

MacNeice, Louis (1954a), *Autumn Sequel: A Rhetorical Poem in XXVI Cantos*. London: Faber.

MacNeice, Louis (1954b), 'I Remember Dylan Thomas', *Ingot* (Steel Co. of Wales), December 1954, 28–30; reprinted in MacNeice (1987), 194–9.

MacNeice, Louis (1960), 'On First Looking into Graves's Homer', *The Guardian*, 11 March 1960, 7.

MacNeice, Louis (1961), 'Pleasure in Reading: Woods to Get Lost in', *The Times*, 17 August 1961, 11.

MacNeice, Louis (1962), 'Blood and Fate' (review of Robert Fitzgerald's *The Odyssey* and Christopher Logue's *Patrocleia*), *The Listener*, 4 October 1962, 527. Reprinted in MacNeice (1987), 234–7.

MacNeice, Louis (1965), *The Strings are False: An Unfinished Autobiography*. London: Faber.

MacNeice, Louis (1987), *Selected Literary Criticism of Louis MacNeice*, ed. Alan Heuser. Oxford: Clarendon Press.

MacNeice, Louis (1993), *Selected Plays of Louis MacNeice*, ed. Alan Heuser and Peter McDonald. Oxford: Clarendon Press.

MacNeice, Louis (2010), *Letters of Louis MacNeice*, ed. Jonathan Allison. London: Faber.

McWhinnie, Donald (1959), *The Art of Radio*. London: Faber.

Marshall, Norman (1947), *The Other Theatre*. London: Lehmann.

Martindale, Charles and Thomas, Richard F., eds (2006), *Classics and the Uses of Reception*. Oxford: Blackwell.

Marwick, Arthur (1991), *Culture in Britain since 1945*. Oxford: Blackwell.

Marwick, Arthur (1998), *The Sixties: Cultural Revolution in Britain, France, Italy and the United States, c.1958–c.1974*. Oxford: Oxford University Press.

Marwick, Arthur (2002), *The Arts in the West since 1945*. Oxford: Oxford University Press.

Matheson, Hilda (1933), *Broadcasting*. The Home University Library of Modern Knowledge series. London: Butterworth.

'M. C.' (1945), 'Edward Sackville-West's "melodrama for broadcasting based on Homer's *Odyssey*"', *The Manchester Guardian*, 10 October 1945, 3.

Michelakis, Pantelis (2008), 'Performance Reception: Canonization and Periodization', in Hardwick and Stray (2008), 219–28.

Minchin, Elizabeth (1995), 'The Poet Appeals to his Muse: Homeric Invocations in the Context of Epic Performance', *The Classical Journal* 91.1, 25–33.

Mitchinson, David (2007), 'Moore and Mythology', introductory essay in the exhibition catalogue *Moore and Mythology*, 4–15. Perry Green, Hertfordshire: Henry Moore Foundation.

Mole, John (1994), 'Obituary: Patric Dickinson', *The Independent*, 31 January 1994.

Morley, Sheridan (1977), *Sybil Thorndike: A Life in the Theatre*, with Preface by John Gielgud. London: Weidenfeld and Nicolson.

Morris, Mick (2007), '"That Living Voice": Gilbert Murray at the BBC', in Stray (2007a), 293–317.

Morwood, James (2007), 'Gilbert Murray's Translations of Greek Tragedy', in Stray (2007a), 133–44.

Murdock, Graham (1981), 'Organising the Imagination: Sociological Perspectives on Radio Drama', in Lewis (1981), 143–63.

Murray, Gilbert (1902), *The Hippolytus and Bacchæ of Euripides, Together with the Frogs of Aristophanes, Translated into English Rhyming Verse*. London: Allen.

Murray, Gilbert (1905), *Euripides: Electra, Translated into English Rhyming Verse*. London: Allen and Unwin.

Murray, Gilbert (1910a), *Euripides: The Iphigenia in Tauris, Translated into English Rhyming Verse*. London: Allen and Unwin.

Murray, Gilbert (1910b), *Euripides: The Trojan Women of Euripides, Translated into English Rhyming Verse*. London: Allen and Unwin.

Murray, Gilbert (1913), *Euripides and his Age*. London: Williams and Norgate.

Murray, Gilbert (1936), 'A Love-Tragedy from Ancient Greece', *The Listener*, 21 October 1936, 770.

Murray, Gilbert (1938a), 'Why Greek?' (part 1), *The Listener*, 25 August 1938, 373–6.

Murray, Gilbert (1938b), 'Why Greek?' (part 2), *The Listener*, 1 September 1938, 431–4.

Murray, Gilbert (1940), *Aeschylus: The Creator of Tragedy*. Oxford: Clarendon Press.

Murray, Gilbert (1946), 'A Post-War Drama of 415 BC', *Radio Times*, 1 March 1946, 3.

Murray, Gilbert (1947a), 'Greece and her Tradition. Home Service, December, 1940', in Henning Krabbe (ed.), *Voices from Britain: Broadcast History, 1939–45*, 81–5. London: Allen and Unwin.

Murray, Gilbert (1947b), 'A Victorian Looks Back on Twenty-Five Years', *The Listener*, 13 November 1947, 839–40.

Murray, Gilbert (1953), *Hellenism and the Modern World: Six Talks on the Radio-Diffusion Française and the BBC*. London: Allen and Unwin.

Murray, Gilbert (2005), *Gilbert Murray's Euripides: The Trojan Women and Other Plays*, ed. and with introduction by James Morwood. Exeter: Bristol Phoenix Press.

Nagy, Gregory (1992), 'Homeric Questions' (the 1991 Presidential Address), *Transactions of the American Philological Association* 122, 17–60.

Napper, Lawrence (2000), 'British Cinema and the Middlebrow', in Justine Ashby and Andrew Higson (eds), *British Cinema, Past and Present*, 110–23. London: Routledge.

Nelson, Graham (2000), '"It lies obscure in layers of dark": Louis MacNeice's Buried Translations of Greek Tragedy', *Oxford Poetry* 11.1, 54–8.

Newbolt, Henry, ed. (1921), *The Teaching of English in England, Being the Reports of the Departmental Committee Appointed by the President of the Board of Education to Inquire into the Position of English in the Educational System of England*. London: His Majesty's Stationery Office.

Newman, Bertram (1946), 'The "Penguin" *Odyssey*', *Greece & Rome* 15.45, 119–24.

Nicholas, Siân (1996), *The Echo of War: Home Front Propaganda and the Wartime BBC, 1939–45*. Manchester: Manchester University Press.

Nicholas, Siân (2006), 'The Good Servant: The Origins and Development of BBC Listener Research, 1936–1950', in *BBC Audience Research Reports*.

Part 1: BBC Listener Research Department, 1937–c.1950. A Guide to the Microfilm Edition. Wakefield: Microform Academic Publishers. Online at http://www.microform.co.uk/guides/R50035.pdf (accessed 6 September 2012).

Nichols, Kate (2012), 'Marbles for the Masses: The Elgin Marbles at the Crystal Palace, Sydenham', in Viccy Coltman (ed.), *Making Sense of Greek Art: Ancient Visual Culture and its Receptions*, 179–201. Exeter: Exeter University Press.

Nisbet, Gideon (2008), *Ancient Greece in Film and Popular Culture*. 2nd edn. Exeter: Bristol Phoenix Press.

Nowlan, Denis (2005), 'Radio—Where the Pictures are Better', *For a Change*, 1 December 2005. Online at http://www.forachange.co.uk/browse/2083.html (accessed 4 September 2012).

Nussbaum, Martha (2012), *Not for Profit: Why Democracy Needs the Humanities*. Princeton: Princeton University Press.

Oesterlen, Eve-Marie (2009), 'Full of Noises, Sounds and Sweet Airs: Shakespeare and the Birth of Radio Drama in Britain', in Terris, Oesterlen, and McKernan (2009), 51–73.

The Open University (2012*a*), 'History of the OU', published online at http://www8.open.ac.uk/about/main/the-ou-explained/history-the-ou (accessed 22 August 2012).

The Open University (2012*b*), 'Small Screen Heroes: The OU and the BBC', published online at http://www8.open.ac.uk/researchprojects/historyofou/story/small-screen-heroes-the-ou-and-the-bbc (accessed 22 August 2012).

Overy, Richard (2009), *The Morbid Age: Britain Between the Wars*. London: Allen Lane.

Papoutsis, Natalie (2011), 'An Ear for an Eye: Greek Tragedy on Radio', doctoral thesis (on Canadian productions) submitted to the University of Toronto.

Paul, David (1959), 'Juan and So On', *The Listener*, 30 April 1959, 774.

Paul, Joanna (2008), 'Working with Film: Theories and Methodologies', in Hardwick and Stray (2008), 303–14.

Paul, Joanna (2013), *Film and the Classical Epic Tradition*. Oxford: Oxford University Press.

Paulu, Burton (1956), *British Broadcasting: Radio and Television in the United Kingdom*. Minneapolis: University of Minnesota Press.

Paulu, Burton (1961), *British Broadcasting in Transition*. London: Macmillan.

Pegg, Mark (1983), *Broadcasting and Society, 1918–1939*. London: Croom Helm.

Perris, Simon (2008), 'Literary Reception of Euripides' *Bacchae* in English, 1866–2008', doctoral thesis, University of Oxford.

'P. H. S.' (1970), 'Now, Act!', *The Times*, 3 March 1970, 10.

Pinch, Geraldine (2002), *Egyptian Mythology: A Guide to the Gods, Goddesses, and Traditions of Ancient Egypt*. Oxford: Oxford University Press.
Pomeroy, Arthur J. (2008), *'Then it was Destroyed by the Volcano': The Ancient World in Film and on Television*. London: Duckworth.
Porter, Andrew (1995), 'Riches Restored', *The Observer*, 16 April 1995, C7.
Porter, Jeff (2010), 'Samuel Beckett and the Radiophonic Body: Beckett and the BBC', *Modern Drama* 53.4, 431–46.
Postgate, Raymond (1969), *The Agamemnon of Aeschylus*. Cambridge: Rampant Lions Press.
Priessnitz, Horst P. (1981), 'British Radio Drama: A Survey', in Lewis (1981), 28–47.
Purbeck, Peter (1939), 'Broadcast Drama: *The Persians*', *The Listener*, 20 April 1939, 858.
Raban, Jonathan (1981), 'Icon or Symbol: The Writer and the "Medium"', in Lewis (1981), 78–90.
Raikes, Raymond (1956), 'A Greek Trilogy', *Radio Times*, 25 May 1956, 4.
Raikes, Raymond (1966), '*The Anger of Achilles*', *Radio Times*, 10 March 1966, 49.
Rattigan, Dermot (2002), *Theatre of Sound: Radio and the Dramatic Imagination*. Dublin: Carysfort Press.
Read, Herbert (1948), '*Aristotle's Mother: An Argument in Athens*', in Rayner Heppenstall (ed.), *Imaginary Conversations: Eight Radio Scripts*, 35–47. London: Secker and Warburg.
Reed, Philip (1989), 'A Cantata for Broadcasting: Britten's *The Company of Heaven*', *The Musical Times* 130.1756, 324–31.
Rees, Roger, ed. (2009), *Ted Hughes and the Classics*. Oxford: Oxford University Press.
Reith, John C. W. (1924), *Broadcast over Britain*. London: Hodder and Stoughton.
Reith, John C. W. (1928), 'Introduction', in British Broadcasting Corporation (1928), 31–5.
Reith, John C. W. (1949), *Into the Wind*. London: Hodder and Stoughton.
Reynolds, Gillian (1970), 'Wives Disguised', *The Guardian*, 7 March 1970, 8.
Rexine, John E. (1962), '*The Anger of Achilles: Homer's Iliad*, translated by Robert Graves', *The Classical Journal* 57.6, 281–2.
Ridley, M. R. (1947), 'Drama', in British Broadcasting Corporation (1947b), 9–17.
Rieu, E. V. (1945), *Homer: The Odyssey*. Harmondsworth: Penguin.
Rodger, Ian (1958), 'A Greek Week', *The Listener*, 30 October 1958, 705.
Rodger, Ian (1959), 'An Early Gagster', *The Listener*, 5 November 1959, 798–9.
Rodger, Ian (1982), *Radio Drama*. London: Macmillan.
Rolo, Charles J. (1943), *Radio Goes to War*. London: Faber.

Rood, Tim (2004), *The Sea! The Sea! The Shout of the Ten Thousand in the Modern Imagination*. London: Duckworth.

Rose, Jonathan (2001), *The Intellectual Life of the British Working Classes*. New Haven: Yale University Press.

Rubens, Beaty (1989), 'Getting Odysseus Taped', *Omnibus* 18, 25-6.

Rubens, Beaty and Taplin, Oliver (1989), *An Odyssey Round Odysseus: The Man and his Story Traced Through Time and Place*. London: BBC Books.

Rutherford, Richard (1996), *Homer*. *Greece & Rome*: New Surveys in the Classics 26. Oxford: Oxford University Press.

Rylance, Rick (2005), 'Reading with a Mission: The Public Sphere of Penguin Books', *Critical Quarterly* 47.4, 48-66.

Sackville-West, Edward (1943), '*The Odyssey* in Terms of Modern Radio', *Radio Times*, 19 November 1943, 4.

Sackville-West, Edward (1945), *The Rescue: A Melodrama for Broadcasting Based on Homer's Odyssey. Orchestral Score by Benjamin Britten. With Six Illustrations to the Text by Henry Moore*. London: Secker and Warburg.

Scannell, Paddy (1996), *Radio, Television and Modern Life: A Phenomenological Approach*. Oxford: Blackwell.

Scannell, Paddy (2007), *Media and Communication*. London: Sage.

Scannell, Paddy and Cardiff, David (1991), *A Social History of British Broadcasting*, vol. 1: *1922-1939: Serving the Nation*. Oxford: Blackwell.

Schmid, Wilhelm and Stählin, Otto (1929), *Geschichte der griechischen Literatur*, vol. 1. Munich: Beck.

Sear, Richard (1964), 'Chaste? It was Bawdy', *The Daily Mirror*, 16 January 1964, 14.

Shahabudin, Kim (2006), 'The Re-Presentation of Ancient Greece in Post-War Popular Cinema', PhD thesis, University of Reading.

Sheppard, J. T. (1929), 'At the Broadcast Play: The *Electra* of Euripides', *The Listener*, 24 July 1929, 126-7.

Shingler, Martin and Wieringa, Cindy (1998), *On Air: Methods and Meanings of Radio*. London: Arnold.

Sidnell, Michael J. (1984), *Dances of Death: The Group Theatre of London in the Thirties*. London: Faber.

Sidnell, Michael J. (1986), '"Another Death of Tragedy": Louis MacNeice's Translation of *Agamemnon* in the Context of his Work in the Theatre', in Martin Cropp, Elaine Fantham, and S. E. Scully (eds), *Greek Tragedy and its Legacy: Essays Presented to D. J. Conacher*, 323-35. Calgary: University of Calgary Press.

Siepmann, Charles A. (1941), 'Can Radio Educate?', *Journal of Educational Sociology* 14.6, 346-57.

Siepmann, Charles A. (1950), *Radio, Television and Society*. New York: Oxford University Press.

Silvey, Robert (1974), *Who's Listening? The Story of BBC Audience Research*. London: Allen and Unwin.
Simpson, Roger (2008), *Radio Camelot: Arthurian Legends on the BBC, 1922-2005*. Woodbridge: Brewer.
Smith, R. D. (1974), 'Castle on the Air', in Brown and Reid (1974), 87-95.
Sommerstein, Alan (2007), 'Lysistrata Turns a Somersault: Comedy, War, and Eric Linklater', *Classics Ireland* 14, 1-43.
Stallworthy, Jon (1995), *Louis MacNeice*. London: Faber.
Stanton, William (2004), 'The Invisible Theatre of Radio Drama', *Critical Quarterly* 46.4, 94-107.
Steiner, George (2004), 'Homer in English Translation', in Fowler (2004), 363-75.
Stevens, Wallace (2006), *Collected Poems*. London: Faber.
Stobart, John Clarke (1911), *The Glory that was Greece: A Survey of Hellenic Culture and Civilisation*. London: Sidgwick and Jackson.
Stranger, Ralph (1928), *Wireless: The Modern Magic Carpet*. London: Partridge.
Stray, Christopher (1998), *Classics Transformed: Schools, Universities, and Society in England, 1830-1960*. Oxford: Clarendon Press.
Stray, Christopher, ed. (2007*a*), *Gilbert Murray Reassessed: Hellenism, Theatre, and International Politics*. Oxford: Oxford University Press.
Stray, Christopher, ed. (2007*b*), *Remaking the Classics: Literature, Genre and Media in Britain, 1800-2000*. London: Duckworth.
Tagore, Rabindranath (1985), *Selected Poems*, translated by William Radice. Harmondsworth: Penguin.
Taplin, Oliver (1985), *Greek Tragedy in Action*. First published 1978. London: Methuen.
Taplin, Oliver (1999), *Greek with Consequence. Classical Association Presidential Address 1999*. London: Classical Association.
Taplin, Oliver (2002), 'Contemporary Poetry and Classics', in T. P. Wiseman (ed.), *Classics in Progress: Essays on Ancient Greece and Rome*, 1-19. Oxford: Oxford University Press.
Taplin, Oliver (2006), 'Greek Tragedy, Chekhov, and Being Remembered', *Arion* 13.3, 51-65.
Taylor, John Russell (1964), 'Farce with a Message', *The Listener*, 23 January 1964, 167.
Terris, Olwen, Oesterlen, Eve-Marie, and McKernan, Luke, eds (2009), *Shakespeare on Film, Television and Radio: The Researcher's Guide*. London: British Universities Film and Video Council.
Thomas, Dylan (1985), *The Collected Letters of Dylan Thomas*, ed. Paul Ferris. London: Dent.
Thorndike, Sybil (1925), 'Where Radio Drama Excels', *Radio Times*, 3 July 1925, 49-50.

Thorpe, Adam (2003), 'The Best Plays You've Never Seen', *The Guardian*, 5 July 2003, section G2, 18.
Thwaite, Anthony and Beny, Roloff (1981), *Odyssey: Mirror of the Mediterranean*. London: Thames and Hudson.
Todd, Robert B., ed. (2004), *The Dictionary of British Classicists*. 3 vols. Bristol: Thoemmes Continuum.
Trewin, J. C. (1952), 'Greeks and Trojans', *The Listener*, 24 January 1952, 157.
Trewin, J. C. (1953), 'End and Beginning', *The Listener*, 10 September 1953, 439.
Trewin, J. C. (1954), 'We'll Hear a Play', *The BBC Quarterly* 9.2, 85–91.
Trewin, J. C. (1955), 'Glory That Was Greece', *The Listener*, 18 August 1955, 271.
Trewin, J. C. (1956), 'Mainly Classical', *The Listener*, 31 May 1956, 733 and 735.
Trypanis, Constantine (1962), '*The Oresteia*', *Radio Times*, 25 January 1962, 26.
Turton, Godfrey (1937), 'Broadcasting a Greek Play', *Radio Times*, 23 April 1937, 6.
Tydeman, John (1981), 'The Producer and Radio Drama: A Personal View', in Lewis (1981), 12–27.
Tydeman, John (1998), 'Obituary: Raymond Raikes', *The Independent*, 8 October 1998, 6.
Van Steen, Gonda (2000), *Venom in Verse: Aristophanes in Modern Greece*. Princeton: Princeton University Press.
Van Steen, Gonda (2007), 'Translating—or not—for Political Propaganda: Aeschylus' *Persians* 402–405', in Francesca Billiani (ed.), *Modes of Censorship and Translation: National Contexts and Diverse Media*, 117–41. Manchester: St Jerome.
Vellacott, Philip (1956), *Aeschylus. The Oresteian Trilogy: Agamemnon; The Choephori; The Eumenides*. Harmondsworth: Penguin.
Vellacott, Philip (1960), *The Bad-Tempered Man; or, The Misanthrope*. Oxford: Oxford University Press.
Vellacott, Philip (1963), *Medea and Other Plays*. Harmondsworth: Penguin.
Vellacott, Philip (1991), *An English Reader's Guide to Aeschylus' Oresteia*. 2nd edn. Cambridge: Monophron.
Wade, David (1977), 'Bottom of the Class', *The Times*, 25 June 1977, 12.
Wade, David (1981), 'British Radio Drama since 1960', in Drakakis (1981), 218–44.
Walker, Roy (1957), 'Venus v. Mars', *The Listener*, 5 December 1957, 957.
Walton, J. Michael (2006), *Found in Translation: Greek Drama in English*. Cambridge: Cambridge University Press.
Warden, Claire Altree (2007), 'The Shadows and the Rush of Light: Ewan MacColl and Expressionist Drama', *New Theatre Quarterly* 23, 317–25.

Warden, Claire Altree (2011), 'Politics, War, and Adaptation: Ewan MacColl's *Operation Olive Branch*, 1947', in Wrigley (2011), 536-8.
Warner, Rex (1947), *The Prometheus Bound of Æschylus*. London: Bodley Head.
Warner, Rex (1949), *Xenophon*. Harmondsworth: Penguin.
Webb, Ruth (2009), *Ekphrasis, Imagination and Persuasion in Ancient Rhetorical Theory and Practice*. Farnham: Ashgate.
Wellington, Lindsay (1957), 'The New Pattern of Sound Broadcasting', *Radio Times*, 27 September 1957, 3.
Wertenbaker, Timberlake (2002), *Plays 2*. London: Faber.
White, Fred M. (1926), 'When Radio Comes to the Village', *Radio Times*, 17 September 1926, 521-2.
Whitehead, Kate (1989), *The Third Programme: A Literary History*. Oxford: Clarendon Press.
Williams, Stephen (1948), 'Guying the Greeks', *Radio Times*, 23 January 1948, 6.
Williams, Stephen (1949), 'Return to Ithaca', *Radio Times*, 2 September 1949, 9.
Williams, W. E. (1946), 'French into English', *The Observer*, 8 December 1946, 2.
Williams, W. E. (1947), 'Voice from Athens', *The Observer*, 9 February 1947, 2.
Williams, W. E. (1948), 'Word from Greece', *The Observer*, 15 February 1948, 2.
Wilson, Duncan (1987), *Gilbert Murray OM, 1866-1957*. Oxford: Clarendon Press.
Wilson, Peter (2007), 'Retrieving Cosmos: Gilbert Murray's Thought on International Relations', in Stray (2007*a*), 239-60.
Winkler, Martin (2009), *Cinema and Classical Texts: Apollo's New Light*. Cambridge: Cambridge University Press.
Wolfe, Kenneth M. (1984), *The Churches and the British Broadcasting Corporation: The Politics of Broadcast Religion, 1922-1956*. London: SCM.
Woodward, E. L. (1948), 'General Cultural Development', *The BBC Quarterly* 3.1, 24-32.
Woolf, Virginia (1942), 'Middlebrow', in *The Death of the Moth and Other Essays*. London: Hogarth.
Workman, Simon (2010), 'Louis MacNeice: Radio, Poetry and the Auditory Imagination', doctoral thesis submitted to Trinity College, Dublin.
Wrigley, Amanda (2006), 'Aeschylus' *Agamemnon* on BBC Radio, 1946-1976', *International Journal of the Classical Tradition* 12.2, 216-44.
Wrigley, Amanda (2007*a*), 'Aristophanes Revitalized! Music and Spectacle on the Academic Stage', in Hall and Wrigley (2007), 136-54.
Wrigley, Amanda (2007*b*), 'Stages of Imagination: Greek Plays on BBC Radio', in Stray (2007*b*), 57-73.

Bibliography

Wrigley, Amanda (2009a), 'Engagements with Greek Drama and Homeric Epic on BBC Radio in the 1940s and 1950s', doctoral thesis submitted to The Open University.

Wrigley, Amanda (2009b), 'Louis MacNeice's Radio Classics: "all so unimaginably different"?', in Lowe and Shahabudin (2009), 39–61.

Wrigley, Amanda (2010a), 'Robert Bridges' Masque *Demeter* and Oxford's Persephones', *New Voices in Classical Reception Studies* 5, published online at www2.open.ac.uk/ClassicalStudies/GreekPlays/newvoices/Issue5/Wrigley. pdf.

Wrigley, Amanda (2010b), 'A Wartime Radio *Odyssey*: Edward Sackville-West and Benjamin Britten's *The Rescue* (1943)', *The Radio Journal: International Studies in Broadcast and Audio Media* 8.2, 81–103.

Wrigley, Amanda (2011a), 'Greek Drama in the First Six Decades of the Twentieth Century: Tradition, Identity, Migration', in Wrigley (2011), 371–84.

Wrigley, Amanda (2011b), *Performing Greek Drama in Oxford and on Tour with the Balliol Players*. Exeter: University of Exeter Press.

Wrigley, Amanda, ed. (2011), *Translation, Performance and Reception of Greek Drama, 1900–1960: International Dialogues*, a double special issue of *Comparative Drama* 44.4–45.1.

Wrigley, Amanda (2012), 'Classics on TV: Greek Tragedy on the Small Screen', *Journal of Classics Teaching* 26.

Wrigley, Amanda (2013a), 'Introduction: Louis MacNeice, Classical Antiquity and BBC Radio: From Wartime Propaganda to Radio Plays', in Wrigley and Harrison (2013), 1–30.

Wrigley, Amanda (2013b), 'Practising Classical Reception Studies "in the Round": Mass Media Engagements with Antiquity and the "Democratic Turn" Towards the Audience', in Hardwick and Harrison (2013), 351–64.

Wrigley, Amanda (2014), 'Aristophanes at the BBC, 1940s–1960s', in S. Douglas Olson (ed.), *Ancient Comedy and Reception: Essays in Honor of Jeffrey Henderson*, 849–70. Berlin and Boston: de Gruyter.

Wrigley, Amanda (2015), '*The Anger of Achilles*, A Prize-Winning "Epic for Radio" by Robert Graves', in Gibson (2015), 315–31.

Wrigley, Amanda (2016a, forthcoming), *Greece on Screen: Greek Plays on British Television*. Under consideration.

Wrigley, Amanda (2016b, forthcoming), 'Greek Tragedy in the BBC and ITV Schools Television Curricula, 1950s-60s', in Hobden and Wrigley (2016).

Wrigley, Amanda (2016c, forthcoming), 'Higher Education, Public Engagement: BBC-Open University Co-productions of Drama on BBC2 in the 1970s', *Journal of British Cinema and Television*.

Wrigley, Amanda (2016d, forthcoming), 'Mass Media Aeschylus', in Rebecca Kennedy (ed.), *The Brill Companion to the Reception of Aeschylus*. Leiden: Brill.

Wrigley, Amanda and Davis, Robert (2011), 'Greek Immigrants Playing Ancient Greeks at Chicago's Hull-House: Whose Antiquity?', *Journal of American Drama and Theatre* 23.2 (special issue on Capitalism and Identity), 7–29.

Wrigley, Amanda and Harrison, Stephen, eds (2013), *Louis MacNeice: The Classical Radio Plays*. Oxford: Oxford University Press.

'W. T. R.' (1940), 'Prizewinning Play—by Aeschylus', *Radio Times*, 23 August 1940, 4.

Wyke, Maria (1997), *Projecting the Past: Ancient Rome, Cinema, and History*. London: Routledge.

Wyndham Goldie, Grace (1937), 'Broadcast Drama: Something for Everybody', *The Listener*, 24 November 1937, 1144.

Index

Page references in italic type are to illustrations.
Abbreviations used: 'ad.', 'adaptation'; 'tr.', 'translation'.

Abbey Players 123, 281
Acharnians, Aristophanes, Dickinson's
  tr. produced by Raikes
    (1955) 264–6, 271 n. 62, 291
Aeschylus, *see* individual plays
Aesop 89, 282, 283
Agamemnon, Aeschylus:
  radio 14–15, 221–46, and by:
    Bradnum (1958) 233, 293
    Gielgud (1946) 222–4, 286
    Gielgud (1960) 234, 294
    Raikes (1950) 66, 100, 224–6,
      229, 289
    Raikes (1953) 131, 226–7, 229, 290
    Theocharis (1976) 238–46, 296
  stage, Group Theatre (1936) 153, 221
  tr. / ad.:
    Alfred 234, 294
    Josipovici 83, 238–46, 296
    MacNeice 66, 100, 153, 170, 221–8,
      286, 289, 290
    Postgate 233, 293
  see also Oresteia
Alcestis, Euripides:
  radio:
    Burnham (1937 and 1940) 128, 283
    Hauser (1950) 53 n. 69, 131, 142, 288
    passages (1928) 86, 122–3, 281
  tr. / ad.:
    Fitts and Fitzgerald 128, 283
    Ford 142, 288
    Murray 122–3, 126, 131, 281, 283
Alexander Nevsky, MacNeice 169
Alfred, William 294
Allen, Mary Hope 68, 286
ancient Greek language:
  abolition of 'compulsory Greek' 40
  performances in 43, 63 n. 98, 64–5,
    137, 229, 287, 288, 290, 292, 295
  see also education, classical
ancient Rome 3, 25 n. 13, 91, 93, 95, 124,
    149, 151, 152, 169, 170, 171,
    174, 209–10, 243 n. 68, 281
ancient sites 86, 226, 281

The Anger of Achilles, Graves 14,
    207–19, 290, 295, 296
Antigone, Anouilh 78, 288
Antigone, Sophocles:
  radio:
    Gielgud and Tucker (1947) 131,
      135–6, 287
    Gielgud (1959) 235, 237, 294
    Gunn (1924) 118, 280
    Raikes (1950) 53 n. 69, 78, 289
  stage, Glasgow (1922) 118
  tr. / ad.:
    Fitts and Fitzgerald 289
    Harrower 280
    Murray 131, 135–6, 287
    Trypanis 235, 237, 294
Aristophanes 86, 284
  see also individual plays and *Enemy
    of Cant*
Arundell, Dennis D. 290
Austen, John 119

Bacchae, Euripides, Cavander's tr. produced
    by Lefeaux (1964) 64, 295
Baker-Smith, Malcolm 284
Bakewell, Michael 291
Bantock, Granville 157, 282, 284
Baring, Maurice 86, 281
Barker, Harley Granville, *see* Granville
    Barker, Harley
Barnes, George 80, 104, 137
BBC:
  Drama Department 14–15, 47, 52,
    59–62, 72, 92, 131, 136, 139,
    142, 171, 213, 218, 238, 250–1
  Education Department 174, 280
  Features Department 44–5, 59–62,
    72, 156, 209, 250
  Home Service 7, 50, 51, 53, 217, 227
  Light Programme 50, 51
  Music Department 191–4
  National Programme 50, 51
  propaganda, wartime 43–9, 143,
    146–50, 151–72

322 Index

BBC: (cont.)
   Radio 3 238
   Radiophonic Workshop 214
   Third Programme 7, 50, 51, 52,
      53, 60, 79–81, 131, 208,
      213 n. 113, 217, 222, 227–8,
      238–9, 276–7
   see also listeners; radio; television;
      and individual programmes
Beckett, Samuel ix, 11 n. 6, 59,
   60, 238
Beckwith, Reginald 287
Berkeley, Lennox 180, 286
Bernard, Anthony 289, 291, 296
Bernard, James 291
Beware the Gods,
   Dunning-Gribble 175, 283
Blair [=W. W. Blair-Fish] 287
Bliss, Arthur 187, 192–3
Boult, Adrian 192
Bower, Dallas 169
Bradnum, Frederick 233, 293
Brandel, Marc 268
Brecht, Bertolt 100, 112
Brian, Havergal 238, 246
Bridgewater, Leslie 287
Bridson, D. G. 43–4, 59
Britten, Benjamin 165–6, 191–4, 202–4,
   221, 223; see also The Rescue
Buckland, John 287, 296
Bulloch, S. A. 281
Burnham, Barbara 89, 125–8, 282, 283,
   285
Burrell, John 285

Campaign for Better Broadcasting 239
Campbell, Archibald Young 85, 136,
   280
Carne-Ross, D. S. 181, 182, 211, 293
Carpe Diem, MacNeice 152 n. 5, 161
Casson, Lewis 118, 130, 280
Casson, Stanley 86, 281
Cavander, Kenneth 63–4, 89, 249, 291,
   295, 296
The Children's Hour 89, 283
choruses in Greek drama 99 n. 68, 125,
   126, 127, 226, 231, 237
Christopher Columbus, MacNeice 169
classical education, see education
classical reception studies 18, 19, 20, 22,
   25–8, 58
classics, impact of radio on 69, 94,
   249–50

Cleverdon, Douglas 59, 209, 295
Cordier, Charles 142, 291
Cotton, Donald 295
Cottrell, Leonard 226 n. 16, 291
Council for the Encouragement of Music
   and the Arts 8, 47, 201
'Croker, Charles' 86, 281
Cruickshank, Andrew 287
cultural 'brows' 7, 36, 50–2, 75, 79–81,
   131, 246
Cupid and Psyche, MacNeice 152, 169,
   274–5
Curran, Charles 238

The Dark Tower, MacNeice 170
Demuth, Norman 290
Dickinson, Patric 15, 67, 69, 142,
   179–80, 263–71, 285,
   286, 291, 293
Doctor Who ('The Myth Makers')
   246 n. 73
Drama Department, see BBC
Drinkwater, John 86, 281
Dyskolos, Menander 293
   Vellacott's tr. produced by Raikes
   (1959) 248–50, 294

The Early Christians, MacNeice 164–5,
   285
Eastwood, Thomas 294
education:
   19th-century reforms 29
   classical 6–7, 22–3, 31, 37, 79
   Education Act of 1944 49, 50
   English literature 7, 41
   potential of radio as 36–7, 42, 58, 75,
      79, 84–94
   schools:
      BBC pamphlets for 4, 88
      evidence for listening in 22, 77–8,
         88, 90, 91–2, 145
      impact of radio on teachers 9, 58,
         76, 90, 91–2, 262–3
      radio broadcasts for 64, 86, 88, 89,
         145, 148, 174, 179, 280, 282,
         283, 296
Ekklesiasouzai, Aristophanes,
   Dickinson's tr. produced by
   Raikes (1970) 264, 296
Electra, Euripides:
   radio:
      Gielgud (1948) 131, 135–6,
         141, 287

Index

Rose (1929) 86, 98, 119–20, 124, 281
Watts (1953) 55, 290
tr. Murray 55, 98, 119–20, 131, 135–6, 141, 281, 287, 290
Electra, Sophocles, Trypanis's tr. produced by Gielgud (1963) 235, 295
Eliot, T. S. 121 n. 16, 228, 243, 250, 251 n. 13
Elliott, Michael 64, 127, 133 n. 47
Enemy of Cant, MacNeice 15, 21–4, 55, 66, 83, 140–1, 161, 170–1, 247–8, 250–63, 274, 287
Enter Caesar, MacNeice 152 n. 5
Entertainments National Service Association 201
Epitrepontes, Menander:
 radio:
  Grantham (1952) 137, 290
  Lefeaux (1956) 142, 292
 tr. Murray 137, 142, 290, 292
Esslin, Martin 53, 60, 112, 238
Euripides 86, 89, 145, 282; *see also* individual plays

features, defined 61–2; *see also* BBC, Features Department
Features Department, *see* BBC
film, ancient world on 16 n. 9, 49 n. 48, 207, 277–8
First World War 38, 167–8
Fitts, Dudley 219, 283, 289
FitzGerald, Prudence 268
Fitzgerald, Robert 283, 289
Fogerty, Elsie 39, 125–6, 128, 282, 283
Ford, Ford Madox 288
The Four Freedoms, MacNeice 164–9, 191, 285
Fraser, Eric iv, 26, 83, *124*, *129*, *138*, *190*, 223, 227, *237*
Frogs, Aristophanes:
 radio:
  Campbell (1928) 136, 280
  Gielgud (1947) 68, 136, 137–41, *138*, 287
  Gielgud (1951) 131, 141, 289
 stage:
  Cambridge Greek Play (1947) 131, 137, 287
  Somerville College (1911) 122
 tr.:
  Hickie 136 n. 57
  Murray 68, 131, 136, 137–41, *138*, 287, 289

Galantière, Lewis 288
Gerhard, Roberto 214, 216, 295, 296
Gide, André 84, 206, 289
Gielgud, John 72 n. 118, 228, 235, *235*
Gielgud, Val 23, 45, 47, 55–6, 59–60, 63–4, 66, 68, 69, 72–3, 99, 101, 107, 125, 131, 135, 136, 137–41, 146, 180, 187, 204, 223, 228–37, *235*, 238, 245–6, 263, 284, 285, 286, 287, 288, 289, 291, 293, 294, 295
Gilliam, Laurence 60, 187, 284
The Glory that is Greece, MacNeice 89, 146, 160–3, 274, 284
Goehr, Walter 284
The Golden Ass, MacNeice 152, 169, 274–5
Grantham, Wilfrid 290
Granville Barker, Harley 121
Graves, Robert, *see The Anger of Achilles*
Gray, Frances 105, 112
Greece Fights On, MacNeice 163–4, 285
Greece Lives, *see The Glory that is Greece*
Greek drama, *see* individual plays
Grigson, Geoffrey 79
Grisewood, Harman 264
Gurney, Peter 216, 294
Guthrie, Tyrone 102, 120, 280

Haley, William 50, 51, 52
Harding, E. A. 263
Harrison, Tony 97–8
Harrower, John 280
Hauser, Frank 142, 288
Hays, Bill 246 n. 73
'H. D.' [=Hilda Doolittle] 291
Helen, Euripides, Vellacott's tr.
 produced by Raikes (1954) 95–6 n. 61, 291
Heppenstall, Rayner 46, 208–9, 287
Herodotus 163, 216 n. 119, 282, 294
Hippolytus, Euripides:
 radio:
  Bakewell (1955) 291
  Burnham (1936) 17, 41–2, 91, 99 n. 68, 123–5, *124*, 282
  Campbell (1928) 280
  Gielgud (1945) 53, 131–2, 285–6
  Raikes (1953) 95 n. 61, 290
 stage:
  OUDS (1955) 63, 235–6 n. 47, 291
  Society for Oxford Home-Students (1910) 122

Index

Hippolytus, Euripides: (*cont.*)
  tr. / ad.:
    Cavander 235–6 n. 47, 291
    MacNeice 153–4
    Murray 17, 41–2, 53, 91, 99 n. 68, 123–5, *124*, 131, 282, 285–6
    Vellacott 95 n. 61, 290
Hoggart, Richard 30
Homer 13, 173–219, 284; see also *Iliad*; *Odyssey*
Home Service, see BBC
Hopkins, Antony 22, 66–7, 231, 255, 259–60, 287, 288, 291, 292
Hotchkis, John 66, 226–7, 236, 289, 290, 291, 293, 294, 295
Hughes, Richard 119

Iliad, Homer:
  film 208 n. 85
  radio 64, 86, 174, 181, 280, 281–2, 293, 296
  tr. / ad.:
    Cavander 64, 89, 179, 296
    Lattimore 213
    Logue 107–8, 181
  see also *The Anger of Achilles*; Dickinson
Illif, Noel 287, 288
Imaginary Conversations series 46, 208, 209, 286
imagination 5, 10, 57, 75–6, 90, 97–113, 173, 277–8
Imison, Richard 218, 296
Ion, Euripides, ad. by 'H. D.' produced by Raikes (1954) 68 n. 112, 291
Iphigenia among the Taurians, Euripides:
  radio:
    Guthrie (1925) 118, 144, 280
    Raikes (1949) 95 n. 61, 288
  stage:
    Cambridge Festival Theatre of Amner Hall 118
    Oxford High School (1910) 122
  tr. / ad.:
    Murray 118, 144, 280
    Vellacott 95 n. 61, 288
Iphigenia in Aulis, Euripides:
  radio:
    Raikes (1951) 91, 289
    Raikes (1975) 92 n. 49, 296
    Young (1991) 68 n. 112
  stage, various 92

tr. / ad.:
  Raikes 93, 289, 296
  Southey 68 n. 112

Jauss, Hans-Robert 19, 22–3
Joad, C. E. M. 89, 282
Johnston, Denis 157, 284
Josipovici, Gabriel 83, 238–46, 296

King, Colette 66, 125, 234–7, 293, 294, 295

Lawrence, T. E. 175
Lattimore, Richmond 213, 239, 296
League of Nations 12, 118, 143, 144, 150
Lefeaux, Charles 291, 292, 295
Linklater, Eric 45–6, 284, 285
listeners:
  evidence for 6, 7, 20, 22, 26, 54–7, 77–8, 84, 88, 90, 91; 93, 102, 106–13, 127–8, 130–1, 132–3, 135–6, 140, 168–9, 180, 183–4, 201–5, 222–4, 227, 229–32, 260–2, 270–1, 274–6
  demographic composition of 57, 75, 77–8
  experience of programmes 17–18, 22–5, 55, 65–6, 71–2, 97–113
  Listener Research Reports 7, 54, 261 n. 32
  listening groups 9, 86–7
  numbers of 51, 53, 54, 59, 75, 77–9, 81
  preparation for programmes 17–18, 91
  in Second World War 49, 77–8
  see also BBC; education
The Listener 42, 68, 80, 86, 124, 145, 149, 248
Livingstone, Richard 88, 282
Lloyd-Jones, Hugh 43, 229, 248–50, 292, 293, 294
Logue, Christopher 107–8
Long Live Greece, see *Greece Fights On*
Lysistrata, Aristophanes:
  radio:
    Illif (1947) 266 n. 48, 287
    Raikes (1957) 264–8, 270, 293
    television, FitzGerald (1964) 268–70
  tr. / ad.:
    Beckwith and Cruickshank 266 n. 48, 287
    Dickinson 264–70, 293

MacColl, Ewan 43
Mackail, J. W. 31
McLeish, Kenneth 246 n. 73
MacNeice, Louis:
  and BBC 12–13, 29, 44–5, 67–8,
    151–72, *154*
  and propaganda 44–5, 151–72
  on radio form 61–2
  in *Radio Times* 132–3, 222–4, 227, 251
  writing for radio, *see* individual works
  writing, other:
    Agamemnon tr., *see Agamemnon*
    'Autumn Journal' 154, 172, 273, 277
    'Autumn Sequel' 62
    Odyssey series (1960) 180–4, 294
    Pax Futura film script 169 n. 58, 170
    Roman humour monograph 152, 154
McWhinnie, Donald 289
The March of the 10,000, MacNeice 158–60, 284
Masefield, John 38, 175, 295
Matheson, Hilda 77, 85, 113, 122, 125
Medea, Euripides:
  radio:
    Burnham (1942) 64, 126, 130–1, 284–5
    Casson (1925) 118, 144, 280
    Gielgud (1949) 131, 288
    Raikes (1962) 64–5, *65*, 95–6 n. 61, 295
  stage:
    CEMA 47
    Christ Church (1925) 118
    County High School for Girls 118
    Oxford (1908) 122
  tr.:
    Murray 118, 126, 130–1, 144, 280, 284–5, 288
    Vellacott 64–5, 95–6 n. 61, 295
Menander 292; *see also* individual plays
Metaxas, Ioannis 161–3
modernism 29, 32 n. 30
Monday Night Theatre 290
Moore, Henry 26, *186*, *195*, 196, *200*, 205–6
Morley, Royston 284
Morpurgo, Michael 111
Murray, Gilbert:
  talks on ancient Greece 12, 17, 39, 60–1, 89, 143, 145–50, 226 n. 16, 283, 284, 285, 290, 292

  talks on politics 12, 87, 142–50, 284
  translations of Greek drama:
    produced on radio 11–12, 17, 41–2, 53, 55, 60–1, 68, 73, 91, 117–42, 247, 280, 281, 282, 283, 284, 285, 286, 287, 288, 289, 290, 292
    stage performances and readings 38, 58, 121
Murray, Stephen *65*
music in radio programmes 65–7, 100, 105, 106, 131–2, 191–4, 214, 226, 231; *see also* individual composers
Mycenae's Second Glory (1955) 291

Nagy, Phyllis 68 n. 112
Nairn, J. Arbuthnot 86, 281
'national theatre of the air' 39, 40 n. 18
Nazism 45, 130, 155
Newby, P. H. 209–10, 218, 238
Nowlan, Denis 103

Odyssey, Homer:
  radio 16 n. 11, 64, 86, 174, 180–4, 280, 282, 283, 294, 296
  tr. / ad.:
    Cavander 64, 89, 179
    Lawrence 175
    Pope 175
    Rieu 79
  see also Beware the Gods; *The Dark Tower*; *The Rescue*; *Twenty Years is a Long Time*
Oedipus at Colonus, Sophocles:
  radio:
    Campbell (1928) 85–6, 280
    Gielgud (1959) 235, 293
  stage, OUDS (1958) 235–6 n. 47
  tr. Trypanis 235, 293
Oedipus Tyrannus, Sophocles:
  radio:
    Bulloch (1932) 123, 281
    Gielgud (1957) 293
  stage, Oxford Poetry Society 234
  tr. / ad.:
    Trypanis 293
    Yeats 123, 281
Ogilvie, Frederick W. 155
Old Vic Company, London 64, 67, 130, 284–5
The Open University 40 n. 19, 69

Oresteia, Aeschylus:
 radio 221-46, and by:
  Campbell (1928) 85, 280
  Gielgud (1962) 66, 82, 236-7, *237*,
   238, 239, 246, 294
  Raikes (1956) 42, 95-6, 228-33,
   246, 292
 television, *The Serpent Son*
  (1979) 246 n. 73
 tr. / ad.:
  Trypanis 66, 236-7, 294
  Vellacott 42, 95-6, 228-33, 292
 see also Agamemnon
Orwell, George, *1984* 56
Oscar, Henry 280
Owen, Alan 295

Page, D. L. 92 n. 49, 289
Parry Gunn, A. 280
Peace, Aristophanes, Dickinson's tr.
 produced by Raikes
  (1957) 264-6, 293
Penguin Classics 9-10, 76, 79, 94-6,
 229, 249 n. 7
Pericles, MacNeice 164-8, 191, 285
Perikeiromene, Menander:
 radio:
  Burnham (1942) 126, 136-7, 284
  Lefeaux (1956) 142, 292
 tr. Murray 126, 136-7, 142, 284, 292
Persians, Aeschylus:
 radio:
  Burnham (1939) 89, 126, 128-9, 283
  Gielgud (1958) 235, 293
  Imison (1965) 28, 238, 296
  passages (1929) 86, 281
  quoted (1941) 162
 stage, Worcester College (1939) 129
 tr. / ad.:
  Campbell 281
  Murray 126, 128-9, 283
  Rudkin 28, 238, 296
  Trypanis 235, 293
Phèdre, Racine 42, 124, 286
Phillips, Stephen 281
Philoctetes, Sophocles:
 radio:
  Richmond (1947) 287
  Lefeaux (1963) *iv*, 64, 83-4, 295
 television, by Eyre (1961) 64
 tr. / ad.:
  Blair 287
  Cavander *iv*, 64, 83-4, 295

philosophy, Greek 88-9, 124, 146,
 282, 283; *see also* Plato;
 Socrates
Pittas, Christos 239, 243, 296
Plato 89, 95, 208, 282, 283, 287
Plautus 263, 264
Pope, Alexander 175
Portrait of Athens, MacNeice 171, 289
Postgate, Raymond 233, 293
Potter, Stephen 106, 192 n. 45
Prix Italia 216-17, 239, 296
Prometheus Bound, Aeschylus, Warner's
 tr. produced by Allen (1948) 68
propaganda, wartime, *see* BBC
Pughe, Cynthia 294

Radice, Betty 95
radio (BBC):
 audience, *see* listeners
 'blindness' 101-2, 106
 communal listening 18
 democratic nature of 54, 56, 71-2, 75,
  77-97
 intellectual prejudice against 58, 67,
  155, 156 n. 19
 and literature 70-2, 103, 110, 123
 producer, role of 62-3, 67, 103, 156,
  221, 225, 249
 publication of scripts 26, 152 n. 5,
  196, 205-6, 266-7
 reading habits, impact on 17-18, 58,
  94, 145
 theatre, relationship with 58, 101,
  103, 117-23
 and women 37, 68 n. 112, 77, 101,
  125-6, 167-8
Radio Times *iv*, 68, 80, 83, 91, 119,
 124, *124*, 127, 129, *129*,
 132-3, *138*, 158, 161,
 190, 217, 222-4, *223*,
 227, *237*
Raikes, Raymond 59, 64-6, 82, 92-3,
 95-6, 213, 216-17, 224-6,
 229-33, 246, 248-50, 265-6,
 288, 289, 290, 291, 292, 293,
 294, 295, 296
Raphael, Frederic 246 n. 73
Raybould, Clarence 192-3, 285, 289
Read, Herbert 46, 286
Reed, Henry 89, 104, 282, 283
Reinganum, Victor 127
Reith, John 4, 6, 35-6, 44 n. 29, 51, 55,
 59, 85, 144, 277

Index

The Rescue, Sackville-West and Britten 13–14, 45, 67, 100, 105, 106–8, 175–6, 179, 184–206, *186, 190, 195, 200,* 285, 288, 289, 291–2, 294–5, 296
Rhesus, Euripides, Murray's tr. produced by Oscar (1926) 119, 121, 144, 280
Richardson, Joanna 142, 291
Richmond, John 287
Rieu, E. V. 79, 95, 96, 184
Rilla, Walter 164
Robinson, Lennox 118
Robson, Flora 118
A Roman Holiday, MacNeice 152, 169
Rose, Howard 281
Rubens, Beaty 173
Rudkin, David 28, 296

Sackville-West, Edward 53, 131, 284, 285, 286; *see also The Rescue*
The Sacred Band, MacNeice 164 n. 38, 285
Salamis, battle of 89, 128, 162–3, 282
Salute to Greece, MacNeice 158, 284
Samia, Menander, Richardson and Dickinson's tr. produced by Lefeaux (1955) 142, 291
Saturday Night Theatre 53, 59
schools, *see* education
Sculthorpe, Peter 240
Second World War 6, 8, 12, 43–4, 46, 64, 77–8, 89, 129–30, 133, 146–8, 151–72, 187–206; *see also* listeners
Searle, Humphrey 216, 246 n. 73, 294
Searle, Ronald 212
Seven against Thebes, Aeschylus:
  radio:
    Burnham (1940) 126, 129–30, *129,* 283
    Theocharis (1981) 243 n. 68
  tr. / ad.:
    Josipovici 243 n. 68
    Murray 126, 129–30, *129,* 283
Shakespeare 70, 117, 145, 175
Sheppard, J. T. 120, 137
Skutsch, Otto 210
Sly, Allan 283
Socrates 45–6, 88, 89, 95, 148, 282, 283, 284, 285
Somerville, Mary 88 n. 40, 174, 280
Sophocles, *see* individual plays

Southey, Rosemary 68 n. 112
Sparta 163, 165–7, 254, 268–9, 281
Spencer, C. R. 282
Stevens, Wallace 110
Stobart, J. C. 36, 161 n. 31, 174, 280

television (BBC) 40 n. 19, 56, 59, 127, 246 n. 73, 268–70
Theocharis, John 239, 240, 296
Thermopylae, battle of 161, 163
Third Programme, *see* BBC
Thomas, Dylan 21, 252
Thorndike, Sybil 47, 97, 102, 118, 119, 128, 130, 290
Thornton, J. C. 210
Thucydides 146, 151, 165, 168, 263
Thurburn, Gwynneth 125–6, 282
Thwaite, Anthony 180, 294
Trachiniae, Sophocles, Wertenbaker's tr. produced by Bailey (1999) 16 n. 11, 68 n. 112
translation, forms of 31, 40–1, 79–82, 84, 86, 137–41, 173; *see also* individual Greek texts
Tredennick, Hugh 287
Trimalchio's Feast, MacNeice 152, 169
Trojan Women, Euripides:
  radio:
    Burnham (1937) 89, 99 n. 68, 126–7, 282
    Gielgud (1946) 127, 131, 133–4, 286
    Raikes (1952) 95 n. 61, 290
  stage, Society for Oxford Home-Students (1912) 122
  television, Wrede and Elliott (1958) 64, 127, 133 n. 47
  tr. / ad.:
    Cavander 64
    Murray 89, 99 n. 68, 126–7, 131, 133–4, 282, 286
    Vellacott 95 n. 61, 290
Trypanis, Constantine 66, 69, 234–6, 293, 294, 295
Tucker, Rex 287
Twenty Years is a Long Time, Garrett 176–8, 288
Tydeman, John 113

Vellacott, Philip 95–6, 228–30, 248, 288, 290, 291, 292, 294, 295
Vergi, Elsa 43, 64–5, *65,* 229, 290, 292, 295
Virgil 174, 243 n. 68

Wanamaker, Sam 207
Warner, Rex 68, 97
Watts, Peter 290
Wertenbaker, Timberlake 16 n. 11, 68 n. 112
What Now?, MacNeice 164, 167–9, 285
Wheeler, Penelope 38, 126
Whelen, Christopher 65, 291, 293, 295
Whitehouse, Mary 268–9
Williamson, Hugh Ross 89, 282
Wood, Helena 141, 290

Woolf, Virginia 30
World Theatre 7, 53, 59, 131, 133, 135, 226–7, 286, 287, 288, 289, 290
Wrede, Casper 64, 127, 133 n. 47, 235–6 n. 47
Wyndham Goldie, Grace 128

Xenophon 158–60, 284

Yeats, W. B. 123, 154, 281